Quality Performance in Human Services

Quality Performance in Human Services
Leadership, Values, and Vision

edited by
James F. Gardner, Ph.D., M.A.S.
and **Sylvia Nudler, M.A.S.**

The Council on Quality and Leadership
in Supports for People with Disabilities
Towson, Maryland

HV
41
.Q38
1999

·P A U L·H·
BROOKES
PUBLISHING CO.

Baltimore · London · Toronto · Sydney

Paul H. Brookes Publishing Co.
Post Office Box 10624
Baltimore, Maryland 21285-0624

www.pbrookes.com

Typeset by Barton Matheson Willse & Worthington,
Baltimore, Maryland.
Manufactured in the United States of America by
Edwards Brothers, Inc., Ann Arbor, Michigan.

CAK 2047

Library of Congress Cataloging-in-Publication Data

Quality performance in human services : leadership, values,
  and vision / edited by James F. Gardner and Sylvia Nudler.
        p.   cm.
    "The Council on Quality and Leadership in Supports for People with
  Disabilities, Towson, Maryland."
    Includes bibliographical references and index.
    ISBN 1-55766-360-2
  1. Total quality management in human services.   2. Human services—
  Management.   I. Gardner, James F., 1946–   .   II. Nudler, Sylvia.
  III. Council on Quality and Leadership in Supports for People with
  Disabilities (Towson, Md.)
HV41.Q38   1998
361.3'068—dc21   98-30589
                                                                      CIP

British Library Cataloguing in Publication data are available from
the British Library.

Contents

About the Editors

James F. Gardner, Ph.D., M.A.S., President and Chief Executive Officer, The Council on Quality and Leadership in Supports for People with Disabilities, Suite 406, 100 West Road, Towson, Maryland 21204. From 1977 to 1986, Dr. Gardner served as Director of Community Programs and then as Vice President for Community Program Development at The Kennedy Institute at The Johns Hopkins University.

Dr. Gardner received his doctoral degree in a dual program of American Studies and American Social History from Indiana University. He was awarded a Joseph P. Kennedy, Jr., Post-doctoral Fellowship in Medical Ethics at the Harvard Medical School. Dr. Gardner later completed the Masters in Administrative Sciences program at The Johns Hopkins University. Dr. Gardner holds faculty appointments at The Johns Hopkins University and the University of Maryland. He has written and edited numerous publications in the field of human services.

Dr. Gardner is a nationally recognized leader in the application of quality improvement methods to the field of human services. Through presentations at national conferences, in his teaching and writing, and during organizational consultations, Dr. Gardner argues that the measurement of quality must move from compliance with organizational processes to facilitating person-centered outcomes for people.

Sylvia Nudler, M.A.S., Vice President and Chief Operating Officer, The Council on Quality and Leadership in Supports for People with Disabilities, Suite 406, 100 West Road, Towson, Maryland 21204. Ms. Nudler is responsible for planning, marketing, and fiscal and administrative management of The Council. Prior to joining The Council in 1989, Ms. Nudler was Division Administrator of The Education Center of Sheppard Pratt, a leading mental health community and continuing education program in Maryland. Ms. Nudler is a graduate of the University of Maryland and holds a master's degree in administrative science from The Johns Hopkins University. She is the co-author of *Paraprofessionals in Mental Health* (Irvington, 1983).

Contributors

Michelle D. Aman, M.S.
Resource and Support Supervisor
Black Hills Workshop
3650 Range Road
Post Office Box 2104
Rapid City, South Dakota 57709

Janet Bast, M.A.
Research Fellow
Institute on Community Integration
University of Minnesota
102 Pattee Hall
150 Pillsbury Drive SE
Minneapolis, Minnesota 55455

Vince Braun
Vice President
Black Hills Workshop and Training
   Center
3650 Range Road
Post Office Box 2104
Rapid City, South Dakota 57709

Greg Butschky
804 Old English Court
Apartment 1B
Bel Air, Maryland 21014

Tina Campanella
Vice President
ProLerna
Suite 406
100 West Road
Towson, Maryland 21204

Michael S. Chapman, M.Ed.
Vice President
Accreditation and Evaluation
   Systems
The Council on Quality and
   Leadership in Supports for
   People with Disabilities
Suite 406
100 West Road
Towson, Maryland 21204

Vernon DeHaven
804 Old English Court
Apartment 1B
Bel Air, Maryland 21014

Gary Donaldson, M.A., M.Ed.
President
Strategic Performance Solutions
   Corporation
9614 Sutherland Road
Silver Spring, Maryland 20901

Arthur Dykstra, Jr., M.A.
President and Chief Executive
   Officer
Trinity Services, Inc.
100 North Gougar Road
Joliet, Illinois 60432

Laura Gessel
2200 Monitor Drive
Apartment 2C
Park City, Utah 84060

Amy Sue Hewitt, Ph.D.
Program Coordinator
Institute on Community Integration
Research and Training Center on
   Community Living
University of Minnesota
204 Pattee Hall
150 Pillsbury Drive SE
Minneapolis, Minnesota 55455

Gillian A. King, Ph.D.
Research Program Manager
Thames Valley Children's Centre
779 Base Line Road East
London, Ontario
CANADA N6C 5Y6

K. Charlie Lakin, Ph.D.
Director
Research and Training Center on
    Community Living
University of Minnesota
102 Pattee Hall
150 Pillsbury Drive SE
Minneapolis, Minnesota 55455

Mary Law, Ph.D.
Professor
School of Rehabilitation Science
McMaster University
1280 Main Street West
Hamilton, Ontario
CANADA L8S 4K1

Elizabeth MacKinnon, M.S.
Manager, Early Childhood Services
Thames Valley Children's Centre
779 Base Line Road East
London, Ontario
CANADA N6C 5Y6

Dawn Merriman
Family Services Coordinator
2515 Rockhurst Road
Salina, Kansas 67401

Don Merriman, B.S.
2515 Rockhurst Road
Salina, Kansas 67401

Mary Moynihan, M.Ed.
Consultant
Wesmar Associates
7 Pembroke Road
Lewes, Delaware 19958

Susan N. O'Nell
Project Coordinator
Institute on Community
    Integration
Research and Training Center on
    Community Living
University of Minnesota
204 Pattee Hall
150 Pillsbury Drive SE
Minneapolis, Minnesota 55455

Kathryn R. Perkins, M.S.
Principal
LifeWorks Consulting
1714 J Landmark Drive
Forest Hill, Maryland 21050

Dennis E. Popp, M.S.W.
Chief Executive Officer
Black Hills Workshop and
    Training Center
3650 Range Road
Post Office Box 2104
Rapid City, South Dakota 57709

Christine Rich, B.S.
Program Manager, Eastern Region
State of Connecticut Department of
    Mental Retardation
376 Pomfret Street
Putnam, Connecticut 06260

John Ricketts
2300 Monitor Drive
Apartment 20A
Park City, Utah 84060

Dianne J. Russell, M.S.
Research Coordinator
Neurodevelopmental Clinical
    Research Unit
Assistant Professor of
    Rehabilitation Science
McMaster University
T-16
1280 Main Street West
Hamilton, Ontario
CANADA L8S 4K1

Peter Sajevic
President
Nekton-Norton
One Griggs Midway
1821 University Avenue
St. Paul, Minnesota 55104

Tony Sampson
4849 Magpie Lane
St. Charles, Maryland 20603

Robert L. Sandidge
Opportunity Planning Associates
1421 Lowe Drive
Post Office Box 424
Algonquin, Illinois 60102

Robert L. Schalock, Ph.D.
Professor and Chair
Department of Psychology
Hastings College
800 Turner
Hastings, Nebraska 68901

Anne C. Ward
Opportunity Planning Associates
425 North Douglas Avenue
Arlington Heights, Illinois 60004

David Warner
2300 Monitor Drive
Apartment 11B
Park City, Utah 84060

Jeannie Warner
2300 Monitor Drive
Apartment 11B
Park City, Utah 84060

Mary Ann Whetzel
1624 Michelle Court
Bel Air, Maryland 21014

Preface

The discussion of quality and leadership in services and supports rests on the premise that quality is determined by responsiveness to the person served rather than compliance with organizational process or regulations and standards. We begin this book with the understanding that although there may be many stakeholders in the provision of services and supports, there is only one customer or end user—the person receiving the services and supports.

Drawing on the work of Law, King, MacKinnon, and Russell (Chapter 5), we use the term *personal outcomes* to indicate the outcomes that people expect in their lives as the result of service and support provision. Personal outcomes identify expectations that surpass the content of goals and objectives found in the traditional (re)habilitation planning methodology. Personal outcomes also address different expectations than do outcomes related to clinical status or functional capabilities. This is not an argument that clinical and functional outcomes are not important or that they make no contribution to quality in services and supports. We believe that clinical and functional outcomes are an important bedrock for the attainment of personal outcomes. But this book is about quality, leadership, and organizational capacity to facilitate personal outcomes.

The book evolved from work and discussions that focused on conceptual and implementation issues related to personal outcomes. Many of the ideas and practices described in these chapters have been discussed, debated, and argued within the organizational discussions of The Council on Quality and Leadership in Supports for People with Disabilities (The Council). Since the early 1970s, The Council has conducted a national dialogue on quality in services and supports. The discussion has involved representatives of our sponsoring organizations; private and public providers of services and supports; recipients of services and supports; and local, state, and federal agencies.

This book, in part, originated in the discovery that the contemporary approaches to leadership theory and development were very similar to what we were learning about methods for facilitating outcomes for people receiving services and supports. We recognized a similarity in the literature on action research and organizational development (French & Bell, 1984); on participant action research (Campbell, 1996; Heller, Pederson, & Miller, 1996; Whitney-Thomas, 1997); and our observations of organizational behavior and leadership in involving the end user in decisions about his or her personal outcomes, organizational priorities, and budget decisions.

We identified contributors based on their recognized expertise and understanding of personal outcomes. Over the years, we have worked with many of these authors as friends, colleagues, and business partners. Common concerns about the connections and relationships among personal outcomes, organizational behavior, quality, and leadership brought them together in this effort. We asked these authors to join us in an exploration of quality in services and supports and individual and organizational leadership. We suggested the general topics for their chapters and provided feedback on drafts of the material. We edited the final drafts to ensure a uniformity in style and continuity across chapters. We did not, however, edit the manuscript to produce a consistent definition of terms or a uniform personal outcome implementation methodology.

Contemporary leadership theory suggests that leadership is developed and exercised through a process of learning by doing. This approach to leadership suggests that leadership is more akin to the meditation, learning, and teaching of the wise philosopher than to the traditional action image of the leader as a warrior hero. Through a process of learning by doing, leaders discover themselves, redefine their expectations about themselves and others, and better understand the people on whom they depend in the exercise of leadership. The lessons of leadership teach us that leaders often cannot predict the results of their actions. Instead, successful leaders have the confidence to believe that their experiences will teach and that they will complete their journeys in better positions than where they began. In a similar manner, leaders discover their leadership capacity through performance rather than through study and preparation.

Leadership learning through action is the same type of learning that people engage in as they discover and realize personal outcomes. People enter into uncharted territory to explore and experience new opportunities and challenges. Through this process, they begin to attach and refine their own meanings to general categories of outcomes and to discover their preferences and priorities. People prioritize outcomes through the experiences of the discovery process. People's definitions of their personal outcomes cannot be known outside the context of the experience and discovery process.

The process of learning through experience and action means that our ability to predict the future is severely limited. The action learning model often conflicts with previous models for planning and learning in which the outcomes were determined at the beginning and the experience consisted of accomplishing the prede-termined outcomes. Instead, the action learning model uses a pro-cess of discovering the outcomes and then developing the organiza-tional processes to facilitate the outcomes.

Our questions about the dynamics of organizational change also prompted the decision to begin this volume. In our early work with personal outcomes in 1992–1994, we encountered many situa-tions in which organizations identified barriers to facilitating per-sonal outcomes and making organizational changes (e.g., bureau-cracy, regulations, reimbursement methods and rates) as the rationale for making no changes. Yet, another organization, located in the same geographical area and confronting the same realities, proceeded with high energy into the arena of organizational change and personal outcomes. At first, we attributed this difference to val-ues and vision. We discovered, however, that values and vision, al-though important and necessary, were not enough. When we added the variable of leadership to values and vision, we believed that we were getting close. We are now at the point of believing that or-ganizational change and implementation of personal outcomes re-quire values and vision; leadership, however, is also necessary. In addition, successful organizations make use of specialized methods, technologies, knowledge bases, and skills in the implementation of new ways of doing business. We believe that without leadership, values, and vision, the quest for quality will fail. Leadership, val-ues, and vision, however, may not be enough. Organizations need leaders and managers who have the skills, knowledge, and abilities to make organizations work.

Perhaps it is not surprising, then, that various chapters em-phasize information collection and data analysis. Chapters by Dyk-stra (Chapter 7); Campanella (Chapter 8); Chapman (Chapter 12); Popp, Aman, and Braun (Chapter 14); Lakin, Bast, Hewitt, O'Nell, and Sajevic (Chapter 15); and Rich (Chapter 16) stress the impor-tance of reliable information and ongoing analysis of data and information.

Section I provides an overview of the changing definition of quality in service and manufacturing settings. Gardner (Chapter 1) provides a historical overview of the changing definition of quality in evaluating both production and service industries. In Chapter 2, he also explores the evolving definition of quality in the field of human services. Moynihan and Perkins (Chapter 3), with invited contributors, explore conversations and correspondence in which the recipients of services and supports identify their personal defi-nitions of quality. Schalock (Chapter 4) and Law, King, MacKinnon, and Russell (Chapter 5) discuss the use of personal outcomes in the measurement of both organizational and individual services and support quality. The common theme through these chapters is the definition of quality in the personal outcomes context. Quality is identified, defined, and evaluated by the recipient of services and support. The second, and perhaps understated, theme is that these personal outcomes can be measured in a valid and reliable manner. From an implementation perspective, organizations and community systems can begin self-assessment, organizational development, planning, and renewal around the personal priorities of people receiving services and supports.

Section II also indicates the importance of values, vision, and an orientation toward people in developing and maintaining services and supports of high quality. Values provide the anchor for the organization; vision offers a glimpse of what the organization might become at some future point. The people are the resources that make the organization change. Dykstra (Chapters 6 and 7) describes the contributions of leadership in setting forth vision and values and the importance of managing people as the key organizational resource. Campanella (Chapter 8) introduces the concept of personal outcomes as an organizing methodology for managing organizational change. Facilitating personal outcomes requires the right organizational values, a vision that offers people permission to exercise leadership, and a human resources system that encourages and rewards people for exercising leadership. In Chapter 9, Gardner explores the contemporary definitions and approaches to quality.

Section III examines organizational dynamics and offers four approaches for managing the quality of services and supports. The four approaches build on vision and values, and they require the exercise of leadership. Leadership in action begins with the values and assumptions held by people providing services and supports. Gardner (Chapter 10) presents a model for systems thinking that enables the practitioner to find applications and implications for the personal outcomes approach throughout the organization. Introducing personal outcomes into an organization is not simply a new form of assessment or goal planning. The successful introduction of personal outcomes will result from a series of interrelated changes throughout the organization. Leaders, however, must challenge people's values and help them to reframe values and assumptions. Learning to lead often begins when one reframes old realities and discovers new and deeper meanings. In Chapter 11, Sandidge and Ward examine reframing as a fundamental leadership and management skill. Chapman (Chapter 12) discusses management of data and information and the contribution that they can make to leadership and organizational change. Campanella (Chapter 13) focuses on the key variable of personal choice as a new organizational design feature. Basing organization process on the personal choices of the people receiving services and supports reinforces the need for reframing and systems analysis as key leadership skills.

Section IV demonstrates that different organizations operate with different approaches to outcomes. Popp, Aman, and Braun (Chapter 14) frame personal outcomes in the context of technology and information management. Lakin, Hewitt, Bast, O'Nell, and Sajevic (Chapter 15) center their treatment of personal outcomes on implementing systems change with Medicaid waivers and personal outcomes in Minnesota, whereas Rich (Chapter 16) employs a total quality management approach to implement personal outcomes in Connecticut. Donaldson (Chapter 17) discusses personal outcomes in terms of corporate business strategy in the community. All four discussions are grounded in organizational values and the need for leadership in services that support people with disabilities.

We urge the reader to embark on this venture in partnership, participation, and learning from our actions without having to know all of the answers ahead of time. Entering into partnerships requires the lessening of control. Leadership requires more listening and learning and less control. This is a challenge to dedicated people in human services programs in which both leadership and quality used to be defined in terms of control, predictability, and consistency. This is a challenge of significant impact to people receiving services and supports. We are confident that all of the authors in this volume will extend your visions of leadership and quality in services.

REFERENCES

Campbell, J. (1996). Toward collaborative mental health outcomes systems. *New Directions in Mental Health, 71,* 69–78.

French, W., & Bell, C. (1984). *Organization development: Behavioral science interventions for organizational improvement* (3rd ed.). Mahwah, NJ: Prentice-Hall.

Heller, T., Pederson, E.L., & Miller, A.B. (1996). Guidelines from the consumer: Improving consumer involvement in research and training for persons with mental retardation. *Mental Retardation, 34,* 141–148.

Whitney-Thomas, J. (1997). Participatory action research as an approach to enhancing quality of life for individuals with disabilities. In R.L. Schalock (Ed.), *Quality of life: Application to persons with disabilities* (Vol. 11). Washington, DC: American Association of Mental Retardation.

Acknowledgments

Quality Performance in Human Services: Leadership, Values, and Vision evolved from an ongoing, interactive learning process. We are particularly indebted to the thousands of people in North America receiving supports and services who have met with us during accreditation reviews and quality enhancement consultations and who have communicated to us their own definitions and meanings of outcomes.

Providers of services and supports shared with us their successes and dilemmas in facilitating outcomes for people. Employees representing all perspectives in the organization have enabled us to better understand the connection between the attainment of personal outcomes and the creative and hard work in arranging the organizational processes that facilitate the outcomes.

Since the first work on the *Outcome Based Performance Measures* in 1991, the employees of The Council on Quality and Leadership in Supports for People with Disabilities (The Council) have demonstrated a commitment to innovation in quality enhancement. They have conducted numerous experiments and field trials to explore the application of the outcomes in quality-enhancement work. Using the accreditation process as a learning opportunity, The Council has been able to try new ideas, test their effectiveness, and determine their applicability.

We would like to acknowledge the contributions of The Council's board of directors. We want to particularly thank those board members who ventured into the field, met with people receiving supports and services, evaluated our personal outcomes and measurement methodology, and provided us with critical feedback. Their contribution was paramount to the ultimate acceptance of the personal outcome methodology by the The Council's board of directors and the field of human services.

Finally, our learning and work were made possible by the support of the leadership of The Council. The support and encouragement of the chairs of The Council during the 1990s made our work exciting and rewarding. Thank you Ed Newman, David Ethridge, Dennis E. Popp, Nancy MacRae, Arthur Dykstra, Jr., and Nancy Santilli for your leadership.

In conclusion, we note that all royalties from this publication will be donated to the Foundation for Quality and Leadership for the purpose of supporting new research and innovative approaches to the enhancement of quality in human services to ensure that people receiving supports and services have full and abundant lives.

To my wife and best friend, Diane Gardner
James F. Gardner

To my parents, who gave me the values
Sylvia Nudler

Quality Performance in Human Services

I

Contemporary Perspectives on Quality and Leadership

In this section on contemporary perspectives on quality and leadership, Gardner (Chapter 1) places the concept of quality in historical perspective. He notes that the concept of quality has evolved with designated processes in the manufacturing sector to responsiveness to the customer in the service sector. Both Gardner and Schalock (Chapter 4) point to the challenges facing providers, professionals, families, and people with disabilities as formal service systems reorganize structures, incorporate person-centered planning, and introduce support models in place of programs.

In Chapter 2, Gardner identifies trends in quality enhancement in human services and systems serving people with disabilities. He summarizes some of the technology used in the measurement of personal outcomes. Gardner; Schalock (Chapter 4); and Law, King, MacKinnon, and Russell (Chapter 5) note the distinction between traditional outcomes that might measure organizational activity of standardized functional outcome scales and person-focused outcomes. Gardner employs the term *personal outcomes*; Schalock uses *value outcomes*; and Law, King, MacKinnon, and Russell describe *life habit or role-related outcomes* to describe the outcomes as defined by the person receiving the support or service. Each of these authors notes the distinction between the score on the "domain" scales that results in a normed outcome score and personal outcomes in which each individual's outcomes represent a unique sample of one. Gardner; Schalock; and Law, King, MacKinnon, and Russell illustrate from different perspectives the changing definition of quality in human services. In contrast to definitions that rest on conformity to standards or regulations, these authors note the connection between measures of quality and the unique perspectives of the individual receiving services and supports. This view of quality is, perhaps, more influenced by the literature of the late 1990s on consumer responsiveness than the total quality management/ continuous quality improvement literature of the early 1990s.

In Chapter 3, Moynihan and Perkins relate conversations with people with disabilities and their definitions of quality in services and supports. The language of people with disabilities is clearly similar to the personal outcomes described by other authors in this section. Especially noteworthy are the common themes of respect from, friendships with, and responsiveness of the people providing support. In Chapter 4, Schalock connects historical and contemporary trends to a Quality Evaluation Model that balances the need for accountability with the value of personal outcomes for both planning and quality review. The reader might also compare Schalock's treatment of the changing conception of disability and the enhancement of role status with Law, King, MacKinnon, and Russell's treatment of the topic in Chapter 5.

In Chapter 5, Law, King, MacKinnon, and Russell discuss the importance of person-centered outcomes in clinical services. They point to the challenges and opportunities that person-centered outcomes present to professionals who must make the shift to engaging in facilitation, negotiation, communication, and problem solving rather than playing the role of the therapist. They also connect the type of personal outcome to other organizational variables such as mission, resources, and personnel. Each author in the section stresses the importance of the program participant as a major contributor of data and information.

1

Quality in Services

James F. Gardner

At the end of the 19th century, the United States was a society of island communities. Communication among the island communities was restricted, and power was dispersed. Education was pragmatic, and there was little incentive for specialization and accumulation of knowledge. Government and democracy were grounded in local autonomy. Managerial government did not exist, and community affairs were enacted informally (Wiebe, 1967).

In the early 20th century, however, industrialization, immigration, and urbanization changed the fabric of American society. In contrast to the informal and personal communities of the 19th century, the new interactions were driven by regulated hierarchies of urban industrial life. During a period of great change, the new experiment in bureaucratic order stressed rules and impersonal sanctions. This progressive response to urban bosses, robber barons, and social disorder stressed continuity and predictability in a changing society. Centralization of authority, hierarchy, conformity with regulations, and bureaucracy offered an alternative to an out-of-control urban industrial society (Wiebe, 1967).

In the early 20th century, Frederick Taylor launched the field of scientific management by using empirical data to identify better ways to perform job tasks. Frank Gilbreth spread the gospel of efficiency by defining "therbligs" as the basic physical movements that workers performed. Max Weber described bureaucracy as the impersonal rational basis for the administration of large-scale undertakings. Henry Fayol's 14 principles of management, first published at the beginning of the 20th century in Europe, included authority, discipline, unity of command, centralization, order, and equity. These principles of industrial-urban management framed the discussion of quality. At the time, *quality* was defined as conformity with regulation and specification (Wren, 1979).

Hierarchies dominated industries that spanned the North American continent. As the railroads, telegraph, and telephone industries grew, companies had to replicate organizational structure in diverse geographic locations. The individual units of these companies each needed executive managers, general managers, and subordinates to summarize information, pass orders, and monitor activity (Savage, 1990). The functions of hierarchy reinforced older doctrines of division of labor, job specialization, control, and chain of command. This fragmentation of work spread through manufacturing and services industries in the 19th and early 20th centuries so companies began to formalize policy and procedure, establishing rules for every imaginable situation. Lines of authority, reporting systems, and chains of command were well established.

In the automobile industry, Henry Ford introduced the moving assembly line. Each worker on the line performed a single assembly function. Although this simplified the tasks, it introduced the requirement for coordinating the workers in their single tasks and in assembling the final product of all their labor. This led to the rise of the professional functional manager and the separation of management functions. Division of labor, job specialization, and chain of command shaped the world of the professional manager and the assembly line worker (Hammer & Champy, 1993).

Hierarchy and job specialization also led to a separation between thinking and doing. This division between thinking and doing was a natural consequence of Taylor's emphasis on specialization through simplification of industrial job tasks, the use of predetermined rules to coordinate those tasks, and the use of monitoring and performance measurements. Planning was separate from execution. Thinking was separate from, and superior to, the performance of the work itself. The consequences of this industrial model were that organizations failed to learn from, listen to, and benefit from those who were actually doing the work.

The progressive commitment to conformity with regulation, centralization, and hierarchy continued through the Depression of the 1930s, the second World War, and into the second half of the

20th century. Following World War II, the United States emerged as the global industrial power. American firms manufactured and exported goods throughout the world. Weak competition and unlimited markets placed an emphasis on mass production, often at the expense of quality.

A HALF CENTURY OF CHANGE

Contemporary discussions of quality are no longer grounded in the industrial-regulatory perspective. In contrast, current definitions of quality are rooted in more recent changes in society. Bell (1976) noted that the United States was entering a postindustrial era in which telecommunications and computers would shape the fabric of society. Bell noted that the manufacturing sector of the economy was being surpassed by the provision of human, professional, and technical services. The replacement of the manufacturing sector by the service sector was accompanied by an emphasis on the theoretical knowledge that made computers, polymers, and biotechnology possible. The capital and labor of the industrial era were being replaced by the information and knowledge of the postindustrial era. Drucker noted that "knowledge workers" made organizational hierarchy and centralized direction obsolete and that "knowledge, therefore, has to be organized as a team, in which the task decides who is in charge, when, for what, and for how long" (1978, p. 290).

The advent of the postindustrial, knowledge-based society challenges the foundations of industrial era management. The assault on the industrial hierarchy has been intensified with the evolution of computers and the growth of information processing. Computers have revolutionized work and organizations. Computers, robots, and computer-aided manufacturing now produce goods and provide services. But workers have not become slaves to the machine. In contrast, the use of computer-assisted design and production has freed workers from manual labor and enabled them to consider improvement in design and production. Rather than performing direct labor, workers engage creativity and critical thinking to increase productivity. Zuboff (1988) demonstrated how the use of computers is creating a world in which hierarchy, defined position, chain of command, control, and job responsibilities are fading.

PRODUCTION VERSUS SERVICE SECTOR QUALITY

The worldwide growth of service economies and the information revolution have elevated the importance of customer service. Because consumers have individual preferences and needs and because these change over time, services must be flexible to accommodate the consumer. These criteria are different from those in the manufacturing setting where *quality* is defined as conformity with specified standards. Standardization of quality is of critical importance in the manufacturing environment. In contrast, quality in services may vary with each customer interaction. Anderson, Fornell, and Rust (1995) referred to this as *customization quality*. In service settings, the measure of quality is the measure of customization (Danaher & Rust, 1996).

Zeithaml, Parasuraman, and Berry identified three themes in the research literature that distinguished service quality from quality in manufacturing and production settings:

- Customers find it more difficult to evaluate service quality than product quality.
- The delivery of the service cannot be separated from the outcome of the service.
- "Only customers judge quality; all other judgments are essentially irrelevant" (1990, p. 16).

Rosander (1989) cited the need for a new approach to management and quality in service settings because the role of people, the role of the customer, knowledge, and the concept of quality are all different than in the production of goods. In addition, he noted the following:

- Services cannot be measured like the physical properties of a manufactured good.
- Services cannot be stored or stockpiled.
- Services cannot be inspected. Services can be observed and conclusions drawn, but they cannot be inspected in any literal sense. Products and physical conditions associated with service can be inspected, but these do not define the quality of the service.
- Service quality cannot be determined ahead of time. Quality is determined at the moment that the service is rendered. The customer cannot evaluate the service until it is delivered and experienced.
- Services involve human reliability to a much greater extent than the reliability of products used in performing the service.
- Services are provided by the lowest paid worker in the company. The quality of the service is determined by the employee waiting on the customer not by the quality of the chief executive officer of the senior staff.

The major distinguishing characteristic of service settings are the people involved. Services are characterized by face-to-face contact between employees and customers. There are no intermediaries or negotiators. The employee determines quality by individual responsiveness. The important role of the individual employee heightens the need for effective supervision and management. Monitoring and feedback for employees is essential (Rosander, 1989).

THE CUSTOMER FOCUS OF SERVICE SETTINGS

Albrecht urged organizations to manage quality by paying attention to *moments of truth*, which he defined as "any episode in which the customer comes into contact with the organization and gets an impression of its service" (1992, p. 116). The details of a business do not exist in the mind of the customer in the same manner that they govern the daily work of employees. For the customer, a service organization exists only in the moments that the service is rendered. Albrecht explains: "Quality in the twenty-first century must start with the customer, not with the tangible product sold or the work processes that create it. This is a profound change in focus, from activities to outcomes" (p. 54).

In the factory setting, many units of the same product are manufactured according to specifications. The units all have a distribution, a mean, and a variance. The goal of quality control is to limit the variance around an acceptable mean so that the units meet specifications. In service settings, however, quality is an individual matter. There is no distribution, mean, or variance. There is only a sample of one customer at a time. Organizations can develop internal means and averages for internal process performance, but these have no meaning for customers. Service companies develop a knowledge base about their customers through multiple samples of one (Rosander, 1989).

Despite the popularity of total quality management (TQM), continuous quality improvement, and organizational reengineering, most American companies, including the well-known Malcolm Baldrige National Quality Award winners, fail to be customer focused (Johnson, 1995). They are market driven rather than customer driven. They pay great attention to market analysis but little attention to the samples of one—the single customer at a single interaction.

In many service industries, the products or deliverables that define the service are becoming commodities. The hamburgers provided through the large, national fast-food restaurants are commodities. Personal computers, videotape players, and clinical services are commodities. How then, asked Davis (1987), do you customize a commodity? His answer is to standardize the commodity, but also to customize the services that surround it.

This customer focus is not limited to the private sector. Osborne and Gaebler asked their readers, "When was the last time you felt like a valued customer at your child's school? How about your motor vehicle office? Your city hall?" They concluded that most traditional public institutions continue to provide "one size fits all services" (1992, p. 166). But, they were able to point to entrepreneurial government organizations that have begun to listen to and learn from their customers. They contrast the GI Bill, which allowed World War II veterans to pick their own university with government-paid tuition with the Veterans Administration hospitals, which were government funded and operated. There is little question that the GI Bill proved to be more responsive to the individual veteran.

The advantages of the customer controlling the resources, and hence the choice of service providers, offers the following advantages (Osborne & Gaebler, 1992, pp. 181–182): Customer-driven services

- Force service providers to be accountable to their customers
- Depoliticize the choice of provider decisions
- Stimulate more innovation
- Give people choices among different kinds of services
- Waste less because they match supply to demand
- Empower customers to make choices, and empowered customers are more committed customers
- Create greater opportunities for equity

MEASURING QUALITY IN SERVICES

Measuring quality in services requires a range of methods because people define quality differently. In addition, the level of employee discretion and decision making will vary with the customer's definition of quality. Both Albrecht (1992) and Zeithaml et al. (1990) have developed measurement systems for assessing quality in services.

Albrecht has developed a four-factor approach to measuring quality. Each factor varies according to the quality objective and the level of employee discretion for achieving the objective. The four levels as illustrated in Figure 1.1 are as follows:

- **Managing risks** This is a defensive quality assurance methodology. The objective is to minimize injury, accidents, and legal liability.
  Employee discretion—Individual employee behaviors are rigidly defined. Behaviors are specifically defined for each situation.
- **Managing resources** This is an internally focused quality assurance methodology. The objective is to minimize cost to the organization.
  Employee discretion—Organizational procedures allow some discretion in performing individual tasks, but there is little discretion in the nature of or the timing of the work tasks.
  Measurement method—An audit makes sure that employees are following the procedures. The audit assumes that the quality procedures are appropriate.
- **Managing customer "tangibles"** This methodology addresses the objective experience that the customer has with the product or service. The product or service must perform as intended. The product or service must meet customer expectations.

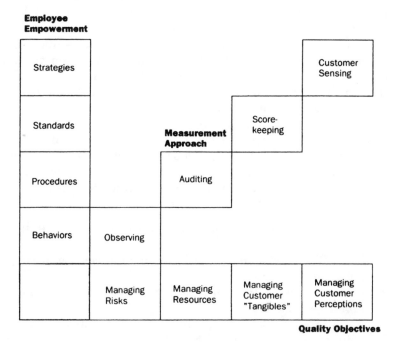

Figure 1.1. Four-factor service quality grid. (From Albrecht, K. [1992]. *The only thing that matters: Bringing the power of the customer into the center of your business* [p. 179]. New York: Harper Business; reprinted by permission.)

Employee discretion—Employees can depart from procedures as long as their actions produce outcomes that meet the standards. *Measurement method*—Scorekeeping with proper objectives enables the organization to measure the number of moments of truth that meet standards.

- **Managing customer perceptions**   This methodology focuses on the subjective value that customers find in the service.
  Employee discretion—Employees design strategies that go beyond predetermined behavior, procedures, or standards. Well-informed, knowledgeable employees exercise best judgment in discovering and managing customer perceptions.
  Measurement method—Customer sensing means that the employee discovers what is of greatest importance to the customer. This measurement is defined by the customer.

This four-factor service quality approach illustrates the interaction among organizational objectives, the level of employee decision making, and the measurement system. As the quality objective moves from managing risk to managing customer expectations, the level of employee discretion increases. Managing a customer's expectations requires greater knowledge of the customer, skills, and abilities in the interactions with the customer and execution of the specific service task. In addition, as the expectations of employees increase, the sophistication of the measurement system multiplies. Organizations cannot expect employees to exercise great discretion in devising strategies to manage customer perceptions when the measurement system provides feedback based on behavioral observations and performance audits.

Based on a series of focus group interviews, Parasuraman, Zeithaml, and Berry (1988) developed an instrument, SERVQUAL, to measure service quality across industries. In summarizing the research, Zeithaml et al. (1990, p. 26) identified five distinct dimensions of service quality:

- Tangibles—the appearance of physical facilities, equipment, and people
- Reliability—the ability to perform the promised service dependably and accurately
- Responsiveness—the willingness to help customers and provide prompt service
- Assurance—the knowledge and courtesy of employees and their ability to convey trust and confidence
- Empathy—the caring and individualized attention provided to customers

In analyzing the results from focus group meetings, Zeithaml et al. concluded that the most important measure was reliability. This was true across the different types of service settings. The conclusion for service providers from customers is to "appear neat and organized, be responsive, be reassuring, be empathetic, and most of all be reliable—do what you say you are going to do" (p. 27).

Subsequent studies have raised questions about the reliability of SERVQUAL across different service industries (Reeves, Bednar, & Lawrence, 1995), but the basic dimensions remain intact. After an examination of the research in service quality, Reeves et al. concluded that dissatisfaction with services was related to the aspects of service delivery that did not involve human contact. This might consist of Zeithaml and colleagues' (1990) category of reliability and Albrecht's designation of customer tangibles. In contrast, service satisfaction was linked clearly to those parts of the service experience that involved personal interactions. For organizations that provide repeated and ongoing services, the research stresses the importance of building a relationship with the customer in addition to the performance of discrete service transactions.

MANAGING QUALITY IMPROVEMENT

The literature on TQM and continuous quality improvement has offered a range of programs, techniques, and approaches to quality improvement. Common themes, however, cut across the different approaches. The quality improvement literature does provide consistency on the themes of variation, inspection for quality, and suboptimization. Considerable differences, however, are found in the recommendations for the rate of change in making quality improvement.

Variation

The statistical strength from TQM and continuous quality improvement programs is found in statistical process control and, in particular, in control charts. The control charts, popularized in the 1980s by the late W. Edwards Deming, graphically depict process or product variables over time. The charts indicate whether actual measures fall within upper and lower control limits. Figure 1.2 illustrates a control chart.

Deming identified two possible causes for variation—special causes and common causes. Tasks performed, not performed, or performed incorrectly are labeled special causes. The special causes are within the control of the individual worker. Deming estimated that 6%–15% of problems in quality were due to special causes. The re-

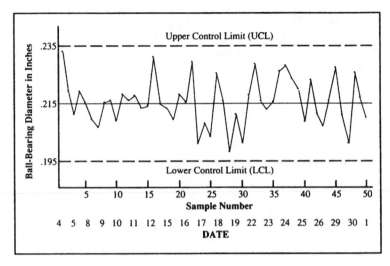

Figure 1.2.   Control chart. (Reprinted by permission of the publisher. From *Putting total qual-ity management to work: What TQM means, how to use it and how to sustain it over the long run* [p. 13], copyright © 1993 by Sashkin, M., & Kiser, K., Berrett-Koehler Publishers, Inc., San Francisco. All rights reserved.)

maining 85%–94% of the problems were classified as common causes and were attributable to the manufacturing or services process itself. No remedial action taken by individual employees can correct systems design problems (Sashkin & Kiser, 1993).

Deming concluded that most of the reasons for poor quality were rooted in the common causes inherent in poor design, inferior raw materials, or defects in tools and processes. Exhorting employ-ees to work more quickly and smartly provides no relief from sys-tems problems. For Deming, top management, not the hourly or line workers, is responsible for the majority of problems in quality in manufacturing and services.

Inspection

Quality improvement practitioners are unanimous in their declara-tion that inspection alone is not a reliable quality improvement technique. Traditional inspection systems based on checking and controls add little value to the service for the customer. Instead, the checking and controls ensure that employees are not abusing work processes or misperforming work tasks.

Defect detection has been the primary quality assurance tech-nique in services and manufacturing settings since the beginning of the industrial revolution (Lareau, 1992). The problem with detect-ing defects after the fact is that the number of defective parts is not limited to ones discovered. Detecting one instance of poor service is an indication that many more have taken place and will continue to happen in the future.

End-of-the-line inspection creates two technical problems. The first problem is that even trained personnel will not identify every defective part or sloppy service. Human attention and perception is not geared for repetitious, boring jobs. For example, the military changes radar screen monitors every quarter hour in critical situations (Lareau, 1992). Adding another level of inspectors will not solve the problem. If the first inspector catches 90% of all defects and a second inspector catches 90% of the remaining defects, you have doubled your cost; but 1% of the defects still escape detection.

The second problem is more pervasive. The focus on inspection diverts attention away from the work processes that are responsible for the defect. Attention, energy, and money become localized at the back end of the problem. Employees develop a belief that quality is the responsibility of the quality assurance inspectors. They see little reason to examine their own work processes to explore possibilities for quality improvement. Johnson summarized the limitations of inspection:

- Inspection does not lead to improvement; it identifies symptoms, not causes.
- Inspection is a defensive strategy. The purpose is to keep customers from complaining, not expressing delight.
- Inspection standards are flexible. Processes and products that fail in slow demand time pass during busy times.
- Because it takes place at the conclusion of the production, it indicates that the process itself cannot consistently produce quality.
- "Inspection is the most wasteful activity in business today" (1989, p. 36).

Inspection, as a part of quality performance improvement, can detect defects and out-of-compliance performance. The inspection, however, must be linked to organizational processes that improve the service quality. Quality improvement programs built on inspection alone do not succeed. Inspection is a legitimate, but not the only or even most important, component for managing high-risk situations. High-risk enterprises like hospitals, air traffic control systems, and nuclear power plants display a high degree of formalism in policy and procedure to guide work performance. Low-risk activities such as a street vendor business or a small home repair company require less formalization and bureaucracy.

Suboptimization

Organizations or units of organizations suboptimize when they become more efficient at performing the wrong tasks. Most typically this occurs when units in organizations concentrate their energy and resources in the pursuit of unit goals that do not further the organization's mission or goals (Juran, 1992). For example, suboptimization occurs when the manufacturing department maximizes production of units that do not meet customer specifications or that are difficult to service.

The human inclination to develop primary loyalties with coworkers often leads units or departments to develop close common bonds. In fact, the major identification is with the people in the unit rather than with other people in the company. This leads to an "us" versus "them" mentality. Each unit or department begins to define itself as different from the rest of the organization, and units and departments begin to emphasize their own goals.

Suboptimization also leads to another organizational phenomenon. As groups begin to build walls, work evolves in the direction of functions. Groups begin to stake out the territory and defend their own turf. Over time, units emphasize their own functions at the expense of integrated, organization-wide problem solving. Over time, units generate policies and procedures to increase power and control. TQM programs attempt to tear down the foxhole mentality of individual departments and focus instead on the cross-cutting quality improvement strategies.

BEYOND TOTAL QUALITY MANAGEMENT

Proposals for quality improvement have offered different formulas for the timing and scope of organizational change. TQM and continuous quality improvement emphasize the ongoing, continuous shaping of quality. With an emphasis on statistical process control, the quality improvement efforts are rooted in the continuous improvement of the special and common causes of quality problems (Sashkin & Kiser, 1993).

In contrast, Hammer and Champy (1993) defined *business reengineering* as starting all over again. They indicated that business reengineering is not about fixing process, and it is not about statistical process control to refine organizational process. In contrast, reengineering emphasizes breakthroughs not by refining existing processes but rather by junking existing process and implementing new processes. Business reengineering represents an assault on the industrial paradigm of the early 20th century. Hammer and Champy call for an end to the division of labor, hierarchy, and economies of scale.

McArthur and Womack (1995) suggested that organizations pursue both approaches—incremental and revolutionary change—simultaneously. On a business track, the senior management focuses on improving or changing the business of the company. This requires the use of cross-functional and interdepartmental teams. In contrast, a separate organizational track emphasizes incremental change with traditional quality improvement methods.

The issues of rapid and incremental change and continuous or discontinuous change can be illustrated by examining S-curves (Foster, 1986). The S-curves illustrated in Figure 1.3 plot the relationship between effort and performance. The bottom part of the curve is flat because start-up time and early effort do not yield equal performance. The midpart of the curve shows rapid ascent as the investment in start-up and early effort pays off. The top of the S-curve flattens out as the organization can no longer achieve performance improvement with the existing technology or business strategy. Change management requires decisions about whether to push up the accent slope of the S-curve or to jump to the next S-curve and begin again with a new technology or new business strategy.

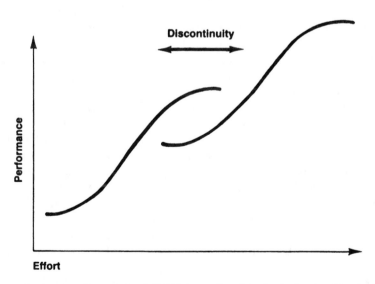

Figure 1.3.   S-curves. (From Foster, R. [1986]. *Innovation: The attacker's advantage* [p. 102]. New York: Summit Books; reprinted by permission.)

The two-pronged approach to change is a fundamental strategy for successful organizations. Kanter (1983) noted that successful companies manage innovation at the same time that the organizational structure carries out the routine business of the organization. Organizations develop one set of systems to provide continuity and maintain order. At the same time, they establish other systems to engage in disruptive behavior associated with change. The organization is anchored to the status quo but also explores change. For Kanter, senior management teams with cross-cutting responsibilities provide integrating mechanisms between and among segmented departments. Behind the ongoing maintenance-oriented organization, there is a parallel organization that can link separate departments and units to solve problems and guide change. There is, Kanter noted, "predictable routine punctuated by episodes of high involvement in change efforts" (1983, p. 359).

LEADERSHIP, QUALITY, AND CHANGE

In describing the linkages among leadership, culture, and change, Bennis noted the presence of "the compelling moral necessity for the new way" (1989, p. 29). Deal and Kennedy described leaders as organizational heroes, "symbolic figures whose deeds are out of the ordinary" and noted that "managers run institutions; heroes create them" (1982, p. 37). Managing has to do with order and procedure and clarity. Heroes and leaders flirt with disorder in pursuit of vision and commitment. These authors describe leaders who do not fit the image of scientific manager, strategic planner, or financial analyst. In contrast, they describe leaders who have deep commitment and who challenge traditions. These leaders convey that commitment through personal action and by example.

Wheatley (1994) echoed a similar theme. She noted that the leader's task is to communicate guiding visions, basic values, and the organization's beliefs. With clear vision, values, and beliefs as guides, leaders can allow individuals to make their own way in seeming chaos. Leadership drives quality improvement. Sashkin and Kiser (1993) emphasized the point by noting that only when the top management is unconditionally committed to quality does the quality improvement effort have a chance to succeed.

Leadership is fundamental for quality improvement efforts because people watch what leaders do with their time. In order to communicate the importance of quality in services, leaders must demonstrate service quality in their actions (Lareau, 1992). Leaders also can teach and coach employees on a real-time basis. Finally, they can take time to discover and lead innovation.

The key to excellent services is service leadership. Management is not enough. Zeithaml et al. (1990) identified the characteristics of service leaders:

- **Service vision**   Excellence in service is part of the strategy for doing business. Superior service is a winning strategy in terms of building customer loyalty and generating profits. This commitment to the service vision of quality requires steadfast watchfulness. Service quality is not a program; rather, it is day-in, day-out, constant hard work.
- **High standards**   Service leaders pay attention to the small items. They are zealots about getting it right the first time. These leaders realize that good service may not be sufficient to differentiate them from the competition.
- **In-the-field leadership style**   Service leaders use a hands-on approach to develop a sense of teamwork and service vision among all employees. They emphasize two-way, personal communication and interaction as they role-model leadership.

Lacking this leadership orientation, top-level officials may experience difficulties in leading the service quality initiative. For some officials, their role is based on power and hierarchy not on knowing how things work. They really do not know where causes of poor quality are found. Compounding this lack of knowledge, their orientation is to functional departments such as finance, sales, or distribution, not to quality, which cuts across functional lines. Some officials mistakenly attempt to assign quality to a department. Finally, some top-level officials miss the point on both leadership and service quality when they substitute slogans, quick-fix approaches, and new techniques for leadership and hard work.

CONCLUSIONS

The progressive movement in the early 1900s provided the urban reformers with the policy, procedures, and decision-making rules to bring about social stability. The progressive reformers enacted legislation that regulated the quality of food, drugs, and drinking water. The civil service legislation was enacted, and the pervasive corruption and lawlessness of the urban bosses was contained.

The concern for uniformity, conformity, and exactness appeared in business and commerce in North America and Western Europe as national economies evolved from an agricultural to industrial basis. Taylor's industrial engineering, Weber's bureaucracy, Fayol's management principles, and Ford's mass production reinforced each other. The industrial definitions of quality, work performance, and management were developed during the first half of the 20th century.

During the second half of the 20th century, the United States, Japan, and Western Europe began the evolution from industrial to postindustrial societies. Provision of services replaced the manufacture of goods as the focus of the national economy. This transition from an industrial to a service-based economy has not been accompanied by a similar change in the definitions of service quality and management. The recent popularity of TQM, continuous quality improvement, and process reengineering have demonstrated the need for change.

Service quality is grounded in defining customer expectations, individualizing the delivery of services one customer at a time, measuring with the customer in mind, organizing around the customer, and leading through focus and clarity of purpose.

REFERENCES

Albrecht, K. (1992). *The only thing that matters: Bringing the power of the customer into the center of your business.* New York: Harper Business.

Anderson, E.W., Fornell, C., & Rust, R.T. (1995). *Customer satisfaction, productivity, and profitability: Differences between goods and services* [Working paper]. University of Michigan, Ann Arbor.

Bell, D. (1976). *The coming of the post-industrial society.* New York: Basic Books.

Bennis, W. (1989). *Why leaders can't lead: The unconscious conspiracy continues.* San Francisco: Jossey-Bass.

Danaher, P.J., & Rust, R.T. (1996). Rejoinder. *Quality Management Journal, 3*(2), 85–88.

Davis, S. (1987). *Future perfect.* Reading, MA: Addison-Wesley.

Deal, T.E., & Kennedy, A.A. (1982). *Corporate cultures: The rites and rituals of corporate life.* Reading, MA: Addison-Wesley.

Drucker, P. (1978). *The age of discontinuity.* New York: Harper Torchbooks.

Foster, R. (1986). *Innovation: The attacker's advantage.* New York: Summit Books.

Hammer, M., & Champy, J. (1993). *Reengineering the corporation: A manifesto for business revolution.* New York: Harper Business.

Johnson, H.T. (1995). Discussion. *Quality Management Journal, 3*(1), 31–34.

Johnson, P.L. (1989). *Keeping score: Strategies and tactics for winning the quality war.* New York: Harper Business.

Juran, J.M. (1992). *Juran on quality by design.* New York: The Free Press.

Kanter, R.M. (1983). *The change masters: Innovation and entrepreneurship in the American corporation.* New York: Touchstone Books.

Lareau, W. (1992). *American samurai: Why every American executive must fight for quality.* New York: Warner Books.

McArthur, C.D., & Womack, L. (1995). *Outcome management: Redesigning your business systems to achieve your vision.* New York: Quality Resources.

Osborne, D., and Gaebler, T. (1992). *Reinventing government: How the entrepreneurial spirit is transforming the public sector.* Reading, MA: Addison-Wesley.

Parasuraman, A., Zeithaml, V.A., & Berry, L. (1988). SERVQUAL: A multi-item scale for measuring consumer perceptions of service quality. *Journal of Retailing, 2,* 12–40.

Reeves, C.A., Bednar, D.A., & Lawrence, R.C. (1995). Back to the beginning: What do customers care about service firms. *Quality Management Journal, 3*(1), 56–72.

Rosander, A.C. (1989). *The quest for quality in services.* New York: Quality Resources.

Sashkin, M., & Kiser, K.J. (1993). *Putting total quality management to work: What TQM means, how to use it and how to sustain it over the long run.* San Francisco: Berrett-Koehler.

Savage, C. (1990). *Fifth generation management: Integrating enterprises through human networking.* Bedford, MA: Digital Press.

Wheatley, M. (1994). *Leadership and the new science: Learning about organizations from an orderly universe.* San Francisco: Berrett-Koehler.

Wiebe, R.H. (1967). *The search for order.* New York: Hill and Wang.

Wren, D. (1979). *The evolution of management thought.* New York: John Wiley & Sons.

Zeithaml, V.A., Parasuraman, A., & Berry, L.L. (1990). *Delivering quality service: Balancing customer perceptions and expectations.* New York: The Free Press.

Zuboff, S. (1988). *In the age of the smart machine: The future of work and power.* New York: Basic Books.

2

Quality in Services for People with Disabilities

James F. Gardner

The evolution in services and supports for people with disabilities has provided a framework for the discussion of the quality of those services and supports. The movement from large residential settings to community-based systems of support redefined quality and exposed areas of both agreement and disagreement among families, providers, professionals, and public officials. The national debates on such terms as *deinstitutionalization, normalization, behavior management,* and *least restrictive environment* have revealed wide differences in values and definitions of quality.

Since the early 1990s, however, a consensus has been emerging. The consensus finds expression in the use of the term *support* to describe a new type of service relationship. Supported employment, supported living, and family support are designed to offer support to individuals and families to address their own priorities. Another expression of this consensus is the emergence of person-centered planning models that are challenging the older and more established forms of habilitation planning. Finally, there is an increasing recognition that formal systems will not be able to provide the full range of services and supports needed by people with disabilities. Some blending of both formal and informal support networks will emerge as cost containment continues to gain momentum.

But, this consensus does rest on the recognition that quality begins with a definition that is person centered. Managing for quality requires that the priorities of people with disabilities directly shape the design of the services and supports that they receive. Although learning from and listening to the person with the disability is the prerequisite for services of quality, there are many management strategies for successful implementation.

A MATTER OF DEFINITIONS

The definitions of *good* and *quality* and the suggestions for examining quality have been the center of the world's religions and philosophies for several thousand years. More recently, advent of the industrial revolution and mass machine production in the late 18th century thrust the question of definition of *quality* from the study of religion and philosophy to that of industrial engineering, operations research, and statistical quality control.

Quality in Services

In a review of the definitions of *quality,* Reeves and Bednar concluded that "the concept has had multiple and often muddled definitions and has been used to describe a wide variety of phenomena" (1994, p. 419). *Quality* has been defined as excellence, as value, as conformance to specifications, and as meeting and exceeding customers' expectations. In the mid-1990s, *quality* was most frequently defined as conformance with specifications. Since the 1950s, however, the service economy in the United States and Western Europe has expanded. In 1900, only three out of ten workers were employed in the service economy. By 1990, that figure had grown to almost eight out of ten workers. In the late 1990s, the most frequent definition of *quality* is that of meeting and exceeding customers' expectations (Reeves & Bednar, 1994).

Albrecht (1992) argued that quality in the 21st century will begin with the consumer not with the products, services, or work processes that create them. Organizational systems, policies, and procedures are guides for serving consumers not ends in themselves. In the customer-value paradigm, "the primary focus of measurement is on outcomes" (p. 41). Zeithaml, Parasuraman, and Berry (1990) also stressed the role of the customer in evaluating service quality. They wrote, "Only customers judge quality; all other judgments are essentially irrelevant" (p. 16).

Quality in Services for People with Disabilities

In the provision of services and supports for people with disabilities, *quality* is most frequently defined in the context of quality assurance. As Bradley (1990) noted, the purpose of quality assurance is to enhance systems as well as to ensure conformance with specifications. This is consistent with the definitions of quality assurance in the Malcolm Baldrige National Quality Award categories. Quality Assurance of Products and Services measures the extent to which the organization's systems are effective in maintaining quality control of all operations. Quality Assurance Results focus on the degree of the organization's success in improving quality, as determined by quantitative measures. These Baldrige Award categories clearly indicate that quality assurance is more than discovering and eliminating defects.

Quality assurance has generally been associated with the necessity of maintaining an agreed-on level of quality in public and private services to people with disabilities. Quality assurance systems require the development of standards, periodic reviews based on the standards, and feedback and control functions based on the review. Quality assurance mechanisms provide assurance to the community that standards will be maintained, provide evidence for state compliance with federal requirements, and provide feedback to providers of services. Unfortunately, quality assurance in disability services is generally associated with inspections and surveys that measure compliance with organizational processes, funding requirements, and federal and state regulations (Bradley, 1990).

The negative connotation of quality assurance, in part, resulted in the popularity of the term *quality enhancement* to describe quality improvement efforts that were not grounded in compliance inspections. The positive, proactive approach of the quality enhancement efforts were also influenced by the total quality management (TQM) literature of the 1980s and 1990s. Deming's admonition to "cease dependence on mass inspections [and] to improve constantly and forever the system of production and management" (1986, pp. 23–24) symbolized the difference between traditional quality assurance approaches and the emerging quality enhancement models.

HISTORICAL CONTEXT FOR QUALITY

The evolution of the definition, focus, and measures of quality have been in response to the changing patterns of service and social and political expectations expressed in federal legislation. The civil rights movement influenced these patterns as litigation and class action suits forced states to alter traditional practices in regard to providing services for people with disabilities. Jaskulski (1991) noted four distinct periods, each with a different focus and measure of quality (see Figure 2.1).

1970s Institutional Reform

In 1962, the original President's Panel on Mental Retardation assessed the status of residential settings for people with mental retardation in the United States. In general, the panel concluded that the level of quality was low as were society's expectations for people with mental retardation and for the institutions in which they lived (Scheerenberger, 1987).

During the 1960s and 1970s, several photographic essays starkly revealed the absence of quality in services that existed in most residential facilities. The *Philadelphia Inquirer* depicted a dehumanizing environment for public residential facilities. Blatt and Kaplan (1966) published *Christmas in Purgatory*, depicting the horrible conditions in residential settings in three eastern states. In 1972, Rivera again brought the same problem to national attention through a televised exposé of the Willowbrook State School in New York (Scheerenberger, 1987).

These revelations resulted in attempts to reform and improve residential institutions. The President's Committee on Mental Retardation prioritized the improvement of standards. Building upon work in the early 1960s, the American Association on Mental Defi-

Era	Focus	Measure
1970s Institutional reform	Protection, health, safety, and supervision	Environmental inputs
Early 1980s Deinstitutionalization	Habilitation planning	Organizational process
Late 1980s Community options	Independence, productivity, integration	Outcomes for people
1990s Non–facility-based services	Empowerment, inclusiveness, quality of life	Satisfaction, well-being

Figure 2.1. Evolution of approaches to delivery of quality in services and supports: 1970s–1990s.

ciency in 1966 formed the National Planning Committee on Accreditation of Residential Centers for the Retarded with the American Psychiatric Association, The Council for Exceptional Children, The Association for Retarded Citizens (now called The Arc), and the United Cerebral Palsy Associations. This National Planning Committee evolved into the Accreditation Council for Facilities for the Mentally Retarded, a part of the Joint Commission on Accreditation of Hospitals. In 1971, The Accreditation Council published its *Standards for Residential Facilities for the Mentally Retarded.* The following year, a federal district court (*Wyatt v. Stickney,* 1972) required the State of Alabama to comply with the Accreditation Council Standards at the Partlow State School and Hospital. Finally, in 1974 the federal government used the 1971 Accreditation Council Standards as the basis for the federal regulations for the Intermediate Care Facilities for the Mentally Retarded (ICF/MR) program (Intermediate Care Facilities Rule, 1978).

These early standards, in an era of institutional reform, emphasized individual protection, health, safety, and supervision. The measures of quality defined *inputs*—resources in the form funding, staffing, equipment, furnishing—that were associated with quality.

Early 1980s Deinstitutionalization

During the 1970s, the movement for institutionalization reform gave way to deinstitutionalization. The argument for closing institutions, first voiced by Samuel Gridley Howe in 1852, acquired acceptance in the 1970s and became a national goal during the early 1980s. Between 1970 and 1995, the number of people residing in state institutions declined from 187,897 to 63,258 (Lakin, Prouty, Smith, & Braddock, 1996). The questions surrounding quality shifted during this time from "How many people should live here?" to "Where else might people live?" Deinstitutionalization was coupled with the principle of normalization, and service providers attempted to enhance personal growth and development through habilitation planning.

During the early 1980s, habilitation planning was added to basic protections in framing the definition of quality. The measurement of quality in services expanded beyond organizational inputs. *Quality* was defined in terms of organizational process—what the organization did with the inputs. As such, licensing, certification, and accreditation organizations measured organizational processes with questions such as

- Who participated on the interdisciplinary team?
- When were the assessments completed?

- Were the behavioral objectives specific and measurable?
- How often did the individual program coordinator review the plan?

The focus on organizational process as a measure of quality cut across organizational settings. The generic individual program plan was reconstituted as the individualized written rehabilitation plan (IWRP) in vocational rehabilitation services, the individualized education program (IEP) in educational settings, and as the individual habilitation plan (IHP) for purposes of accreditation. For example, the IHP emphasized thorough professional assessment, the development of goals and specific behavioral objectives, the ongoing collection of data, and the review and modification, if necessary, of the plan on a regular basis.

Late 1980s Community Options

During the late 1980s, the focus of quality began to shift from conformity with habilitation processes to outcomes resulting from the habilitation process. Concerns surfaced about "paper compliance" (i.e., measuring quality by the presence of files and plans) and compliance with regulations and standards as ends in themselves. In the late 1980s, the Administration on Developmental Disabilities used the terms *independence, productivity,* and *integration* to describe quality in services and supports for people with disabilities. During this period, critics of the ICF/MR program noted the high monetary and human resources costs of ensuring compliance with certification requirements. The passage of the Home and Community Based Waiver (PL 97-35) and the Community Living Arrangements (PL 101-508) represented attempts to finance community alternatives to the ICF/MR with less rigid regulatory requirements.

1990s Non–Facility-Based Services

In the late 1980s and early 1990s, the concept of support services led to the separation of services from facilities and locations. Family support services, supported employment, and supported living emphasized that resources and supports can be provided to people in the locations where they live and work. Providing supports in natural settings empowers people with disabilities and their families, increases social inclusion, and promotes both autonomy and interdependence. Individuals are able to define the when, how, and why for support services, and the provision of the support services can strengthen the ties of family and community. Individuals also define quality in their own terms.

CURRENT DILEMMAS

The evolution of quality through these four eras reveals how remnants of the past remain in practice in the late 1990s. New approaches to services and supports, and the rules and procedures that follow the implementation of new approaches, are usually added to existing rules and regulations. Regulations and procedures arising from contemporary practice do not replace older regulations and procedures. The new does not replace the old; the new is added to the old.

The result is a quality assurance/enhancement methodology that resembles a layer cake. As presented in Figure 2.1, the various quality approaches are wedged below one another. Addition rather than replacement poses no problem as long as we recognize that the different frames will emphasize and promote different definitions of quality. The problem arises when the federal or state governments or private organizations expect to promote quality in all four frames through a process that works in only one frame.

For example, a concern for health and safety is nonnegotiable. Organizations receiving public support have a fiduciary responsibility to protect the health and welfare of those people to whom they provide services and supports. Inspection, as a methodology, can detect dangerous situations from fire hazards to unsanitary food preparation to violations of building code. Quality assurance through inspection can prevent disasters. The new approaches to quality enhancement are no substitute for providing the basic protections in the areas of personal safety, health, and freedom from abuse and neglect.

However, the same methods that result in greater health and safety will not necessarily result in greater person-centered outcomes or in greater satisfaction. Facilitating outcomes and individual satisfaction requires different approaches to quality and quality improvement. Figure 2.2 illustrates the limitation of inspection as an all-purpose quality-enhancement methodology. At the bottom of the figure, at Point 1, a dollar of resources for inspection produces a dollar of quality in return. As dollars are added, the level of quality increases from AA to BB on the left-hand axis. As quality goes up, however, there is a diminishing return on the dollar investment so that at Point 2, a dollar expended returns only 5 cents in further protection. In fact, at some point additional inspection produces no new gains in quality. Inspection hits a ceiling at which there is no further return on investment.

In order to realize gains in quality, service systems have to go beyond inspection to other methods of quality improvement. These

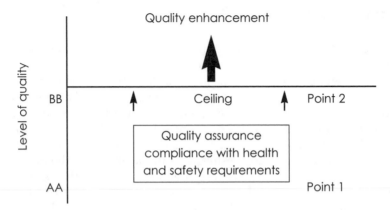

Figure 2.2. Demonstration of the limitations of inspection as a quality-enhancement methodology.

quality enhancement methods incorporate personal outcomes, individualized planning models, techniques for self-managed work teams, methods for promoting organizational learning, and new leadership models. In addition, the promotion of inclusion, personal planning, and interviews, and the emphasis on community participation, social inclusion, and natural support models, appear to be proactive methods for ensuring the basic protections for health, safety, and welfare.

A MATTER OF MEASUREMENT

The changes in the definition of quality have resulted in different definitions of measurement terms. The most common terms are inputs, processes, outputs, and outcomes.

Inputs

The resources that fuel services and supports for people with disabilities are called *inputs*. Typical resources are funding, personnel allocations, buildings, equipment, and furnishings. Credentials of staff, staffing ratios, and building requirements represent attempts to manage quality through the definition of input requirements. Inputs are generally easy to define and measure.

Processes

Measures that define how the organization uses its resources are called *processes*. Organizational policies and procedures, job descriptions, funding requirements, and regulations can dictate how the organization uses its resources. Personnel expectations are often governed by practices and expectations associated with programs. Designated programs models such as supported living or employment services dictate particular processes. *Quality* is defined as a measure of conformity or compliance with the process requirement. Written documentation is often used to determine compliance with organizational process requirements.

Outputs

Measures of the results of organizational processes are called *outputs*. Output measures might include the number of people placed in supported employment options, the number of assessments completed, or the number of units of service or support provided. Outputs are generally easy to identify and measure. Providers frequently cite organizational outputs as measures of quality in reports to government agencies and funding sources.

Outcomes

Measures that represent the impact of the service and support on the individual are called *outcomes*. There is no clear consensus on the definition of the term *outcome*; however, an adaptation of Law's (1998) categorization of outcomes suggests that outcomes can be differentiated among clinical, functional, and personal outcomes.

Clinical Outcomes *Clinical outcomes* refer to changes in symptom status. For example, the clinical outcome that results from services and supports (in the form of medication) for a person with depression is a reduction in the symptoms of depression. This is clinically recorded in charts and records and through a utilization review.

Functional Outcomes *Functional outcomes* focus on increasing functional status in designated areas. For example, physical therapy is provided for an individual to increase range of motion, which then enables the person to execute additional activities of daily living. This increase in activity of daily living skills is measured through standardized scales. The standardized scales make possible comparisons to norms for various groups of people.

New technology and equipment can enhance functional outcomes, such as by increasing communication and mobility abilities. Communication and mobility can be measured with standardized scales that are normed for various populations.

Personal Outcomes *Personal outcomes* focus on the items and issues that matter most to people in their lives. Personal outcomes provide the context for considering services and supports to attain clinical or functional outcomes. The positive change in the clinical symptoms of seizure disorders results in greater possibilities for employment. An increase in activity of daily living skills or community mobility capability should facilitate a priority personal outcome. The following are just a few examples:

- With medication, William's symptoms of depression are greatly reduced. The clinical outcome is connected to the personal outcome when he joins a wine-tasting club. However, he is not satisfied with symptom reduction and increased social functioning. He wants to work. He wants to use the increased functioning in a personally valued setting.
- With physical therapy, Mary Ellen increases range of motion. The increased range of motion enables her to perform more activities of daily living. In addition, she wants to get out of the 14-person group home and live with two close friends.
- The new motorized wheelchair gives Michael the function of mobility. He is no longer content to be transported to the sheltered workshop for the day. He wants to get together with some friends, do volunteer work at the hospital during the week, and go fishing on the weekend.

QUALITY OF LIFE

Differences in definition also extend to the concept of quality of life (QOL). There is an ongoing debate between quantitative and qualitative researchers. The quantitative researchers dismiss qualitative approaches because these approaches are subjective and do not demonstrate reliability or generalization of findings. Qualitative researchers reply that the quantitative methods oversimplify complex human experience, and this simplification can lead to depersonalization and devaluation of life experience (Dennis, Williams, Giangreco, & Cloninger, 1993).

Parmenter (1994) reviewed social and psychological indicators of QOL. He concluded that social indicators such as income or marital status and psychological indicators such as health, work, or learning obscured individual QOL status (Parmenter, 1994). Quoting from the work of Flanagan (1978), Parmenter noted that "the effects on each individual's quality of life should be evaluated in terms of his or her personal values and needs" (1994, p. 251). Taylor and Bogdan noted that "Quality of life is a matter of subjective experience. . . . People may experience the same circumstances differently. What enhances one person's quality of life may detract from another's" (1990, pp. 34–35). Goode also noted that "quality of life needed to be evaluated from the subjective standpoint of the individual" (1994, p. vi). The Principles and Recommendations of the National QOL Project stressed

> QOL is a concept that gives primacy to the individual's point of view. It can and should account for the experiences of persons with severe cognitive, emotional or physical disabilities and reflect the very different ways such persons may see the world and set goals within it. (Parmenter, 1994, p. 148)

Brown, Bayer, and MacFarlane (1988), Murrell and Norris (1983), Parmenter (1994), and Schalock (1990) defined QOL within the context of the fit between the individual and his or her environment. Goode (1988) also stressed the interconnection between the QOL of an individual and those people within the immediate environment with whom he or she interacts. Noting the social nature of QOL, Goode (1988) argued that services and supports be based on an understanding of the relationship between "QOL family supports, independent living, personal and attendant care, and staff quality of work life" (p. 149).

Schalock (1996) suggested that QOL is less important as an entity in itself and more valuable as a concept that can provide insight into improving life conditions for all people. More important, Schalock suggested that we use data not to evaluate QOL as a score but rather to determine the person's well-being; identify priority outcomes; and give formative feedback to family, staff, and involved community members. Taylor (1994) made a similar point in noting that QOL is a useful sensitizing concept; that is, the concept of QOL forces us to understand how people with disabilities experience the world and how they feel about their lives.

PERSON-CENTERED PLANNING

The service-oriented definition of *quality* as meeting and exceeding customers' expectations is clearly evident in the emerging variations of person-centered planning (Dennis et al., 1993). The forms of person-centered planning place a primary emphasis on the person with the disability. Services and supports are designed and provided so as to meet (and perhaps exceed) identified expectations. O'Brien and Lovett (1992) identified the common characteristics of person-centered planning, which include the following:

- The person and those who love him or her are the knowledgeable authorities on the person's life course. Professional and technical information may be important but only when presented in the context of knowing the person and his or her desired future.

- Knowledge is generated by learning from shared action. Uncertainty about what to do can be decreased and managed when people agree that they will learn from trying new experiences.
- Common patterns of community life are challenged.
- Respect and recognition of the dignity and completeness of the individual are essential.
- People participating in the learning-through-action model must demonstrate an ability to learn, grow, and change.

PERSONAL OUTCOMES

Several organizations in the United States and Canada have combined the approaches found in outcome studies, person-centered planning, and QOL studies. The Canadian Association of Occupational Therapists, The Centre for Health Promotion at the University of Toronto, and The Council on Quality and Leadership in Supports for People with Disabilities (formerly, the Accreditation Council) have designed person-centered outcome methodologies that are based on individually defined priorities. These person-centered outcomes can be used for both individual planning and retrospective assessment of the success of those plans. The three efforts, while different in intent and scope, share similar characteristics:

- An in-person interview and dialogue reveal priority outcomes.
- The outcomes are not ratings on preset scales; rather the outcomes are the identified priorities that people want in their lives.
- Valid and reliable methodologies can determine whether the outcomes are achieved.
- Valid and reliable methodologies can identify the organizational processes that facilitated the outcomes.

Canadian Association of Occupational Therapists

The Canadian Association of Occupational Therapists, in collaboration with Health and Welfare Canada, have designed the Canadian Occupational Performance Measure (COPM), which is used to identify and assess individual outcomes in the areas of self-care, productivity, and leisure (Law et al., 1990). The purpose of the COPM is to evaluate individually defined outcomes after occupational therapy services. Initial discussions between the therapist and the individual identify the individual's priority outcomes. After identifying priorities, the individual rates the importance of the issue, current performance capability, and personal satisfaction with that ability.

During these assessments, "the true priorities of the client became evident, and these priorities were often different than the therapist's initial ideas" (Law et al., 1990, p. 85). During the development of the COPM, some therapists discovered differences between individuals and their families. In describing the pilot testing of the COPM in four countries, Law et al. noted that

> Some therapists were clearly uncomfortable with the client being the primary person to identify problems for intervention. However, in a client-centered approach, it must be clients who identify which problems exist for them and which are the most important. The therapist has skills in knowing how to address the problems that the client has identified. (1994, pp. 196–197)

Centre for Health Promotion at the University of Toronto

Researchers at the Centre for Health Promotion at the University of Toronto have developed a QOL project that measures how an individual rates both the importance of and satisfaction with nine different areas in three categories:

- Being—Who You Are as a Person
  1. Physical Being
  2. Psychological Being
  3. Spiritual Being
- Belonging—How You Fit In with People and Places
  4. Physical Belonging
  5. Social Belonging
  6. Community Belonging
- Becoming—Activities that Facilitate Personal Goals, Hopes, and Wishes
  7. Practical Becoming
  8. Leisure Becoming
  9. Growth Becoming

Basic principles guided the development of the QOL instrument (Centre for Health Promotion, 1995). Assessment would take place in the same general life realms shared by all people; but within those general life realms, individuals would define their own areas of importance. In addition, individuals would assign personal ratings of importance and satisfaction with the specifics in the life realm areas. Finally, because people live in environments, QOL indicates a person's view of self, the environment, and the manner in which a person fits with the environment.

The development of the QOL instrument revealed a dilemma. On the one hand, the authors wanted a quantitative methodology for assessing QOL that could yield data for purposes of statistical analysis, be generalized from samples to larger units, and be used to guide public policy. On the other hand, they recognized the limitations of reducing a complex, deeply personal definition of QOL into a contrived and expertly designed system for analysis. In the end, they attempted

> To devise methods and measures which would allow individuals to tell their own stories, identify their own important life areas, and express personal satisfaction. (Raphael, Brown, Renwick, & Rootman, in press)

The QOL instrument reflects the premise that the individual's QOL is, in the final analysis, a "personal construction based upon one's specific life circumstances" (Raphael et al., in press). In addition, the instrument reflects the belief that there is a difference between the outcome and the means to the outcome. Moreover, there may be many means by which an individual arrives at his or her own important outcomes.

The Council on Quality and Leadership in Supports for People with Disabilities

The Council published the *Outcome Based Performance Measures* in 1993 after field testing the instrument at 10 sites in the United States and Canada. Based on individual and focus group meetings with people who had a wide range of disabilities, the *Outcome Based Performance Measures* contained 30 outcome realms. Between 1993 and 1995, The Council conducted more than 450 interviews during accreditation reviews. After conducting a factor analysis of those interviews, The Council reduced and modified the outcomes and published the *Personal Outcome Measures* in 1997 (Gardner, Nudler, & Chapman, 1997; The Council, 1997). The *Personal Outcomes* represent both a format for personal-futures planning and a methodology for entering into a dialogue with people to determine if their preferred outcomes are present in their lives.

The *Personal Outcomes* serve as a quality design guide because they enable the individual to identify the outcomes that are of most importance to him or her. Although the 25 personal outcome realms are uniform, each individual will identify how and why the category has meaning for oneself. People attach very different meaning to the generic categories of work, residence, friendship, community participation, health, and safety. Organizations can use a variety of person-centered approaches to identify outcomes. Having assisted the individual in giving definition to priority outcomes, the organization's employees can then utilize their education, skills, and experience to facilitate the outcomes. This presents a clear separation of ends and means. People with disabilities identify the ends. Employees, with input from the person, present a range of options, or means, for facilitating the outcome.

The *Personal Outcome Measures* can also be used for purposes of either internal self-assessment or external independent assessment through accreditation. The ability to designate outcomes as present or not and individualized organizational processes as present or not can provide quantitative measures that indicate an organization's capability in facilitating outcomes for people. The data can also provide information on the relationships among outcomes, individual profiles, organizational characteristics, and individualized supports and services.

In addition to identifying person-centered outcomes, the *Personal Outcome Measures* match an individualized organizational process with each outcome present for the person. This reverses the traditional approach to the exploration of organizational process that examines policy and procedure prior to and apart from the consideration of outcomes. Using the *Personal Outcome Measures,* the organization first identifies the individual's priority outcomes, then determines whether they are present to the extent desired by the person. If an outcome is present, the assessors work backward to determine the individualized organizational process(es) that facilitated the outcome. Process is examined in the context of the person-centered outcome. Organizational policies, procedures, and processes that have been individualized and that contribute to outcomes are strengthened. Processes that do not contribute to outcomes are reexamined.

Because individuals with disabilities define the meaning of each of the outcomes, the *Personal Outcome Measures* can be applied across different cultural settings. A Native American in the Southwest, a Vietnamese immigrant, and an African American in Boston can define each of the *Personal Outcome Measures* in his or her own manner. Keith, Heal, and Schalock (1996) reported considerable international consistency in the rating of concepts that professionals around the world used in describing QOL for people with disabilities. The 10 items were very similar to the 10 categories of outcomes contained in the *Outcome Based Performance Measures* (The Council, 1993).

These examples of personal-outcome approaches differ from outcome methodologies that measure functions or behaviors on a scale. For example, outcomes in activity of daily living skills might measure eating, grooming, and toileting behaviors on a 1–5 scale. In a similar manner, outcomes in social functioning might measure how often a person with depression visits with family, goes shopping, or attends the theater. These functional/behavioral outcomes can be normed so that organizations can determine whether the group norm or an individual score is changing. In contrast, personal outcomes cannot be normed. There is no mean or standard deviation with personal outcomes. Each person is a sample of one. The nature of personal outcomes prevents one person's definition of community participation from being averaged with another person's definition.

Although this focus on valued outcomes provides important information about outcome attainment of individuals and groups, it does not provide an individualized understanding of the person. The scales will reveal the scores on the various domains, but there is, in some instances, no indication of whether the domain is important to the individual or even how the individual would prioritize the domain. Knoll (1990) observed that the general focus of outcome studies provided little information for use in program design or evaluation.

QUALITY AND LEADERSHIP IMPLICATIONS

The definition of quality and the context for measurement has evolved since the 1960s. This evolution has been cumulative, and new insights have been added to traditional approaches. The result is that definitions of *quality* include concerns for protection, health and safety, attention to organizational process, an emphasis on person-centered outcomes, and a focus on satisfaction, well-being, and QOL. Each of these concerns is legitimate, however, the organizational processes, management priorities, and leadership focus for each of these legitimate priorities will be different. For example, the organizational policies and procedures and the management processes that promote protection, health, and safety may not be the same responses that maximize person-centered outcomes and QOL for people receiving services. Compliance with environmental standards may promote safety and protection but not lead to person-centered outcomes. In addition, facilitating person-focused outcomes may require very different organizational processes than those that secure subcontract work. Furthermore, the organizational processes, policies, and procedures that maximize outcomes for one person may be a burden to another person.

In order to cope with the multiple dimensions of quality, organizations can focus on eight major points: 1) focus on the person; 2) quality is part of the design; 3) person-centered outcomes challenge the program's focus; 4) focus on the few, critical variables; 5) quality costs less; 6) professional roles change; 7) outcomes require organizational learning; and 8) values and principles are not good enough.

Focus on the Person

Service organizations often encounter multiple demands. For example, the franchise book dealer in the local mall must be responsive to the national franchise, the mall management, and the customers who purchase merchandise. Providers of service to people with disabilities must answer to funders, regulators, families, advocates, and contractors. Providers of service must satisfy all the stakeholders, but the test of quality is determined by the satisfaction of the user of the service. The other stakeholders are important, but the person using the service defines quality from his or her individual perspective. Services and supports are provided to facilitate individual outcomes.

Quality Is Part of the Design

Quality is built into programs and services when we learn who people are, what outcomes they want in their lives, and then design services and supports accordingly. Person-centered outcomes provide the design for services and supports. Without knowledge of the outcomes, there can be no design; without the preliminary design, services and supports are unconnected to the person. Monitoring services that are not designed around the individual reveal only services that are unconnected to outcomes.

Person-Centered Outcomes Challenge the Program's Focus

Programs are professional artifacts that have very little meaning to people with disabilities. Professionals create programs to ease the dilemmas of administering services, to reduce ambiguity about personal differences, and to make measuring easier. Managers measure and report program outputs as indicators of quality and success. Programs may be quite efficient and effective in terms of operations but actually be unresponsive to individual outcomes. Managers suboptimize—that is, become more efficient at doing the wrong thing—when they confuse means with ends. Services are means. They are designed and provided to facilitate outcomes.

Focus on the Few, Critical Variables

The Pareto principle (Rowe, Mason, Dickel, & Snyder, 1989) reminds us that relatively few variables account for most of the outcomes. In general, a few people do most of the work, and a few cost centers produce most of the profit. Standards and regulations need to be focused on the critical variables that account for most of the variance in quality. Table 2.1 depicts 10 tasks that each take 1 hour to accomplish. Each of the tasks accounts for some percentage of the quality variance. Tasks 1, 2, and 3 account for 40%, 20%, and 15% of the quality—a total of 75%. Tasks 8, 9, and 10 account for a total of 1.5% of the quality. Organizations will realize the greatest payoff in quality if they concentrate on Tasks 1, 2, and 3. There is also little doubt about what Tasks 1, 2, and 3 might be:

1. Learn who the individual is.
2. Identify the person's priority outcomes.
3. Introduce services and supports to facilitate those outcomes.

Quality Costs Less

The cost of quality is not the added cost of doing business differently. The true cost of quality is continuing to provide services and supports that are unconnected to outcomes. The real cost of quality is continuing to do business that does not work.

Professional Roles Change

Person-centered outcomes require that professionals play two distinct roles—that of learner and that of facilitator. Professionals

Table 2.1.   Illustration of the Pareto principle

Variable	% of quality outcome	Cumulative %
1	40	40
2	20	60
3	15	75
4	10	85
5	6	91
6	4	95
7	3.5	98.5
8	0.8	99.3
9	0.5	99.8
10	0.2	100

must first understand the person's prioritized outcomes. This understanding requires that the professional listen, observe, ask, discover, question, and redirect. This learning precedes any decisions about what role the professional might play in facilitating the outcome. Identifying priority outcomes enables the professional to ask, "What skills, abilities, and knowledge can I use to facilitate this outcome?" Very often, assessment provides information about processes and methods for accomplishing outcomes. Assessment, by itself, does not identify outcomes; people define their own outcomes.

Outcomes Require Organizational Learning

Person-focused outcomes shift the definition of *quality* from compliance with organizational process requirements to responsiveness to the individual. Quality, then, is directly related to our knowledge of the person. This learning also requires self-understanding on the part of staff. Only when we understand ourselves, our own values, and our assumptions can we begin to understand others.

In addition, this learning results from taking action and learning from our interactions. Traditions in human services place learning before action. Thus we assess and assess and then hold team meetings and then implement. This reverse-action research model suggests that we make informed decisions, provide learning experience, and reflect on what was learned from the experience.

The new process of decision making is dynamic and sometimes unsettling. The learning organization, however, invites questioning, questions certainty, and encourages innovation and self-evaluation. In the learning organization, ambiguity increases, personnel exert less direct control of individuals' outcomes, and change becomes more frequent.

Values and Principles Are Not Good Enough

Quality in services and supports requires values and principles. However, values and principles do not always result in services and supports of high quality. Beyond values, managers need commitment and skills. Many organizations have well-developed principles and articulate sound values; however, they often lack the commitment and skills to make and sustain changes needed to respond to people's priority outcomes.

CONCLUSIONS

The social and economic trends affecting quality in service industries are also evident in the provision of services and supports to people with disabilities. There is clear recognition that supports are designed around the individual and that fitting people into service slots is no longer acceptable.

The discussion of QOL, person-centered planning, and personal-outcome measures are indicators that *quality* can be defined in personal terms, and that this level of quality in supports and services can be both planned and measured. This focus on the individual and his or her outcomes demonstrates how an organizational process can be very positive for one individual and very ineffective for another. Contemporary practice is forcing a discussion on just how organizational process (the work that organizations perform) is directly resulting in people's priority outcomes.

REFERENCES

Accreditation Council for Facilities for the Mentally Retarded (ACF/MR). (1971). *Standards for residential facilities for the mentally retarded.* Chicago: Joint Commission on the Accreditation of Hospitals, The Council.

Albrecht, K. (1992). *The only thing that matters: Bringing the power of the customer into the center of your business.* New York: Harper Business.

Blatt, B., & Kaplan F. (1966). *Christmas in purgatory.* Needham Heights, MA: Allyn & Bacon.

Bradley, V.J. (1990). Conceptual issues in quality assurance. In V.J. Bradley & H.A. Bersani, Jr. (Eds.), *Quality assurance for individuals with developmental disabilities: It's everybody's business* (pp. 3–16). Baltimore: Paul H. Brookes Publishing Co.

Brown, R.I., Bayer, M.B., & MacFarlane, C. (1988). Quality of life amongst handicapped adults. In R.I. Brown (Ed.), *Quality of life for handicapped people* (pp. 107–123). London: Croom Helm.

Centre for Health Promotion. (1995). *Quality of life project: Instrument package and manual.* Toronto: University of Toronto, Centre for Health Promotion.

Community Living Arrangements Act, PL 101-508, 42 U.S.C. §§ 1396u *et seq.*

The Council on Quality and Leadership in Supports for People with Disabilities (The Council). (1997). *Personal Outcome Measures.* Towson, MD: Author.

Deming, W.E. (1986). *Out of the crises.* Cambridge: Massachusetts Institute of Technology, Center for Advanced Engineering Study.

Dennis, R.E., Williams, W., Giangreco, M.F., & Cloninger, C.J. (1993). Quality of life as context for planning and evaluation of services for people with disabilities. *Exceptional Children, 59,* 499–512.

Flanagan, J.C. (1978). A research approach to improving our quality of life. *American Psychologist, 33,* 138–147.

Gardner, J.F., Nudler, S., & Chapman, M.S. (1997). Personal outcomes as measures of quality. *Mental Retardation, 35,* 295–305.

Goode, D.A. (1994). The national quality of life for persons with disabilities project: A quality of life agenda for the United States. In D.A. Goode

(Ed.), *Quality of life for persons with disabilities: International perspectives and issues* (pp. 138–175). Cambridge, MA: Brookline Books.

Home and Community Based Waiver Act, PL 97-35, 42 U.S.C. §§ 1115 *et seq.*

Intermediate Care Facilities for the Mentally Retarded Rule, 43 Fed. Reg. (1978).

Jaskulski, T. (1991). *Affecting the quality of services: Perspectives on quality and home and community based services for people with developmental disabilities.* Columbia, MD: Jaskulski & Associates.

Keith, K.D., Heal, L.W., & Schalock, R.L. (1996). Cross-cultural measurement of critical quality of life concepts. *Journal of Intellectual and Developmental Disabilities, 21,* 273–293.

Knoll, J.A. (1990). Defining quality in residential services. In V.J. Bradley & H.A. Bersani, Jr. (Eds.), *Quality assurance for individuals with developmental disabilities: It's everybody's business* (pp. 235–262). Baltimore: Paul H. Brookes Publishing Co.

Lakin, C.K., Prouty, B., Smith, G., & Braddock, D. (1996). Nixon goal surpassed—two fold. *Mental Retardation, 34,* 67.

Law, M., Baptiste, S., McColl, M., Opzoomer, A., Polatajko, H., & Pollock, N. (1990). The Canadian Occupational Performance Measure: An outcome measure for occupational therapy. *Canadian Journal of Occupational Therapy, 57,* 82–87.

Law, M., Polatajko, H., Pollock, N., McColl, M., Carswell, A., & Baptiste, S. (1994). Pilot testing of the Canadian Occupational Performance Measure: Clinical and measurement issues. *Canadian Journal of Occupational Therapy, 61,* 191–197.

Murrell, S.A., & Norris, F.H. (1983). Quality of life as the criteria for need assessment and community psychology. *Journal of Community Psychology, 11,* 88–98.

O'Brien, J., & Lovett, H. (1992). *Finding a way toward everyday lives: The contribution of person centered planning.* Harrisburg: Pennsylvania Office of Mental Retardation.

Parmenter, T.R. (1994). Quality of life of people with developmental disabilities. *International Review of Research in Mental Retardation, 18,* 247–287.

Raphael, D., Brown, I., Renwick, R., & Rootman, I. (in press). Assessing the quality of life of persons with developmental disabilities: Description of a new model, measuring instruments, and initial findings. *International Journal of Disability, Development, and Education.*

Reeves, C.A., & Bednar, D.A. (1994). Defining quality: Alternatives and implications. *Academy of Management Review, 19,* 419–445.

Rouse, A.J., Mason, R.O., Dickel, K.E., & Snyder, N.H. (1989). *Strategic planning: A methodological approach* (3rd ed.). Reading, MA: Addison-Wesley.

Scheerenberger, R.C. (1987). *A history of mental retardation: A quarter century of promise.* Baltimore: Paul H. Brookes Publishing Co.

Schalock, R.L. (Ed.). (1990). *Quality of life: Perspectives and issues.* Washington, DC: American Association for Mental Retardation.

Schalock, R.L. (1996). Reconsidering the conceptualization and measurement of quality of life. In R.L. Schalock (Ed.), *Quality of life: Conceptualization and measurement* (Vol. 1, pp. 123–139). Washington, DC: American Association For Mental Retardation.

Taylor, S.J. (1994). In support of research on quality of life, but against QOL. In D. Goode (Ed.), *Quality of life for persons with disabilities: International perspectives and issues* (pp. 260–265). Cambridge, MA: Brookline Books.

Taylor, S.J., & Bogdan R. (1990). Quality of life and the individual's perspective. In R.L. Schalock (Ed.), *Quality of life: Perspectives and issues* (pp. 27–40). Washington, DC: American Association on Mental Retardation.

The Accreditation Council on Services for People with Disabilities (The Council). (1993). *Outcome Based Performance Measures.* Towson, MD: Author.

Wyatt v. Stickney, 344. F. Supp. 387, 400 § 22d (M.D. Ala., 1972).

Zeithaml, V.A., Parasuraman, A., & Berry, L.L. (1990). *Delivering quality service: Balancing customer perceptions and expectations.* New York: The Free Press.

3

A Personal Perspective

Mary Moynihan, Kathryn R. Perkins,
Greg Butschky, Vernon DeHaven, Laura Gessel,
Don and Dawn Merriman, John Ricketts, Tony Sampson,
David and Jeannie Warner, and Mary Ann Whetzel

Person-centered planning and supports in human services reflect the trend in service economies to base services on consumers' wants and preferences. Consumer-focused businesses that offer services are striving to discover and develop the most effective ways of learning what their customers value. The paradigm shift in human services is placing the definition of wants and preferences in the hands of the individuals receiving the supports and services.

Consumers of services in the general public have some common characteristics across most industrialized countries. Due in part to low birth rates and longer life expectancies, we find that consumers of human services are older, more educated, more knowledgeable, and more demanding of high-quality services than ever before (Naumann & Giel, 1995). In the postindustrial, service-oriented society, people receiving services expect good customer value.

Most people who experience a disability personally know what they like and what they do not like in the services that they receive, but it is difficult for many to describe the services they receive in terms of quality. This may be due, at least in part, to the relatively recent trend toward respecting their opinions of the services. In addition, there is still some underlying and residual fear of the possible repercussions of expressing dissatisfaction. To some degree, both individuals and families have had their sense of quality dulled by years of low-quality services.

As people are asked for feedback regarding their satisfaction with services, their knowledge base expands and fear of reprisal begins to diminish. Service providers can no longer be content with meeting last year's expectations (Naumann & Giel, 1995). It is imperative that service providers seek ways to encourage and actively solicit both consumers and their families to participate in planning for their organization's future. Every organization must know what the people who they serve want in the future and how they want the services that they need to be delivered.

In the service sector, it is nearly impossible to separate the actions and behaviors of employees from the perceived degree of excellence of the service. Only individual staff members are the point of delivery, and quality for service recipients is intertwined with the actions of the staff who serve them. When asked to reflect on quality in the services that people with disabilities receive, both the individuals and their families look to particular staff members as hallmarks of an organization's quality. It is the interpersonal actions of staff that self-advocates often use to define quality or lack of quality.

This chapter views quality from the perspective of those people *receiving* services and not from the perspective of those who *provide* services. As each self-advocate, parent, and family in the chapter presents their expectations for service delivery in their own words, keep in mind their differing, and personal, definitions of quality.

THE SELF-ADVOCATE'S PERSPECTIVE

David and Jeannie Warner are married, live in an apartment, and receive services from a provider organization. They offer this view on quality in services.

Jeannie

Several people have made a difference in my life. My grandma taught me how to crochet with yarn, and my step-mom taught me that I could do more than I knew. I got self-confidence! She also helped me to get into this program. Jean Richter (staff person) introduced David and me. We were happy together, and we got married. David is my life, my friend. He is my life saver.

I don't think that service providers should have information about my personal goals and priorities unless I want them to have it. I share a little with them; but because it's personal, it depends on why they want to know. People who work with people who have disabilities should treat them like real people. To me, quality means that when I say something, people take me seriously.

David

The person who is most important to me is my wife, Jeannie. She has filled my life so that I'm not lonely. In the future, I would like to have a log cabin. I want staff members who work with people with disabilities to treat them with respect. We need people we can trust, people who treat us with more respect and kindness without sarcasm. That's what quality means to me—I want respect from others.

Tony Sampson lives in a townhouse in St. Charles, Maryland. He works in a commissary on a naval air base.

Tony

I have lived alone for 2 years. I'm close to shopping and places where I need to go. Carol Coles has made a big difference in my life since my dad died. Dad helped me with my bills. Now Carol helps me to pay them. She also takes me to the store, to college, and other places. She helps me maintain my house, and she shows me how to clean it.

The most important thing about Carol is that she is always on time. She also shows me how to behave. For example, she showed me how to talk to people. This helps me to be a little more mature, to meet people, to have friends.

The most important thing in my life right now is to live the American Dream like my dad did. I want to get a driver's license, buy a car, and get a job that pays good money. If I won the lottery, I would own a house and a car.

I want to live the life of normal people, not people with disabilities. I hope to make it to the other side, forget the workshops. I want to go from the client world to the adult world. I'm in the middle right now. I'm going to college to study office technologies. The agency that provides my home supports is sending me to college. They help with transportation, and they went with me to the guidance counselor at college to help me pick my courses. Next I want to go to driving school.

The best advice for staff is to respect us. Just because some of us have mental retardation doesn't mean we have to be treated like children. I learned a lot about this at a convention. I know that not every organization treats people like little kids.

Sometimes staff members say things like, "What did I just tell you?" and "I want you to go sit over there and think about what you've done." I am not a kid. And correcting me in front of other people makes the other guy think that I have problems.

Some agencies make you watch movies that are for kids. They say violence isn't good for some people who are immature. I don't see why they can't show movies for adults.

Agencies can give us better training instead of contract work. Rather than putting nuts and bolts together, we need jobs and career development classes. We need computers and more on-the-job training. Staff members need to help us understand the grievance policies at our jobs and what to do when things go wrong. All they do is put us in restaurants and places doing janitorial work. Agencies that serve us are good, but they could be better.

Teaching skills for independence and showing respect are the two most important things staff members can do. Teach us how to find jobs, how to get and keep jobs. I'm getting those things now, so I would say I am getting quality services. This is because I'm easy to get along with and I listen. I know other people who deserve better than what they are getting.

Mary and Pam[1] recently began sharing an apartment in Maryland. Both work at a workshop, and Mary has a part-time job working with animals.

Mary

My staff person has made a big difference in my life. I've had her for 3 or 4 years. I was living with her for a little while. When I left her house, she told me I had to get out and start mingling with other people. She takes care of my checkbook. Right now I don't want to do that. She taught me to wash my own clothes. She has given me things, like a birthstone and a watch. She calls me her big sister.

Agencies have a hard time finding staff. Sometimes staff members have to use their own cars to drive us places. They don't like it. If we could get a new van, we could go out more often. We use cars from other houses, and it's not fair to them or to us.

The most important thing to me is getting along with people, being kind, and helping people out. I help feed someone at the work-

---

[1]Mary and Pam's names have been changed at their request to protect their identities.

shop. Working with cats and dogs is important to me. I pet them, feed them, and help out the lady who runs the place. It's also important for me to see my mother and father's graves. I go to see them every 3 months. I have to do that. It's very important to me.

Pam

It's important to me to get to church. Sometimes it's hard to get a ride there. I like to take walks and do my laundry. I want to go bowling with Mary or go to the movies. I want to take Mary to play golf one day. I want to go out and do stuff. Staff members should ask us what we want to do. I don't want to go to with them to visit other houses (in the residential program).

Sometimes the staff members are strict. I tell them that they're not my mother. When I use the telephone, they ask me who I'm calling and say, "Aren't you supposed to ask?" That's my choice to use the telephone.

Staff need a break sometimes. They need time off. They need a break from us, and we need a break from them.

Mary Ann Whetzel, Greg Butschky, and Vernon DeHaven are members of People First of Harford County, a self-advocacy group. Mary Ann lives with her mother and brother. Greg and Vernon have shared an apartment for more than 5 years. Mary Ann and Vernon are employed in restaurants, and Greg is employed in a department store.

Mary Ann

I like what I do when it comes to working. I like being able to do things myself. It's important to have staff members who help out when you need the help. Mike, my job coach, comes by to check on how things are going. Sometimes I get a little nervous. If someone gets me upset, I talk to Mike. I'm breaking out of my shell more though. Now if there's something I don't understand I go to someone at work. Last week I went to the person who does the schedule. There was a little mix up. I told her I didn't understand, and it got settled.

I'm learning to tell people what's on my mind and how I feel. My friends help me and People First helps me, too. Going to public schools and speaking about disabilities helped me to break out of my shell. Vernon went first, now I go and others go, too.

I love people. I get along with anyone. I don't like it when some staff members talk to us like they don't care. For example, a staff person who drives the van sometimes points at us and says, "How come you weren't ready?" He should respect us. That means listening to what we have to say. Mike, my job coach, listens. If I call him with a problem he says, "Don't worry, Mary Ann, we'll figure it out."

I like what I do, and I love my apartment. Someday I hope to get my own place. That's the goal I'm working toward.

Greg

I have a good job, and it pays well. My co-workers are nice. Will gives me comic relief, and James and I talk about music. The rest of them tease the life out of me! When I first left the workshop, I had a case of the last day/first day jitters—you know, last day at the workshop, first day at the new job. I was as quiet as a church mouse. Mrs. Cole, my new supervisor, said, "We have a new associate named Greg." I barely said anything. I was in a corner eating alone when some co-workers said, "Don't eat by yourself. Come over here and eat with us." Then I thought, "Hey this is going to be OK." They were nicer to me than I was to them. They tease me now, but it's good, positive teasing.

Greg and Vernon

Robin (support staff) made a big difference in our lives because she cared. She did a lot of extras that were not necessary. She took us to see her son play ball. We went with her husband to see their son play lacrosse. They didn't have to do that. She was fun to be with, too. We could tease her. Staff members should know when to kid around and when to stop, when we want to be serious.

Staff members have to know what they're doing. They need to know what the person they are supporting can and can't do. They should ask us what kind of help we need. If the person can't tell them, staff members should be able to look around and see what needs to be done and help them do it. Staff members should help us with things we can't do. Like when a person doesn't know how to clean, the staff members should say, "That needs to be dusted a little more." It should be said in the right tone of voice. The staff should care about our feelings. That's what makes an "A plus" support staff.

People who don't have as many skills need more and better help. Staff members should give individuals more support if they see that some people need it. They should help them out more. We're lucky. What one of us can't do, the other (roommate) does. We trade off and help each other.

It's important to have a team effort in your working and living conditions. Our living conditions are beautiful right now. We have a roof over our heads, and we can pay our rent. We went through different roommates but they didn't work out as well as the two of us. We're both goofy sometimes. We share everything, including the urge to strangle each other at times. We have our arguments, but we get it out in the open and after that we're calm again. We help each other out. When one of us is having problems, the other will ask if he needs help.

That kind of team effort is important with support staff, too. Staff and clients need to work together. We've been through different ones. That's how we know that team effort can be beautiful. Good staff train you and they can make your wheels move faster, but they have to do it at your pace. Staff should show us how to do things, then step back and watch us do it. For example, we sometimes need someone to get us motivated with housework. The staff used to make chore lists, which wasn't bad. We now do that on our own. Staff members can help us figure out how to do things, help us to keep organized. They remind us or help us put stuff on the calendar. When we don't have drop-in staff, we motivate each other. We say things like, "Wrestling comes on at 11. We have to get the house clean before then." One of us will do the bathroom, the other will clean the living room.

It's also important for staff to get there on time. The first thing we ask staff is "Are you reliable?" Reliability is a big thing. If they say they are going to be here and we should be ready by 7 o'clock sharp, then they should be here at 7 sharp to pick us up. We understand traffic and stuff happens, but it's not proper etiquette to be late. We don't want to spend our lives waiting.

When we need help, staff should be available. We should be able to call and say, "I need to go to the grocery store," and they will come over and take us. We need support with transportation because we have limited options for transportation. Family helps, but we still need better weekend public transportation. We need a Saturday bus run. People First is going to the town hall to ask for it. We need support from the community. It would help everyone— elderly people, people with disabilities, people who don't have cars. Other places have bus runs on Saturday and better public transportation. We take one challenge at a time. When we get through this transportation issue, things will be 100% better.

Staff need to have some knowledge about us, like medical things and our doctor's appointments. They should know what we need help with, like cooking. But let us do the things we can do, then butt out. They should be somewhat knowledgeable about whether we are eating good food, but if we want a chili dog for dinner once in a while that's none of their business. We understand that they want us to eat hot meals and to be healthy. We want to be healthy, too, to an extent. If you believe everything the doctor says is good for you, you'd starve. Sometimes we listen to the doctor, and sometimes we don't. We know what to get at the grocery store and what we like. Staff members shouldn't tell us that we can't buy something.

When staff members leave, it's hard to get good quality people to replace them. You can't just hire any Joe off the street. People aren't answering ads to become staff because of the money. We have had good staff, but some people are just here for the money. If staff members got paid better money, they (People First) could hire the right staff. This would stop the revolving door effect.

John lives in his own apartment, gets himself to work at an independent job, and is supported by a provider organization. He has experienced a few different living situations.

John

My life changed a lot when Craig Carroll helped me get out of one facility and into a group home and then to move into this apartment. One of the most important things that really changed my life was getting a job. Now I want to save money.

Things work best when I work at doing things with the staff. Quality means good work and getting things done.

Anna Lohr lives with her husband in Philadelphia. Anna has provided more than 2 years of national service through Americorps. Anna has cerebral palsy and often uses a Liberator to assist her in speaking.

Anna

We have a homemaker; she's been with us for 4 years. We love her because she goes out of her way for us; she would do anything for us. When my husband had to go to the hospital, she drove separately and met us there. Sometimes she meets us at the movies; she does this when she's not being paid. She will also go to the university where my husband is an Americorps member and assist him at lunchtime.

I think our homemaker does this work because it makes her feel good. People who provide services to assist other people need to have a good personality. Some homemakers can't cook. It is important to be able to cook.

I really don't like it when people talk about me, especially when they refer to me as "not normal." This seems to happen especially in hospitals.

THE PARENTS' PERSPECTIVE

Don and Dawn Merriman are the parents of Craig. As a family, they have been the recipients of early intervention and educational services and are on the brink of receiving services from adult community-based providers.

Don and Dawn

Because our son's disability was caused by birth trauma, we may have spent more time in denial than most families. We kept waiting for him to "get better." For us as parents, early intervention was critical. We're sure that early intervention was of more benefit to us as parents than it was directly for our son.

We were asked to write letters of support for staff nominated for special educator of the year when our son was 5 years old. Through that process, we identified the most valuable lesson that we learned from the people who worked with our son during his preschool years. It was that no matter what skills he learned or didn't learn, he was a valuable person to his family and to people in his community. Of course, we as parents loved and valued our son; but to see people unrelated to him respect and value this child with severe and multiple disabilities was a lesson that would give us hope and optimism for what life could offer our son. His life was not to be one in which people felt sorry for him but one of building on his strengths and finding support for his disabilities. We were very fortunate to work with truly caring people who did their job very well.

We were treated as part of a team. Our questions and suggestions were valued, and most important, people answered our questions and acted on our suggestions. The people who worked with our son told us that we were the experts when it came to him because we spent more time with him and knew him better than anyone else. They truly valued our input, and we knew it by their actions. They didn't just shake their heads in agreement—they worked with us to accomplish goals that we as a team identified for our son.

Because the early education services received by our son were achieved by cooperation of multiple agencies, we were exposed to an individual outside the realm of special education who worked for an adult services provider agency. She was a major factor in that we were able to talk to someone who knew more than just special education services. She worked with adults with disabilities and could answer "what if" questions about our son's future. The most important lesson she shared with us was that our son did not have to be able to perform certain skills before he could experience life and make choices. He should not have to "fit in" to a system, but rather, the systems were there to provide support to him as he needed no matter how severe his disabilities.

Our son will be 18 years old soon. He is a caring and, for the most part, happy young man. Sometimes we think it might be easiest to have him live with us until we die. We know that he would not experience the most in life if he lives with his parents for our whole lives. Try as we might, we do what we think is right, not always what he would choose. It is important to our family that a normal separation process occur that will allow all of us to grow. Change is exciting, uncomfortable, rewarding, and hard.

Our priorities for our son are for him to live in a setting that he likes, to work and play at activities that are important to him, to be valued in his community, and to have as many choices as possible concerning his life.

Quality will be measured differently by individuals. How well quality is achieved will depend on how service providers listen and act on the identified wants and needs of individuals with disabilities and their families. One good question to ask is "If I became disabled, would I want to receive services from this agency?"

Individuals, families, and service providers must work together to make the most possible choices available to individuals with disabilities. In order for this to happen, individuals and families must have input in the development of services from the beginning.

THE FAMILY'S PERSPECTIVE

Laura receives services through a community-based provider agency. Laura's parents, Bonnie and Dave, and her sister share this family perspective.

Laura

Chrysalis has made the biggest difference in our family's lives. The staff at Chrysalis advocated for Laura's psychiatric treatment, have set the necessary limits, and have always been respectful of our goals and desires for Laura. When Laura moved into her apartment, there were competent people who were willing to be tenacious about Laura's medical/psychiatric issues, and, at the same time, they genuinely cared about Laura and her social and emotional needs as well those of the family.

In our family, it is important that we support each other in times of need and joy. We are willing to share our personal priorities with service providers and professionals because we think that as they understand our family's priorities they can understand what to expect from our family to support Laura. This will enhance Laura's quality of life, and everyone can work as a team.

We believe that people working in services that support people with disabilities must show a caring attitude but also should set goals and expectations with rewards. They should work as a team with the family.

We believe that a service or support works when there are competent, accountable staff who are willing to be candid, empathetic, and accessible. Staff also need to be aware and to implement goals in cooperation with the family. For us, Chrysalis of Park City, Utah, is equated with quality. Chrysalis serves Laura and our family, and they are always striving to make changes for the better.

CONCLUSIONS

Each of these personal accounts is unique and speaks of the experience of one person or one family, and yet there are some strands that unite them. People who experience disability either personally or through someone they care about want those who provide human services to listen to them. Listening means attending carefully to what is said as well as to what is meant; seeing actions as a way of communicating; and most profoundly, possessing the spirit of taking other people seriously (Lovett, 1996).

Listening is an essential building block to achieving quality in services. It has been identified by award-winning companies as crucial to their success (Hinton & Schaeffer, 1994); and in human services, given the nature of the work, it is imperative that we listen to our customers. Success, as measured through *personal outcomes* will occur only when we truly listen to our customers, thereby recognizing their voices. In order to have a voice one first must have something to say; second, a way to say it; and third, someone to hear it (O'Brien, 1997).

Being listened to is often perceived as an indicator of respect. In several of these personal expressions on quality, the writer is telling us that he or she wants to be respected or wants people with disabilities to be supported by people who respect them and respect those who truly care about them. Respect is defined as showing consideration for someone—a simple request. Given the frequency with which it is offered as an indicator of quality in human services by those who receive these services, it must not be so simple. As has already been stated, individual staff members are the point of service delivery in human services and as such are the vessels of respect. Therefore, the human services organization must hold respect for people as a core value—one that permeates the organization—if it is to provide services that meet the quality standards of its customers. The message is clear: Assist me to have a voice, listen to what I say when I tell you what I want, respond in a way that tells me I'm a person first and foremost, and respect me by acting on what I say.

REFERENCES

Hinton, T., & Schaeffer, W. (1994). *Customer-focused quality: What to do on Monday morning*. Upper Saddle River, NJ: Prentice-Hall.

Lovett, H. (1996). *Learning to listen: Positive approaches and people with difficult behavior*. Baltimore: Paul H. Brookes Publishing Co.

Naumann, E., & Giel, K. (1995). *Customer satisfaction measurement and management: Using the voice of the customer*. Cincinnati, OH: Thomson Executive Press.

O'Brien, C.L. (1997, April). *Challenges to organizations in supporting relationships for people with disabilities*. Third Annual Invitational Conference, The Council on Quality and Leadership in Supports for People with Disabilities, Kansas City, MO.

4

A Quest for Quality

Achieving Organizational
Outputs and Personal Outcomes

Robert L. Schalock

Human services organizations are being challenged to provide quality services within the context of two powerful, potentially conflicting forces: person-centered values and economic-based restructured services. These two forces represent the context within which any service delivery system must operate to achieve quality organizational outputs and personal outcomes. They also represent the contextual variables that will influence significantly the "quest for quality" that is reflected in the late 1990s emphasis on quality of life, total quality management (TQM), and quality outcomes for people with disabilities.

The focus on person-centered values stems from a number of sources. First, the human rights and self-advocate movements emphasize equality, inclusion, equity, empowerment, respect, and community-based supports. Second, public laws, such as the Individuals with Disabilities Education Act (IDEA) of 1997 (PL 105-17), the Vocational Rehabilitation Act Amendments of 1992 (PL 102-569), the Americans with Disabilities Act (ADA) of 1990 (PL 101-336), and the Developmental Disabilities and Bill of Rights Act of

1990 (PL 101-496) stress person-referenced outcomes related to independence, productivity, community integration, and satisfaction. Third, research documents that people can be more independent, productive, community integrated, and satisfied when quality-of-life concepts are the basis of individualized services and supports (Butterworth, Steere, & Whitney-Thomas, 1997; Karan & Bothwell, 1997; Kiernan & Marrone, 1997; Snell & Vogle, 1997; Whitney-Thomas, 1997).

In contrast, the focus on restructured services stems from a number of social, political, economic, and demographic factors. Chief among these factors are economic constraints; managed care concepts of privatization, capitalization, utilization management, and service substitution; a deprofessionalization of the work force; and a movement toward a market economy in health and rehabilitation care and services (Kirchner, 1996; Rioux, 1996). The net result of these factors has been the movement toward managed health care (Ashbaugh & Smith, 1996), efforts to reinvent government (Osborne & Gaebler, 1992) and restructure corporations (Hammer & Champy, 1993), the appearance of learning organizations (Senge, 1990), the formation of alliances and partnerships (Lindemann, 1996), and the increasing demand for program accountability (Schalock, 1995a).

The purpose of this chapter is to discuss the impact that these two contextual variables—person-centered values and restructured services—have on the quest for achieving organizational outputs and personal outcomes for people with disabilities. The first section discusses the impact of these contextual variables on rehabilitation services, such as 1) a change in the conception of disability, 2) an attempt to conceptualize and measure the concept of quality of life, 3) a change in how organizations see themselves and operate, and 4) an increase in demand for accountability. The reader then is introduced to a program evaluation model that incorporates efficiency and value standards, focusing on organization-referenced outputs and person-referenced outcomes. Examples of four types of outcome-based evaluation analyses incorporated within this model are discussed briefly, demonstrating the model's utility in evaluating both efficiency and value outcomes.

Throughout the chapter, a number of terms are used. *Quality* refers to meeting and exceeding consumers' expectations (Reeves & Rednar, 1994; see also Chapter 1). *Consumers* refer to the heterogeneous constituency composed of customers, stakeholders, and taxpayers who have an impact on rehabilitation services and supports (Schalock, 1995a). *Outputs* measure the results of organizational processes, whereas *outcomes* represent the impact of services and supports on the individual (Trabin, Freeman, & Pallak, 1995).

CONTEXTUAL VARIABLES AND THEIR IMPACT

Person-centered values and restructured services represent the context within which rehabilitation programs are expected to achieve organizational outputs and personal outcomes for people with disabilities. This section discusses the impact that these contextual variables have on services and supports: 1) changing to a contextual conception of disability, 2) attempting to conceptualize and measure quality of life, 3) changing organizations and services, and 4) responding to the increased demands for accountability.

Changed Conception of Disability

Oliver Sacks (1995), in his book, *An Anthropologist on Mars,* asked readers to reconsider what is meant by disease and its impact. He suggested that defects, disorders, and diseases can play a paradoxical role by bringing out latent powers, developments, evolutions, and forms of life that might never have existed or even been imagined. Throughout his work, he provided evidence supporting the following proposition:

> This sense of the brain's remarkable plasticity, its capacity for the most striking adaptations . . . has come to dominate my own perception of my patients and their lives. So much so, indeed, that I am sometimes moved to wonder whether it may not be necessary to redefine the very concepts of "health" and "disease," to see these in terms of the ability of the organism to create a new organization and order, one that fits its special, altered disposition and needs, rather than in the terms of a rigidly defined "norm." (p. xvii)

This movement to rethink disability is reflected in Figure 4.1, which summarizes Pope and Tarlov's (1991) conceptualization of the relationship among pathology, impairment, functional limitations, and disability. In this four-stage model of the disabling process, the "pathology" is associated with an abnormality at the cellular or tissue level, such as tuberous sclerosis. The pathology then produces an "impairment" at the organ or organ system level, such as brain dysfunction. The brain dysfunction then produces a "functional limitation" at the organism level, such as low intelligence. The functional limitation becomes a "disability," however, only when it has an impact on or interferes with the person's social role.

This four-stage model of the disability process has a number of implications for both the reconceptualization of disability and the

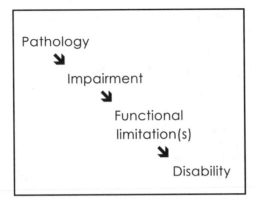

Figure 4.1.   The handicapping process. (*Source:* The Institute of Medicine, 1991.)

services and supports provided to those people engaged in a quest for quality. The following statements are among the most important to consider:

- Disability is neither fixed nor dichotomized; rather it is fluid, continuous, and changing, depending on the person's functional limitations and the supports available within a person's environment (Zola, 1993).
- One lessens functional limitations (and hence a person's disability) by providing interventions or services and supports that focus on prevention, adaptive behaviors, and role status (Coulter, 1996).
- The transformed vision of what constitutes the life possibilities of people with mental retardation and/or developmental disabilities is supported. This transformed vision includes self-determination, strengths and capabilities, inclusion, empowerment, and equity (Luckasson, Schalock, Snell, & Spitalnik, 1996).
- Outcome-based evaluation focuses on the extent to which the functional limitations have been reduced and the person's adaptive behavior and role status have been enhanced (Schalock, 1995a).

Conceptualization and Measurement of Quality of Life

Quality of life is not a new concept; indeed, since antiquity people have pursued the dimensions of a life of quality. What is different in the late 1990s—and what makes the concept of quality of life so important to our field—is the attempt to use this concept as a process and an overriding principle to improve the lives of people with disabilities and to evaluate the outcomes and social validity of current rehabilitation efforts. To do so, however, requires a clear understanding of the concept of quality of life and a valid approach to its measurement. Clarifying these two issues is the purpose of the following section.

Quality of Life Dimensions and Exemplars   There is a growing consensus regarding the eight core dimensions that constitute a life of quality (Schalock, 1997a): 1) emotional well-being, 2) interpersonal relationships, 3) material well-being, 4) personal development, 5) physical well-being, 6) self-determination, 7) social inclusion, and 8) rights. These eight core dimensions, along with suggested core exemplars, are summarized in Figure 4.2. Page constraints preclude an in-depth discussion of each of the components of this heuristic quality-of-life model, and the interested reader can find more details in Schalock (1997a, 1997b).

Core Measures and Measurement Techniques   There is also a growing consensus that measures of quality of life should be explicitly tied to values. An important corollary is that the core measures of quality of life reflect either one's level of satisfaction with life conditions or objective indicators of the core exemplars summarized in Figure 4.2. Methods for evaluating each can be found in Cummins (1996) and Schalock (1997b).

Because quality of life is a multidimensional phenomenon, its measurement involves one or more methods, depending on the investigator's focus and purpose. The use of multiple measurement techniques is based on a number of premises including the following: Quality of life is a multidimensional construct in which culturally consensual values and shared attitudes are reflected; individuals differ in their ability to understand and respond; people use quality-of-life data for different purposes, including self-report, description, evaluation, and comparison; and the use of quality-of-life data can focus on either the individual or a group. Three approaches to measurement are found in the literature—participant observation, performance-based assessment, and standardized instruments (Schalock, 1997a). The major aspects of each are summarized in Table 4.1.

Changing Organizations and Services

Human services are being "reengineered" because of the four "Cs": customer, competition, change, and cost containment. In general, these changes can be characterized as managing for quality and adopting a business mentality. Specific changes include stressing

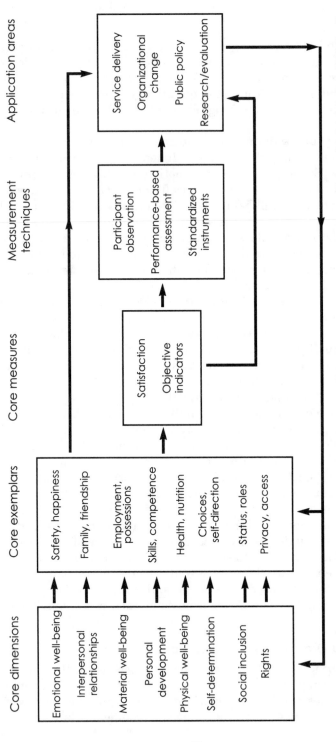

Figure 4.2. A heuristic quality-of-life model. (From Schalock, R.L. [1997]. Can the concept of quality of life make a difference? In R.L. Schalock [Ed.], *Quality of life: Application to persons with disabilities* [Vol. II, p. 261]. Washington, DC: American Association on Mental Retardation; adapted by permission.)

Table 4.1.   Quality-of-life measurement techniques

Measurement technique	Focus	Method
Participant observation	Psychological indicators (e.g., well-being)	Ethnographic Observe what people do
	Personal satisfaction (happiness)	Listen to what people say Participate in people's daily activities
Performance-based assessment	Social indicators	Survey
	Objective exemplar indicators	Database analysis
Standardized instruments	Core quality-of-life dimensions	Rating scales (self/other)

person-centered planning (PCP), implementing a supports model, employing quality enhancement techniques, and focusing on outcomes.

General Changes   The emphasis on managing for quality results in service providers reorganizing resources around individuals rather than rearranging people in program slots (Albin, 1992; Albin-Dean & Mank, 1997; Albrecht, 1993; Deming, 1993; Dillon, 1993; Edgerton, 1996; Gardner & Nudler, 1997; Schalock, 1994; Taylor & Bogdan, 1996). In addition, the techniques used to monitor and evaluate rehabilitation programs also change. For example, outcomes from rehabilitation programs are used to improve organizational efficiency and enhance person-referenced services and supports (Clifford & Sherman, 1983; Mathison, 1991; Schalock, 1995a; Torres, 1992; Trabin et al., 1995). Quality assurance changes to a shared set of activities completed jointly by the provider, consumer advocate, and regulatory body. Results are used to evaluate program effectiveness, implement quality enhancement techniques, and conduct program evaluation (Bradley & Bersani, 1990; Gardner & Nudler, 1997; Grossman, Rowe, Cerreto, & Schalock, in press; Knoll, 1990). Furthermore, organizations are also changing the way they think of themselves. As described by Wheatley,

> Our concept of organization is moving away from the mechanistic creations that flourished in the age of bureaucracy. We have begun to speak in earnest of more fluid, organic structures, even boundaryless organizations. We are beginning to recognize organizations as systems, construing them as 'learning organizations' and crediting them with some type of self-renewal capacity. (1994, p. 13)

This new way of thinking about organizations has resulted in changes in management styles reflected in management for quality (Deming, 1993; Juran 1989), learning organizations (Senge, 1990), reengineered corporations (Hammer & Champy, 1993), and entrepreneurship (Osborne & Gaebler, 1992). The concepts and principles espoused compose a new wave of management strategies that are broadly referred to as continuous improvement, whose common features include the following: a focus on consumers, the establishment of relationships based on mutual trust and respect, the building of staff ownership to improve quality, and the use of systematic strategies for analyzing performance and achieving (quality) improvement (Albin-Dean & Mank, 1997).

The emphasis on restructured services and person-centered outcomes also is bringing about significant changes in how organizations increasingly view themselves as businesses that aspire to the following characteristics (Jacobs & Moxley, 1993; Osborne & Gaebler, 1992; Schalock, 1995a):

- Adopting an organizational policy framework that allows for entrepreneurship, resource development, and capital formation
- Creating, improving, and integrating major organizational systems including marketing, fiscal management, clinical decision making, data-based management, and evaluation
- Securing accreditation but treating it as a quality floor on which to build high performance
- Making TQM and continuous improvement fundamental aspects of organizational culture
- Committing the organization to effective resource utilization management
- Using utilization management, cost control, and risk reduction procedures

Specific Program Changes   In addition to these two general changes—managing for quality and adopting a business mentality—organizations are also experiencing specific changes in how they provide and evaluate services to people with disabilities. Four of these—PCP, supports model, quality enhancement techniques, and focus on outcomes—are described in the following sections.

Person-Centered Planning   PCP involves establishing a partnership with an individual and his or her family to create a compelling image of a desirable future and inviting participation to achieve those goals (Butterworth et al., 1997). Several approaches to PCP have emerged, including personal futures planning (O'Brien, 1987), essential lifestyle planning (Smull, 1994a, 1994b), and whole life planning (Butterworth et al., 1993). Common elements to these approaches include the following (Butterworth et al., 1997):

- The empowerment of the individual
- The use of natural supports
- A changing role for professionals in service planning
- The use of a facilitator
- An opportunity for redefining the person for all participants
- A clear, unrestricted vision for the future
- An opportunity for creative brainstorming

Supports Model   The shift to a supports model is to a large extent grounded in the philosophy of normalization and involves a move away from a defect orientation toward a growth and personal development orientation in prevention (Coulter, 1996), assessment (Butterworth, Hagner, Kiernan, & Schalock, 1996; Schalock, 1995b), diagnosis (Luckasson et al., 1992), service eligibility (Grossman et al., in press), and service delivery (Luckasson et al., 1996, Nisbet & Hagner, 1988; Roberts, Wasik, Casto, & Ramey, 1991; Rusch, 1990; Snell, 1993; Wehman & Moon, 1988). Moving to a system of supports is not easy. The challenges involved are expressed well by Smull:

> Real supported living requires that we learn how people want to live and then support them in the lives that they want (within the constraints of available resources and any issues of health or safety). It requires efforts that help people be supported by their communities and have opportunities to contribute to their communities. Real supported living requires that people with disabilities and the people providing the direct supports be empowered. It requires that agencies move from tidy organizational structures in which people with disabilities 'fit' into program vacancies to a fluid structure that changes with the desires of the individuals supported. It requires that control be shared rather than flowing from the top of a hierarchical arrangement. (1994a, p. 3)

The impact of the supports model on the quest for quality is considerable. Support assessment involves many disciplines working as a team, analyzing a variety of assessment findings that include norm-referenced tests, criterion-referenced measures, observation, and interaction with the person. The anticipated levels of support are based on the strengths and limitations of the person and his or her environment, not simply on the individual. Ongoing supports then are provided to enhance the person's adaptive behavior and role statuses (Schalock, 1995b; Smull, 1994b).

Quality Enhancement Techniques   Once the core quality of life dimensions are identified and the core exemplars suggested in Figure 4.2 are developed and measured, then organizations can implement quality enhancement techniques that should enhance the person's perceived quality of life. A number of suggested techniques are summarized in Table 4.2 and discussed more fully in Schalock (1994, 1995a, 1997b).

Determining whether these quality enhancement techniques do in fact make a difference in a person's life requires the use of a shared quality assurance process. The concept of a shared quality assurance process is based on the movements toward participatory management, consumer-based evaluation, and participatory action research (PAR) (Heller, Pederson, & Miller, 1996; Papineau & Kiely, 1996; Whitney-Thomas, 1997). As shown in Figure 4.3, the key aspects of this shared process include the following (Schalock, 1996):

- There is a parallel set of activities completed by the provider (internal evaluation) and the consumer/advocate/regulatory body (external validation).
- Internal evaluation is a data-based process built around person-referenced valued outcomes and organization-referenced efficiency outputs that are monitored jointly by the service provider and the external evaluator(s).
- External evaluation involves agreeing on which quality outcomes to monitor, providing technical assistance and supports to the development and maintenance of the data system, and validating the outcomes.
- Data from the shared quality assurance process are used for a variety of purposes, including implementing quality management or enhancement techniques or conducting quality evaluation.

Focus on Outcomes   The focus on outcomes within reengineered services and a supports paradigm encompasses the central question of what human services ought to achieve for people receiving them: valued person-referenced outcomes from efficient and effective rehabilitation programs. This focus on outcomes stems from two sources: the quality revolution and consumer empowerment. The quality revolution, which is evident in both industry and human services, stresses that quality is integral to both the process used in service delivery and the outcomes from those services. As such, it has directed organizations toward measuring both agency-referenced outputs and person-referenced outcomes.

- *Agency-referenced outputs* are measures of an organization's processes. Examples include responsiveness, consumer satisfaction, quality improvement, placement rates, unit costs, recidivism, bed days, and waiting lists.
- *Person-referenced outcomes* are measures of the impact of services and supports on an individual's adaptive behavior and role

Table 4.2.   Quality-of-life enhancement techniques

Dimensions	Exemplary enhancement techniques
Emotional well-being	Increase safety
	Allow for spirituality
	Provide positive feedback
	Reduce stress
	Foster success
	Promote stable, safe, and predictable environments
	Maintain as low a psychotropic medication level as possible
Interpersonal relationships	Allow intimacy
	Permit affection
	Support family
	Encourage interactions
	Foster friendships
	Provide supports
Material well-being	Allow ownership
	Advocate for financial security
	Ensure safe environments
	Support employment
	Encourage possessions
Personal development	Provide education and (re)habilitation
	Teach functional skills
	Provide vocational and avocational activities
	Foster skill development
	Provide purposeful activities
	Use augmentative technology
Physical well-being	Ensure health care
	Maximize mobility
	Support opportunities for meaningful recreation and leisure
	Encourage proper nutrition
	Support activities of daily living
	Promote wellness by emphasizing physical fitness, nutrition, healthy lifestyles, and stress management
Self-determination	Allow for choices
	Permit personal control
	Allow decisions
	Assist in developing personal goals
Social inclusion	Interface with support networks
	Promote positive role functions and lifestyles
	Stress normalized and integrated environments

continued

Table 4.2.   (continued)

Dimensions	Exemplary enhancement techniques
	Provide opportunities for community integration and participation
	Support volunteerism
Rights	Ensure privacy
	Encourage voting
	Reduce barriers
	Afford due process
	Encourage ownership
	Encourage civic responsibilities

status. Examples of adaptive behavior include activities and instrumental activities of daily living; self-direction; and skills related to communication, social behavior, employment, functional academics, recreation, and leisure. Examples of role status include home and community living arrangements; employment status; and indicators of home ownership, education, health, and wellness (Schalock, 1995a).

The consumer empowerment movement has forced program evaluators to adapt their practices to a more complex view of social systems, in which the concerns and problems that stakeholders want to address, as well as the relational and political context of the organization, guide the evaluation process. Increasingly, PAR is used to involve consumers in program evaluation activities (Papineau & Kiely, 1996; Schalock, 1995a).

Increased Demands for Accountability

Rehabilitation programs are buffeted by two competing accountability requirements: 1) Demonstrate valued, person-referenced outcomes; and 2) measure organization outputs that reflect efficiency and cost control. Albrecht stated that in the customer-value paradigm, "the primary focus of measurement is on outcomes" (1993, p. 14). Others (e.g., Ashbaugh & Smith, 1996; Braddock & Hemp, 1996; Jacobs & Moxley, 1993; Kane, Bartlett, & Potthoff, 1995) also pointed out the need for organizations to be more efficient under proposed Medicaid spending reductions and anticipated managed care.

The focus on efficiency has come largely from the social-political environment of the late 1990s, with its emphasis on cost containment, lids, and managed care. Increasingly, policy makers and funding sources are concerned about the costs of rehabilitation ser-

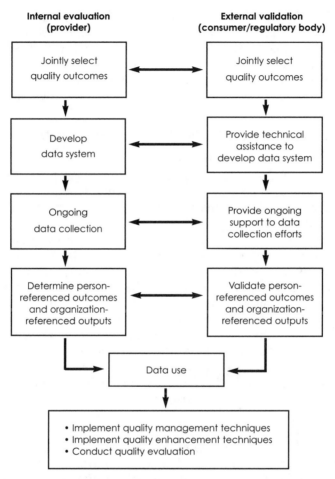

| Internal evaluation (provider) | External validation (consumer/regulatory body) |

Figure 4.3.   The components of a shared quality assurance model. (From Schalock, R.L. [1996]. Quality of life and quality assurance. In R. Renwick, I. Brown, & M. Nagler [Eds.], *Quality of life in health promotion and rehabilitation: Conceptual approaches, issues and applications* [p. 112]. Thousand Oaks, CA: Sage Publications; reprinted by permission.)

vices and the need for those programs to demonstrate cost efficiency and cost savings. To this group, "increased accountability" is equated to increased efficiency, which has become both a mantra and an evaluation standard in the 1990s (Bachrach, 1996; Schalock, 1995a). At the same time, consumers are desiring valued person-referenced outcomes from the services and supports provided to them. They are defining accountability in reference to the extent that services and supports result in enhanced empowerment, independence, productivity, community integration, and satisfaction.

How one can best meet these two competing accountability requirements provides the framework for the Quality Evaluation Model discussed in the next section. The model, which is based on those phenomena discussed thus far in the chapter and the combination of qualitative and quantitative research methods (Sechrest & Sidani, 1995), represents a key technique in one's quest for quality.

QUALITY EVALUATION MODEL AND ITS APPLICATION

As discussed thus far in this chapter, the two contextual variables of person-centered values and restructured services have a profound impact on public policy and service delivery. Not only has the contextual concept of disability shifted, but the disabilities field has also embraced the concept of quality of life as the overarching principle on which to provide services and supports and evaluate person-referenced outcomes. In addition, people in the disabilities field have changed how they view organizations and the services that they provide, stressing the general characteristics of managing for quality and adopting a business mentality, and implementing specific programmatic changes related to PCP, supports, quality enhancement techniques, and outcome evaluation. But the basic question remains, "How do we know whether we have succeeded in meeting the demands for both person-centered outcomes and increased accountability?" Such is the purpose of the Quality Evaluation Model presented in Figure 4.4.

Model Components

As shown in Figure 4.4, the model suggests two standards and two foci that need to be considered in program evaluation. Within each cell of the matrix are the critical performance indicators that are the basis for the measures used.

Standards   The standards component of the Quality Evaluation Model reflects an emphasis on efficiency and value. Efficiency standards are based on economic principles involved in increasing the net value of goods and services available to society; whereas, value standards are based on principles related to excellence, preferences, desirability, or importance (Schalock, 1995a).

Focus   The focus component of the model represents an emphasis on programmatic outputs and person-referenced outcomes. *Outputs* measure the results of organizational processes; *outcomes* represent the impact of services and supports on the individual.

Critical Performance Indicators   The critical performance indicators (CPIs) listed in each cell represent person-referenced out-

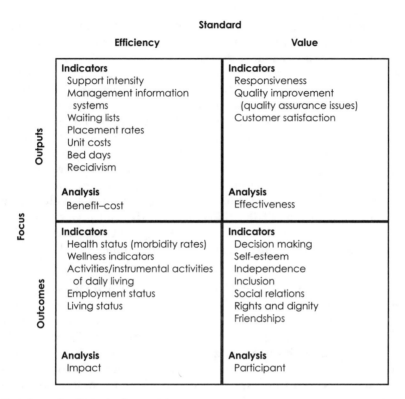

Focus	Standard: Efficiency	Standard: Value
Outputs	**Indicators** Support intensity Management information systems Waiting lists Placement rates Unit costs Bed days Recidivism **Analysis** Benefit–cost	**Indicators** Responsiveness Quality improvement (quality assurance issues) Customer satisfaction **Analysis** Effectiveness
Outcomes	**Indicators** Health status (morbidity rates) Wellness indicators Activities/instrumental activities of daily living Employment status Living status **Analysis** Impact	**Indicators** Decision making Self-esteem Independence Inclusion Social relations Rights and dignity Friendships **Analysis** Participant

Figure 4.4. Quality Evaluation Model.

comes and organization-based outputs that meet the following outcome-based evaluation criteria (Schalock, 1995a): valued by the person, multidimensional, objective and measurable, connected logically to the program, and evaluated longitudinally.

Type of Analysis The type of analysis associated with each cell of the matrix represents four outcome-based evaluation analyses (Schalock, 1995a):

- *Benefit–cost analysis* involves determining whether the program's benefits outweigh the costs. The key components of a benefit–cost analysis include an analytical perspective (participant and rest of society/other taxpayers); estimated costs and benefits; and the inclusion of intangible benefits, such as independence, productivity, community integration, and satisfaction.
- *Impact analysis* involves determining whether the program made a difference compared with either no program or an alternate program. The key components of an impact analysis in-

clude one or more comparison programs or groups and impact statements of statistically significant differences in outcomes among the programs or groups.

- *Effectiveness analysis* involves determining the extent to which a program meets its stated goals and objectives. Key components of an effectiveness analysis include a comparison condition (which can include pre- and postprogram changes in the participants or longitudinal status comparisons) and a longitudinal evaluation of program-related personal outcomes.

- *Participant analysis* involves evaluating person-referenced outcomes from the perspective of the consumer or program participant. Key components of a participant analysis include consumer involvement (as reflected in PAR) and a clear focus on psychological indicators of well-being, personal satisfaction, and/or quality-of-life core dimensions/exemplars (see Figure 4.2).

The four components of the Quality Evaluation Model—evaluation standards, evaluation focus, CPIs, and type of outcome-based evaluation analysis—provide the framework for program evaluation activities related to the quest for quality. As shown in Figure 4.4, *efficiency outputs* from the organizational process include such CPIs as support intensities (which should decrease with effective services and supports), waiting lists, bed days, recidivism, placement rates, or unit costs. *Value outputs* from the organizational process include CPIs such as responsiveness, quality improvement, or consumer satisfaction. *Efficiency outcomes,* which measure the impact or effect of the services and/or supports received from the organization, include health or morbidity status, wellness indicators, activities/instrumental activities of daily living, employment status, or living status. *Value outcomes* include measures of independence, inclusion, social relationships, rights and dignity, friendships, decision making, and self-esteem.

The importance of the Quality Evaluation Model is that it meets the competing accountability requirements of efficiency and value-based outcomes and provides a heuristic model for future work in this area. The next section presents examples of how the model has been applied in program evaluation.

Model Application

There are a number of potential applications of the evaluation model presented in Figure 4.4. Four types of analyses, referenced to each matrix cell, are discussed in this section.

Benefit–Cost Analysis   In reference to the model, benefit–cost analyses relate to efficiency outputs. For example, one of the early studies of benefit–cost analysis involved evaluating the benefits and costs of transitional employment programs in enhancing the economic and social independence of young adults with mental retardation (Kerachsky, Thornton, Bloomenthal, Maynard, & Stephens, 1985). The sample included 437 individuals—226 in the experimental group (who were enrolled in transitional employment programs throughout the United States) and 211 in the control group (who were not enrolled in such programs). Estimated costs to society were $6,232 per participant during the 22-month observation period, whereas social benefits (increased output by participants and the reduced use of other training, service, residential, and transfer programs) totaled only $4,193 per participant. Thus, about 83% of the initial investment was offset during the 22-month observation, but expenses were projected to exceed social costs at 29 months. Nonmonetized benefits to the participants included preferences for work, increased self-sufficiency, and independent living. In a similar study, Lewis, Johnson, Bruininks, Kallsen, and Guilley (1992) evaluated the benefits and costs of supported employment in Minnesota. They reported that benefits exceeded costs in the areas of increased productivity; reduced use of alternative programs; decreased governmental subsidies; and "other benefits" that included increased community integration, quality of life, and self-esteem. Similar benefit–cost analyses demonstrating program-related efficiency outputs have been conducted on preschool education programs (Barnett, 1993), on the Intermediate Care Facilities for the Mentally Retarded (ICF/MR) program (Conroy, 1996), and on supported employment for people with mental retardation (Conley & Noble, 1990; Rusch, Conley, & McCaughlin, 1993) or mental illness (Hill et al., 1987; Rogers, Sciarappa, MacDonald-Wilson, & Danley, 1995).

Impact Analysis   In reference to the model, impact analysis relates to efficiency outcomes. In the Kerachsky et al. (1985) study, for example, significant statistical differences were obtained between the training and nontraining group in percentage of individuals employed in a typical job, average weekly earnings in a typical job, and percentage of individuals in training. In general, relatively small program effects were observed on measures of independence, overall economic status, services received from community agencies, and involvement in activities oriented toward employment. Conroy (1996) also used impact analysis to evaluate smaller ICFs/MR versus other community living arrangements on 35 quality indicator measures. Significant differences between the two programs were obtained on nine measures: 1) behavioral progress over 5 years, 2) choice-making, 3) frequency of integrative experiences indicative of employment, 4) average size of home, 5) group home management style, 6) overall rating of home/program quality, 7) staff expectations regarding growth, 8) written plans for fires, and 9) written plans for medical emergencies. Similar impact analyses demonstrating efficiency outcomes have been conducted on training environments (Schalock, Gadwood, & Perry, 1984), special education programs (Garber, McInerney, & Velu, 1994), classroom placement (Hunt, Farron-David, Beckstead, Curtis, & Goetz, 1994), mental health capitation programs (Reed, Hennessy, Mitchell, & Babigian, 1994), and community residential versus institutional services (Knobbe, Carey, Rhodes, & Horner, 1995).

Effectiveness Analysis   In reference to the Quality Evaluation Model, effectiveness analysis relates to analyzing valued outputs from organizations and determining the extent to which a program or organization obtains its goals and objectives. For example, a longitudinal study (Schalock & Lilley, 1986) evaluated valued outputs from a community-based program for people with mental retardation whose programmatic goals were to place people into more independent and productive environments and enhance their quality of life. Data sets were related to the consumers' current living and employment status, the relationship of consumer characteristics and training variables to successful placement, and measures of the person's quality of life. Individuals involved in the analysis were 85 (42 males, 43 females) service recipients who had been placed 8–10 years prior to the study into either an independent living or an integrated employment arrangement and who had remained within that placement for a minimum of 2 years. Their average age was 30, and their average IQ score (according to the Wechsler Adult Intelligence Scale) was 67 (standard deviation = 12). Three groups emerged on the basis of participants' current programmatic and living/work status: 20% maintained their living and work placements or moved into comparable environments; 47% had changed their placement categories with current statuses including living independently but unemployed or employed only part time, being in a mental health facility, or living with family and unemployed; and 24% returned to the training program. A number of variables were found to discriminate between successful and unsuccessful living and work outcomes, including program, family, and person-related factors. For assessed quality of life, significant correlates included family involvement, income, number of disabilities, and age. Those who were successful had a higher assessed quality of life, including measures of satisfaction.

Another valued outputs analysis involved the analysis of the postgraduation living and work status of special education students who had participated in a community-based job exploration and training program during a 5-year period prior to the analysis. The 108 students involved in the study (Schalock, Wolzen, Elliott, Werbel, & Peterson, 1986) had been classified according to the State Department of Education's definitions as *specific learning disabled* (SLD), *educable mentally handicapped* (EMH), or *mentally retarded* (MR). The sample included 65 students diagnosed as SLD, 31 as EMH, and 12 as MR. Four significant findings relating to valued outputs were obtained: 61% of the graduates were working competitively; 22% were living independently; students diagnosed as SLD were more likely to be employed, live independently, and be self-sufficient than those diagnosed as EMH or MR; and students whose families were moderately to highly involved with the students' programs were more successful on the employment-related outcome measures. Effectiveness analysis also has been used to evaluate psychotherapy programs (Seligman, 1995), programs for homeless veterans with mental illness (Rosenheck, Frishman, & Gallup, 1995), and medical diagnostic testing (Posavac, 1995).

Participant Analysis   In reference to the model, participant analysis relates to valued outcomes. The adoption by the Accreditation Council (Gardner & Nudler, 1997) of outcome-based performance measures represents such an analysis. Ten groups of outcome measures—1) personal goals, 2) choice, 3) social inclusion, 4) relationships, 5) rights, 6) dignity and respect, 7) health, 8) environment, 9) security, and 10) satisfaction—are the basis for program participants to define the meaning and application of outputs for themselves. Organizations then can measure whether the output is present in the manner and, to the extent, defined by the person. In addition, an emphasis is given to the individualized organizational process that facilitates outcomes and the relationship between outcomes and individualized organizational process. An analogous approach is being used by the Massachusetts Department of Mental Retardation to certify agencies (Grossman et al., in press). The survey and certification process is built around six quality-of-life areas: 1) respect and dignity, 2) individual control, 3) community membership, 4) relationships, 5) growth and accomplishments, and 6) personal well-being (health, safety, and economic security). A provider is evaluated and certified based on the quality of supports provided across the entire array of services offered.

Other examples of participant analysis include a study by Schalock and Genung (1993) who surveyed the attitudes of previous program participants as to whether they had experienced a number of desired outcomes from living in the community. Significant positive attainments were reported for making decisions, arranging for assistance, visiting with others, using the community, and owning things. In an analogous study (Schalock, Nelson, Sutton, Holtan, & Sheehan, 1997), former recipients of facility-based mental health services were surveyed regarding their level of current functioning, community adjustment, and quality of life. Survey results then were compared with a matched sample of typical individuals living in the community. The mental health group reported more current problems; used more community resources; had a higher need for living, employment, and self-direction assistance; received most of their support from family members; and had lower measured quality-of-life scores related to satisfaction, productivity, empowerment, and community integration. Participant analyses also have been reported for satisfaction with residential services (Newton, Ard, Horner, & Toews, 1996), satisfaction among a group of people with mental retardation living in the community (Edgerton, 1996), and desires regarding the components of a life of quality among self-advocates (Goode, 1990).

CONCLUSIONS

The 1990s have been referred to as the "decade of quality of life and value clashes." These, in turn, are reflected in the two powerful and potentially conflicting forces that were experienced in the 1990s: person-centered values and restructured services. As discussed in this chapter, these two forces represent the context within which education, health care, and rehabilitation programs will operate as we continue to strive to achieve quality organizational outputs and personal outcomes. These factors represent significant challenges to each of us. From a service delivery perspective, they require organizational changes consistent with the four discussed in this chapter—a changed conception of disability, the use of quality-of-life–oriented program services and supports, and an evaluation of outcomes. From a program evaluation perspective, they require the use of multiple outcome-based evaluation analyses, including benefit–cost, impact, effectiveness, and participant.

It is a safe prediction that the movement toward quality evaluation will continue, and it is this author's firm belief that the Quality Evaluation Model presented in Figure 4.4 can meet the two major contextual variables discussed in this chapter. The model's emphasis on efficiency standards and program outputs will provide objective indicators of restructured human services programs that are more efficient. The model's emphasis on value standards and personal outcomes should meet consumers' desires for person-referenced outcomes that truly make a difference in their lives.

A quest is never ending and requires that one begin with the end in mind. We are seeing an increasing number of state agencies and rehabilitation programs respond to the need to restructure and be more efficient, without losing sight of their responsibility to achieve organizational outputs that are consistent with person-centered values and quality person-referenced outcomes. The organizations that survive into the 21st century will have met this challenge successfully by being innovative and developing their direct services workers. The others will have forgotten the sage advice that the world belongs to those who are flexible.

REFERENCES

Albin, J.M. (1992). *Quality improvement in employment and other human services: Managing for quality through change.* Baltimore: Paul H. Brookes Publishing Co.

Albin-Dean, J.E., & Mank, D.M. (1997). Continuous improvement and quality of life: Lessons from new approaches to organizational management. In R.L. Schalock (Ed.), *Quality of life: Application to persons with disabilities* (Vol. II, pp. 165–180). Washington, DC: American Association on Mental Retardation.

Albrecht, K. (1993). *The only thing that matters: Bringing the power of the customer into the center of your business.* New York: Harper Business.

Americans with Disabilities Act (ADA) of 1990, PL 101-336, 42 U.S.C. §§ 12101 *et seq.*

Ashbaugh, J., & Smith, G. (1996, June). Beware the managed health-care companies. *Mental Retardation,* 189–193.

Bachrach, L.L. (1996). Managed care: IV. Some helpful resources. *Psychiatric Services, 47*(9), 925–930.

Barnett, S.W. (1993). Benefit-cost analysis of preschool education: Findings from a 25-year follow-up. *American Journal of Orthopsychiatry, 63*(4), 500–525.

Braddock, D., & Hemp, R. (1996). Medicaid spending reductions and developmental disabilities. *Journal of Disability Policy Studies, 7*(1), 1–32.

Bradley, V.J., & Bersani, H.A. (Eds.). (1990). *Quality assurance for individuals with developmental disabilities: It's everyone's business.* Baltimore: Paul H. Brookes Publishing Co.

Butterworth, J., Hagner, D., Kiernan, W.E., & Schalock, R.L. (1996). Natural supports in the workplace: Defining an agenda for research and practice. *Journal of The Association for Persons with Severe Handicaps, 21*(3), 103–113.

Butterworth, J., Hagner, D., Heikkinen, B., Faris, S., DeMello, S., & McDonough, K. (1993). *Whole life planning: A guide for organizers and facilitators.* Boston: Institute for Community Inclusion, Children's Hospital.

Butterworth, J., Steere, D.E., & Whitney-Thomas, J. (1997). Using person-centered planning to address personal quality of life. In R.L. Schalock (Ed.), *Quality of life: Application to persons with disabilities* (Vol. II, pp. 5–24). Washington, DC: American Association on Mental Retardation.

Clifford, D.L., & Sherman, P. (1983). Internal evaluation: Integrating program evaluation and management. In A.J. Love (Ed.), *Developing effective internal evaluation: New directions for program evaluation* (No. 20, pp. 124–162). San Francisco: Jossey-Bass.

Conley, R.W., & Noble, J.H. (1990). Benefit-cost analysis of supported employment. In F.R. Rusch (Ed.), *Supported employment: Models, methods and issues* (pp. 271–288). Sycamore, IL: Sycamore Publishing.

Conroy, J.W. (1996). The small ICF/MR program: Dimensions of quality and cost. *Mental Retardation, 34*(1), 13–26.

Coulter, D.L. (1996). Prevention as a form of support: Implications for the new definition. *Mental Retardation, 34*(2), 108–116.

Cummins, R.A. (1996). The domains of life satisfaction: An attempt to order chaos. *Social Indicators Research, 38,* 303–328.

Deming, W.E. (1993). *The new economics for industry, government, education.* Cambridge: Massachusetts Institute of Technology, Center for Advanced Engineering Study.

Developmental Disabilities and Bill of Rights Act of 1990, PL 101-496, 42 U.S.C. §§ 6000 *et seq.*

Dillon, M.R. (1993). Morality and freedom: Challenges to a field in transition. *Mental Retardation, 31,* iii–viii.

Edgerton, R.B. (1996). A longitudinal-ethnographic research perspective on quality of life. In R.L. Schalock (Ed.), *Quality of life: Conceptualization and measurement* (Vol. I, pp. 83–90). Washington, DC: American Association on Mental Retardation.

Garber, H.L., McInerney, M., & Velu, R. (1994). Effectiveness in special education programs: Deriving empirical strategies for efficient resource allocation. *Issues in Special Education and Rehabilitation, 9*(1), 101–112.

Gardner, J.F., & Nudler, S. (1997). Beyond compliance to responsiveness: Accreditation reconsidered. In R.L. Schalock (Ed.), *Quality of life: Application to persons with disabilities* (Vol. II, pp. 135–148). Washington, DC: American Association on Mental Retardation.

Goode, D.A. (1990). Thinking about and discussing quality of life. In R.L. Schalock (Ed.), *Quality of life: Perspectives and issues* (pp. 41–58). Washington, DC: American Association on Mental Retardation.

Grossman, G., Rowe, J., Cerreto, M., & Schalock, R. (in press). A quality of life-oriented outcome based approach to agency certification. *Mental Retardation.*

Hammer, M., & Champy, J. (1993). *Reengineering the corporation: A manifesto for business revolution.* New York: HarperCollins.

Heller, T., Pederson, E.L., & Miller, A.B. (1996). Guidelines from the consumer: Improving consumer involvement in research and training for persons with mental retardation. *Mental Retardation, 34*(3), 141–148.

Hill, M., Banks, P.D., Handrich, R., Wehman, P., Hill, J., & Shafer, M. (1987). Benefit-cost analysis of supported competitive employment for persons with mental retardation. *Research in Developmental Disabilities, 8,* 71–89.

Hunt, P., Farron-David, F., Beckstead, S., Curtis, D., & Goetz, L. (1994). Evaluating the effects of placement of students with severe disabilities in general education versus special classes. *Journal of The Association for Persons with Severe Handicaps, 19*(3), 200–214.

Individuals with Disabilities Education Act (IDEA) of 1997, PL 105-17, 20 U.S.C. §§ 1400 *et seq.*

Jacobs, D.R., & Moxley, D.P. (1993). Anticipating managed mental health care: Implications for psychosocial rehabilitation agencies. *Psycho-social Rehabilitation Journal, 17*(2), 15–31.

Juran, J.M. (1989). *Juran on leadership for quality.* New York: The Free Press.

Kane, R.L., Bartlett, J., & Potthoff, S. (1995). Building an empirically based outcomes information system for managed mental health care. *Psychiatric Services, 46*(5), 459–461.

Karan, O.C., & Bothwell, J.D. (1997). Supported living: Stretching beyond the limits of our conventional thinking and practice. In R.L. Schalock (Ed.), *Quality of life: Application to persons with disabilities* (Vol. II, pp. 79–94). Washington, DC: American Association on Mental Retardation.

Kerachsky, S., Thornton, C., Bloomenthal, A., Maynard, R., & Stephens, S. (1985). *Impacts of transitional employment for mentally retarded young adults: Results of the STETS demonstration.* Princeton, NJ: Mathematica Policy Research.

Kiernan, W.E., & Marrone, J. (1997). Quality of work life for persons with disabilities: Emphasis on the employee. In R.L. Schalock (Ed.), *Quality of life: Application to persons with disabilities* (Vol. II, pp. 63–78). Washington, DC: American Association on Mental Retardation.

Kirchner, C. (1996). Looking under the street lamp. *Journal of Disability Policy Studies, 7*(1), 77–90.

Knobbe, C.A., Carey, S.P., Rhodes, L., & Horner, R.H. (1995). Benefit-cost analysis of community residential versus institutional services for adults with severe mental retardation and challenging behaviors. *American Journal of Mental Retardation, 99*(5), 533–541.

Knoll, J.A. (1990). Defining quality in residential services. In V.J. Bradley & H.A. Bersani (Eds.), *Quality assurance for individuals with developmental disabilities: It's everybody's business* (pp. 235–262). Baltimore: Paul H. Brookes Publishing Co.

Lewis, D.R., Johnson, R.H., Bruininks, R.H., Kallsen, L.A., & Guilley, R.P. (1992). Is supported employment cost-effective in Minnesota? *Journal of Disability Policy Studies, 3*(1), 67–92.

Lindemann, A.J. (1996, October 7). *Human resources for the 21st century: Policies and practices.* Paper presented at the AAMR Region IV Annual Conference, Phoenix, AZ.

Luckasson, R., Coulter, D.L., Polloway, E.A., Reiss, S., Schalock, R.L., Snell, M.E., Spitalnik, D.M., & Stark, J.A. (1992). *Mental retardation: Definition, classification and systems of supports.* Washington, DC: American Association on Mental Retardation.

Luckasson, R., Schalock, R.L., Snell, M.E., & Spitalnik, D.M. (1996, August). The 1992 AAMR definition and preschool children: Response from the Committee on Terminology and Classification. *Mental Retardation,* 247–253.

Mathison, S. (1991). What do we know about internal evaluation? *Evaluation and Program Planning, 14,* 159–165.

Newton, J.S., Ard, W.R., Jr., Horner, R.H., & Toews, J.D. (1996). Focusing on values and lifestyle outcomes in an effort to improve the quality of residential services in Oregon. *Mental Retardation, 34*(1), 1–12.

Nisbet, J., & Hagner, D. (1988). Natural supports in the workplace: A re-examination of supportive employment. *Journal of The Association for Persons with Severe Handicaps, 13,* 260–267.

O'Brien, J. (1987). A guide to lifestyle planning: Using the Activities Catalog to integrate services and natural support systems. In B. Wilcox & B.T. Bellamy (Eds.), *The activities catalog: An alternative curriculum design for adults with severe disabilities* (pp. 104–110). Baltimore: Paul H. Brookes Publishing Co.

Osborne, D., & Gaebler, T. (1992). *Reinventing government: How the entrepreneurial spirit is transforming the public sector.* Reading, MA: Addison-Wesley.

Papineau, D., & Kiely, M.C. (1996). Participatory evaluation in a community organization: Fostering stakeholder empowerment and utilization. *Evaluation and Program Planning, 19*(1), 79–93.

Pope, A.M., & Tarlov, A.R. (Eds.). (1991). *Disability in America: Toward a national agenda for prevention.* Washington, DC: National Academy Press.

Posavac, E.J. (1995). Program quality and program effectiveness: A review of evaluations of programs to reduce excessive medical diagnostic testing. *Evaluation and Program Planning, 18*(1), 1–11.

Reed, S.K., Hennessy, K.D., Mitchell, O.S., & Babigian, H.M. (1994). A mental health capitation program: II. Cost benefit analysis. *Hospital and Community Psychiatry, 45*(11), 1097–1103.

Reeves, C.A., & Rednar, D.A. (1994). Defining quality: Alternatives and implications. *The Academy of Management Review, 19,* 419–445.

Rioux, M.H. (1996, July 8–13). *Disability: The place of judgement in a world of fact.* Paper presented at the 10th World Congress, International Association for the Scientific Study of Intellectual Disability, Helsinki, Finland.

Roberts, R.N., Wasik, B.H., Casto, S., & Ramey, C.T. (1991). Family support in the home: Programs, policy and social change. *American Psychologist, 46,* 131–137.

Rogers, E.S., Sciarappa, K., MacDonald-Wilson, K., & Danley, K. (1995). A benefit-cost analysis of a supported employment model for persons with psychiatric disabilities. *Evaluation and Program Planning, 18*(2), 105–115.

Rosenheck, R., Frishman, L., & Gallup, P. (1995). Effectiveness and cost of specific elements in a program for homeless mentally ill veterans. *Hospital and Community Psychiatry, 46*(11), 1131–1139.

Rusch, F.R. (1990). *Supported employment: Models, methods, and issues.* Sycamore, IL: Sycamore Publishing.

Rusch, F.R., Conley, R.W., & McCaughlin, W.B. (1993). Benefit-cost analysis of supported employment in Illinois. *Journal of Rehabilitation,* April/May/June, 31–36.

Sacks, O. (1995). *An anthropologist on Mars.* New York: Vintage Books.

Schalock, R.L. (1994). Quality of life, quality enhancement, and quality assurance: Implications for program planning and evaluation in the field of mental retardation and developmental disabilities. *Evaluation and Program Planning, 17*(2), 121–131.

Schalock, R.L. (1995a). *Outcome-based evaluation.* New York: Plenum.

Schalock, R.L. (1995b). The assessment of natural supports in community rehabilitation services. In O.C. Karan & S. Greenspan (Eds.), *Community rehabilitation services for people with disabilities* (pp. 184–203). Newton, MA: Butterworth-Heinemann.

Schalock, R.L. (1996). Quality of life and quality assurance. In R. Renwick, I. Brown, & M. Nagler (Eds.), *Quality of life in health promotion and rehabilitation: Conceptual approaches, issues and applications* (pp. 104–118). Thousand Oaks, CA: Sage Publications.

Schalock, R.L. (1997a). Can the concept of quality of life make a difference? In R.L. Schalock (Ed.), *Quality of life: Application to persons with disabilities* (Vol. II, pp. 245–267). Washington, DC: American Association on Mental Retardation.

Schalock, R.L. (1997b). The conceptualization and measurement of quality of life: Current status and future considerations. *Journal of Developmental Disabilities, 5*(2), 1–21.

Schalock, R.L., Gadwood, L.S., & Perry, P.B. (1984). Effects of different training environments on the acquisition of community living skills. *Applied Research in Mental Retardation, 5,* 425–438.

Schalock, R.L., & Genung, L.T. (1993). Placement from a community-based mental retardation program: A 15-year follow-up. *American Journal on Mental Retardation, 98*(3), 400–407.

Schalock, R.L., & Lilley, M.A. (1986). Placement from community based mental retardation programs: How well do clients do after 8–10 years? *American Journal on Mental Deficiency, 90*(6), 669–676.

Schalock, R.L., Nelson, G., Sutton, S., Holtan, S., & Sheehan, M. (1997). A multidimensional evaluation of the current status and quality of life of mental health service recipients. *SigLo CERO, 28*(4), 5–14.

Schalock, R.L., Wolzen, B., Elliott, B., Werbel, G., & Peterson, K. (1986). Post-secondary community placement of handicapped students: A five-year follow-up. *Learning Disabilities Quarterly, 9,* 295–303.

Sechrest, L., & Sidani, S. (1995). Quantitative and qualitative methods: Is there an alternative? *Evaluation and Program Planning, 18*(1), 77–87.

Seligman, M.E.P. (1995). The effectiveness of psychotherapy. *American Psychologist, 50*(12), 965–974.

Senge, P. (1990). *The fifth discipline: The art and practice of the learning organization.* New York: Doubleday/Currency.

Smull, M. (1994a). Moving to a system of supports: Using support brokerage. *AAMR News and Notes, 7*(4), 4–6.

Smull, M. (1994b). Moving toward a system of support. *AAMR News and Notes, 7*(5), 3–5.

Snell, M.E. (Ed.). (1993). *Systematic instruction of students with severe disabilities* (4th ed.). New York: Macmillan.

Snell, M.E., & Vogle, L.K. (1997). Interpersonal relationships of school-aged children and adolescents with mental retardation. In R.L. Schalock (Ed.), *Quality of life: Application to persons with disabilities* (Vol. II, pp. 43–62). Washington, DC: American Association on Mental Retardation.

Taylor, S.J., & Bogdan, R. (1996). Quality of life and the individual's perspective. In R.L. Schalock (Ed.), *Quality of life: Conceptualization and measurement* (Vol. I, pp. 11–22). Washington, DC: American Association on Mental Retardation.

Torres, R.T. (1992). Improving the quality of internal evaluation: The evaluator as consultant-mediator. *Evaluation and Program Planning, 14,* 189–198.

Trabin, T., Freeman, M.A., & Pallak, M.E. (Eds.). (1995). *Inside outcomes: The national review of behavioral healthcare outcomes programs.* Tiburon, CA: Central Link Publications.

Vocational Rehabilitation Act Amendments of 1992, PL 102-569, 29 U.S.C. §§ 701 *et seq.*

Wehman, P., & Moon, M.S. (Eds.). (1988). *Vocational rehabilitation and supported employment.* Baltimore: Paul H. Brookes Publishing Co.

Wheatley, M. (1994). *Leadership and the new science: Learning about organizations from an orderly universe.* San Francisco: Berrett-Koehler.

Whitney-Thomas, J. (1997). Participatory action research as an approach to enhancing quality of life for individuals with disabilities. In R.L. Schalock (Ed.), *Quality of life: Application to persons with mental retardation* (Vol. II, pp. 181–198). Washington, DC: American Association on Mental Retardation.

Zola, I.K. (1993). Disability statistics: What we count and what it tells us. *Journal of Disability Policy Studies, 4*(2), 9–39.

5

Quality Performance

Designing Clinical Services
Around Person-Centered Outcomes

Mary Law, Gillian A. King,
Elizabeth MacKinnon, and Dianne J. Russell

The design and delivery of clinical services has changed rapidly
since the 1970s, and there are no indications that the pace of change
will moderate in the late 1990s. Driven by increased demand for consumer involvement; alternate views of disability; modifications to
the financing, structure, and process of services; and fiscal restraint,
clinical services have been transformed. What these changes have
meant for the measurement of the outcomes of clinical services is the
focus of this chapter. The chapter begins with a description of these
changes and is followed by a discussion of methods that can be used
to design a clinical service system that measures outcomes centered
on the individual(s) receiving services.

PERSON-CENTERED OUTCOMES

In the past, clinical services have been planned and implemented by
professionals with little or no involvement of the people receiving
the services. It was believed that professionals, with their training

and experience, were experts and could apply their knowledge to design an efficient service system. Little attention was paid to the individual needs of those receiving services. Classification and quality improvement schemas were devised so that "patients" could be grouped into clusters and moved through a clinical service system at minimum cost (Humphreys & Lindberg, 1989; U.S. General Accounting Office, 1991). A patient was seen as a "consumer of health care rather than [as a] producer of health" (Avis, 1994, p. 296). Lip service was paid to "patient" outcomes, which often were measured by the number of service units, mortality rate, or cost of services. The application of elementary consumer satisfaction questionnaires was the closest that service organizations came to measuring the preferences and outcomes as perceived by the people receiving the services.

The cost of clinical services has risen dramatically since the 1960s. Health care costs in the United States are estimated to have increased from $27.1 billion in 1960 to $666.2 billion in 1990 (Iglehart, 1992). Efforts to decrease these costs have resulted in changes toward a managed care system, in which purchasers of clinical services have organized to support integrated service delivery models. Criteria for the successful receipt of managed care contracts often emphasize the services that provide the most value for the least cost.

Service quality in clinical services has largely been defined and measured by evaluating the structure, process, and outcomes of services using a framework devised by Donabedian (1988). The *structure* of a service refers to the facilities, programs, and staff that make up the service, whereas *process* includes the manner in which services are delivered and whether process guidelines about time and delivery of service are met. Although structure and process have been evaluated as measures of the quality of clinical services, it is only since the mid-1990s that the evaluation of outcomes has gained increasing attention (Gardner & Campanella, 1995).

As consumers demand increased involvement in the planning of and outcomes of clinical services, there has been a growing recognition that the active participation of people in receiving information and making decisions about clinical services is a fundamental human right (Kennedy, 1981). People are realizing that, unless they are actively involved in defining the preferred outcomes of services, the results of those services often will be disappointing.

The prevalence of disability leading to activity limitations ranges from 6% for children and adolescents to 25% for people older than 75 years of age (U.S. Department of Health and Human Services, 1991). The aging of the population and increased long-term survival of people with impairments and injuries will continue to substantially transform the demographic picture of disability in North America. Concomitant with the increases in prevalence of disability has been a policy shift toward community living for people with disabilities. As institutional costs rose and the quality of care was questioned, policies shifted to move people with disabilities into community living situations. These living arrangements, unfortunately, often were set up without adequate community support or follow-up/monitoring of outcomes.

Disability advocates have stressed that poor quality of life or poor outcomes are not the fault of the individual who has a disability but rest in the relationship between the individual and the environment (Hahn, 1984; Jongbloed & Crichton, 1990). Community environments often are disabling to consumers, preventing them from achieving their daily living goals. It has been argued that these situations will not improve until consumers with disabilities are intimately involved in the planning and delivery of services. To this end, services could focus on planning and social policies aimed at the modification of the environment, not just on methods to change a person with a disability to fit the environment. Quality of life is determined by the interactions and fit between the person and the environments in which he or she lives, works, and plays (Law, 1991).

Redefining Clinical Services

Whereas many of the modifications to clinical services are driven by the desire to decrease costs, a shift to services that are centered on the needs of people also is occurring. There is increasing recognition that people receiving services are an integral part of the "service team" and that their active participation influences the outcome of services (Greenfield, Kaplan, & Ware, 1985; Morris, Goddard, & Roger, 1989). Whether labeled as patient-centered, patient-focused, client-centered, or person-centered, there are common assumptions that define service systems that are directed toward the needs of the person. These include the assumptions that people and their families know themselves best, that each person and his or her family is unique, and that optimal functioning occurs within a supportive family and community context (Rosenbaum, King, Law, King, & Evans, in press). Principles of service delivery to ensure that these assumptions are inherent in all service delivery include the following:

- Services are tailored to the individual rather than fitting the individual into already established programs (Law, Baptiste, & Mills, 1995).

- Each person and his or her family receives information to enable them to define their needs, make choices, and be a partner in clinical decision making (Rosenbaum et al., in press).
- People receiving services and their families are treated with respect, and services are recognizing people's unique values, roles, interests, living environment, and culture.
- Services are provided in a coordinated fashion within the context of the community in which the person lives (Gerteis, 1993).
- Services are provided in a timely, flexible, and accessible manner, emphasizing interventions that promote learning and problem solving (Law et al., 1995).
- Services are structured to minimize bureaucracy so that the focus of service is on the defined needs of the person, not only on what is reimbursable.

Implications for Measuring Outcomes

If the principles of person-centered services are followed, then outcomes will measure the needs and goals that people receiving services (and their families) consider to be important (Gardner & Campanella, 1995; Law et al., 1995). In many instances, this will shift the focus of outcomes measurement from the evaluation of impairments (e.g., strength, memory, self-concept) to the evaluation of everyday tasks (e.g., driving a car, operating a computer, playing cards) and to satisfaction with service. Quality of life is the essential concern of people with disabilities (Shapiro, 1993).

In a person-centered service model, increased attention is paid to the values that are implicit in outcomes measurement (Fuhrer, 1995). Methods of evaluation reflect the values and preferences of people with disabilities rather than characteristics that are most easily measured. Designing these outcome systems may lead to the questioning of standardized measurements that apply the same assessment to all individuals and that include items that are of little or no importance to a person receiving services.

What Are the Outcomes of Clinical Services?

Outcomes provide information about a variety of aspects of clinical services. First and foremost, outcomes are used to make decisions and improve services to individuals. Information about outcomes across individuals is used to improve the services or programs that are part of a clinical services delivery system. Other purposes that outcomes serve in clinical services include demonstration of financial and/or professional accountability, the meeting of legislated directions or accreditation requirements, and the provision of evidence of the effectiveness of services (Law et al., 1996).

Outcomes, therefore, represent the end result of clinical services activities. Results can be measured in many different ways, including describing a person's functional status; noting changes in specific impairments, such as strength or cognitive status; and assessing a person's satisfaction with service and the cost of the service. Outcomes can be measured from a variety of perspectives, including the perspective of the person receiving the service, the service provider, the funder, the organization providing the service, or other community agencies. In measuring person-centered outcomes, it is important that the primary outcome that is measured be based on information gained from the person receiving the service and his or her family.

Using a Conceptual Framework for Measuring Outcomes

Focusing outcomes measurement on the priority outcomes of people receiving services is the important first step in defining the best outcomes to measure. Without a conceptual measurement framework, however, it would be difficult for people and service providers to make decisions about which outcomes to measure in each clinical situation.

There are some examples of the application of a measurement framework in work with adults with disabilities and with adults in rehabilitation (Bunch & Dvonch, 1994; Wright, Linacre, & Heinemann, 1993). The most widely used framework is the Uniform Data System, built around the Functional Independence Measure (FIM[SM]) (SUNY at Buffalo, 1993). Although the model of the Uniform Data System has been useful to provide information about burden of care and resource use, information provided by the FIM is global in nature and is not specific to each individual person and his or her needs. This data system relies on only one outcome measure, which may not be appropriate for the nature or the scope of the services received or the nature of the outcomes desired by the person receiving services. A conceptual framework that incorporates more flexibility in choosing outcomes to be measured would better serve the needs of people receiving clinical services.

Haley, Coster, and Ludlow (1991) outlined three conceptual frameworks for the selection and use of outcomes measures to be used with children who receive services. These frameworks include 1) the International Classification of Impairment, Disability and Handicap (ICIDH) (World Health Organization, 1980); 2) a developmental framework; and 3) an environmental and social framework. The use of a developmental framework is problematic because typical developmental patterns in children with disabilities are not well known. The environmental framework incorporates characteristics of the child as well as the environment in leading to outcomes of the child's functional capacity and functional performance. The incorporation of environmental issues into an environmental and social framework recognizes the impact that environment can have on performance. This framework, however, is not suitable to all clinical services, as it has been developed primarily for pediatric use.

A modification of the ICIDH (Fougeyrollas, Bergeron, Cloutier, & St. Michel, 1991) represents a conceptual framework that can be applied broadly across all clinical services. This framework (see Figure 5.1) fits with the purpose and philosophy of person-centered services, measures outcomes at various levels (e.g., disability, life habits), reflects the perspectives of a number of stakeholders, is not discipline specific, and is relevant to the goals of people receiving services. The modified ICIDH provides a broad perspective for outcomes measurement and allows for a flexible and individualized approach to the selection of outcomes measures.

SERVICES THAT BEGIN AND END
WITH PERSON-DEFINED OUTCOMES

A clinical service process that adheres to the principles outlined in the previous section can be designed to ensure that a person receiving services is a partner in the service plan. The following discussion outlines such a generic process.

1. *Initiate Referral*   Clinical service is initiated upon the referral to a service by a person with a disability, his or her family, or a service provider. Referrals should never proceed without discussion and agreement with the person who is to receive the service; if that is not possible, there should be agreement with his or her caregiver. In many instances, self-referral is most appropriate.
2. *Develop Individualized Person-Centered Assessment*   Assessment of the needs of a person referred for service begins with the service provider learning about the person, his or her needs and values, and the outcomes that are important to him or her. Assessment methods such as storytelling, natural history, or semistructured interviews are often the best way to enable the person to communicate his or her needs. Through this process, the person with a disability or his or her family will be able to articulate specific service needs, and, together, they can determine whether the service provider can help with those issues.

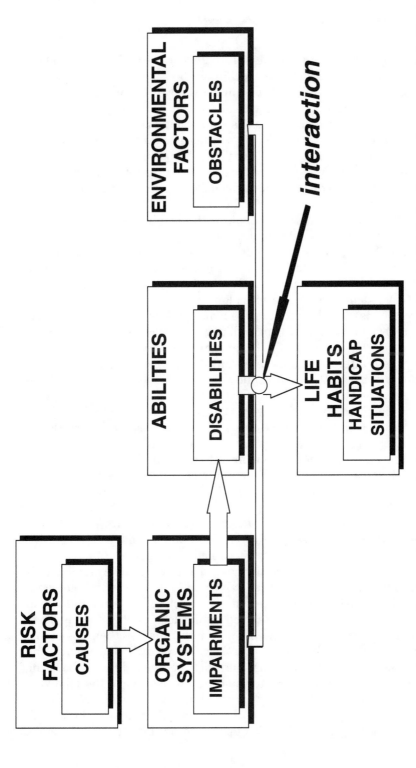

Figure 5.1.   Handicap creation process. (From Fougeyrollas, P., Bergeron, H., Cloutier, R., & St. Michel, G. [1991]. The handicaps creation process: Analysis of the consultation and new full proposals. *International ICIDH Network, 4.2;* reprinted by kind permission from author, Patrick Fougeyrollas, Ph.D., President, Canadian Society for the ICIDH. ©1991 Fougeyrollas, Bergeron, Cloutier, & St. Michel.)

3. *Plan Service and Partnership with Person and Family*   Once the person has defined specific needs, a service plan is developed through a discussion among the service provider and the person receiving the service and his or her family. It is important for service providers to spend enough time with the person and to communicate clearly so that everyone has a full understanding of what will occur throughout the intervention. It is often tempting for service providers to present a plan to a person without adequate discussion. Although a person may agree to such a plan, research indicates that adherence to intervention is enhanced when people with disabilities are involved in setting up the service plan (Greenfield et al., 1985).

4. *Implement Service Plan*   In implementing the service plan, the person with the disability, his or her family, and the service provider work together to solve the functional problems that they have identified. The service plan will not always go smoothly, as obstacles may be encountered along the way. A service plan that allows for flexibility is more likely to be successful.

5. *Evaluate Outcomes*   The end of the service process occurs when, after a suitable intervention time, it is time to evaluate the outcomes. To determine whether the goals of service have been reached, the characteristics that the person had indicated as important and that were the focus of service are reassessed through individualized or standardized assessment methods. At this point, the service process will end if the goals have been reached; or it could continue if the goals have not yet been reached or if new person-defined needs have arisen.

Examples of the Process

The following scenarios present examples of a service process that begins with the person defining his or her needs and ends with assessment of those specifically defined outcomes.

Amanda   Thomas and Susan are parents of Amanda, a 9-year-old girl who has cerebral palsy and a significant developmental delay. In 1996, they received a wheelchair for Amanda, which had been prescribed by a seating clinic close to their home. They have since moved to another city and have referred themselves to a children's rehabilitation center because of difficulties with the equipment. When the occupational therapist asked them about the needs for which they came to the center, Susan gave the following information: "Take the thing apart; I guess you need a screwdriver and everything. You have to pull the whole thing apart. She's a 35-pound child, and she's in this massive thing. I can't use this chair.

I'm home, I'm crying all the time, because my daughter can't go anywhere. I can't take her anywhere. We're trapped."

Although Amanda may have many other needs, it is clear from the interview with her parents that the equipment is their first priority. As her parents indicated, the person-centered outcome in this service process would be the ability of Amanda's parents to take her out into the community to participate in community activities. Following the interview, a service plan was developed in which the therapist and parents together investigated other equipment options and funding possibilities. Funding was found from a local community service to purchase a new wheelchair for the family. In searching for the most appropriate wheelchair, the therapist and Amanda's parents paid particular attention to the size and weight of the chair and were able to find a lightweight chair with a compact modular seating system. Once the wheelchair had been received, the therapist met with the parents to ensure that the wheelchair fit Amanda properly and to provide them with information about the care and maintenance of the equipment. Follow-up evaluation 2 weeks later indicated that the equipment was working well and that Amanda was able to accompany her parents on many community outings.

Joseph   Joseph is a 69-year-old man who is retired from his job as an accountant. A week prior to referral, he had a stroke, which caused moderate paralysis on the left side of his body. Five days after his stroke, he was transferred to the rehabilitation service. He experiences difficulty with walking, transferring in and out of his bed, getting dressed, cutting food, and taking a bath. With people who have had a stroke, rehabilitation often begins with training in basic mobility and in activities of daily living, such as eating, dressing, and bathing. Upon discussion with Joseph, however, it became clear that these basic activities were not his first priority. During the past few years of his retirement, Joseph has spent 2–3 days a week as a volunteer in a local seniors' center. As a volunteer, he helps organize activity schedules using a computerized calendar program and produces the center's newsletter. He stated that it was vitally important to him that he return to these volunteer activities as soon as possible. His first goal for rehabilitation, therefore, was the operation of a computer. When asked about other activities of daily living, he stated that he would like to learn to accomplish his self-care and mobility tasks, but these were not as important to him as his volunteer activities; and he believed that his wife could help him with some of the daily living tasks initially.

The rehabilitation team agreed to focus on his first goal. The rehabilitation team also discussed with Joseph their perception that he would need some walking ability or mobility skills to carry out his volunteer activities. After this discussion, Joseph, along with his wife, agreed that this would be an important second goal for intervention focus.

The service plan was implemented, and outcomes were evaluated 3 weeks later when Joseph was discharged from the rehabilitation program. The outcome evaluation was difficult in this situation because of the individualized nature of the intervention. The rehabilitation program had a policy of using a standardized assessment for all individuals, which focused on basic self-care, mobility, and communication skills. This assessment was completed, and it showed that Joseph had made substantial progress in mobility. He never had any communication difficulties, so the reassessment of this was irrelevant. Although he had made some modest changes in self-care activities, the reassessment of self-care also was not relevant to Joseph. In this situation, an individualized approach to an assessment would be more appropriate in determining the achievement of Joseph's self-defined rehabilitation goals.

PROFESSIONAL ROLES IN PERSON-CENTERED SERVICES

Participating in a person-centered service environment has significant implications for people receiving service, their families, service providers, and organizations. People enter such organizations with needs, concerns, and expectations. Many have never heard of person-centered services, but they do know how they want to be treated and do know what they need. They often do not know "what" can help them realize their needs, and service providers often do not know these expectations. Person-centered service affects the relationship and partnership that develops among the various stakeholders. For organizations, these relationships form the basis of services.

Within a person-centered service environment, responsiveness is considered to be a mandatory attribute. Responsiveness requires a high degree of attention regarding the person, active listening, a readiness to consider options, and a willingness to try different ideas. This is very different from reactivity. These concepts, however, do get confused by service providers when they discuss person-centered service. Some service providers believe that person-centered service means doing everything the person wants (i.e., reactivity). People neither expect nor want a reactive response. Individuals would like to think that their service providers are able to develop their perspectives and approaches differentially to meet the individual's particular needs and goals. Individuals want service providers to respond with thoughtful insight. Schon (1983, 1987) identified this insight as "reflection-in-action," which requires service providers to think on the spot both in terms of the person's response but also in terms of their own.

The implementation of clinical services designed to support person-centered outcomes is challenging and demands new responsibilities from services providers. Instead of being the "expert," service providers assume roles of learner and facilitator—learning what outcomes are important to the person and facilitating the problem-solving process that will help them to achieve those outcomes (see Chapters 1 and 2). For services providers, this means understanding their own values and perspectives about their roles and responsibilities. On the one hand, if a service provider considers him- or herself to be an "expert," then a person-centered services approach will feel alien to him or her. A person-centered services approach, instead, recognizes that the consumers are the experts about themselves. On the other hand, if the service provider considers him- or herself to be a "doer of what the person says," then people do not get to understand their options. They feel abandoned because the service provider does not contribute beyond the individual's perspective. It is important for a service provider to recognize the need for a balance between these two extremes—being an expert or doing only what the individual says. The service provider's role is to understand his or her own expectations for the individual–service provider relationship. What do they expect of families? How do they communicate that expectation? What do they value in a clinical relationship? How do they build relationships? What happens when the relationships do not evolve as expected? These types of introspective questions are difficult for service providers to answer. They require ongoing consideration and discussion, self-disclosure, and a readiness to change intra- and interpersonally. Moving from being "the changer" or "the therapist" to becoming the "change agent" is a difficult dynamic that service providers encounter when working in the person-centered care model.

A service provider, or change agent, in a person-centered service environment is expected to have strong facilitation, negotiation, communication, and problem-solving skills. How does one know as a service provider whether he or she has these skills? How does one attain them? To answer these questions, we first must define these skills. *Experts* and *doers* do not negotiate. A *person-centered service provider,* however, negotiates everything. He or she negotiates all aspects of service, including service location, frequency of contact, service issues, information, intervention options, activities to assist with change, and evaluation of the process. Negotiation, which is built on effective communication skills, can take the form of written or verbal communication. And negotiation, with its heavy emphasis on give and take, is hard work because it requires all parties to come to a common understanding. Furthermore, throughout the negotiation process a service provider needs to facilitate and problem solve. Effective facilitation means bringing together perspectives and helping everyone to understand those perspectives so that change can occur. Problem solving, which relies largely on strong creativity skills, can occur once a common perspective is realized. It is chiefly through these four skills that a person-centered service provider helps individuals achieve their *personal* intervention goals.

The delivery of person-centered service is not without ethical challenges. All service providers have the responsibility to provide care that is of the highest standard and to ensure that personal risks are always considered. There are situations in which the safety of the consumer or others is at risk, and service providers need to make decisions to minimize that risk. It is important to distinguish between situations that involve risk and situations that represent only differences in values. On the one hand, a decision not to bathe and to wear dirty clothes probably represents a difference in values not risk. A service provider can discuss this issue with the individual, pointing out the possible implications of this decision; but in most cases, this decision does not put the person at risk. On the other hand, sending a person with a disability home using a walker when he or she is unable to safely walk a short distance represents a risk of injury from a fall. In this case, a service provider has a responsibility to consider other options that will not lead to injury.

There are other challenges in the day-to-day implementation of services centered on a person's self-defined outcomes and his or her family's needs. In a qualitative study, in which 13 service providers from 6 children's rehabilitation centers were interviewed, Law et al. (1996) found that the concept of family-centered service is not well articulated or defined. It often is described in abstract terms as a philosophy, an approach, an attitude, a value system, or a culture. Participants in the study believed that one of the most significant challenges is how to implement this type of service on a day-to-day basis within the constraints of time and available resources. A sustained and participatory leadership appears to facilitate change toward family-centered service.

Avis (1994) examined the perspectives of people in a day surgical unit and found that people expected that they would be told what to do and did not express a desire for more collaboration. It was not clear whether the people in this study did not want to participate or did not feel that they were able to participate. Service systems often have implicit unequal relationships between people with disabilities and service providers, and overcoming this inequality so that the trust to participate develops, is difficult. Service providers may need to ensure that a clinical climate supports questioning before participation will occur. Waitzkin (1985) found that service providers also overestimate the time that they spend giving information and encouraging questions from people receiving service.

A series of studies of patient-centered care by the Picker/Commonwealth Program for Patient-Centred Care (Gerteis, Edgman-Levitan, Daley, & Delbanco, 1993) found that the service delivery "culture" was a key factor in those institutions that were rated as more patient-centered. These institutions had developed a service system centered on individuals' needs, extending from the mission statement to clinical services to food services. Staff were socialized into the institutional culture, attention was paid to the development of knowledgeable front-line staff, and people were always asked to evaluate service. Furthermore, short-term cost cutting, such as increasing part-time staff or laying off senior or higher-qualified workers, has been demonstrated to significantly decrease quality of care (Bane & Ellwood, 1991; Schlesinger & Heskett, 1991).

MAKING DECISIONS ABOUT MEASURING OUTCOMES

Measuring outcomes sounds like a simple thing to do; yet it is a complex endeavor (Lohr, 1988). Three difficulties often arise. First, it is difficult to determine what specific outcomes *should* be measured. Among the many conceptual and practical issues that need to be dealt with are lack of clarity in the purposes for measuring outcomes, the diversity of possible outcomes, and the lack of a framework from which to select outcomes. A framework provides a sense of the whole picture that needs to be considered—the context for looking at outcomes, the specific decisions that need to be made, and a sense of all possible outcomes. A framework will enable all parties to consciously eliminate certain outcomes and thereby narrow in on the outcomes of most importance to the person receiving service. Second, once outcomes of interest are identified, there may not be appropriate tools to measure these outcomes. This is particularly the case in pediatric rehabilitation (Gowland et al., 1991). Many measures for children have not been validated for children with disabilities. The third difficulty is having the human and financial resources to implement the plan to measure outcomes. Lack of time and resources for planning, training, and implementation are critical practical issues that need to be considered before implementing an outcomes measurement process.

So, the complexity in measuring outcomes comes from the many interrelated decisions that need to be made. There is no recipe or set of rules for how to make decisions about measuring outcomes (Patton, 1990). Designing an evaluation is as much an art as a science (Cronbach, 1982). Knowing the critical questions and decision points, however, will help guide a successful outcomes evaluation. The purpose of this section is to provide a set of questions to guide the important decisions and thereby end up with a well-conceptualized measurement plan. It is important to take the time to make these decisions consciously and in advance rather than by default.

Evaluation can be done by external evaluators or according to a collaborative inquiry model (Edey & Newton, 1995). We recommend the latter approach and, therefore, propose a series of questions to be used by a group of service providers (or by a single clinician when the purpose is to determine appropriate outcomes measures for a specific service recipient). When service providers, managers, and people receiving service are involved in decision making, they are more likely to perceive the findings as credible and to use the findings, as well as learn about the goals and outcomes of their services (Edey & Newton, 1995). If stakeholders do not accept the outcomes as appropriate, then the findings cannot have the desired impact on changes to clinical service (Posavac & Carey, 1992).

A Framework for Defining and Determining Outcomes and Outcomes Measures

The framework we provide does not deal with the whole process of doing an outcomes evaluation study. Our focus is on defining relevant outcomes and determining appropriate outcomes measurement tools that are based on a series of informed decisions. We do not deal with the development of an overall research plan including study design (e.g., when the measurement tools will be administered, to whom, and how) and how the collected data will be analyzed. It is important to recognize that there is not a clear dichotomy between specific person-centered goals and organizational goals that facilitate person-centered outcomes; in fact, in a quality-driven organization, these goals become one and the same.

Key Questions in Defining and Determining Outcomes   The key questions to be answered by the evaluation team or individual clinician are outlined in Table 5.1. The basic flow of the questions is from larger, conceptual considerations (concerning philosophy, goals, purpose, context, and perspective) to more specific, practical issues (concerning implementation resources and psychometric properties of measures). The questions involve 1) defining the organizational context (i.e., the goals of the organization and the program or service), 2) clarifying the purpose for measuring outcomes (improving clinical practice or improving managerial decision making), 3) choosing the environment in which outcomes will be measured (e.g., home, school, workplace, community, center), 4) selecting the perspectives that will be adopted in the measurement of outcomes (e.g., caregiver, care recipient, parent, teacher), 5) deciding on the level of outcome that is of interest (global outcomes versus more specific outcomes), 6) deciding on the specific attributes (i.e., content areas), 7) considering the constraints raised by available resources, and 8) considering the properties of available and relevant outcomes measures. Each of these questions is considered in more detail later in the chapter.

Decision-Making Process for Person-Centered Outcomes
The selection of outcomes has been determined almost exclusively by the values and interests of health care professionals (Butler, 1995). More and more researchers are emphasizing the importance of examining person-centered (Coyte, 1992) or functional outcomes (Haley et al., 1991). People with disabilities are much more interested in functional and role-related outcomes than impairment outcomes (Butler, 1995).

Adopting a person-centered perspective has implications for the answers that will be given to the questions. A person-centered perspective implies that 1) the context or environment of the outcomes measurement likely will be broader than the clinic setting, 2) the perspective(s) adopted will include more than that of the service provider (i.e., family and service recipient perspectives become more important than clinician perspectives), and 3) outcomes of interest are more likely to deal with function or role in society (as well, satisfaction may be an important outcome).

A Nonlinear, Iterative Process The discrete questions and their order may give the impression that there is a logical flow or progression from one decision to another; but this is not so. Making one decision typically can encourage a group to revisit another so that the group refines their plan over several meetings. For example, the group may decide that they would like a tool completed by parents (to capture parents' perspectives). The group then may decide that impairment outcomes are most relevant to their organiza-

Table 5.1.   Questions to help define and determine relevant outcomes and appropriate measures

What are the goals of our organization and what services do we provide, to whom, and why?

Define your organizational context (mission and organizational goals).
Define the service/program and/or individuals for whom outcomes are to be measured.
Identify the service/program's goals.

Why do we want to measure outcomes?

What is the specific purpose of the measurement process? Purposes include clinical decision-making for a specific individual or managerial decision-making (i.e., program evaluation or determination of cost-effectiveness).

What is the context or environment of the outcome measurement?

Outcomes could be measured in an educational, home, or community context.

Whose perspective should be adopted on the attainment of the outcomes?

Possible perspectives include people receiving services, families of service recipients, service providers, or program managers.
Who will use these outcome data and how will the information be used?

What level of outcome (micro versus macro) should be used?

Using the ICIDH framework, should the outcome reflect changes in impairment, disability, or mediating changes in the environment?

What specific attributes should be measured?

Major content areas include communication, motor function, or activities of daily living. Within these groupings, which specific aspects of communication, types of motor function, or activities of daily living are of interest?

What resource-related issues do I need to consider?

Describe important factors that may influence the choice of the outcome measure (e.g., time available, cost limitations).
Do you have the resources to conduct the evaluation as a whole (from conceptualization to implementation to reporting of findings)?

What properties of measures should I consider?

Choose the most appropriate outcome measure based on information provided about the measures that are available, including their psychometric properties.

tion's objectives. Looking at available measures, they may find no tools that capture parents' perspectives of children's impairments for that specific attribute. The group then would need to decide whether tapping parents' perspectives is the appropriate route or whether they really are more interested in measuring outcomes at a disability or life habits level—levels at which parents can more easily make judgments or discriminations (and for which more tools may be available).

Defining the Organizational Context

Defining the organizational context (reviewing the mission and goals of both the organization and the program or service) will help to determine the types of outcomes that are most important to the organization and people receiving services. There should be a logical fit among the organization's mission, the goals of the program or service, and the outcomes selected for examination. For example, if the organization and the people receiving services value the importance of function in everyday life situations, the service provider should not decide to examine impairment attributes.

The organizational context often has a large impact on evaluation activities (Charette, Fortin, & Hurteau, 1995). In an organization with a person-centered perspective, outcomes measurement will concentrate on functional outcomes or recipients' satisfaction with services. In organizations with more traditional perspectives on outcomes, the focus will more likely be on impairment-level outcomes. Outcomes that are appropriate in one context will not necessarily be appropriate in another. Outcomes measurement systems need to be individualized to be appropriate, relevant, and useful.

One question that a person-centered organization should ask about outcomes measurement is whether the program is conceptualized clearly enough so that an evaluation is appropriate. People sometimes jump into measuring outcomes when they are not ready to do so. Before an evaluation of outcomes is undertaken, there needs to be 1) consensus on what the program is trying to achieve (i.e., a clear rationale for the program); 2) a fit among the organizational mission, program goals, and selected outcomes; 3) a clear understanding of the types of services provided and to whom they are provided; and 4) clear descriptions of the service strategies that are used to meet the goals (the link between the service activities and the hoped-for outcomes). Furthermore, services need to be delivered consistently.

Another important question to ask is the following: What are the long-term goals of the service or program? Program goals refer to the long-lasting changes expected to be accomplished by the program (Lodzinski, 1995). Service providers and those receiving services need to specify and agree on key program goals because this will help them choose from the many possible outcomes. Finally, they should ask, "Is the goal to influence impairments (the underlying neurological/biological level), disabilities (function or skills), or life habits (effect on the person's life)?"

What Is the Specific Purpose of the Measurement Process?

One of the most important elements in measuring outcomes is to determine the intended purpose of an activity (Haley et al., 1991). It is important to clarify why the evaluation is being done and for whom (Edey & Newton, 1995) because the purpose has direct implications for the types of outcomes chosen and the measurement system that is set up. Furthermore, problems can arise when the purpose of the evaluation is not clearly negotiated or stated up front (Posavac & Carey, 1992).

The two main reasons for measuring outcomes are 1) to evaluate outcomes for a specific service recipient (to improve services to that individual), and 2) to evaluate the clinical effectiveness of a service or program or to provide information that can be used to determine cost effectiveness (to improve programs or services). With respect to improving services to the individual, the goal is to have clinically useful information. For example, if a child and her parents want to see an improvement in handwriting, outcomes measurement will provide information about whether the activities used to improve that child's handwriting actually made a difference in the legibility of the child's handwriting. If the legibility did not improve (as shown by a comparison between pre- and postintervention measures), the service provider might try new strategies. The service provider could use an individualized or standardized measure. There is no need to summarize the data across individuals because the goal is to know whether the outcomes for that one individual have improved.

The second type of purpose for outcomes measurement is to improve services or programs as a whole. A managerial decision-making system requires aggregation, so identical measures need to be administered for each person involved—ideally at predetermined times. For example, a manager might want to know whether parents are satisfied with their level of involvement in planning services for their child. If parents are not satisfied, this information (and parents' suggestions for improvements) could be used to devise new ways of interacting with parents.

Standardized versus Individualized Measurement Approaches

Two types of measurement approaches can be used to evaluate the effects of clinical services—individualized and standardized approaches (Russell, King, Palisano, & Law, 1995). Either approach could be used for clinical or managerial decision making. The individualized approach may be more suited to clinical decision making but may be used in programwide evaluations when the specific methods provide data that can be aggregated. *Individualized methods* use judgment-based measures of progress that indicate whether each person has achieved the goals of intervention (Russell et al., 1995). These methods provide clear goals and priorities for intervention, and they ensure the ongoing relevance of the person's goals (Russell et al., 1995). *Standardized measures* have manuals reporting required methods of administration and are designed to yield data that can be used to compare groups or individuals. Standardized measures, however, may not measure the specific goals of each person receiving service, and many of these measures have not been validated as responsive to change or appropriate for people with disabilities (Palisano, Haley, & Brown, 1992). Many standardized measures are not sensitive to the small changes seen in people with disabilities (Stephens & Haley, 1991), and the measures do not readily convert into intervention plans or outcome expectations (Kiresuk, Smith, & Cardillo, 1994).

Goal attainment scaling (GAS) is one type of individualized method. GAS is an individualized, criterion-referenced measure of change that involves defining a unique set of goals for each person and then specifying a range of possible outcomes for each goal on a five-point scale. GAS initially was used to measure the impact of intervention in the mental health field (Kiresuk & Sherman, 1968). The primary strength of GAS is the ability to measure intervention-induced change, whereas most standardized measures are designed to measure postintervention status in a fine-tuned way and are not responsive (i.e., able to measure clinically important change over time) (Kiresuk et al., 1994; Ottenbacher & Cusick, 1993; Palisano, 1993). Another widely used individualized measure is The Canadian Occupational Performance Measure (COPM) (Law et al., 1994). This measure detects self-perceived change in self-care, productivity, and leisure activities over time.

In What Environment Should Outcomes Be Measured?

Outcomes can be measured in many different contexts, such as the person's workplace, school, home, community recreation center, or rehabilitation center. A service provider selects an appropriate environment in which to observe or have respondents consider the behaviors or outcomes of interest. For example, parents or teachers may be asked to rate or report on aspects of the child's functioning at home or at school because they have the most opportunity to observe the child's function in these environments. There are also cases, however, in which it may make the most sense for service providers to do observations or ratings in the center or clinic.

Whose Perspective on Outcomes Attainment Will Be Adopted?

The natural tendency may be to have service providers be respondents (Butler, 1995) to outcomes measures. If the organization has adopted a person-centered approach, however, then it makes more sense to take the service recipients' perspectives and have them provide the outcome data. Asking the following questions can help service providers decide who should be designated respondents: 1) Who has the "best" information about the person's improvements, and 2) who will be most credible as a data source in the eyes of those who will receive (and hopefully use) the results of the evaluation? For example, board members, who represent their communities, may value highly the information provided by people receiving services. Other stakeholders may believe that people receiving services do not have the expertise to judge certain outcomes. Program participants often are viewed as one of the most important and accessible data sources, particularly from a person-centered perspective. Service providers, of course, can provide useful information. Once the participants (e.g., service provider, service recipient, family) have decided whose perspective should be adopted, they have essentially decided who the respondent will be on the outcomes measure, which means that the service provider then will need to search for outcomes measures that can be completed by that group of individuals. To provide a well-rounded perspective, service providers can use multiple outcomes and several respondent groups when performing a program evaluation (Posavac & Carey, 1992).

At What Level of Outcome Should the Service Provider Operate?   There are many categorization schemes one could use when considering the universe of possible outcomes (macro versus micro). Based on an analysis of the service organization's mission and service goals, the organization may be interested in impairment outcomes (e.g., range of motion, position, posture), functional outcomes (essential activities required in the person's natural environments of home and school, such as mobility, communication, self-care skills, or social skills), or life habits (role-related outcomes, such as having a job, attending school, participating in social activities). The life habit (or "disability" level) is the level at which boards and communities are most likely to be interested in measuring the impact of services.

What Specific Attributes Should Be Measured?

Once the service organization has selected the general level of the outcomes (e.g., impairment, disability, life habit), the service providers need to consider and choose from a wealth of specific attributes (content elements). For example, Haley et al. (1991) provided a conceptual framework for functional (disability-related) outcomes consisting of three categories (self-care, mobility, and communication and social function), each of which is divided into many attributes (e.g., self-care consists of eating, dressing, bathing, grooming, toileting). Again, the selection of specific attributes to measure should reflect the intent of the program or service (Posavac & Carey, 1992).

What Resource-Related Issues Should Be Considered When Selecting a Measurement Tool?

There are several practical issues that should be considered when deciding among several available outcomes measures. These include the following: 1) the level of training required to administer the measure appropriately, 2) the level of training required to score the measure and interpret the scores, and 3) the cost of the measure and accompanying equipment or manuals. The organization also needs to consider the resources required to implement the evaluation as a whole (Posavac & Carey, 1992). These resources include the time and cost involved to have people attend meetings; document decisions; obtain necessary approvals; coordinate data collection; administer measures; enter and analyze data; and produce easily decipherable graphs, reports, or summary statistics.

What Properties of Measures Should Be Considered When Selecting a Measurement Tool?

Several practical issues are important in deciding the usefulness of an outcomes measure. The primary criterion is whether the results of the measure will give the information needed to plan, evaluate, and ultimately improve outcomes. Other considerations include the acceptability of the measure to the person being assessed and to the assessor. One important consideration is the measure's format. Will the information be best acquired through an interview, questionnaire, or actual performance of activities? This will depend on the amount of time there is to assess and also on the nature of the required information. Questions that the person may perceive as sensitive or personal may best be obtained through a self-administered questionnaire as opposed to a face-to-face interview. If an individual is interested in assessing daily living activities, however, then observation of the person in an appropriate environmental context (e.g., home, school, community) may be a better indicator than an interview, questionnaire, or even an observational assessment completed in a hospital setting. Cost is another obvious consideration in choosing a measure. The cost to run a complete gait analysis or to purchase a test kit with expensive equipment may not make either of these a practical choice. The amount of training required to ensure that the assessor is competent to administer, score, and interpret the results is another consideration when choosing a measure.

To be an effective user of outcomes measures, one needs to understand about measurement properties. Is the measure reliable and valid? *Reliability* refers to the consistency of scores or results with the measure based on repeated uses when the characteristic being measured has not changed. *Validity* refers to the ability of the measure to measure what it is supposed to measure. There are several types of validity including content, criterion, and construct validity (Nunnally, 1978; Streiner & Norman, 1989). *Content validity* refers to the appropriateness of the items to the construct that one is attempting to measure. Do the items relate to all behaviors or characteristics that are relevant and important? *Criterion validity* is the degree to which the measurements obtained by the instrument agrees with another more accurate measure of the same characteristic (Nunnally, 1978). *Construct validity,* the most common method of empirical validation, is established by determining if a measure corresponds to hypotheses that have been set up based on knowledge of the characteristic being measured. One aspect of validity that is important for an outcomes measure is whether the measure has demonstrated responsiveness to change (Kirshner & Guyatt, 1985). A good outcomes measure must be responsive enough to detect clinically meaningful change when it has occurred. There are several standards or guidelines available to help users assess the measurement properties of standardized measures (see American Psychological Association, 1985; Johnston, Keith, & Hinderer, 1992; Kirshner & Guyatt, 1985; Law, 1987).

CONCLUSIONS

In summary, to measure person-centered outcomes properly (and successfully), one must

- Encourage active participation of people in planning and implementing service because participation influences service outcomes.
- Provide information to enable decision making.
- Select methods of assessment that reflect the values and preferences of people with disabilities.

- Consider the mission and goals of the organization and service to make sure that the outcomes selected fit with these goals.
- Be clear about the organization's purpose. Do you want to measure outcomes for a specific person receiving services or evaluate the program as a whole?
- Select an appropriate environment in which to measure outcomes (e.g., school, home, clinic).
- Decide whose perspective should be adopted (e.g., service provider, service recipient, teacher, spouse). Different people value different types of outcomes. Consider who has the best information about the person's improvements.
- Decide on the level of outcomes (micro versus macro) that you want to examine.
- Decide on the specific attributes to measure.
- Consider the resources required to undertake the outcomes measurement.
- Select a reliable and valid measure.

REFERENCES

American Psychological Association. (1985). *Standards for educational and psychological testing.* Washington, DC: Author.

Avis, M. (1994). Choice cuts: An exploratory study of patients' views about participation in decision-making in a day surgery unit. *International Journal of Nursing Studies, 31,* 289–298.

Bane, M.J., & Ellwood, D.T. (1991). Is American business working for the poor? *Harvard Business Review, 69,* 58–66.

Bunch, W.H., & Dvonch, V.M. (1994). The value of FIM scores. *American Journal of Physical Medicine and Rehabilitation, 73,* 40–43.

Butler, C. (1995). Outcomes that matter. *Developmental Medicine and Child Neurology, 37,* 753–754.

Charette, A., Fortin, J., & Hurteau, M. (1995). How context influences evaluation practice: A case study of two university programs. In A. Love (Ed.), *Evaluation methods sourcebook* (Vol. II, pp. 18–29). Ottawa, Ontario: Canadian Evaluation Society.

Coyte, P.C. (1992). Outcome measurement in speech-language pathology and audiology. *Journal of Speech Language Pathology and Audiology, 16,* 275–285.

Cronbach, L. (1982). *Designing evaluations of educational and social programs.* San Francisco: Jossey-Bass.

Donabedian, A. (1988). The quality of care: How can it be assessed? *Journal of the American Medical Association, 260,* 1743–1748.

Edey, S., & Newton, P. (1995). Collaborative inquiry: Integrating evaluation into the workplace. In A. Love (Ed.), *Evaluation methods sourcebook* (Vol. II, pp. 4–16). Ottawa, Ontario: Canadian Evaluation Society.

Fougeyrollas, P., Bergeron, H., Cloutier, R., & St. Michel, G. (1991). The handicaps creation process: Analysis of the consultation and new full proposals. *International ICIDH Network, 4,* 1–25.

Fuhrer, M. (1995). Conference report: An agenda for medical rehabilitation outcomes research. *American Journal of Physical Medicine and Rehabilitation, 74*, 243–248.

Gardner, J.F., & Campanella, T. (1995). Beyond compliance to responsiveness: New measures of quality for accreditation. *Work, 5,* 107–114.

Gerteis, M. (1993). Coordinating care and integrating service. In M. Gerteis, S. Edgman-Levitan, J. Daley, & T. Delbanco (Eds.), *Through the patient's eyes: Understanding and promoting patient-centered care* (pp. 45–71) San Francisco: Jossey-Bass.

Gerteis, M., Edgman-Levitan, S., Daley, J., & Delbanco, T. (Eds.). (1993). *Through the patient's eyes: Understanding and promoting patient-centered care.* San Francisco: Jossey-Bass.

Gowland, C., King, G., King, S., Law, M., Letts, L., MacKinnon, E., Rosenbaum, P., & Russell, D. (1991). *Review of selected measures in neurodevelopmental rehabilitation* (Research Report No. 91-2). Hamilton, Ontario, Canada: McMaster University and Chedoke-McMaster Hospitals, Neurodevelopmental Clinical Research Unit.

Greenfield, S., Kaplan, S., & Ware, J. (1985). Expanding patient involvement in care: Effects of patient outcomes. *Annals of Internal Medicine, 102,* 520–528.

Haley, S.M., Coster, W.J., & Ludlow, L.H. (1991). Paediatric functional outcome measures. *Paediatric Rehabilitation, 2,* 689–723.

Hahn, H. (1984). Reconceptualizing disability: A political science perspective. *Rehabilitation Literature, 45,* 362–365.

Humphreys, B.L., & Lindberg, D.A.B. (1989). Building the Unified Medical Language System. In L.C. Kingsland (Ed.), *Proceedings of the Thirteenth Annual Symposium on Computer Applications in Medical Care.* Washington, DC: IEEE Computer Society Press.

Iglehart, J.K. (1992). Health policy report: The American health care system. *New England Journal of Medicine, 326,* 962–967.

Johnston, M.V., Keith, R.A., & Hinderer, S.R. (1992). Measurement standards for interdisciplinary medical rehabilitation. *Archives of Physical Medicine and Rehabilitation, 73,* 3–23.

Jongbloed, L., & Crichton, A. (1990). Difficulties in shifting from individualistic to socio-political policy regarding disability in Canada. *Disability, Handicap and Society, 5,* 25–36.

Kennedy, I. (1981). *The unmasking of medicine.* London: George Allen Unwin.

Kiresuk, T.J., & Sherman, R.E. (1968). Goal attainment scaling: A general method for evaluating comprehensive community mental health programs. *Community Mental Health Journal, 4,* 443–453.

Kiresuk, T.J., Smith, A., & Cardillo, J.E. (1994). *Goal attainment scaling: Applications, theory, and measurement.* Mahwah, NJ: Lawrence Erlbaum Associates.

Kirshner, B., & Guyatt, G.H. (1985). A methodological framework for assessing health indices. *Journal of Chronic Diseases, 38,* 27–36.

Law, M. (1987). Measurement in occupational therapy: Scientific criteria for evaluation. *Canadian Journal of Occupational Therapy, 54,* 133–138.

Law, M. (1991). The environment: A focus for occupational therapy. *Canadian Journal of Occupational Therapy, 58,* 171–180.

Law, M., Baptiste, S., Carswell, A., McColl, M., Polatajko, H., & Pollock, N. (1994). *Canadian occupational performance measure manual* (2nd ed.). Toronto: CAOT Publications ACE.

Law, M., Baptiste, S., & Mills, J. (1995). Client-centred practice: What does it mean and does it make a difference? *Canadian Journal of Occupational Therapy, 62,* 250–257.

Law, M., Brown, S., Barnes, S., King, G., Rosenbaum, P., & King, S. (1996). *Implementing family-centered service in Ontario Children's Rehabilitation Services.* Hamilton, Ontario, Canada: McMaster University and Chedoke-McMaster Hospitals, Neurodevelopmental Clinical Research Unit.

Lodzinski, A. (1995). Linking program design and evaluation: Five guiding questions for program designers. In A. Love (Ed.), *Evaluation methods sourcebook* (Vol. II, pp. 30–38). Ottawa, Ontario: Canadian Evaluation Society.

Lohr, K.N. (1988, Spring). Outcome measurement: Concepts and questions. *Inquiry, 25,* 37–50.

Morris, J., Goddard, M., & Roger, D. (1989). *The benefits of providing information to patients.* University of York: Centre for Health Economics.

Nunnally, J.C. (1978). *Psychometric theory* (2nd ed.). New York: McGraw-Hill.

Ottenbacher, K.J., & Cusick, A. (1993). Discriminative versus evaluative assessment: Some observations on goal attainment scaling. *American Journal of Occupational Therapy, 47,* 349–354.

Palisano, R.J. (1993). Validity of goal attainment scaling with infants with motor delays. *Physical Therapy, 73,* 651–658.

Palisano, R.J., Haley, S.M., & Brown, D.A. (1992). Goal attainment scaling as a measure of change in infants with motor delays. *Physical Therapy, 72,* 432–437.

Patton, M.Q. (1990). *Qualitative evaluation and research methods* (2nd ed.). Thousand Oaks, CA: Sage Publications.

Posavac, E.J., & Carey, R.G. (1992). *Program evaluation: Methods and case studies.* Upper Saddle River, NJ: Prentice-Hall.

Rosenbaum, P., King, S., Law, M., King, G., & Evans, J. (in press). Family-centered service: A conceptual framework and research review. *Physical and Occupational Therapy in Pediatrics.*

Russell, D., King, G., Palisano, R., & Law, M. (1995). *Measuring individualized outcomes* (Research Report No. 95-1). Hamilton, Ontario, Canada: McMaster University and Chedoke-McMaster Hospitals, Neurodevelopmental Clinical Research Unit.

Schlesinger, L.A., & Heskett, J.L. (1991). The service-driven service company. *Harvard Business Review, 69,* 71–81.

Schon, D. (1983). *The reflective practitioner: How professionals think in action.* New York: Basic Books.

Schon, D. (1987). *Educating the reflective practitioner.* San Francisco: Jossey-Bass.

Shapiro, J.P. (1993). *No pity: People with disabilities forging a new civil rights movement.* New York: Times Books.

State University of New York (SUNY) at Buffalo. (1993). *Guide for the Uniform Data Set for Medical Rehabilitation (Adult FIM), version 4.0.* Buffalo, NY: Author.

Stephens, T.E., & Haley, S.M. (1991). Comparison of two methods for determining change in motorically handicapped children. *Physical and Occupational Therapy in Pediatrics, 11,* 1–17.

Streiner, D.L., & Norman, G.R. (1989). *Health Measurement Scales: A practical guide to their development and use.* New York: Oxford University Press.

Task Force on Standards for Measurement in Physical Therapy. (1991). Standards for tests and measurements in physical therapy practice. *Physical Therapy, 71,* 589–622.

U.S. Department of Health and Human Services. (1991). *Healthy people 2000.* Washington, DC: U.S. Government Printing Office.

U.S. General Accounting Office. (1991). *Medical ADP systems: Automated medical records hold promise to improve patient care.* Washington, DC: Author.

Waitzkin, H. (1985). Information giving in medical care. *Journal of Health and Social Behavior, 26,* 81–101.

World Health Organization. (1980). *International classification of impairments, disabilities and handicaps.* Geneva: Author.

Wright, B., Linacre, J.M., & Heinemann, A.W. (1993). Measuring functional status in rehabilitation. *Physical Medicine and Rehabilitation Clinics, 4,* 475–489.

II

Quality and Leadership Foundations

This section on quality and leadership foundations guides the reader through both conceptual and practical issues. Within each chapter, the authors identify two central themes—vision/mission and people—as the cornerstones of leading quality improvement efforts. In Chapter 6, Dykstra explores the meaning of vision in organizational life and quality performance. He distinguishes visions from goals and identifies principles for developing, communicating, and sustaining the organization's vision. The role of leadership and top management is defined as linking the future vision with organizational practices and decisions. The leaders must communicate both values and vision to energize the organization.

Visions are frequently crowded out by the concerns and demands of the day-to-day requirements of management. Effective leaders are able to balance the daily management responsibilities with the strategic priorities of moving toward the vision. Effective leaders also recognize the importance of helping and enabling others to both see and move toward the vision. In Chapter 7, Dykstra explores the complex and critical area of human resources management. In human services, organizational performance is accomplished by people on behalf of other people. Dykstra introduces the concept of partnerships as a key organizing principle for effective working relationships. He also examines implementation issues of hiring, promotion, compensation, performance appraisal, motivation, and communication in the context of organizational quality improvement.

Campanella's chapter on person-centered services (Chapter 8) brings another perspective to the discussion of leadership. Adopting the principles of person-centered services and supports, Campanella challenges the organization to set aside a program orientation and redefine its mission. She offers a framework for managing this organizational shift that includes the participation of people receiving services, the involvement of staff, realignment of structure and resources, and new leadership roles. Campanella shares Dykstra's emphasis on partnerships and participation. While both authors note the central role of partnership and participation, they take the theme in different directions. Dykstra applies the themes to the employee workforce. Campanella carries partnership and participation to the relationship between the organization and the recipient of the services and supports. Campanella's *process of engagement,* includes such items as engaging in dialogue with people to learn about their priority outcomes, acknowledging people as partners in the exploration, and being creative in supporting people. This process of engagement parallels Dykstra's discussion of performance feedback and performance appraisal. In Chapter 7, Dykstra discusses partnerships as a basic principle in organizing human resources.

Taken together, Dykstra and Campanella reveal that the leadership within an organization and facilitation of outcomes for people rest on some of the same principles—partnership, participation, reframing old assumptions, and listening to and learning from employees and people receiving services and supports. In Chapter 9, Gardner continues this analysis and connects the issues of leadership in the disabilities field with an overview of the contemporary issues in leadership theory and practice. He describes how researchers have studied leadership as a trait, a style, a behavior, and/or a relationship. Gardner emphasizes that leaders exist throughout the organization—they are the people who embody and act on the vision. Both leadership and learning come from doing. Successful organizations provide an environment that fosters growth, promotes learning, and creates self-awareness.

Gardner also discusses the requirement that organizations wanting to promote leadership growth must give their employees permission to make mistakes and learn from those actions. The action research approach of learning from doing is also the core of facilitating outcomes for people. Gardner concludes his chapter with the observation that "organizations that are successful in facilitating personal outcomes for people with disabilities also grow leaders throughout the organization."

6

Quality Performance and Organizational Vision

The Role of Vision in Leadership and Management

Arthur Dykstra, Jr.

Vision answers the organizational question, What is it all about? Vision is about the future in its idealized form, that is, what is hoped for and thought to be possible—the desirable objectives of our corporate dreams. Visionaries look 10–25 years into the future and try to predict the organization in its ultimate light.

Vision, therefore, serves as the engine of progress. Vision links our imagination to our work as we seek to succeed in the uncertain future. Lipton, writing in *Sloan Management Review,* provided additional clarity to the definition of *vision:*

> A vision must focus on the future and serve as a concrete foundation for the organization. Unlike goals and objectives, a vision does not fluctuate from year to year but serves as an enduring promise. A successful vision paints a vivid picture for the organization and, though future-based, is in the present tense, as if it were being realized now. It illustrates what the organization will do in the face of ambiguity and surprises. A vision must give people the feeling that their lives and work are intertwined and moving toward recognizable, legitimate goals. (1996, p. 85)

THE PURPOSE OF VISION

Visions are not about tomorrow or the day after. Visions are not about monthly production figures or accomplishments; they are not about annual report projections or the work of public relations specialists. Visions of the future are not about those things that the organization is presently achieving. Effective visions allow us to project into the future and transform our imaginations into reality—particularly the reality of the future state of the organization.

When people discuss the nature and impact of organizational vision, it is remarkable how frequently the middle-age members of the discussion will cite the vision of the National Aeronautics and Space Administration in the early 1960s: to place a man on the moon by the end of the decade. What a compelling sense of direction. Many people thought that this vision was mere science fiction or the result of too many glasses of wine.

Conference speakers, seeking to inspire audiences with the significance of organizational vision, frequently quote the biblical imperative, "Where there is no vision, the people perish" (Ecclesiastes 29:18). Recognition of the importance of vision to the basic issues of human survival has been with us for a long time. Whether any particular local organization should survive may not be critical in the context of the challenges facing humankind—disease, poverty, global warming, or the pursuit of peace—but for the specific organization seeking to survive into the future, no concern serves as vital a function as having an organizational vision. A well-formulated and well-communicated vision allows the employees of that organization to be hopeful for the future and to believe that what they are doing today will have meaning in the future. In "Building Your Company's Vision," Collins and Porras emphasized the motivational value of the corporate vision:

> It makes no sense to analyze whether an envisioned future is the right one. With a creation—and the task is creation of a future, not prediction—there can be no right answer. Did Beethoven create the right Ninth Symphony? Did Shakespeare create the right Hamlet? We can't answer these questions; they're nonsense. The envisioned future involves such essential questions as Does it get our juices flowing? Do we find it stimulating? Does it spur forward momentum? Does it get people going? The envisioned future should be so exciting in its own right that it would continue to keep the organization motivated even if the leaders who set the goal disappeared. (1996, p. 75)

Creating a corporate vision is difficult work, and its success depends on experience, knowledge, intuition, networking, and the lessons learned from the errors of the past. Thoughtful visions capture the deepest purposes of the organization and reflect the values and ideas that accompany such purposes. But visions need to be distinguished from daydreams, the appealing observations found in fortune cookies, and the software results of computerized vision packages. All too often, the content of corporate vision posters, plaques, and videotapes are the work of sophisticated entrepreneurial fortune tellers who have substituted employee surveys, group exercises, and leadership interviews for tea leaves and tarot cards. The role of the organization's leaders is to build vision from values and to communicate both vision and values to energize the organization.

A typical organization might employ 250 staff members, operate several day programs, and own 5 support buildings and 10 vehicles. What might the future hold for this organization as found in a vision statement? The vision might be to employ 500 people, operate 10 sheltered workshops and 8 support buildings, build 1 large building to save on costs, and own a fleet of vans. Part of the vision might be to be debt free and have $5 million in the supporting foundation. This vision is tied to the values associated with the acquisition of buildings, equipment, and money. Unfortunately, this vision seems limited because it does not inspire the organization to its highest potential.

Alternative visions, however, flow from different values. As an alternative to the vision presented in the previous paragraph, an organization's vision statement that is intended to motivate the employees of the organization serving people with disabilities might read as follows: "It is our vision to be the service and support choice of people with disabilities in northern Illinois." Such an alternative vision would be based on the following themes:

- The organization would own no buildings except for one that might be needed for meetings and support activities.
- People presently being served in large congregate program sites would be visited on their jobsites or after work.
- Those people unable to work would receive services within community settings such as factories, libraries, shopping malls, and municipal buildings.
- Only as many staff members as necessary would be employed, based on the emergent needs and desires of the person seeking services or supports.
- Most employees would work or travel out of their own homes to the homes of those served.

Unlike the first vision in which the organization basically continues to do what it is already doing, the second vision statement could dramatically change the substance of the organization's work. Such vision is compelling because it is dynamic and allows for the organization's evolution toward the desired end; yet, it allows the organization to be creative as it responds to future demands. Although both vision statements shape the present and the future direction of the organization, the second vision statement ensures that use of the organization's assets are guided by the people *receiving* the services or supports. This is much different from the previous vision that merely touts the goals of growing larger and serving more people.

A compelling vision, embraced by organizational members, results in a heightened consciousness of the future in the minds of the organization's leaders. The organization's leaders should continually ask themselves and others the question, How does what I am doing today relate to the vision of the future? To answer the question, the nature and content of the vision are consciously considered in all of the organization's functions, including budgeting, program design and conflict resolution, resource acquisitions, and so forth. Furthermore, leaders must be careful to balance present needs with future needs for the organization's resources; that is, the present should not be sacrificed for the future.

One of the practical uses of *transcendent vision*—a vision that is greater than the organization's daily goals and objectives—is that it provides a strong anchor in hazardous waters. In times of internal distress or external peril, going back to the vision can be a source of encouragement. A well-crafted vision provides an intellectual rallying point and can help to combat any feelings of, "What's the use?" or organizational feelings of meaninglessness.

THE LINK BETWEEN VISION AND QUALITY PERFORMANCE

Having defined and explored vision, the discussion turns to a brief consideration of quality performance. It is difficult for organizations to continuously improve if the focus is only on the present and on improving present functions and activities by some stated amount or measurable degree. It is tempting to think incrementally: If we can serve 50 people, then let's serve 100; if we can place 100 people, then let's place 200; if we can operate 5 support businesses, then let's operate 10. Quality performance, reviewed through the perspective of a guiding vision, may require a dramatic departure from present activities. If the vision takes hold, then the organizational emphasis may change dramatically; it changes from programs to people, from services to supports, from process to outcomes, from details to dynamics, and from buildings to behaviors.

BARRIERS TO ORGANIZATIONAL VISION

Organizational vision is both simple and complicated—that is, the best vision statements are simple and straightforward; changing the vision statement is complicated. Good organizations and well-intentioned managers often confuse vision with goals and performance statements. Three of the barriers that block organizational vision are seeing only the present, personality limitations, and organizational instability.

Seeing Only the Present

Whether too busy or too preoccupied, some organizational leaders are unable to create a vision for the future because they are concerned with only the present. In other instances, after having taken the time to create a corporate vision, the leaders do not take the time to ensure that action continues in pursuit of the vision. Unless leaders are constantly vigilant of the time that establishing and promoting a vision can take, present demands on their time and energy will drive out future opportunities. The day-to-day routine will consume each day unless one has a great deal of discipline. Parkinson's Law still applies, "Work expands to fill the time available." Successful leaders, however, are able to balance the day-to-day management priorities with the strategic priorities of moving toward the vision. Effective leaders simply set aside the time for the management of strategic vision, and they make time to engage other employees in the strategic decision-making process.

Personality Limitations

Visions are blocked in some organizations because of the cognitive and creative shortcomings of the chief executive officer (CEO) or corporate leadership. As Lipton shared,

> A survey of 1,500 senior leaders, 870 of them CEOs, from twenty different countries, asked for the key traits or talents the CEOs should have by the year 2000. The principal behavior trait they most frequently mentioned was that the CEOs convey a 'strong sense of vision'; ninety-eight percent saw that trait as most important for the year 2000. Of the critical knowledge and skills for CEOs of the present and future, the leaders cited 'strategy formulation to achieve a vision' as the most important skill for now and in 2000, by a margin of twenty-five percent over any other skill. (1996, p. 84)

Organizational Instability

It is very difficult to create or sustain an organizational vision in the midst of significant corporate instability such as downsizing, geographic relocation, or major financial setbacks. Likewise, organizations that have experienced long periods of administrative or legal oversight in response to regulatory violations may have a difficult time overcoming mind-sets of learned helplessness. Organizations caught in periods of learned helplessness place the blame for their problems on outside forces and take no responsibility for their conditions. Learned helplessness, lack of responsibility, and a preoccupation with internal events prevent organizations from believing that they can formulate a vision statement and achieve those visions.

SUPPORTS FOR ORGANIZATIONAL VISION

Other practices and behaviors—such as finding and developing the vision, and combining vision and leadership—must be in place for a unified vision to take hold at an organization. Sustaining the vision, however, takes even more effort, which includes gaining the commitment of top leadership, aligning organizational practices with the vision, establishing personal responsibility, expanding the organization, aligning the organization's constitution and by-laws with the vision, and writing a mission statement.

Finding and Developing the Vision

A vision develops when there is an acceptance and realization by members of the organization that present organizational performance can be improved. Dissatisfaction with the status quo has led to the formation of many compelling visions. There are times when the sense of a more desirable future occurs spontaneously to an individual who is carrying out the work of the organization. In other instances, the formation of a vision is the product of many people who come together in a deliberate manner and engage in thoughtful dialogue with respect to the future of the organization. As many organizational members as possible should participate in creating the initial vision. The process should be open and inclusive but not follow a course of development that is unfamiliar to the organization. It is likely that the essence of the vision will come from one or two people. But the point is that everybody should be involved to the extent that they are interested, even if it is only providing the finishing touches.

Developing the vision may take place during one extended session or evolve over a course of days, weeks, or months. There are times when a facilitator is employed from outside of the organization, while the actual course of creating the vision occurs throughout the work of the organization's internal membership. It is also not unusual for organizations to bring outside experts into the process to present their ideas and explain their points of view. Contrasting positions with respect to significant issues are explored, studied, and deliberated.

The next level of participation should occur as the draft of the vision statement is circulated through the organization. Employees should be invited to meetings in which they can discuss and ask questions about the vision. They should have an expectation that the vision will take on a clearer focus and that it will be refined during the reaction period.

For a vision to become a part of an organization's culture, the organization's leaders must be constantly conscious of the vision. It needs to be discussed at staff meetings, written about, reacted to, and reflected in decision making. If understood properly, employees will realize the evolutionary nature of the vision. As steps are taken to forward it, the challenges become clearer. To employees at all levels of the organization, the vision needs to be made relevant so that the purpose is seen as meaningful, something worth striving for. Having an organizational vision must be as commonplace as having a place to work.

Combining Vision and Leadership

Jaques (1989) examined the relationship between top management and the creation of the corporate vision. Jaques suggested that each organizational level has its own degree of challenge and that the level of complexity increases as one moves toward the top of the organization. Remapping an organizational vision is complicated business, especially as one recognizes the 20- to 30-year time span being projected in the formation of the vision. It is in the creation of the organizational vision that corporate leaders will come to realize that "the complexity of a problem does not lie in the complexity of the goal, but in the complexity of the pathway that has to be constructed and then traversed in order to get to the goal" (1989, p. 23).

If top management writes (or has written) a lofty sounding vision statement and announces it in a festive atmosphere amid much hoopla, it likely will not work. The likelihood that employees will react with more than lip service and public displays of allegiance is slim. Private reaction will tend toward cynicism and an attitude of,

"So, what else is new?" Vision seminars and pep rallies rarely influence employees' behavior for any significant length of time. Instead, the vision should be focused on the goals of the organization and should become an integral part of the everyday activities of the organization.

Establishing a Single Vision   If a vision of the future is focused and channels the efforts of organization's decision making, there can be only one vision. Multiple visions confuse people and distract from the desired unity of purpose and direction. That is not to say that there cannot be subordinate, synergetic visions that come out of divisions or departments and merge into the overarching corporate vision. Furthermore, the vision for each organization must be unique to that organization; it must reflect that organization's culture and context. If a meaningful vision is to be developed, then there must be a deep knowledge of the organization's dynamics, history, resources, environmental boundaries, and workforce.

Excellent organizations are generally characterized by leaders who think ahead. The search for the highest quality performance comes from those who are concerned with achieving the highest quality. Along these lines, Jaques developed the interesting idea of *time span of discretion,* a construct that suggests that,

> The longer the time-span of a role, the higher the level of work. . . . The highest level of work to be accomplished at the CEO level is conceptual work—developing strategic plans, evaluating cultural forces as they impinge or might impinge upon the organization, determining cultural pathways, and forecasting financial implications. . . . As time-span gets greater, the feeling of weight of responsibility increases, and the greater the working capacity you must have in order to cope. (1989, pp. 16, 37)

With such considerations in mind, it becomes more apparent why CEOs are more concerned about creating a meaningful vision than are those at lower levels of the organization. CEOs and top management staff are much more likely to be involved in matters that could be described as environmental conditions—issues that can only be anticipated, reacted to, or managed. This is much different from spending the days as a front-line supervisor, solving problems that can be solved and answering questions that can be answered. The work of the CEO is much less controllable.

The Art and Science of Vision Creation   Many authors writing on the subject of leadership have argued that one of the most critical functions in which a leader can engage is to create the future for the organization through a well-constructed vision. This process of creating a vision depends heavily on the contributions of both science and art. Corporate leaders seeking to create or find an organizational vision may not take comfort in the fact that creating a vision is not a scientific endeavor. It is impossible to create a control group and an experimental group, run trials under specified conditions, measure the results, and draw relevant conclusions. In as much as the task or challenge of creating a vision is not a matter of prediction and control, it is tempting to conclude that the process is really an art. After all, creating a vision requires imagination and intuition, and no two visions are exactly alike. Artists, however, create works that are usually judged by subjective standards. Well-crafted visions will necessarily be subject to objective standards, including their impact on the bottom line. The application of objective evaluations may not occur for a period of years, but eventually judgments with respect to the merit or soundness of the vision will be made. Leaders should recognize that scientific laws and theories, mathematics, and statistics come together in the formation and evaluation of visions with individual creativity, personal temperament, and risk taking.

SUSTAINING THE VISION

A great deal of enthusiasm and interest can generally be mustered in developing the corporate vision. The vision is new, it provides a distraction from the challenges of the present, and it looks toward the prospect of greener pastures. When each employee returns to his or her worksite, desk, or office, however, the tendency is to lose sight of the vision. For some employees and organizations, the vision vanishes when the lights are turned out at the end of the day. In other circumstances, the vision fades gradually and eventually disappears.

In other organizations, the vision for the future is always in sight—sometimes closer, sometimes farther away, but always in sight. A number of factors come together in attempting to understand why organizational visions endure and flourish in one corporate environment and not in another.

Gaining the Commitment of Top Leadership

Organizational reality suggests that most organizations function with an inner circle of influence around the CEO. These key people must believe in the vision if it is to be pursued and become an integral part of corporate life; their belief, or for that matter their unbelief, will be revealed in their language. An organization sustained by a strong vision will find its employees mentioning the following from time to time:

- "If we are going to create a system in which everybody receives services and supports, then we had better examine how we are spending our money today."
- "How does this program relate to our vision of the future?"
- "Buying or constructing another building seems to be out of line with our future plans."

Aligning Organizational Practices with the Vision

Sustaining the vision requires more than words. Organizational deeds must be congruent with organizational words. Lofty desires and expressions of the ideal must have real-life significance for vision to prevail. In practical terms, this requires a road map or strategic plan that can be followed and from which progress can be judged. The organization must set goals, and parties must agree on responsibilities. Although the essence of a vision can be known and perceived, the exact details of how to achieve the vision are rarely known in advance. Achieving the vision becomes an ongoing process.

While the vision is in the process of being discovered or redefined, organizations can improve the quality of services and supports that they provide. Continuous quality improvement will sustain multifaceted visions. In a similar manner, human resources management, reviews that offer helpful feedback, and hiring practices contribute to a workforce that can consider and implement the vision-creation process.

Establishing Personal Responsibility

A vision perceived in a culture of personal responsibility is much more likely to prevail than a vision introduced into an environment in which dependency and hierarchy are the governing dynamics. To the extent possible, all of the employees must be engaged in carrying out their parts—large or small—in fulfilling the vision. Employees who have a sense of inner self-direction and permission to take significant actions will believe that they can make contributions to the vision statement. The organization must reward creativity, initiative, and risk taking.

Expanding the Organization

Organizations that are expanding their services, engaging in new behavior, renewing themselves, reaching out to new clients, and serving more people are much more likely to rely on and value the importance of vision than organizations that are laying off employees, are under regulatory siege, or who feel that they are already "big enough." This is not to argue that bigger is better, but the dynamics of growing and change invariably involve momentum and inertia. As a result, more opportunities are encountered and more possibilities are generated by organizations in dynamic situations. The familiar observation applies: It is easier to steer a moving vehicle.

Motivated, future-oriented workers stretch themselves. Nothing is as rewarding as achieving. To continue to perform the same work, that is, to do the same thing—only better—with the same number of people, in the same location, at the same time, and at the same pace is characteristic of organizations with energizing visions. Visions that call for massive changes and great effort often accomplish more through their ability to inspire than do mundane visions calling for insignificant changes. Along these lines, Farson (1996) argued that big changes are easier to make than small ones. In examining the civil rights movement, Farson pointed out that the pace of progress in integration, economic equality, and reduction of discrimination has been glacially slow in the two generations since the movement began in the 1950s. "The bold act that most dramatically and quickly brought about racial integration in a major institution of our society," wrote Farson, "was President Harry Truman's elimination of Jim Crow laws in the armed services, which he accomplished by executive order" (p. 110). Sudden, monumental changes take hold more quickly and survive longer than gradual, incremental steps toward progress. This is what Martin Luther King, Jr., referred to as the "tranquilizing drug of gradualism" (Farson, 1996, p. 110).

An organization creating a glorious future must align all of its resources. In addition to emphasizing the central role of organizational personnel in fashioning the vision, senior management also must direct attention to the organization's constitution and by-laws, its mission statement, and its plan for achieving the goals that it set out in the vision.

Aligning the Organization's Constitution and By-Laws with the Vision

An organization in the process of creating a vision probably already has a constitution and by-laws. The documents and all of the implications included in their pages must be viewed through the lens of the future. Each organization will have its unique concerns, governance structure, membership, purpose, tax status, and so forth. All of these variables need to be reviewed for their support of the desired future.

Writing a Mission Statement

Once the organization has achieved a working acceptance of the vision, the next step is to direct organizational energy toward the development of a mission statement. The mission statement identifies the desired goals of the immediate future; that is, it objectifies what the organization is trying to accomplish now and over the next several years. Individuals involved in the business of the organization need to have an awareness of both further states—mission and vision—and to know the difference between the two directional forces. A possible mission statement for the organization that is discussed in previous sections might be as follows: "To be a leader in providing the highest quality, socially responsible, and cost-effective services and supports to people with disabilities so that they may achieve their full potential and have the opportunity to live abundant lives."

Once the organization's members begin to understand these statements, the organization needs to take the next step and set goals that can be achieved in attempting to realize the accepted vision. Rarely, however, will all employees have a full understanding of the vision and purpose. Turnover prevents organizations from providing sustained educational and in-service programs to all employees. In addition, some employees who have been doing the same job for a considerable length of time will not be able to think in terms of vision or mission. Their attention is taken up by the day-to-day details of the organization.

In attempting to sustain the vision of the organization, the reward and recognition system must be directed toward the future. The reward and recognition must be clear and unambiguous. If leaders can define the vision with clarity, then most employees will perform and move in the direction of the vision. Bonuses, if they are utilized, and pay raises must reflect the value of moving toward the future. A compensation system that merely reflects increases in the cost-of-living or an attitude of, "We survived another year," does not reinforce movement toward the vision.

FROM VISION TO ACTION

In many respects, a vision is really an observation of the future, but not everybody has the ability to create a vision. Think back to when you were a youngster; it is a warm summer day, and you and your friends are lying on the ground and watching billowing clouds. One friend says, "Look at the lion." Another says, "Look at the spaceship"; and still another remarks, "That looks like a cowboy." Some of your friends can see more in the clouds than others. One friend is sure to remark, "I don't see anything; where is it?" But before you can pinpoint the exact location, the cloud becomes something else. The development of corporate visions is similar; some of the participants can see many things, some a few, and others none. Visions are obviously more substantial than cloud formations, but the key to clarifying vision is to free oneself from the demands of the present so that one can observe the future.

Recruiting Visionaries

People who are able to explore the future in a way that compels others to add their talents and insights may not be easily found; and they may not be contented by routine tasks. Visionaries need to be recruited into organizations in which their ideas will be taken seriously, even if their ideas are not always acted upon. It is rare for corporate members who are forward thinking and who have established the discipline to follow through to go unnoticed in the corporate environment. Such individuals are tremendous assets because they serve as the intellectual leaders of the organization.

Collaborating on a Single Vision

The following example offers a compelling testimony for the role of organizational vision. Fritz (1996) analyzed the art of filmmaking to gain a better understanding of the importance of vision. In making a typical Hollywood movie, the director shoots each scene in the order that is most convenient in terms of the locations, actors, and crew—not in the order that we finally see the movie. Much more film is shot than is used in the final product. The editor pulls together what he or she needs from hours of footage, sometimes with the help of the director. The director, therefore, must have a strong vision of the finished film during all stages of production. The actors, as well, must be able to envision their roles within the story. They may have to perform in the climactic scene at the very beginning of shooting and wrap up the project by doing something as mundane as getting out of a car for a transitional scene. The actors and director also collaborate with the screenwriter, cinematographer, producer, editor, and crew on their vision of the film. As Fritz wrote,

> In filmmaking, vision is not a vague notion made up of fuzzy inspirational feelings and sweet-sounding platitudes. It is a profound understanding of

the desired state. It is clarity. It is the standard of measurement against which all actions are judged and adjusted. It creates continuity with drastically changing circumstances. (1996, p. 186)

CONCLUSIONS

The journey from creating organizational vision to making those visions a reality may be a long and challenging one, but the success of the quest relies on two rather simple admonitions: Plan ahead, and follow through. In addition, the clarity of the vision must be contained in the simplicity of the message. Visions, like missions, convey meaning and energy when they are concise and to the point.

REFERENCES

Collins, J.C., & Porras, J.I. (1996, September–October). Building your company's vision. *Harvard Business Review,* 65–77.

Farson, R. (1996). *Management of the absurd: Paradoxes in leadership.* New York: Touchstone.

Fritz, R. (1996). *Corporate tides: The inescapable laws of organizational structure.* San Francisco: Berrett-Koehler.

Jaques, E. (1989). *Requisite organization: The CEO's guide to creative structure and leadership.* Arlington, VA: Cason Hall.

Lipton, M. (1996, Summer). Demystifying the development of an organizational vision. *Sloan Management Review,* 83–92.

RECOMMENDED READING

Oakley, E., & Krug, D. (1993). *Enlightened leadership: Getting to the heart of change.* New York: Simon & Schuster.

7

Quality Performance and Human Resources

Arthur Dykstra, Jr.

Much has been written regarding the responsibilities and opportunities of being a leader. Shaping, directing, modeling, and encouraging the commitment to quality are responsibilities that a leader cannot delegate to others. Quality, as an organizational goal, can be achieved only if all of the stakeholders are involved—hourly workers, first-level supervisors, middle managers, and executive staff. Yet the contribution of the chief executive officer (CEO) cannot be minimized. The CEO sets the quality pace of the organization, defines the expected performance, and gives staff feedback with respect to ongoing improvement efforts. It is the CEO's role to encourage staff to further accomplishments and to articulate the organization's vision.

Organizations cannot achieve dramatic gains in service or product quality easily or quickly because an organization's system of values—and not the mere application of "cookbook techniques"—will invariably point the way toward increased organizational quality. Handy argued that quality is no longer a matter of inspection or statistical review:

> In a more competitive world, organizations will only survive if they can
> guarantee quality in their goods or their services. Short-term profit at the

expense of quality will lead to short-term lives. In that sense, quality is, to my mind, the organizational equivalent of truth. Quality, like truth, will count in the end. No one, and no organization, can live a lie for long. Hard to define, impossible to legislate for, quality, like truth, is an attitude of mind. (1990, p. 145)

Motivated and energetic employees need to be linked together around sound quality improvement principles and practices that facilitate high-quality outcomes. Linkage can occur through face-to-face meetings, team projects, newsletters, e-mail, seminars, or staff retreats. Such efforts should include the use of checklists, flowcharts, graphs, and other feedback mechanisms that will lead to the creation of a critical mass of employees who are focused on personal outcomes as the measure of quality.

Organizational quality improvement does not occur by chance. It does not occur naturally or spontaneously. Organizational quality improvement requires leadership, energy, and focus. Above all, organizational quality improvement requires persistence and patience. Whether organizations proceed gradually or rapidly and whether change is total or incremental, leaders need to demonstrate persistence and resolve.

Just as exceptional leadership can lead to organizational outcomes of the highest quality, poor leadership can result in poor performance and erode quality. Discouraged supervisors and middle managers often are frustrated by CEOs who exhibit no commitment to quality improvement, organizational change, and greater employee autonomy. Explanations for such CEO behaviors are plentiful. Examples include the following: The CEO simply does not get it—"it" being the proper understanding of the role or the duties that go with the top position; the CEO lives by the standard, "It's good enough for government work"; or the CEO is interested in concerns other than organizational performance. Whatever the cause, the consequences are the same: Staff members become discouraged, performance is uneven across the organization, and products or services are mediocre.

Quality as a concept is an organizational ideal. It never exists in its perfect form or in the manner for which one would ultimately hope. As a result, quality represents a constellation of ideas that guide organizational efforts toward the goal of becoming better. Quality is an ever-developing indicator of how well the organization is performing. The concept of quality exists in our minds as well as in the minds of those who observe our behavior. In this regard, quality is a matter of both words and deeds.

Quality as a performance goal has to be articulated in words that are meaningful for employees. The organization must explain quality in organizational practices, policies, and procedures. The organization needs agreed-on definitions of quality so that all employees can recognize quality in services and supports. In practice, however, quality is a matter of deeds. An organization is not likely to be described as high quality merely on the basis of its words, whether they are found in the mission statement or in the annual report. Behavior must be present that is exemplary in representing recommended practices as well as being reflective of current available knowledge. Leaders should recognize that even though a person is striving to do his or her best and is committed to excellent performance, he or she may not be doing the right thing from a technical or scientific perspective. Knowing how to do the required behavior and being motivated to accomplish it must be combined for quality practices to occur. Services and supports of high quality result from this combination of motivation, leadership, knowledge, and experience.

The remainder of this chapter focuses on those activities and practices that support the people or employees who are performing the work of the organization for the benefit of others. Within the field of management, these support activities are identified as issues of human resources.

IMPORTANCE OF HUMAN RESOURCES MANAGEMENT

The familiar saying "Caring for the people who care for others" may seem somewhat folksy, but it is the fundamental tenet of any human resources activity. Organizations cannot deliver high-quality services, especially those that are based on person-to-person transactions, for any significant period of time without concerning themselves with the employment and management practices that affect these same people. A workforce that is discouraged, oppressed, or abused cannot carry out its responsibilities in a high-quality manner. In such situations, employees frequently become preoccupied with their own negative circumstances and fail to perform as they were trained.

Quality performance is in many ways predicated on the quality of the human resources practices of the organization and in many ways determines the quality of the products or services. The responsibility for human resources practices rests with all the employees of the organization, but the primary leadership responsibility rests with the senior management.

A small organization employing less than 100 employees may not have a full-time staff member who fulfills the human resources function. Instead, such responsibilities might be shared by several employees. In small organizations, people know each other, and informal practices dominate organizational life. Issues may be dealt with only when they occur. The CEO, financial manager, or a central office staff member frequently steers or manages the human resources activities. Often, in smaller organizations, human resources–related issues are dealt with and discussed but never classified as human resources issues, per se.

Many authors have described the side effects of organizational growth—the trend toward becoming bureaucratic perhaps being identified most frequently. The human resources function is often one of the first organizational units that sprouts up; and instead of the organization's collectively dealing with human resources issues, a separate department takes charge of the issues that might matter most to the organization. The apprehension here is not the necessary evolution of a human resources department but rather that there is often a shift in the responsibilities of human resources from top management to other levels of the organization. It is very much akin to the practice of creating a quality assurance department and asking that employees working in the department take the responsibility for the organization's quality practices and improvement strategies. In rather rapid fashion, other managers begin to focus on other issues—issues other than constant commitment to quality—that are less vital to the organization.

In organizations following sound program and fiscal practices, quality results from human resources employees' and other staff member's learning the organization's practices. On a practical basis, this means that top leadership is continuously struggling with such human resources issues as hiring, compensation, performance appraisals, communication, and job design. Specially trained individuals can research compensation and performance evaluation systems, for example; but the primary responsibility for relationships can never be subordinated or delegated. Relationships in organizations are not a matter of information sharing or dissemination but rather involve emotion, dispute resolution, concerns of fairness, honesty, and respect. Stated another way, human resources activities demonstrate how the people in an organization care for one another so that they might care about the people whom the organization serves and the work that it does.

It is unlikely that the dynamics of the organization are the same on Friday as they were on Monday. The policies and procedures, the organizational structure, the budget, and the personnel manual are probably the same, but it is quite likely that during the week one or more employees have been hired, terminated, or retired. Feelings have been hurt, rumors have circulated, sexual affairs may have occurred, employees may have been sick, others were passed over for promotions, some employees may have received new computers while others did not, meetings were held, minutes were taken, lunchtime or afterwork baby showers may have been held, or wakes were attended. Still other employees may have been selected for an award, received a letter of discipline, been in an accident, attended a workshop or seminar, or sold a fellow employee a used car. The work of the organization must go on and does go on even in the midst of such activity. Not to be cognizant of the significant ramifications of employee-to-employee relationships is to be organizationally naïve. To ignore or to pretend that such employee behavior does not have an impact on service quality or habilitation efforts is to be organizationally negligent.

Human resources practices must support the mission of the organization in theory as well as in practice. Personnel handbooks written in user-friendly language and illustrated with cartoons might serve as camouflage to regulatory agencies, but such manuals will not fool the organization's employees. The employees will be watching, observing, and comparing notes whenever the occasion presents itself. Therefore, it is important that organizational goals and values should be continuously addressed through an ongoing dialogue that acknowledges the changing dynamics within the organization.

Development of Partnerships

Human resources efforts that are founded on a commitment to relationships and partnerships will flourish as part of the quality consciousness of the organization. These human resources efforts contribute energy to the organization. In contrast, efforts directed at compliance criteria (e.g., satisfying funding authority mandates) or support activities can be maintained, but they will absorb organizational energy rather than create it. These relationships and partnerships occur through the various levels of organizational influence, among the top executives, middle managers, and front-line employees. Time is set aside to review current practices, to seek and accept feedback, and to make ongoing changes to benefit the workforce. As in other aspects of organizational life, not all ideas will be implemented—some because of cost, others because of context or culture. Partnership as an organizing human resources principle is an enabling, optimistic, truth-telling force in organizations that enforce its pursuit. Williams stated that

> Partnering puts a new emphasis on the working relationship. It began with a commitment to cooperation by the top management . . . It is a commitment to fairness and openness. It requires acceptance of one's own mistakes and refraining from exploitation of the other's mistakes. (1996, p. 1)

In essence, partnership recognizes the benefits of cooperation over competition, of engagement over withdrawal, of truthfulness over manipulation, and of equality over hierarchy. Other qualities of partnerships include the following:

- Partners do not do bad things to each other, do not exploit each other, and do not say one thing and do another. Partners do not help themselves to unequal shares of the payroll and do not blame others for organizational problems.
- Partners worry about the life challenges faced by others. Partners work to strengthen the organization—they see more than their own department or responsibilities. Partners seek to share, not hide, their resources.
- Partners come together, enrolled in a higher purpose, but it is not to fight against a motivationally manufactured enemy (i.e., a fictitious enemy manufactured by managers for the purposes of motivating staff). Partners share responsibility for problem solving.
- Partners share the losses as well as the gains. They are each other's agents.

A commitment to partnership does not happen accidentally or easily. True partnership is a matter of emotional and intellectual covenants. It binds the participants so that they are free to carry out the work of the organization without fear, mistrust, or insecurity. An organization that is fraught with internal competition, baronial warfare, secrecy, and scapegoating will find it very difficult to provide quality services. An organization that is serious about pursuing partnership should have a written partnership agreement that is signed by all of the relevant parties. Human resources measures will, as a result, be developed to enhance the organization, not to control the employees.

HUMAN RESOURCES PRACTICES

Having considered the importance of quality as it relates to employee behavior, especially in the context of service organizations, the chapter turns its attention to many of the most significant human resources practices. In 1993, the U.S. Department of Labor designated certain human resources procedures as High Performance Work Practices (i.e., those behaviors that contribute to greater employee effectiveness and organizational achievement). Included in this list were employee recruitment, selection, and training; formal information sharing; attitude assessment; job design; grievance procedures; labor-management programs; performance appraisal; promotion; and incentive compensation systems. Huselid investigated these practices and reported that "across a wide range of industries and firm sizes, [there is] considerable support for the hypothesis that investments in such practices are associated with lower employee turnover and greater productivity and corporate financial performance" (1995, p. 667). There is growing evidence that human resources practices have a major impact on organizational performance. Each of the following activities can have an impact on quality performance: hiring and promotion activities, compensation practices, performance accounting and appraisal systems, employee appeals processes, communication practices, and job design.

Hiring and Promotional Activities

Although each of the activities identified in this section contribute to quality outcomes, none is so critical as the decision of whom to hire. As a matter of organizational management, this principle is self-evident; converting self-evident principles into actual practice is another matter. In many organizations, new employees are hired by supervisors and managers who have little experience in hiring and even less training in employee selection. The more experienced staff members are engaged in other, more important organizational deliberations. Yet, the irony is that the experienced staff often find themselves spending their time on staff discipline, grievance hearings, and unemployment or workers' compensation issues, or on crafting strategies to deal with overtime expenditures.

Although the topics of employment screening, testing, and interviewing fall beyond the scope of this chapter, one phenomenon does deserve attention. Organizations could achieve better employment outcomes if the person doing the interviewing would talk less and listen more. Given the opportunity, most candidates for employment will communicate why they should or should not be hired. Organizations, unfortunately, devote too little time listening to and learning about potential employees. To improve the employee selection process, interviewers can use job previews, behavioral questioning, response vignettes, and similar approaches. On a broader level, companies can conduct internal self-assessments on the organizational hiring process by asking questions such as the following:

- Who does the hiring? And why?
- When is it done?
- Where does it occur?
- What is the employment application process?
- Is the application useful?
- How long is the lag time between application and interview?
- Where do we advertise job openings? To whom?
- What do we want in terms of qualifications?
- How many people apply?
- How many applicants are interviewed?
- How many employees are hired?
- How many applicants turn our job offers down? Why?

An organization concerned with quality not only addresses these questions but many more, including the cost of the process. In the same regard, the organization should be able to characterize the attributes of the person who does not fit well into the organization—that is, the person who should not be hired.

The best person to make the hiring decision—when prepared in terms of training and experience—is the person who will supervise the employee when he or she joins the organization. In large organizations, the temptation is to let the human resources staff do the interviewing, preservice training, and benefit explanations. This occurs because of the consequences of bureaucracy, because the belief that management staff is too busy, and because human resources staff are professionally trained. The limitation of this approach is that there is no initial buy-in, bonding, or initial acknowledgment of a partnership and relationship between the new employee and the community that he or she is joining.

Promotional practices are another key human resources consideration. To assess promotional practices, an organization can ask a parallel set of self-assessment questions:

- Who is promoted? Why?
- Do promotions tend to occur internally, or are positions generally filled from the outside?
- Are employees aware of promotional opportunities? If so, by what mechanism?

One of the tragedies of human services organizations is that individuals who work directly with the individuals being served, often in a one-to-one or group basis, cannot be (or are not) financially rewarded for the outstanding work that they do. As a result, these employees, because of greater salary opportunities, often end up in management or supervisory positions for which they are not suited. Managing others is not easy. Not all employees have the skills, talent, and motivation for management.

In the trend toward flatter organizations with less hierarchy, the opportunity for promotions may be decreased. Organizational leaders will have to confront this reality. For some employees, receiving ongoing compensation increases without a change in title will be acceptable. For others, a promotion to a new set of challenges or opportunities is very important. Managers and employees should recognize individual differences in motivation as a critical dimension in organizational performance, and the corporate structure and internal process should be constructed to allow for these differences.

Compensation Practices

The issue of compensation, or wages, can generally be sorted into amount, major areas of concern, and methods. In terms of emphasis, the issue of "how much to pay" typically takes precedence over the issues of "for what," "how," and "when." In organizations that do not have multiple income streams, the issue may be decided rather simply (i.e., How much do we have?). All that remains in this situation is to calculate an annual cost-of-living increase (e.g., 3%) and distribute that to all eligible employees on an annual basis.

In organizations solely dependent on state dollars, salary increases are linked to state appropriations. Within this approach, again using a 3% increase as the example, it is not uncommon for management to establish the norm of merit increases or compensation. This results in a performance appraisal that finds some employees receiving less than 3% and some employees receiving more, based on common performance indicators. The governing factor is the 3% increase available in the "personnel: wages and salary" column found on the chart of accounts. Organizations typically award this annual increase at the beginning of the calendar or fiscal year or on the anniversary of the employee's hiring.

To ask the question, "For what should the employees be paid?" may seem irrelevant or unnecessary; such is not the case, however. The previous discussion alluded to a compensation system based on an annual cost-of-living adjustment that included a slight increase based on merit. In actual practice, many CEOs simply give all employees the same percentage salary increase, except for their immediate subordinates who get a slightly higher percentage. The public logic is frequently expressed as "The wages are so low and the increases so small that we thought everyone should get the same." Often, however, this occurs because the organization has not established a compensation system that rewards individual contributions. The organization simply cannot distinguish objectively one employee's productivity from another's. In addition, managers are often afraid to make wage distinctions among employees; it is not easy to explain to an employee why he or she is making less or was recommended for a lesser increase than another person.

The alternative is to initiate a variable compensation plan whereby employees are paid on the basis of performance. Many approaches are possible; a few are described here briefly. Effort is not made, however, to evaluate the strengths of one system over another. Certain variable pay plans begin with a slight cost-of-living increase, with the remainder of the compensation occurring through periodic bonus payouts—usually on a quarterly basis. Some systems are based on the performance of single employees, similar to the ideas of sales commissions. Others combine more than one element (e.g., employee and work group or team performance); still others add a third element—overall agency and organizational financial strength. How the elements—employee, team, organization—are weighted, in terms of accounting for the most variance with respect to the dollars available, varies from one organization to another.

There is a national trend toward establishing incentive compensation systems. An organization seeking to avail itself to the best management practices must keep itself informed of the changes in the compensation field. Furthermore, organizations periodically should address the issues of compensation by asking some of the following questions:

- Will the organization have differential pay for different shifts? For holidays or weekends? For different assignments? If so, how will the amount be decided?
- How often will the organization pay its employees? Weekly, every 2 weeks, twice per month, or monthly?
- Who gives the employees their checks? And how do they do it?
- How are payroll check errors corrected? Is the error taken seriously by management? How quickly is it fixed?

It is also worth noting that compensation analysts have begun to pay more attention to the spread between the highest and lowest paid employees within an organization rather than to the differences among employees at different organizations. This mode of analysis suggests that the highest paid employee should make no more than 10 times the compensation of the lowest paid worker. In the late 1990s, many large American corporations maintain a compensation ratio of 50 or 100 to 1 (Crystal, as cited in Bower, 1997).

Performance Accounting and Appraisal Systems

Apart from compensation considerations, most organizations realize the importance of employee feedback. How does an employee know how he or she is doing? How can he or she improve? What should he or she do more of? Less of? There are correct answers to these questions; but, unfortunately, they are rarely given in organizational practice. Organizational feedback should be provided by the employee's immediate supervisor on a regular basis, and, under ideal circumstances, on a one-to-one basis. Performance feedback between employee and supervisor, unfortunately, is more rare than common. Typical excuses for the lack of feedback are that supervisors are too busy, untrained in the feedback process, reluctant to deal with emotional responses, or have failed to establish objective standards for feedback. The method used for providing employee feedback has an impact on employee performance. There is no uniform approach that is optimal for all organizations. Organization history, culture, leadership, and employee expectations influence the feedback methodology. Many books have been written about the advantages and disadvantages of the various performance appraisal approaches. The organization must select and correctly use the approach that is appropriate to its culture and values. On a regular basis, the organizational leadership should consider the following questions:

- Is a written document to be used in performance appraisal?
- Is one form used for all employees?
- Does it use a "check the correct box" approach?
- How often is the form or document completed? Quarterly? Annually?
- Where does it go?
- Where is it filed?
- Does the employee have the opportunity to discuss (i.e., agree or disagree with) the evaluation?

Performance feedback and appraisal is directly linked to organizational performance. Jaques and Clement offered a valuable insight with respect to performance accounting and performance evaluations and appraisal:

Every managerial leader must also recognize the fundamental difference between performance accounting and personal effectiveness appraisals.

An individual's performance is the relationship between targeted output and achieved output. Personal effectiveness appraisals are judgments made by an individual's manager about how well the subordinate has done in producing the outputs, taking into consideration all of the relevant circumstances. Thus, while accounting data and performance feedback are important, they do not, by themselves, tell how well or how poorly subordinates have worked at their assigned tasks. To tie individual personal effectiveness appraisals solely to quantitative information about performance imposes a serious injustice on subordinates.

Once this distinction between performance accounting and personal effectiveness appraisals is clear, it becomes equally clear that, while objective measures can be used for performance accounting, personal effectiveness appraisals call for managerial judgment. (1991, p. 188)

Apart from the customary annual recording of an employee's performance, many organizations will seek to give feedback to the newly hired employee on a more frequent basis (e.g., every 30 days of the trial service or probation period). Some organizations require a formal performance appraisal when an employee is promoted, transferred, or disciplined. Beyond the formally scheduled appraisal schedule, however, the most effective and reinforcing review process is to provide one-to-one feedback and listen to the response. Not providing periodic employee feedback and then suddenly pulling out the appraisal form from the drawer and marking everything as "needing improvement" cannot be tolerated. The common sense logic of human resources management is that there be no surprises in employer–employee relationships and feedback. Any surprise indicates a breakdown in the feedback process.

Employee Appeals Processes

Every organization, regardless of size, must have an accessible pathway for resolving differences. In small organizations, the path may lead directly from the program to the CEO. In larger organizations, the path may wind through a committee or designated staff members. The approaches to employee appeals are varied; some organizations use a committee of peers, others use non-involved support or management staff from another program. Whatever the path may be, the organization must provide an unbiased review of the employees' concerns. The steps of the appeals process must be followed carefully, especially in instances of employee discipline or termination.

Communication Practices

Communication influences organizational behavior. There is no substitute for direct communication—whether in a group meeting or private conference. This is especially significant during times of organizational change or restructure. Employees want to know how the contemplated action will affect them, if at all. It is important to listen and respond promptly and accurately to employees' concerns. One of the most serious problems existing in organizations today is the failure of supervisors or managers to spend time on a one-to-one basis with the employees under their supervision. Mechanisms such as newsletters, informational memorandums, and web sites are also helpful—sometimes to reinforce a message or to communicate general information. But, these other mechanisms do not substitute for a personal relationship. For successful communication among the various levels of an organization to occur, leaders must engage in continuous self-assessment and ask the following questions:

- Are the messages and information of top leadership being shared with all of the employees?
- Are the concerns of the first-line workers making it to top corporate leadership?
- Are middle managers talking to other middle managers?
- Where are the communication barriers? And what is being done to break them down?
- What messages are not communicated?

Effective communication cannot be assumed, even if it is a stated organizational goal. It must be worked on all of the time.

Job Design

What do employees do? Who decides on the tasks? How do the tasks change? These are the critical issues of job design. To be effective, employees must be engaged in meaningful activities that are valued by the organization. Job design is the mechanism whereby critical issues such as the amount of supervision, level of authority, and the significance and range of tasks being performed can be evaluated. If properly aligned, these elements are a major source of external motivation and job satisfaction.

Job design is crucial in organizations that serve people with disabilities. There is a significant difference between assisting a person to perform a task and allowing a person to perform a task alone. Teaching a person with a disability how to prepare and cook a meal is not the same as cooking the meal while the person watches. Understanding this difference and acting on it are likewise not the same thing. Performing the task rather than teaching and facilitating occurs because the staff members may mistakenly view a person with disabilities as if he or she were a child and respond to him or her just as they did in raising their own young children. At other times, staff members underestimate the abilities of the people whom they are assisting and believe that the individuals cannot learn the suggested new behavior. In other instances, staff members lack the skills necessary to teach the task, and, so in frustration they do it themselves.

What is especially complicated in job design is to accept and recognize the individual differences of the program participants and to realize that a successful technique used with one person may not work with another. In an organization concerned with quality outcomes, diligent attention should be given to the nature of the work and to how it is performed at every level of the organization.

IMPORTANCE OF EMPLOYEE RECOGNITION

A 12-year-old boy was pitching in the top of the third inning of his little league baseball game and, even at this young age, he had earned a reputation for his fast ball. The batter on this day, unfortunately, lined a fast ball right back into the pitcher's mouth. His mother and father, who were watching the game, immediately ran to the pitcher, as did the coach. They all agreed that he needed to go to the emergency room to receive stitches in his upper lip. He reluctantly agreed to leave the game and go to the hospital but only under one condition—that he be allowed to return to the game. When all of the adults tried to assure him that this was unnecessary, he remarked, "I have to, the team needs me. The team needs me."

Quality would not be an issue in an organization in which all the employees believed that they were needed by their co-workers and bosses—for that matter, quality would probably not be an ongoing issue in an organization in which a quarter of the workforce felt needed. The fulfillment of human need is a powerful motivator and a source of reinforcement. Recognizing employees for their contributions is a vital source of individual and corporate self-esteem and commitment. Every organization is concerned with the motivation of its workforce, from hourly workers and middle managers to top executives. Gellerman observed that "every employee is motivated; the only unmotivated employees are dead ones" (1992, p. 78).

Organizational leaders assess and periodically reassess their approach to employee recognition. Nothing sustains employees as much as a culture of appreciation and encouragement. Nothing works like saying, "Thank you." But the thought and action must be genuine. Organizations must concern themselves with their values every day not just once a month or once a year. Employees soon lose their "I'm Number One" key chains and break or misplace their coffee mugs with the inspirational mottos. Organizations should avoid establishing inflexible employee recognition programs because these frequently result in a mandated set of instructions regarding smiling, how to say "good morning," and the reassignment of parking spaces. It does not take long in such environments for mindless routines and gimmicks to become the established approach.

To avoid inflexible recognition programs, leadership behavior is paramount. It counts for far more organizational performance than all policies, procedures, and practices. Employees continuously observe the behavior of those in charge and emulate that behavior. Role modeling by those in positions of authority is critical. Shaking hands, thanking, congratulating, and encouraging must happen on an ongoing basis. Again, there must be an intellectual as well as an emotional commitment to the activity. An organizational leader cannot just be appreciative when he or she feels like it; instead the leader should show appreciation when the situation calls for it.

Organizations also must develop formal and informal methods or programs of recognition and appreciation. In some instances, such recognition may be the result of a memorandum, a visit from an organizational mascot, or a small present. Outstanding performance, exemplary attitude, and acts of special kindness should be recognized. Such approaches tend to create organizational excitement, especially if they are unpredictable and well deserved. The organization also needs to utilize recognition and positive reinforcement mechanisms that transcend daily acts of appreciation. These approaches represent a planned approach used by the organization and are just as important in commitment as the other human resources practices. They are the mechanisms used in between the daily and yearly recognition practices.

Annual recognition of outstanding organizational performance is also crucial. Once again, the awards should reinforce the organization's values and vision. Celebrations are vital to organizational renewal. Employee recognition rituals—including decisions with respect to financial awards, frequency, extent of publicity, and ceremonies—should be linked to organizational values and vision. In a complementary way, organizations might choose to recognize small groups or teams of employees for particular accomplishments. A team award is powerful in communicating the value of cooperation. It is important to recognize employees for their personal and organizational worth. Organizational leaders must be committed to a culture of appreciation every day. Although recognition and appreciation are a daily occurrence, they are still rituals that reinforce values, mission, and vision. Never offer recognition and appreciation for behavior and performance that does not reinforce the organization's values, mission, and vision.

Morrison outlined some of the practical ways in which managers can recognize their employees. Other than the commonly referred to pay, promotions, and perquisites, she added the following forms of recognition:

> Participation—inclusion in decision-making; Autonomy—freedom to act on one's own without supervision; Resources—staff, budget, and time to do the job; Respect and Credibility—one's priorities and opinions are considered and valued; and Faith—the expectation that one's productivity will continue in increasingly responsible positions. (1994, p. 62)

LEADERSHIP AND MANAGEMENT ISSUES

Human resources practices are fundamental to quality performance; these activities cannot be subordinate to fiscal or programmatic concerns. The challenge of leadership is to recognize which things need to be done simultaneously and which need to be done sequentially. The balance is demanding and ever-changing, but the dynamics cannot be neglected.

Age, Size, and Structure

A newly incorporated organization will necessarily approach human resources in a different manner than a well-established organization. Newer, smaller organizations frequently can use informal practices and approaches that are not possible when levels of middle managers or multiple sites are added. Smaller organizations may, as previously suggested, handle personnel matters on a shared or multiple-role basis; whereas larger organizations often have sizable human resources departments. Bureaucratic forces begin to emerge as an organization grows. Managers should attempt to use the positive elements of bureaucracy and guard against the frivolous.

Structure also has an impact on human resources. Hierarchical organizations require very different reporting relationships than flat organizations. When everyone knows everyone else, the reporting methods are very different from the situation in which employees from one department or division rarely interact with those from another.

Many variables affect an organization's human resources efforts in addition to age, size, and structure: resource availability, unionization status, staff availability (in terms of the local labor pool), and staff development and learning opportunities.

Resource Availability

Organizations vary dramatically in terms of available financial resources—as a result of their developmental history, because of their
dependence on state or federal funding levels, or because of cutbacks
or recessions. Other organizations are tied to foundations that have
a solid basis of fundraising or endowment. Salary levels, benefits
packages, reward systems, and promotional activities are affected
by financial circumstances. Other key practices, however, exist and
must be appropriately addressed, regardless of the financial circumstances. An organization forced to lay off a portion of its workforce is
much different from a rapidly growing, expanding organization.

Unionization Status

Unions and the subsequent labor contracts can have a powerful
influence on human resources practices. The classic triad of union
interests—wages, hours, and working conditions—clearly impinge
on human resources strategies. The opportunity for creativity and
variation is usually arrested by union issues of seniority and past
practices. The speed of organizational change may be much slower
in unionized organizations.

Staff Availability

Securing qualified employees may be the primary issue on the
minds of the leadership staffs of human services organizations. A
labor pool that is very small because of the competition for workers
creates a great challenge. As a result, the energy and concern invested in recruitment and retention practices may be the dominant
human resources theme.

Staff Development and Learning Opportunities

The manner in which an organization approaches issues of staff
recruitment, supervision, feedback and learning, and staff development influences the quality of the services and supports experienced by that organization's consumers.

CONCLUSIONS

For an organization to be successful, six essential forces must coa-
lesce in the pursuit of quality: 1) the organization's values and vision, 2) the organization's financial practices and stewardship,
3) the soundness and effectiveness of the principles used in actually
performing the work of the organization (whether it be habilitative,
educational, or treatment activities), 4) the staff development or

learning processes, 5) the experiences that are available and engaged in, and 6) the organization's human resources practices.

REFERENCES

Bower, M. (1997). *The will to lead.* Boston: Harvard Business School Press.

Gellerman, S.W. (1992). *Motivation in the real world.* New York: Dutton.

Handy, C. (1990). *The age of unreason.* Boston: Harvard Business School Press.

Huselid, M.A. (1995, June). The impact of human resource management practices on turnover, productivity, and corporate financial performance. *Academy of Management Journal,* 635–672.

Jaques, E., & Clement, S.D. (1991). *Executive leadership.* Arlington, VA: Cason Hall.

Morrison, A.M. (1994). Diversity and leadership development. In J. Renesch (Ed.), *Leadership in a new era* (pp. 53–68). San Francisco: New Leaders Press, Sterling & Stone.

Williams, T.D.W. (1996). *Partnering: An overview of the application of the partnering process to the current business environment.* Seattle, WA: Resolutions International.

RECOMMENDED READINGS

Bowen, D.E., & Lawler, E.E. (1992, Spring). The empowerment of service workers: What, why, how, and when. *Sloan Management Review,* 31–39.

Choi, T.Y., & Behling, O.C. (1997, February). Top managers and TQM success: One more look after all these years. *Academy of Management Executive,* 37–47.

Denhardt, R.B. (1981). *In the shadow of organization.* Lawrence: University of Kansas Press.

Hofstede, G. (1994). *Uncommon sense about organizations.* Thousand Oaks, CA: Sage Publications.

Ivancevich, J.M. (1995). *Human resource management.* Chicago: Irwin.

Weisbrod, B.A. (1988). *The nonprofit economy.* Cambridge, MA: Harvard University Press.

8

Managing
Organizational Change
and Transition Through
Personal Outcomes

Tina Campanella

Business leaders recognize the importance of ongoing change for maintaining performance improvement and ensuring the survival of their organizations. Organizations that do not change are vulnerable. Even the most successful companies must reevaluate continuously to respond to what is changing in the world—customers, technology, markets, and the workforce. Change should be an accepted phenomenon within organizations—especially in organizations concerned with quality.

Creating a culture that acknowledges continuous change as an organizational constant is a challenge. Change is associated with feelings most people would prefer to have less of in their lives, such as uncertainty, chaos, loss of control, and pain. Change—both planned and unplanned—however, is a natural by-product of the human services process. As people with disabilities using services and supports achieve goals and experience personal growth, organizational priorities must shift. Advances in technology and professional knowledge also create the need for continuing change to keep practice current with accepted standards. In addition, routine organizational events such as staff turnover, budget changes, and changes in regulations or funding that support services' activities require change within the organization; otherwise, effectiveness and performance suffer.

PERSON-CENTERED SERVICE ORGANIZATIONS

Operating with a focus on consumers has become an accepted standard within the service industry. The successful service organization is flexible and willing to change in response to the needs of the people it serves. The service organization's core competency for long-term success is understanding and responding to the needs and desires of the people who will use the organization's services. Developing this competency requires more than just customer surveys or listening to personal needs. Whitely and Hessan (1996) described this challenge as a process for moving from listening to the consumer to "hardwiring" the voice of the customer into the organization. This strategy takes what is learned from listening to each consumer and uses the information to redesign operations to ensure delivery of what each person really wants (Whitely & Hessan, 1996).

Examples of organizations failing to meet this challenge are found in everyday experiences. When the mechanic at your local garage explains why your car cannot be fixed on time or the waiter at a new restaurant explains that you cannot have an entrée prepared the way you want it, they are displaying a fundamental failure in listening to customers' needs. Even worse, however, is the failure of a service business to vigorously address this process breakdown and use these interactions as opportunities to improve performance. By tolerating an environment in which consumers' needs are not addressed, the service organization displays its lack of understanding about the essential nature of its business. Like the local garage or the restaurant whose business is not really about fixing cars or preparing food, the service organization's business is about providing service to the consumer.

Flaws in service delivery are easy to identify in the single-focus service organization such as the auto repair shop and the restaurant. Performance problems and breakdowns can be more difficult to see in organizations that assist people with disabilities (e.g., helping them to find and keep homes or work, helping to establish themselves within the community). Expectations for service to people are influenced by what service deliverers believe is possible for their customers. The very reasons that a person with disabilities seeks supports from service organizations may be identified as potential barriers to achieving the person's desired outcome. For example, people looking for assistance to reestablish themselves after hospitalization for mental illness may be seen as incapable of living on their own because of their illness. In this case, emphasis is being placed on addressing clinical diagnosis instead of on listening to the person.

The consumer-driven approach to services demands that we reexamine our overall expectations about people as well as for service quality. Strategies for quality improvement rely on a set of assumptions about people and organizations. The use of traditional program standards to set expectations considered process to be the most important factor and expected service practices to meet the criteria of uniformity and consistency. These organizations operated within a paradigm in which people believed that certain key practices such as assessment and planning needed to be carried out in the same way for every person. Although these assumptions provided direction for practice, they have been challenged by definitions of quality in services and what is known about providing individualized supports for people.

Trends in the late 1990s place primary importance on people. Guidance for individual action must be derived from an understanding of each person and his or her desires for personal outcomes. The organization's mission and values provide guidance for defining the organization's role in supporting people to achieve these desired ends. Through interaction with the person, the organization's process is defined for responding to each person's unique requirements for support. Nonprescriptive guidelines for professional practice allow organizational resources to be used in different ways for different people to achieve individualized results. The ability to understand and respond to individual differences is the key variable in organizational performance. This focus on the person lays a new foundation for practice and new methods for promoting quality in services.

PEOPLE AND PROGRAMS—AN OXYMORON

In human services organizations, the "program" approach to service delivery has been used for definition and guidance about how to support people: Employment programs find jobs for people; residential programs provide housing. Whereas this approach serves to clarify responsibilities, program constructs also can interfere with identifying and addressing individual needs by taking attention away from listening to and understanding personal needs. Effort and emphasis are placed on addressing individuals' needs that are viewed as consistent with the program's goals. For example, employment programs rarely seek to understand what occurs in people's lives beyond the workplace. Individuals are assisted to acquire work skills or to find employment, but the question of how a job may or may not fit with each person's other life priorities is not addressed. This process of limited focus and attention leads to a poor outcome for the individual. As a consequence, there is a significant effort to move away from programs as a primary organizing principle in human services.

The traditional tools and techniques for the operation and delivery of human services are products of the professions. Services were designed using professional frameworks for understanding people. The professional "service prescription" included the expectation that therapy or treatment played a useful role in people's lives. Service systems emerged as a means to coordinate the action of multiple professionals and to allow the work of providing service to people with different disabilities to remain controlled and predictable. This produced an outcome of consistency for the human services worker but did not always provide an outcome of accommodation or support for people with disabilities and their families.

In contrast, the person-centered services organization responds to what is important for each person seeking support from the organization. Paying attention to the personal outcomes desired by people assists organizations to learn how each person defines and prioritizes issues in his or her life. The organization uses what is learned about each person's life priorities to make decisions about the support relationship and the allocation of resources. Engaging people in discussions about life priorities becomes a primary service activity and provides data and direction for service evolution and improvement.

USING PERSONAL OUTCOMES AS GUIDES FOR CHANGE

Tension between the needs of people and the work of the service organization often comes from commitment to the program construct. Staff within an organization designed around programs must decide what is most important—adherence to program practice or responding to individuals' needs. The process of creating program models and seeking support and funding for program development encourages people to develop deep commitment to the program. The benefits for people become but one aspect in the overall evaluation of program success. Over time, the program takes on a life of its own. Under this paradigm, people in need of support are expected to adapt to the structure of the program instead of the program adapting to the needs of the individuals.

An organization using outcomes for people to define service priorities operates differently from an organization using a program approach to service delivery. In an outcome-focused organization, the staff focus on developing individualized supports and producing service processes that respect individual choice. Although there is some consistency in the general outcome areas that people identify as important, specific definitions for personal outcomes are made by each consumer. Personal outcomes reflect the consumers' preferences and individual life circumstances. When used to direct services, outcomes spotlight what is important to each person. Service action and practice, therefore, are based on what makes the most sense to and for the person in relation to the achievement of his or her outcomes.

Implementing an outcome approach to service does not require that all current practices be discarded or changed. It does demand that organizations place a primary emphasis on the person and the service provider's knowledge of the individual's desired outcomes. Individual outcomes for each person must be defined before decisions about service practice are made. Without an understanding of what is important to each person, services become routine and, at times, may conflict with the person's perception of what is important. The following questions can help to begin assessment of the connection between people being supported and how work is done within an organization:

- How is the need for change identified in this organization?
- Who gets included in decisions about individual supports? How?
- Whose permission is most important to get before making changes in the support process?
- How do staff members describe barriers to individualizing supports and services?

The specific answers to each question are less important than the information about organizational priorities that asking these questions produce. Person-centered organizations look to the people seeking support to guide decisions and to evaluate success. Working to achieve outcomes promotes a partnership relationship through which people with disabilities help to define and direct the work of the organization.

BASIC PRINCIPLES IN SERVICE

Providing a range of supports that assist people to overcome barriers to achieving personal outcomes is the basic business of the human services organization. This job is challenging. There is no scientific process to ensure that good things happen for people. Supporting outcomes requires engagement with people in active pursuit of individually defined priorities. The process of active engagement with the person begins at the point of service initiation. Staff work with the consumer to define individual priorities through dialogue and interaction. This process is implemented for every person. It reflects the organization's commitment to respect for the unique, individual identity of each person.

The process of engagement does not stop with the initial identification of outcomes. Provisions for continued learning from the person keep the service process on track. Adjustments in the type and intensity of supports are made as more is learned about the person and his or her desired outcomes. Staff ensure that a balance between individual and organizational responsibility is maintained through ongoing interactions and assessment of individual support needs. The goal of outcome-based support is to provide only the amount and type of intervention needed to assist the person to attain his or her desired outcomes.

Actions that provide the greatest support for people as they develop and work toward the achievement of important life outcomes are grounded in principle not procedure. These principles keep the focus of service interactions on each person and his or her desired outcomes. The following are examples of some basic principles that guide person-centered service practice: actively learn about outcomes from people, acknowledge people as partners in the service process, clearly define support roles for the organization and staff, and be creative in developing supports for people.

Actively Learn About Outcomes from People

Knowledge about what is important to people supported by an organization cannot be assumed. Effective service organizations develop mechanisms to continually monitor each individual's priorities. Interactions with people begin with engaging the person in active exploration of issues and options; and this continues throughout the service relationship.

Acknowledge People as Partners in the Service Process

As attention shifts from programs to supports, the role of the person being supported is redefined. No longer is the person a target of service; instead, he or she becomes an active player in the service process. The service organization's role is to provide opportunities and resources to assist the person in choosing and achieving outcomes. Supports help the person to increase individual capability and to remove barriers. Acting in partnership requires shared responsibility for movement toward desired outcomes.

Clearly Define Support Roles for the Organization and Staff

The role and responsibility shared by the organization and staff in support of outcomes for people cannot be uniformly defined. Answering the question "What should we do?" requires reflection about individual desires, capabilities, and needs and the organization's commitments and resources. Mission statements give parameters for identifying and tailoring supports for each consumer. Roles are defined through person-by-person interaction, using the organization's mission statement as a guideline.

Be Creative in Developing Supports for People

Because people have different preferences and desires, they need staff to be creative in their thinking about ways to use resources for support. Creativity requires thinking beyond the boundaries of existing options. It also may require envisioning things that have never been accomplished before. This is an essential aspect of supporting people with disabilities to achieve outcomes. Staff members need to remember that defining or evaluating the person's desired outcomes is not part of their job. Rather, their job is to support the exploration and movement toward outcome attainment.

A FRAMEWORK FOR
PERFORMANCE IMPROVEMENT WITH OUTCOMES

Quality improvement requires a combination of leadership, commitment, and belief in the possibility of change. The biggest dilemma facing managers is how to design an approach that is simple, clear, and consistent that also leaves room for creativity. Organizational change efforts often get bogged down in the technical processes of quality improvement. Quality improvement committees are formed to address identified problems, data are collected, and new processes are designed and implemented. People struggle to use quality tools, such as surveys, decision trees, process controls, and benchmarking, only to eventually lose momentum and touch with the priorities that originally motivated the change effort. Over time, little is truly changed.

Producing change in human services organizations requires a strong connection to the constituencies of the organization. Alliances between the providers of services and the users of services can be productive sources of creativity and motivation for service improvement. The most obvious and important constituency is the primary user and beneficiary of services—people with disabilities and their families. Quality improvement strategies are a structural support for responding to the need for change in a coordinated and deliberate fashion.

Development of an Outcome-Based Approach

An outcome-based approach to organizational change places the people with disabilities at the center of organizational consciousness. One obvious benefit of using data from personal outcome measurements to guide change is that the collected information reflects the impact of these multiple constituencies. Collecting data on outcomes for people provides a focus for beginning an internal dialogue about improvement.

Outcome data collected from consumers can describe the status of outcomes for a group of people according to each person's individual criteria. Furthermore, the data reflect the effectiveness of the organization in individualizing processes and supports for each person. Moreover, they present a snapshot of organizational performance in supporting critical outcomes for people that can be used to analyze the organization's strengths and weaknesses in many critical performance areas. Without data about what is happening for people, assessment and improvement discussions often are driven by feelings, perceptions, and personal or professional opinions about services.

The elements for an outcome-directed approach to performance improvement are practical steps for implementing person-centered principles of service in organizations. They are presented as a step-by-step process to guide organizations through decision making. Decisions about how to organize and support personal outcomes are rarely simple and clear; instead, these decisions are usually complex and require coordinated analysis of many variables. Outcome-based quality improvement processes support staff so that they can routinely engage in this analysis at many levels throughout the organization. Organizational improvement planning is not a magical process. It can help people to work through perceived and real barriers to providing meaningful supports for people. It also can create a sense of cohesion and commitment to a common goal. Engaging in the planning process, however, does not ensure successful change in organizational performance.

Developing plans to direct improvements in service organizations differs from traditional planning. Annual planning processes and plans often produce goals that flow from current activity and reflect incremental improvements within existing structures (Hamel & Prahalad, 1989). Planning for quality improvement requires a process that challenges current practice and produces strategic plans for fundamental change in the organization to enhance performance. The goal of effective improvement planning is to create capacity and understanding within the organization to support a new way of doing business. This requires more that just detailed instructions and action plans that tell people what to do. The seven elements of effective improvement planning are 1) defining mission and purpose, 2) identifying outcomes for people, 3) aligning services and supports with outcomes, 4) developing resource management and procurement plans, 5) addressing human resources needs, 6) reviewing and adjusting organizational structure for support, and 7) tracking performance and providing feedback.

Defining Mission and Purpose   Most organizations have developed a statement of mission and purpose. The following questions concerning the organization's mission can be addressed during improvement activities: 1) Do staff members understand the organization's mission? 2) Can all staff members describe how they contribute to implementation of the mission? and 3) How functional is the mission? It is commonly accepted that the organization's mission must be visible and known by all. But even in organizations in which the mission hangs on the wall or is carried in the wallets of all staff members, real understanding of the mission can be weak.

The organization's mission and purpose provide the foundation for assessing the organization's performance and priorities in a quality improvement process. A mission statement answers the basic questions of "Why does the organization exist?" and "What is our role in the lives of people we support?". The mission statement of a service organization should clearly state who is supported and the expected relationship and responsibilities of the service transaction. The mission statement should reflect a clear commitment to personal outcomes as well as to clinical and functional goals. Without a clear statement of mission and values, it is difficult if not near impossible, to assess whether organizational performance is consistent with expectations. Lack of clarity about mission also deprives staff of direction about organizational priorities.

Successful improvement processes create opportunities for all staff members to discuss the mission in personal terms. The meaning conveyed by the mission must be clear so that staff can translate the mission into day-to-day action. Discussions of the organization's mission and values can occur in many forums. Often, they are the primary subject of formal training sessions and staff retreats. In reality, the discussion of mission and purpose most likely needs to be a standard part of many different interactions between leadership and staff as well as any staff meeting or other group agenda.

Identifying Outcomes for People   The second critical step in service improvement planning is to understand which outcomes are most important to the people supported by the organization. This is best accomplished through the systematic collection of data on the outcomes desired by the organization's consumers. This process requires that the organization have a mechanism for documenting and collecting information about each person's unique requirements. Conducting interviews with a sample of people supported by the organization in different ways makes this a manageable task and provides a database that represents the organization's performance in supporting personal outcomes.

Collecting data on outcomes begins the internal dialogue about improvement priorities. Outcome measurement data that are collected from a representative sample of people illustrate a number of things. They describe the status of outcomes for the individuals in the sample according to each person's own criteria; and they reflect the effectiveness of the organization in individualizing supports for each person in the sample. Some organizations find it useful to compare perceptions of performance with actual performance data on outcomes. This can be done through a process of asking staff members to note what they believe to be significant capabilities, strengths, and accomplishments in relation to each group of personal outcomes before actual data on personal outcomes are collected or reviewed. Based on this self-reporting, a rating is then given to each outcome indicating whether it represents an area of strength or an area for improvement. These data then are compared with the data collected through personal interviews.

Aligning Services and Supports with Outcomes   The alignment of services and supports with the priority outcomes for people enables the organization to see where supports and services match up with people's needs. The desired goal is to deliver only those services that are effective in supporting people to achieve the outcomes that are meaningful in their lives. If the services do not contribute to people's desired outcomes, then the organization is expending resources on activities that do not produce people's desired results.

The process of alignment starts with reviewing data collected about people's outcomes. Data collected also must include information about the presence of individualized processes that support outcomes. It is important to look at organizational performance for both outcomes and processes to complete an analysis of strengths and gaps in services.

The data can be studied in a variety of ways for performance analysis. Two critical questions to consider are 1) What outcomes and processes are present for a majority of people? and 2) What outcomes and processes are not present for a majority of people? The information generated through this questioning process provides direction for the continued examination of organizational performance. Those areas in which process is present (even when outcomes are not) can be identified as strengths. Learning about the type of organizational actions that are effectively supporting people indicate supports and resources that are essential for people. The areas in which process is not present (even where outcomes are present) reflect areas in which there is a difficulty with resources. This may be a breakdown in the effective use of resources or a lack of resources in the type or quantity required by people supported by the organization. Performance improvement requires further examination of these areas.

Developing Resource Management and Procurement Plans

A challenge of leadership is to connect organizational resources to the people needing support. This analysis begins with information about the outcomes that are most important for people and the organization's strengths and weaknesses in the processes that support outcomes. The organization first asks questions about how specific processes are working (or not working) and about which resources are needed but are unavailable. Then, leaders ask questions about how existing resources can be shifted and used differently to support people. Finally, managers consider what additional resources are required and whether the organization will secure these through internal development or alliances with other potential community partners.

Organizations frequently cite lack of adequate funding as the most common reason for poor performance. The same organizations, however, may not have conducted a review of how resources are being used to support people's outcomes. Outcome measurement data can help managers begin a reevaluation of resource usage. Discussions among staff following the collection of outcome data from people receiving services can answer questions such as the following:

- Which resources are not being used in a manner that supports outcomes?
- Which resources are not contributing to outcomes at all?
- Which resources are needed but are not available?

Resource analysis is enhanced by collecting specific information about organizational processes that contribute to outcomes (e.g., identifying organizational practices or activities that promote community participation or the best possible health). By learning about why certain practices work and in which situations, the organization has guidance for expanding the most relevant and useful resources. If practices are found to be ineffective at supporting outcomes, then these activities may be discontinued to free resources for other purposes. These additional data provide information about organizational actions that contribute to the improvement process. The individual data provide staff with individual stories that illustrate the need for changes in practice.

Addressing Human Resources Needs   People resources and the competency of an organization's employees are its greatest assets and challenges for organizational management. Human resources are the primary method for ensuring that services satisfy the customer. Staff must have the knowledge, skill, and authority to respond to and satisfy needs in the service delivery process. Corrections after the interaction or delays in response time can, in themselves, be indicators of service problems. Constant reevaluation of employee knowledge, learning, and support needs determines service quality.

Overreliance on standardized policy and procedure can prevent or discourage staff from individualizing supports. Conversely, lack of policy or procedure can allow too much room for individual action. Organizations need policy that describes the principles that should guide staff actions. Policy also serves to describe the boundaries—making clear where staff members have the discretion to act and where they do not.

Human services organizations require knowledgeable staff who can direct the flow of appropriate resources for each person. This is accomplished through a combination of training and supervision. Training and supervision feedback enable staff to put principles into action. Daily feedback on the principles of policy in action enable staff to learn how to make use of the organization's policy information. Supervisors exercise primary responsibility for translating the organization's policies into action.

Reviewing and Adjusting Organizational Structure for Support During the improvement process, the value of making changes in organizational reporting relationships or groupings is considered in the context of creating new or more functional working relationships. For example, in some organizations service coordinators or case managers assigned to programs often fail to provide comprehensive and effective coordination for people. The service coordinator's focus and interactions often are limited by the boundaries of the program and by supervision. Information needed may be unavailable or located in another program. Possible structural responses to this situation could include removing service coordination from the program responsibility or having service coordinators from different programs meet together to work through information and resource-sharing needs.

Organizing staff and resources through structure is a tool that promotes effective and efficient patterns of work. The structure of an organization reinforces the mission and values of the organization. Structure also can facilitate the functional efficiency of organizational operations. In many instances, programs or professions dictate structure. A commitment to personal outcomes requires flexibility in structure. Organizational structure is modified to enable people to provide the supports that facilitate outcomes.

Tracking Performance and Providing Feedback The last step in the improvement process is planning and providing opportunity for tracking progress and providing feedback concerning the organizational successes and challenges in the improvement process. Quality improvement plans are statements of direction and commitment. They identify staff members' responsibilities for the effectiveness of service activities. Plans are written to provide information to employees and to people receiving support and their families.

People often agonize about developing improvement plans. The process, however, not the plan, drives action. Plans document key information for communication and evaluation. The development of performance improvement plans define

- Desired change (statement of goal or outcome)
- Strategies for achieving the desired end
- Action steps for implementing strategies
- Expected time lines for implementation
- Assignment of responsibility

The plan is an expression of the organization's vision for change and reflects the values and priorities of the organization. The information is more important than the format. A written plan describes priorities and procedures for the organization's performance improvement effort. Sharing information about quality improvement links all employees to the improvement effort. Communication facilitates the exchange of information, joint problem identification, and problem solving. Communication also creates an internal benchmark against which future performance can be measured.

Implementing the Steps to Effective Improvement Planning

Although the steps in the previous section are discussed sequentially, they do not necessarily require sequential implementation. In fact, as individual comfort level increases, skills improve, and the system evolves within the organization, these steps are implemented simultaneously. Staff directly supporting people with disabilities face daily decisions about the type and intensity of service interactions necessary to facilitate individual outcomes. As middle managers problem solve with staff, they identify whether their current plans support individuals and optimize shared resources. A coordinated quality improvement effort enables the data collected by staff about desired outcomes and needs for support to be aggregated so that decisions about resources and design issues can be made based on real information about organizational strengths and challenges.

A productive planning process evolves over time from leaders' interactions and dialogue about performance. Performance improvement takes place when people work together, ask questions, gather data, and evaluate alternatives for action. The plan or planning format is not important. Implementation is sustained by the commitment for action developed among participants in the planning process.

Learning about the outcomes that people with disabilities value is a powerful tool for change in the human services organization. Staff should understand that services and supports are justified only when they result in personal outcome. Using an outcomes-based approach, however, requires discipline. It involves more than just asking people what they want. The process of outcome measurement forces people to carefully collect information about people's life priorities. This allows an evaluation of how the person's current circumstances match their expectations.

Staying focused on people is difficult in human services organizations because many priorities compete for attention. Program funding, regulations, staffing, and many other day-to-day realities draw attention from what is most important to the people using the organization's services and supports. In addition, understanding outcomes for one person, or a small group of people, will not be enough. Some generalizations can be made with these data, but care must be given to avoid overgeneralization about the needs of people sharing common characteristics. Achievement of outcomes requires continuous learning about personal priorities and accommodating different priorities within the organizational system. The following are prescriptions for accommodating organizational change:

1. *Focus on one person at a time.*   Making change within a large organization can be overwhelming. One practical and simple strategy is to focus attention on one person at a time. The strategy recognizes the power of experience. People learn best from real-life examples.

2. *Celebrate success.*   Small steps toward success can lose power if not highlighted and celebrated. Organizations often expect staff to implement new procedures and processes without support or feedback. Individual success stories effectively communicate desired results and reinforce individual efforts. Celebration of small successes provides opportunity for everyone to assess and adjust action based on concrete descriptions of real situations.

3. *Measure, measure, measure.*   Making changes in organizational process will not guarantee meaningful change. New methods of work without a means for individualizing and evaluating effectiveness are likely to fail. Data provide an objective point of reference in the change process. Although people often experience change emotionally, data can bring the group focus back to reality. Measuring the process produces learning. Furthermore, people often have experienced measurement as punishment. Performance standards led to compliance behavior. People were chastised if performance benchmarks were not achieved. Measurement does not have to be a negative experience. Data that are used for analysis, not judgment, can support the critical thinking and creative problem solving that is the fuel for continuous improvement.

4. *Create a learning culture.*   Whereas planning for change can result in new behaviors and processes, Beckhard and Pritchard propose that "learning by doing" (1992, p. 9) is probably the most important part of the change process. The complexity of large-scale change in organizations demands that attention be given to what is learned through implementation. The periodic

modification of original plans does not reflect a flaw in the planning process but rather the organization's commitment to success. The reinforcement of patterns of behavior that reflect learning through experience builds a culture of success.

Although many organizations recognize the need for learning from action, few take steps to ensure that this occurs during the change process. Improvement plans are developed and then delegated to others for implementation. Few managers recognize the need to create an authority structure within the organization that holds specific responsibility for mentoring the implementation process and incorporating the learning that occurs with experience. Furthermore, a project's success should be measured throughout the change process not just at the end. Because measured results often demonstrate that the amount of change occurring is not consistent with expectations, periodic reevaluation that allows for modification of plans in accordance with experience keeps the momentum going and allows many more people within the organization to contribute to and direct performance improvements.

MANAGING THROUGH TRANSITIONS

In his discussion of organizational transitions, Bridges noted that "it isn't the changes that do you in, it's the transitions" (1991, p. 3). Although people often talk of the complexity of making change in organizations, what they are really referring to is the difficulty of helping people to make transitions from what is familiar to what is unknown. These personal transitions are at the heart of successful change.

Resistance, a natural product of the change process, is easily recognized. Few people welcome the prospect of leaving behind familiar patterns of behavior. Although resistance is not desired, its presence indicates that people feel the effects of change efforts. Lack of resistance in any major change initiative may signal a lack of progress with implementation. Information and education can facilitate and support the implementation of change. People often resist new ways of acting because they are comfortable with what they know, and they are unsure of what is to come. Opportunities to explore new ideas and ways of operating can support people to be successful with making change.

Changing Roles

Another element of transition is to readjust organizational roles. Using personal outcomes to drive services will require a transition in staff roles. The traditional role of "caregiver" with the accompanying responsibility of minimizing negative consequences conflicts with the new role of promoting the achievement of outcomes. Adoption of this new role occurs through personal, not professional, interaction. Once priorities are understood, staff members use their skills, training, and experience to facilitate outcomes.

Outcome-driven supports create individual networks that reach beyond the traditional boundaries of the organization to assist people to achieve their goals. Because the development of individual supports is guided by the person's priorities, each person's network of supports will reflect the people, places, and resources that are most important and meaningful to the individual. A person's network of personal support may include family, friends, co-workers, and neighbors, as well as staff.

Achieving the person's outcome is not solely a support staff responsibility. There are many things that may influence the achievement of personally valued outcomes in people's lives, including the activities of organizational management. Role transitions also will occur for the organizational leadership. There is a distinct difference between traditional requirements for managing organizational functions and leading an organizational learning and improvement effort. Managing is typically associated with the bureaucratic processes of tracking and control. Leading, however, reflects a balance between involvement in day-to-day activities and maintenance of a focus on the larger strategic picture. Although management processes encouraged the inclusion of people in different organizational roles in planning and decision-making tasks, the traditional hierarchical management approach leaves overall responsibility clearly with the manager. This creates tension for many managers. Managers are torn between sharing responsibility for making decisions and still being held responsible for the decisions. Understanding leadership requirements may assist with resolving this dilemma.

MANAGEMENT AND LEADERSHIP RESPONSIBILITIES

Leadership does not mean that the leader gives up responsibility or only pays attention to the "big picture." On the contrary, to ensure good leadership, the leader's presence must permeate the organization. A leader's attention is focused on the outcome or vision of the future. In discussions with support staff, the leader asks, "How does this contribute to the outcome we want?".

Leadership means questioning support structures and inviting ideas and suggestions for change from throughout the organization. Leaders recognize that support staff may operate within different frames of reference. Leaders do not try to second guess; instead, they seek to deepen and clarify staff members' understanding of the organizational mission and desired outcomes so that everyone can be more successful and productive. A prime responsibility of leaders is to ensure that the organization supports the staff to achieve the mission by providing the necessary tools, resources, and assistance.

Coaching is an important part of leading change. This process encourages managers to identify and clarify their expectations and to set goals for performance that guide performance. Setting individual expectations and goals is critical for supporting performance improvement. Coaching and mentoring interactions also help to improve communication about work among all staff members.

Individual experience and application of principles associated with supporting outcomes must be connected to a larger organizational change effort. The manager is responsible for laying the foundation for ongoing improvement. Major change in any human services organization is based on values and policies about people. This type of change is pervasive, and there is an impact on all aspects of the organization. No person or activity will remain untouched. Employee attitudes on issues such as autonomy, capability, and choice making will change. But does this mean that the improvement process should focus on changing attitudes? Leaders often face the choice of initiating change in attitude or behavior. Changing attitudes is intensive and expensive. It requires leadership that is well trained and an investment in hours of employee involvement that does not relate directly to the accomplishment of work tasks. In contrast, change processes can target staff behaviors. Training programs designed to instruct staff in new processes such as person-centered planning are based on the belief that if performance expectations change, changes in attitude and performance will follow. These approaches, however, often fail due to lack of clarity about expected results. Behavior change, in the absence of specific outcome criteria, frequently fails to produce long-term change.

Outcome-based approaches to change, however, focus on results. The process moves backward through the performance cycle to have an impact on process; behavior; and, ultimately, attitudes. People learn new ways of working through understanding which organizational processes facilitate outcomes in individual situations. Another benefit of changing processes to support different outcomes is that the approach does not emphasize personal or group failure.

Instead, it provides an opportunity for each employee to contribute to the improvement effort without being identified as the problem. The problem is framed as a lack of alignment between organizational action and the outcomes desired by people. The proper alignment is not determined by external forces but through an understanding of each person's unique circumstances. The challenge for the work group, therefore, is to understand individual requirements and engineer processes that will support the identified priority outcomes. The following discussion highlights some issues—maintaining the clarity of vision, recognizing and rewarding success, and sustaining and redirecting energy through vision—that require leadership during the change process.

Maintaining the Clarity of Vision

Organizations pay too little attention to the process of developing improvement plans. The form or structure of the plan is less important than the "picture" that the plan describes. Plans that capture the vision of a new or different future as "pictured" by organizational leadership and key stakeholders have a greater chance for success than plans that are well formulated but do not address the priorities or constituency. Participation of stakeholders is critical to successful implementation, and leaders create the shared understanding and commitment to change that supports progress.

Recognizing and Rewarding Success

The type of support and rewards needed to reinforce new patterns of action is different for different people. Top managers may be independent, self-directed, self-rewarding learners. Their job tasks involve engagement in planning and strategic discussions that support individual and collective learning. Direct support staff by contrast often depend on leadership to provide behavioral cues about desired performance. There are many ways to recognize and reward people, including verbal praise, promotion, awards, and publication of efforts. The means used should fit the situation and person, but an effective reward system is essential for reinforcing desired new behaviors.

Sustaining and Redirecting Energy Through Vision

Strong leadership vision keeps everyone focused on the main goal. Consistency in quality improvement priorities is especially critical to the success of change efforts in service organizations. Lack of clarity about the focus and purpose of services creates chaos in practice. Service process and organizational requirements can override the individual rationale for service action. When many different activities occur in the name of quality (e.g., task forces, licensing reviews, health inspections, self-assessments), the staff's energy can be pulled in many different directions. Strong leadership vision sustains momentum by redirecting energy and attention from lesser priorities.

REDEFINING MANAGEMENT'S ROLE

The role of management and leadership in an organization concerned with outcomes for people is being redefined. Emphasis shifts from control thinking and acting to vision communication and nurturing capabilities. Skills and behaviors that lead people in critical thinking replaces management emphasis on behavior control. This new leadership mandate begins with assuming responsibility for supporting staff in the same manner that staff are expected to support people with disabilities. Using the same principles of individual respect and involvement, the manager concerned with achieving outcomes for people works with staff to understand the range of unique circumstances among employees.

Leaders clarify the organization's mission that guides implementation of outcomes with people. This enables staff members to define the organization's role in the lives of the people for whom they provide support. Through interactions with individuals receiving supports, staff members define the responsibility of the organization for providing services. The leadership delegates responsibility for making decisions about service interactions by providing the resources and supports for staff to support individual outcomes. The leader also prevents the organization from returning to comfort and complacency with accomplishments.

The questions that leaders must ask are characterized by the degree of change or challenge to existing practice. Leaders support staff by providing safety in changing the organizational role. This change often exceeds what staff members are typically comfortable making as individuals. The following are some questions that leaders can ask as they shift the organization's paradigm to a person-centered, outcomes-based service provider:

- Who are we? What is our organizational identity?
- What have we learned about people and outcomes?
- What stories do we have to tell that will increase our understanding?
- What trends can we find in our experience and success?
- What opportunities are there for growth and change?

The ultimate role of the leadership is to lead by example. Leaders model the values for the organization to make them come alive for the staff. Commitments to learning and change are communicated by the behavior of top management. Managers who are more concerned with maintaining stability than with providing effective service cannot promote the flexibility needed to be responsive to the individuals whom they serve.

CONCLUSIONS

Changing an organization's orientation to a clear and firm focus on people is a long-term project. It requires careful examination of how organizational processes contribute to each person's life priorities. Direction is obtained through shared learning about achievement of personal outcomes. The required change cannot be accomplished through simple modification of policy or changes in practice. Instead, meaningful and lasting change takes time. A leader cannot change the way employees think about and interact with people supported by his or her organization simply by altering policy procedure or organizational structure. Fundamental change in the work of the organization must occur through long-term interactions among all of the stakeholders. Responsiveness to people reflects the integration of technical knowledge about the support process with the values of the service role. Ultimate success in becoming a person-centered organization comes from building the organization's capacity for learning, problem solving, and change, which enables the organization to respect and respond to the unique needs of each person seeking support.

REFERENCES

Barker, J.A. (1992). *Paradigms: The business of discovering the future.* New York: Harper Business.

Deal, T.E., & Kennedy, A.A. (1982). *Corporate cultures: The rites and rituals of corporate life.* Reading, MA: Addison-Wesley.

French, W.L., & Bell, C.H. (1978). *Organization development.* Upper Saddle River, NJ: Prentice-Hall.

Hamel, G., & Prahalad, C.K. (1989, May–June). Strategic intent. *Harvard Business Review,* 63–76.

Rogers, E.M. (1995). *Diffusion of innovations* (4th ed.). New York: The Free Press.

Schon, D.A. (1983). *The reflective practitioner.* New York: Basic Books.

Whitely, R., & Hessan, D. (1996). *Customer-centered growth.* Reading, MA: Addison-Wesley.

Woodward, H. (1994). *Navigating through change.* Burr Ridge, IL: Irwin Professional Publishing.

RECOMMENDED READINGS

Beckhard, R., & Pritchard, W. (1992). *Changing the essence: The art of creating and leading fundamental change in organizations.* San Francisco: Jossey-Bass.

Block, P. (1993). *Stewardship: Choosing service over self interest.* San Francisco: Berrett-Koehler.

Bridges, W. (1991). *Managing transitions: Making the most of change.* Reading, MA: Addison-Wesley.

Dykstra, A. (1995). *Outcome management: Achieving outcomes for people with disabilities.* East Dundee, IL: High Tide Press.

Senge, P. (1990). *The fifth discipline: The art and practice of the learning organization.* New York: Bantam Doubleday.

Tunks, R. (1992). *Fast track to quality.* New York: McGraw-Hill.

9

Perspectives
on Leadership

James F. Gardner

Academic journals and the popular press provide a detailed discussion of leadership. Unfortunately, the academic perspective, which is based on empirical research, stresses the quality of the research rather than the practical applications of leadership (Yukl, 1994). In contrast, the popular press produces readable, and sometimes compelling, formulas for successful leadership, management, and organizational success. But because the popular accounts of leadership frequently are based on case studies and other anecdotal approaches, readers are often cautious about generalizing the theories and advice to the real world of the organization. The purpose of this chapter is to provide an overview of the discussion of themes in leadership in organizational settings. Rather than exploring the detailed research in specific issues or repeating the admonitions and advice of leading consultants, this chapter describes an emerging orientation to leadership.

THE IMPORTANCE OF LEADERSHIP

Social and economic changes in the 1990s have increased the emphasis on leadership. In the industrial era with centralized bureaucracies, acknowledged leaders occupied the top of organizational hierarchies. In the decentralized postindustrial society, leaders and leadership are distributed throughout organizations.

Automation and computerization have transformed the unskilled laborer of the mid-20th century into the knowledge worker of today. Freed from the time and drudgery of physical labor, employees in the late 1990s are able to plan and design new and better machines and design and implement new processes that enhance efficiency and effectiveness. In the agricultural age, workers battled nature. In the industrial era, workers harnessed the machine. In the information age, knowledge workers will have to learn to get along with each other. Paradoxical as it may seem, greater technology and automation require greater interpersonal and leadership skills because knowledge workers are being freed from their repetitive, machine-based jobs to work together, plan, and create new methods for accomplishing the work of the organization.

The increasing complexity and sophistication of medical and rehabilitative technology has altered the coordination of work. In the simple and routine performance of individual tasks, specific plans, policies, and procedures can guide employees; as individual performances are linked in sequence and across space, schedules and flowcharts are added to the plans and policies. Complex technologies, however, require more than schedules and plans. Mutual feedback, whether human or cybernetic, guides the utilization of complex technology. The surgical team in the operating room, the space shuttle crew, and the rehabilitation team all conduct their business through mutual feedback.

In a human services organization, mutual feedback can provide the leader with information and data from both employees and people with disabilities. No longer are annual performance evaluations for employees or annual individual program plan reviews for people with disabilities sufficient to guide organizational activity. Instead, leadership requires coordinating mutual feedback among all shareholders. In this paradigm, leaders must recognize that everyone within the organizational system is always learning and changing. All parties react to the activity of the organization while simultaneously affecting the future direction of the organization. The effective leader recognizes the real-time nature of change and encourages feedback from all of the organization's representatives.

The certainty and continuity of the low-technology, centralized, and bureaucratic hierarchy have declined. Human services organizations are no longer able to provide directives and rules that guide employees and people with disabilities in decision making in all instances. In contrast, the constantly changing environments provide the learning laboratory for designing new and better criteria for decision making.

A Paradigm Shift

Managing and leading the organization in today's marketplace requires a different set of values, experiences, and expectations than management and leadership in the mid-1950s (Raelin, 1991). In the 1990s, knowledge professionals bring creative insights, technical skills, and sophisticated content mastery to the job. Employees want greater discretion in accomplishing their work, and people with disabilities want organizational activity that facilitates their priority outcomes. In addition, the restructuring and downsizing occurring since the early 1980s have reduced organizational layers and increased the span of control (i.e., the number of people supervised by a manager). Workforce shortages and greater diversity in work places add to the pressures on leaders. Older leadership models based on a command-and-control model are becoming extinct, whereas new models that offer increased worker discretion and autonomy are gaining momentum.

Numerous social, economic, and technological advances have increased the importance of leadership and people-oriented interaction. In the industrial age, organizational structures and rules, consistent and routine technology, and continuity in workers' roles and responsibilities provided substitutes for leadership. Organizations with marginal leadership survived because of these compensating variables. Many of the traditional compensating variables are eroding, leaving some leaders vulnerable and ill prepared for new circumstances.

Service Industry Growth

The continued growth of service industries has influenced the discussion of quality and the roles and responsibilities of leaders. In the production of goods, quality can be associated with the final product. As such, the final product can be inspected for conformity with specifications. Goods can be stockpiled or delivered just in time to the customer. The provision of a service, however, lacks a final product specification. In service delivery, the customer defines the specification of the service. Quality is determined at the time the service is rendered; there is no product that can be stockpiled, returned, or repaired.

This emphasis on the customer and the "moment of truth" when the service is rendered means that the definition of quality can vary from consumer to consumer and that any single person's criteria for quality may change over time. As a result, leaders are developing greater awareness of markets, consumers' preferences, and organizational capabilities for delivering those preferences. With this outside/inside perspective, leaders fuse organizational energy and resources to deliver services of high quality to consumers. Leaders in organizations serving people with disabilities recognize that personal outcomes have replaced program requirements as the starting point for organizational action planning. The definition of *quality* in services has changed from compliance with program and organizational process to being responsive to the person with the disability.

INSIGHTS FROM THE RESEARCH ON LEADERSHIP

The term *leadership* has varied meanings. Researchers define the term according to their individual interests. As such, each researcher begins with differing interests, insights, and expectations. As a result, the individual definition of *leadership research* does not focus the investigation. In addition, the variables often discussed with leadership, such as power, authority, vision, management, and responsibility, are often ambiguous and discussed without precision. Stogdill (1974) provided an analysis of leadership by examining such research perspectives as

- Leadership as a focus of group process
- Leadership as personality and its effects
- Leadership as the art of inducing compliance
- Leadership as the exercise of influence
- Leadership as behavior
- Leadership as a form of persuasion
- Leadership as an instrument of goal achievement
- Leadership as an effect of interaction

Stogdill concluded that "there are almost as many definitions of leadership as there are persons who have attempted to define the concept" (1974, p. 7). Yukl (1994) classified leadership research into six general approaches: trait approach, behavioral approach, power-influence approach, situational approach, participative leadership, and transformational and cultural leadership.

- *Trait Approach*   Numerous researchers in the 1930s and 1940s failed to find a set of traits that would consistently account for leadership success. The significant limitation in the research was the lack of attention to the intervening variables in the causal chain.

- *Behavioral Approach*   The failure of the trait research led researchers in the 1950s to investigate what leaders do on the job. Some investigators studied the nature of managerial work, whereas others compared the behavior of effective and ineffective leaders. The research on behavior and effectiveness has emphasized the micro level of leadership as a dyadic or group process. The results of the large research effort, unfortunately, have been "contradictory and inconclusive" (Yukl, 1994, p. 75).

- *Power-Influence Approach*   The power-influence approach attempts to describe leadership in terms of the interaction between leaders and followers. The research does indicate "that effective leaders rely more on personal power than position power" (Yukl, 1994, p. 217). Most of this research, unfortunately, concentrates more on "how managers gain power over subordinates than in how leaders empower subordinates to become change agents and lead the organization" (p. 248).

- *Situational Approach*   In contrast to universal approaches that define a "best" leadership style for all situations, the situational or contingency approach indicates that there is no best leadership style that can be applied to all situations. Although the various theories provide insights into the reasons for leadership effectiveness, conceptual weaknesses limit their utility in practice. And as some critics contend, few leaders have the time to analyze all of the variables to identify the best practice in each situation.

- *Participative Leadership*   The participative leadership approach emphasizes the benefits of shared leadership, delegation, and self-directed teams. Although the research is not conclusive, it does suggest that participative leadership, delegation, and self-directed teams do facilitate greater motivation, commitment, and better quality of products and services and organizational efficiencies in certain circumstances than when the leader or supervisor makes decisions alone.

- *Transformational and Cultural Leadership*   Transformational leaders develop a vision, bring internal and external stakeholders together around that vision, formulate strategies to reach the vision, and cement the new values and assumptions in the organizational culture. Theory and research on organizational culture have isolated key aspects of leader behavior and organizational mechanisms that influence organizational culture. A potential downside to the transformational leadership style is a lack of introspection. Leaders and followers are so attracted by a single vision that they become locked in "groupthink" and fail to consider alternative visions or strategies.

THE ART OF LEADERSHIP

The limited contribution of academic investigators to the practical side of organizational life has resulted in a deluge of management, leadership, and organizational management literature from the popular press. Some of this literature is trendy and questionable. Much of it promises a quick fix through "ten essential principles," "five leadership strategies," or some other number of recommendations for organizational leadership. Books on leadership lessons have been based on the lives and writings of personalities from Abraham Lincoln, Attila the Hun, Captain Kirk, and Moses. Animals apparently provide appealing metaphors for management and leadership authors. We are provided advice by the *Flight of the Buffalo* (Belasco & Stayer, 1993), the *Strategy of the Dolphin* (Lynch & Kordis, 1988), and *Teaching the Elephant to Dance* (Belasco, 1990).

The more meaningful descriptor of the emerging management and leadership literature is that of art. In *Managing as a Performing Art,* Peter Vail used the performing arts to express the "dynamism, fluidity, extraordinary complexity, and fundamental personalness of all organizational change" (1989, p. xiv). Max DePree, in *Leadership Is an Art,* noted that "leadership is an art, something to be learned over time, not simply by reading books. Leadership is more tribal than science, more a weaving of relationships than an amassing of information" (1989, p. 3). These themes of dynamism, complexity, personalness, and relationships extend throughout much of the leadership literature from the 1990s. They interconnect with other themes of organizational learning, personal reflection, and reframing.

The metaphor of leadership as art indicates that leadership develops through performance and reflection on performance. Feedback from all representatives in the organization contributes to this reflection and encourages additional personnel toward development of leadership skills. The metaphor of leadership as an art indicates that there are no proven methods of leadership that can address all situations. Like jazz or improvisational theater, leadership is learned and expanded through the performance itself. Leadership arises not out of textbooks or pseudoacademic self-help guides but rather out of doing and learning from doing.

LEADERSHIP AND THE NEW SCIENCE

The distinction between art and science has traditionally rested on the presence of guidelines and rules that guide decision making. Art is depicted as "figuring it out as you go along," because there are few established guidelines. Science, in contrast, implies a full set of guidelines and empirical evidence to guide choice making. But, the new science of quantum mechanics suggests that science often presents unknowns and that science is more similar to art than dissimilar.

Some portion of contemporary leadership theory is drawn from the transformation in scientific thinking from a work of Newtonian Physics to the world of quantum mechanics and chaos theory. The machine was the metaphor for the Newtonian world. Made up of many smaller parts, the machine could be broken down and analyzed. After examining the individual parts, the machine could be reassembled. Comprehension and knowledge followed the analysis of smaller and smaller pieces of reality. This same model was applied to large hierarchical and bureaucratic organizations. Through the use of technical analysis, managers focused understanding on individual functions and units of activity. At the turn of the 20th century, Max Weber developed the language of bureaucracy, which included *division of labor, hierarchy of authority, hiring by technical qualifications,* and *rules* and *controls.* Several years later, Henry Fayol (Wren, 1979) defined the 14 principles of management (see Table 9.1). The Newtonian world of science and the scientific and administrative theory that supported the bureaucratic world began to falter even as they arose. The machine was no longer the relevant metaphor for the organization. Modern science suggests that art may provide a better metaphor.

In the world of quantum theory and chaos theory, the classical notion of ever smaller solid objects dissolves into wave-like patterns of probability. The result, Capra noted, is that "the sub-atomic particles—and therefore, ultimately, all parts of the universe—cannot be understood as isolated entities but must be defined

Table 9.1.   Fayol's 14 principles of management

Division of work	Authority	Discipline
Unity of command	Unity of direction	Subordination of individual interest
Remuneration	Centralization	Line of authority
Order	Equity	Stability of tenure of personnel
Initiative	Esprit de corps	

Source: Wren (1979).

through their interrelations" (1982, p. 80). The subatomic world appears as a web of relationships within a unified whole (Capra, 1991). Referring to the world of quantum physics, Wheatley (1994) noted that connections and relationships rather than separate entities are the fundamental realities of life. Wheatley asked,

> If the physics of our universe is revealing the primacy of relationships, is it any wonder that we are beginning to reconfigure our ideas about management in relational terms[?]. . . Even organizational power is a quantum event. One evening I had a long exploratory talk with a wise friend who told me that 'power in organizations is the capacity generated by relationships.' It is a real energy that can only come into existence through relationships. Ever since that conversation, I have changed what I pay attention to in an organization. Now I look carefully at how a workplace organizes its relationships; not its tasks, functions, and hierarchies, but the patterns of relationships and the capacities available to form them. (1994, pp. 12–13, 38–39)

Leaders are responsible for encouraging the messy and sometimes confusing development of systems of associations and connections within organizations. These systems of interactions cannot be determined ahead of time; they cannot be predicted. In contrast, leaders provide positive energy that enables employees to explore associations and connections. Leaders create an environment in which people can learn, take chances, and make mistakes. In this manner, people create the relationship systems for accomplishing the work of the organization (Wheatley & Kellner-Rogers, 1996). Senge defined leaders as designers, stewards, and teachers: "They are responsible for building organizations where people continually expand their capabilities to understand complexity, clarify vision, and improve shared mental models—that is, they are responsible for learning" (1990, p. 340). Senge's view of leadership is not consistent with the traditional view of leaders as heroic individuals who have answers, make the key decisions, energize people and, ultimately, save the day. This traditional view was based on the belief that the leaders at the top of the hierarchy alone possessed the ability to take command, and the majority of employees at the bottom of the hierarchy were unmotivated and unwilling to take responsibility. Change, therefore, came from the few great leaders located in the upper echelons of the organization.

LEADERSHIP MYTHS AND COMPETENCIES

Management and leadership books and manuals published in the late 1990s provide a wide range advice—from sound to dubious—on how to manage and how to be a leader. Many of the recommendations in these volumes, however, are based on the same, seldom-challenged myths. McLean and Weitzel (1991) identified a number of leadership myths. Some of them are as follows:

- *Charisma Is a Necessary Leadership Quality*   Commitment to and communication of the organizational vision and an ability to support and sustain others in quest of the vision is the more important quality than possessing charisma. Al Gore and Frank Perdue are not particularly charismatic, but they are leaders with visions.
- *Leaders Can Never Be Wrong*   Thomas Edison tried more than 3,000 laboratory experiments before he finally produced a working light. In other words, he was wrong many times before he was right.
- *Leadership Means Being Consistent*   In a constantly changing world, consistency for consistency's sake alone is an organizational dead weight. Employees need to know what is expected of them. Communicating change and the reasons for change are a leader's priorities.
- *Leaders Should Always Know the Goal in Advance*   Leaders need visions that give energy to organizations. They need to communicate those visions and build coalitions of support for the organizing visions. Leaders, however, formulate the organization's goals and strategies out of a dialogue with employees, customers, suppliers, and others. Our research indicates that the answers begin to emerge only after the organization begins to act.

In contrast to these myths, Bennis (1989b, 1993) has written frequently of the four competencies of leadership. In a study of 90 effective leaders, Bennis found the following four competencies:

- *Management of Attention*   Leaders communicate a focus of commitment that draws people into a consensus. They set forth an unambiguous vision, goal, or direction.
- *Management of Meaning*   Leaders communicate that vision through the assembly of facts, concepts, and anecdotes into meaning for followers. Leaders use metaphors, stories, models, and symbols to clarify visions. They make visions tangible and real to others.
- *Management of Trust*   Leaders must display consistency in their values and vision. This reliability over time infuses trust into the organization. Trust is an essential part of all organizations.
- *Management of Self*   Self-awareness and self-dialogue are critical. Knowledge of one's own skills, attitudes, limitations, and

lack of understanding is the basis for learning. Knowing when and how to act provides the beginning of learning.

FROM WARRIOR TO PHILOSOPHER

In contrast to the antiquated image of a leader as a warrior, more recent depictions cast the leader as a knowledgeable philosopher and describe leadership in terms of self-knowledge and reflection. Covey (1990) urged potential leaders to develop a personal mission statement. This personal mission statement defines the core values and principles that guide the leader in day-to-day decision making. Possession of these core values and principles enables the leader to move quickly and decisively in rapidly changing environments. Covey noted that "the key to the ability to change is a changeless sense of who you are, what you are about and what you value" (p. 108). The "leader as philosopher" builds upon, and perhaps modifies, these core values by engaging in continuous learning about him- or herself. Bennis (1989a, 1989b) described leadership in terms of self-knowledge and self-discovery. He described a process of inventing oneself through self-knowledge. Kouzes and Posner (1987) noted that the search for leadership in oneself is a quest for self-development. Wheatley and Kellner-Rogers (1996) emphasized that self-reflection leads the individual to the possibilities for change. Senge stated that

> The ability of such people to be natural leaders, as near as I can tell, is the by-product of a life time of effort—effort to develop conceptual and communication skills, to reflect on personal values and to align personal behavior with values. (1990, p. 359)

Self-discovery and personal awareness are part of a continuous process of questioning basic assumptions. At times, it is similar to a dialogue with oneself. According to Kouzes and Posner, leaders routinely ask questions such as the following:

- What are my strengths and weaknesses?
- How can I improve my abilities?
- How committed am I to my basic values and mission? To those of the organization? Are the two compatible?
- How much do I really understand about this organization? The external environment?
- Am I prepared to handle the complex problems facing the organization?
- Are people prepared to follow me?
- Am I the person to lead at this time? (1987, pp. 305–308)

Bennis presented a different list of questions for a self-dialogue:

- What do you believe are the qualities of leadership?
- What experiences were vital to your development?

- What were the turning points in your life?
- What role has failure played in your life?
- How did you learn?
- Are there people in your life, or in general, whom you particularly admire?
- What can organizations do to encourage or stifle leaders? (1989a, p. 7)

The leader as a philosopher approaches mistakes in a manner altogether different from the leader as a warrior. The leader as a warrior fears mistakes because they threaten his or her claim to invincibility. Mistakes threaten a manager's claim on power because of the cultural expectation that the leader is always the smartest. Modern-day bureaucracies push top-level managers to such rarefied heights of authority that the managers are not allowed to make mistakes. Mistakes and leadership, however, are mutually exclusive. When leaders are not allowed to make mistakes, they avoid mistakes by not acting. But, not acting precludes any further learning and erodes the process of self-discovery. The path to learning and self-discovery requires decision making and action; and these, in turn, require permission to make mistakes while engaging in the journey. Belasco and Stayer concluded that "knowledge is nothing without action. Nothing changes until you do something. What you do will directly determine what you learn" (1993, p. 313).

As opposed to the warrior leader, the philosopher leader does not worry about mistakes because, as Bennis wrote, "these leaders put all of their energy into their task[s]" (1993, p. 57). Philosopher leaders stay focused on positive goals. They avoid wasting negative energy on worry and mistakes. In addition, philosopher leaders treat mistakes as opportunities for learning. Successful managers reframe mistakes as the opportunity for self-discovery through decision making and action. Effective leaders do not seek failures, but they recognize the opportunity to learn from each failure. They reframe failures as learning opportunities rather than as tragedies. Belasco and Stayer (1993) recalled establishing a "Shot in the Foot Award" for the employee who both made the biggest mistake and learned the most from that mistake.

In analyzing the leadership style of Moses, Wildavsky noted that Moses' pattern of leadership was not "a matter of going from one success to another but of salvaging some success from each defeat" (1984, p. 207). What enabled Moses to endure defeat after defeat was his vision or purpose. The vision, noted Bennis and Nanus is "a target that beckons" (1985, p. 89). Having vision is different than having personal values or principles. The vision is the definition of the organization's future direction. The role of the leader is to guarantee that the organization follows the vision. At times, this will require charm and charisma. At other times, leaders may need to be hard and insensitive to keep the organization consistent with the vision and goals (Deal & Kennedy, 1982). Leadership style may change with the circumstances, but it always serves the mission and goals of the organization.

Hence, the main role of the leader is to develop a shared vision and goal for the organization. Leaders need for members of the organization to "buy in" to the vision and goals. Clear visions and futuristic goals, however, are pointless if they are not communicated, understood, and shared. This points to the distinction between visionaries and leaders. Visionaries develop futuristic goals and visions, but they stop short of communicating their goals and building coalitions around the visions. Effective leaders, however, communicate and develop coalitions of support around energizing visions. Lynch and Kordis (1988) urged leaders to communicate their visions using concrete ideas that encourage members of the organization to identify what the vision means for them individually. Without the shared vision, employees will go about incorporating their own interpretation of the vision into the fabric of the organization. Multiple definitions of vision dissipate organizational energy into different, and sometimes contradictory, directions.

The shared vision is the platform that supports other organizational endeavors. Strong strategic plans achieve the vision. Careful planning and communication bring employees into action; and the actions taken are evaluated in terms of their contributions to the vision. Although vision is no substitute for employee skills, motivation, and good management, it is possible to bring together skills, technology, and good people to achieve success through a common vision.

The importance of vision points to the difference between management and leadership. Management without leadership is, noted Covey, "like straightening deck chairs on the Titanic" (1990, p. 102). Both Bennis (1989a, 1989b) and Drucker (1954) have noted the difference between the terms *management* and *leadership*. Management is doing the job right. It is a matter of technique and method, analysis, and review. Leadership, in contrast, is doing the right job. Leadership requires vision and values, synthesis, and feedback. Covey conveyed the difference between leaders and managers by describing a group of workers cutting and hacking their way through a jungle. As producers and problem solvers, they cut through the obstacles to accomplish their job. The managers do the planning, sharpen the tools, train in brush hacking, and establish work and compensation schedules. But, the leader, wrote Covey, "is the one who climbs the tallest tree, surveys the entire situation, and yells, 'Wrong Jungle'" (1990, p. 101).

Good management cannot create leaders. Instead, good management can create environments in which leaders and leadership qualities can incubate and evolve. Because leaders are made by their experiences and by their learning in action, organizations need to provide potential leaders with the opportunities to "learn through experience in an environment that permits growth and change" (Bennis, 1989a, p. 182). These same qualities that grow leaders—learning in action and learning through experience in an environment that permits growth and change—facilitate outcomes for people with disabilities. These are the organizational dynamics that promote learning, growth, and self-awareness. It is probably no accident that organizations that are successful in facilitating personal outcomes for people with disabilities also grow leaders throughout the organization.

REFERENCES

Belasco, J.A. (1990). *Teaching the elephant to dance.* New York: Crown.
Belasco, J.A., & Stayer, R.C. (1993). *Flight of the buffalo: Soaring to excellence, learning to let employees lead.* New York: Warner Books.
Bennis, W. (1989a). *On becoming a leader.* Reading, MA: Addison-Wesley.
Bennis, W. (1989b). *Why leaders can't lead: The unconscious conspiracy continues.* San Francisco: Jossey-Bass.
Bennis, W. (1993). *An invented life: Reflections on leadership and change.* Reading, MA: Addison-Wesley.
Bennis, W., & Nanus, B. (1985). *Leaders: The strategies for taking charge.* New York: Harper & Row.
Capra, F. (1982). *The turning point: Science, society, and the rising culture.* New York: Simon & Schuster.
Capra, F. (1991). *The tao of physics* (3rd ed.). Boston: Shambhala.
Covey, S.R. (1990). *The seven habits of highly effective people: Powerful lessons in personal change.* New York: Simon & Schuster.
Deal, T.E., & Kennedy, A.A. (1982). *Corporate cultures: The rites and rituals of corporate life.* Reading, MA: Addison-Wesley.
DePree, M. (1989). *Leadership is an art.* New York: Doubleday.
Drucker. P.F. (1954). *The practice of management: A study of the most important function in American society.* New York: Harper & Row.
Kouzes, J.M., & Posner, B.Z. (1987). *The leadership challenge: How to get extraordinary things done in organizations.* San Francisco: Jossey-Bass.
Lynch, D., & Kordis, P.L. (1988). *Strategy of the dolphin: Scoring a win in a chaotic world.* New York: William Morrow and Co.
McLean, J.W., & Weitzel, W. (1991). *Leadership—magic, myth, or method?* New York: American Management Association.
Raelin, J.A. (1991). *The clash of cultures: Managers managing professionals.* Cambridge, MA: Harvard Business School Press.

Senge, P. (1990). *The fifth discipline: The art and practice of the learning organization.* New York: Doubleday Currency.

Stogdill, R.M. (1974). *Handbook of leadership: A survey of theory and research.* New York: The Free Press.

Vail, P.B. (1989). *Managing as a performing art: New ideas for a world of chaotic change.* San Francisco: Jossey-Bass.

Wheatley, M.J. (1994). *Leadership and the new science: Learning about organization from an orderly universe.* San Francisco: Berrett-Koehler.

Wheatley, M.J., & Kellner-Rogers, M. (1996). *A simpler way.* San Francisco: Berrett-Koehler.

Wildavsky, A. (1984). *The nursing father: Moses as a political leader.* University: The University of Alabama Press.

Wren, D. (1979). *The evolution of management thought.* New York: John Wiley & Sons.

Yukl, G. (1994). *Leadership in organizations* (3rd ed.). Upper Saddle River, NJ: Prentice-Hall.

III

Examining
Organizational Dynamics

This section on examining organizational dynamics presents four methods or techniques that leaders can use to analyze group behavior, shape organizational culture, and implement different action strategies. These strategies—systems analysis, reframing, data and information analysis, and understanding and supporting individual choice—link organizational learning with organizational action. Each of these strategies requires an examination of data and information from different perspectives. Leadership that rests on understanding and learning, as described by Gardner in Chapter 9, can channel organizational energy into action strategies.

The systems analysis presented by Gardner in Chapter 10 depicts the service or support organization as a grouping of six interrelated systems: work content, work process, people, structure, mission, and external environment. Change, whether in the form of person-centered planning, supported living, or voucher systems, cannot be confined to one system. In contrast, transitions may initially be focused within one system, but they quickly can have an impact on other systems. Understanding systems enables leaders to find connections among seemingly random events. Systems thinking also allows leaders the opportunity to minimize the disruptions that can ripple across different systems without visible or obvious cause.

Focusing on the impact of events in different systems enables leaders to examine the events and activities of organizational life from different perspectives. In Chapter 11, Sandidge and Ward examine reframing as a basic management and leadership skill. They note that when the leader can generate multiple interpretations of events through reframing, more choices for strategic action emerge. Sandidge and Ward examine reframing at the individual, group, and organizational levels. Reframing applies to people with disabilities, employees, and members of the community. Reframing is a requirement for employees and community representatives who begin to listen and learn about people's outcomes. Employees and community representatives need to make the transition from their roles of therapists, clinicians, professionals, or staff members to listeners and then facilitators. Likewise, people reframe through their language when they redefine others as patients, clients, or residents. Examples of paradigms that represent alternative frames through which we both view and define people with disabilities include medical, technological, community inclusion, and the advocacy/rights paradigms.

In Chapter 12, Chapman approaches personal outcome data and information as an opportunity to reexamine organizational processes and the relationships among the organization's resources, processes, and the personal outcomes for the people served. Establishing clear definitions of the needs and intended uses of information and data are exercises in reframing. The use of objective personal outcome data and information enables leaders to reframe organizational activities and practices within the context of personal outcomes and corresponding organizational processes. Chapman also stresses that understanding personal outcomes for the people receiving services and supports is the fundamental learning activity for the organizational leadership. A key role of the organization's leader is to acquire knowledge about people's outcomes, the organization's and community's resources that can be employed to facilitate the outcomes, and the ongoing self-assessment of personal outcome attainment by people receiving services and supports.

Section III concludes with an examination of choice as an organizational design feature. In Chapter 13, Campanella discusses choice as the design principle for leaders in organizations serving people with disabilities. With the deemphasis on centralization and hierarchy, the importance of individual choice and the fluidity in management that must accompany choice become paramount. The elements of learning responsibility and providing examples, opportunities, and experience for making choices are guiding principles in decisions about organizational structure, staffing, and the content of work. The leadership of the organization is responsible for ensuring that there are occasions for learning by example, opportunities to try responsible behaviors, and ongoing experience in developing responsible behavior around making choices. Enabling people to make choices and exercise control will redistribute power and influence in the organization. It will cause a change in organizational dynamics as people with disabilities exercise choices and make decisions that direct the organization.

10

Organizations as Systems

James F. Gardner

This chapter uses one family's Thanksgiving Day traditions to help explain how a service organization can use a systems approach to management. Thanksgiving has always been my favorite holiday. The parades, ceremony, ritual, and requirements of other secular and religious holidays never intruded on our family gathering. There was no drawn-out holiday season characterized by hurry and stress. Also, unlike Memorial Day or Labor Day, Thanksgiving was just a day and not a weekend for journey and vacation. As a family, we knew what to expect of Thanksgiving. Over the years, the traditions evolved but never unexpectedly. At the end of the evening, before relatives departed, we talked about what to do next year.

Thanksgiving represented both a daytime social event and an evening dinner. The earliest tradition was to watch the Detroit Lions play the Chicago Bears on television. Later, as the children became restless during the game, 10-pin bowling became an afternoon ritual. When teenagers became too sophisticated to be seen in the bowling alley, we attended a matinee at the movie theater. In the late afternoon and evening, the preparation of Thanksgiving dinner assumed primary importance.

Over the course of the years, we tried many different methods for cooking the turkey and accompaniments. My grandfather preferred to use an outdoor charcoal grill, whereas my mother preferred an electric range. Some years we used an outdoor gas grill; one year my sister, unfortunately, tried to cook the bird in a microwave—causing us to order a whole dinner for 18 people from a restaurant the following year. Over the years, we debated the merits of adding chestnuts to the dressing and serving sauerkraut with the turkey.

The different approaches to the social event and evening dinner reflected the individual preferences of the participants, their social and cooking skills, and their abilities to compromise and support each other. As we grew older, we exercised new roles and skills. Grandparents served as reminders of past practice. Parents and older children performed the cooking and social/recreational tasks. Teenagers learned the art of making stuffing and gravy; cooking apple and mince pies; and later in the week, making turkey soup from the remaining carcass.

For all the people involved, Thanksgiving was enjoyable. Over time, we learned how to organize the event. We all agreed on the time and location for our gathering. We also agreed on the purpose. We tried to simplify the day. Dress was informal, and there was no exchange of gifts. The person hosting the dinner assigned responsibility to the participants for bringing prepared food to the dinner. Responsibility for preparing the food also was organized by the host family. Over the years, each family organized the responsibilities on the basis of the people attending (in both numbers and individual interests), the layout of the house, and the cooking skills and preferences of the participants. One structural constant across all of the years was the separation of most of the men and children from the then predominately female kitchen staff. I am sure that the exile to the football game; the bowling alley; and, later, the movies was structured to protect the grandmothers, mothers, aunts, and sisters preparing the Thanksgiving dinner. Another structural constant was that cooking the turkey on the charcoal grill was a man's responsibility. Finally, although many people assumed responsibility for planning and preparing the meal, carving the turkey fell to the leading male figure of the family hosting the dinner.

A SYSTEMS APPROACH

These patterns of family activity, interactions, and cooperation often appeared chaotic. At times, seemingly trivial and unconnected events produced major consequences. Consider these scenarios in the following categories: goal, work content, work process, people, structure, and outside forces. First, we apply these categories to the Thanksgiving meal; and in the section that follows, we apply similar categories to a detailed explanation of a systems model of organization developed by French and Bell (1984).

Goal

The participants (the families) shared a common vision about Thanksgiving. This shared vision guided assumptions about the event and shaped individual and group behavior. In addition, we constantly asked each other about preferences and priorities as we planned for next year's event. This was a conscious, verbal discussion. We constantly updated our goal based on the collective sense of individual and family preferences. Whenever we neglected this discussion, the common vision and definition slipped a bit during the year. In the late 1980s, some severe interpersonal problems within one family prevented this discussion for several years. During this time, the simple tasks of scheduling, cooking, delegating, and even passing food at the table became complicated.

Work Content (What We Do)

Whereas we acknowledged the social/recreational goal of Thanksgiving, we all performed specific responsibilities. The task for men and children was to stay away from the kitchen. The family hosting the dinner coordinated shopping for groceries. Women polished the silver, set the tables, and prepared the meal. Everyone passed the bowls and platters during the meal. Everyone contributed to the clean up and dishwashing after dinner. In 1988, however, Grandfather Ed felt that cooking the turkey on the grill conferred authority in the kitchen. He began to coordinate the roasting of the turkey with activity in the kitchen, but he soon retreated to the outdoor grill when challenged by the kitchen crew.

Work Process (How We Do the Work)

Over the years, we designed various methods for removing fathers, husbands, and children from the kitchen and dining room. Before small children became a factor, the men watched the football game. As children became a factor, the methods of separation moved on to bowling and then the movies. Some cousins, particularly females, became concerned about public visibility in bowling alleys. For several difficult years we had to negotiate groupings of bowlers and movie viewers.

The method of cooking also changed. Depending on the leadership (conferred by the location of the gathering), the methods changed from charcoal grill to gas stove and from microwave to home delivery. Questions of chestnuts and sauerkraut also reflected leadership decisions and delegation of decision making.

People

Both individuals and groups influenced the goals, content, and process of our work. Sometimes inconsistencies and disagreements in people's values and assumptions showed up in the areas of goals, work, and process. One year, Brother William argued for presents and formal dress at next year's dinner. This resulted in some argument, but in the end, William adjusted his expectations to the group norm. Another year, Uncle Mike's family decided that they were going to help with the dinner, which produced confusion in the kitchen about who would cook the meal. This provided an opportunity for Grandfather to usurp the leadership, cook the turkey on the grill, and add chestnuts to the dressing. Finally, as the children grew into older adolescence, they wanted to include friends and dates in our Thanksgiving celebration. This led to a discussion as to whether those who would be invited had values and assumptions that were consistent with our traditions and whether they had social and cooking skills that would enable them to accept responsibilities.

Structure

The participants organized to prepare and enjoy Thanksgiving dinner. That organization also enabled participants to socialize and perform work in a generally pleasant manner. Sometimes the structure caused problems. Mary Ellen once delegated cooking and preparation to individuals who lacked cooking skills. In 1984, the women spent so much time keeping the men and children out of the kitchen that they mistimed cooking the potatoes, squash, beans, gravy, rolls, sauerkraut, turkey, and dressing. In most years, the children tried to escape the clean up after dinner.

Outside Forces

As Thanksgiving became more and more commercialized, we had to struggle to keep the event simple and family focused. Businesses attempted to increase holiday sales by making Thanksgiving the beginning of holiday shopping. Parades, department store sales, and sporting events vied for our attention. Our goals and traditions were threatened by outside forces.

FROM HOLIDAYS TO ORGANIZATIONS

The literature on leadership has emphasized the importance of understanding organizations as systems. Synthesis of information to uncover larger patterns of interaction and connection in organizations has replaced analysis of smaller parts of the organization. Synthesis leads to wholeness, relationships, and increased understanding. Through synthesis, leaders can discover larger patterns of interaction and relationships within the organization. The systems dynamics that occurred during my Thanksgiving dinners take place in organizations that provide services and coordinate supports for people with disabilities. The same variables that explain Thanksgiving dinner can identify patterns of behavior and interactions in organizations.

The external environment includes the forces outside of the organization, such as government regulators and funding sources, competitors, the local economy and job market, and other factors in the community. Individuals receiving services and supports are located at the center of the organizational goal subsystem. The systems analysis depicted in Figure 10.1 is adopted from French and Bell (1984). This systems analysis conveys four important principles:

1. The organizational systems are interconnected. These subsystems are linked—in organizations and in my Thanksgiving dinner. The work that is performed is linked to the methods for doing the work; and both the methods and the work depend on people and how they are organized.

2. Intervention and change cannot be confined to one system. It is, for example, impossible to change work methods without causing change in other systems, such as the people and work tasks. In a similar manner, changing the goals or structure of the organization will result in change in other organizational subsystems. For whatever reason, dinner preparation always took an extra 2 hours when Aunt Helen coordinated the event. That meant the kids came back from bowling with nothing to occupy their time. Men began to roam into the kitchen in search of snacks. Those cooking disagreed on responsibilities. A few of the sophisticated teenagers began to question the wisdom of continuing this family tradition.

3. Change, or disequilibrium, is introduced into the organization from two directions—by individuals at the center of the organization and by circumstances in the external environment. The challenge to the organization is to accommodate the changes by reconfiguring the subsystems. In addition, organizations face the seeming contradiction that changes in the environment and changes resulting from people served by the organization may be at odds. The two sources of change—the environment and

Figure 10.1.   A systems model.

the people served—may pull the organization in different directions. The commercialization of Thanksgiving challenged our traditions. Belief in our traditions weakened when our structures and people did not provide optimum support.

4. Leadership generally originates in the people subsystem, but it can then incubate in any of the other subsystems. Leadership for quality can take many different paths. Some leaders focus on clear mission statements and organizational goals. Some leaders stress work content, whereas others limit the scope of the work content and concentrate on the work methods and processes. Some leaders stress structural approaches to facilitating outcomes; other leaders emphasize the informal aspects of the people subsystem. Aunt Jane provided leadership by actually doing the work. She ran the kitchen by being there and by coordinating the cooking. Sister Ginger managed the work content and cooking process through organization that actually consisted of schedules, charts, and cooking instructions that hung on walls and from the ceiling.

A SYSTEMS MODEL

As discussed previously, organizations consist of interconnected subsystems. For example, an automobile contains an ignition, electrical, brake, engine, drive, and steering system. Humans have circulatory, nervous, skeletal, digestive, and endocrine systems. The following systems model was adapted from French and Bell (1984).

Goal Subsystem (Why We Work)

As noted in Figure 10.1, the goal subsystem is located at the center of the organization. The goal subsystem contains the mission, goals, and objectives of the organization. The mission, goals, and objectives of the organization are most frequently found in the organization's promotional literature and legal documentation. The goal subsystem contains the priority goals of the organization that are reflected throughout the departments of the organization. These priority goals provide the glue that binds the organization together. Departmental and program goals, which are generally developed after the organization's goals are established, should reflect the organization's goals and should direct organizational activity toward organizational goals. My family's goal for Thanksgiving was to celebrate family and strengthen family connections. The work of cooking the meal, the structure of the day, and the individual contributions for task accomplishment all flowed from the goal.

Organizations also constantly examine the alignment between organizational mission and departmental goals. In organizations with mission statements promoting personal outcomes, departments and other subunits also pursue personal outcomes rather than clinical or functional outcomes. In some cases, departments and programs establish goals that do not directly support the organizational goals. Departments and programs, in fact, become more and more efficient at achieving their own day-to-day goals and become further and further removed from achieving organizational goals. It is a leader's job to coordinate and align these disparate goals. As Law, King, MacKinnon, and Russell suggest in Chapter 5, organizations that serve people with disabilities must synchronize their missions with either clinical, functional, or personal outcomes.

Work Task Subsystem (What We Do)

The work of the organization consists of the tasks and duties that staff perform. For a typical human services organization, these would include providing individual and group counseling, identifying people's priority outcomes, completing forms, and providing transportation to and from the clinic.

Origins of Work Tasks   Work tasks are generally defined by job descriptions and program criteria. For example, the job description of the psychiatric technician in a partial hospitalization program identifies his or her primary duties and responsibilities (e.g., psychosocial functional skill development, medication monitoring, psychobehavioral assessment). These duties and responsibilities are exercised in the context of the program expectations associated with the partial hospitalization program. Although the individual duties and responsibilities and the program model will contain some flexibility to accommodate individual differences among people receiving the services, the typical expectation is that the person will adjust to the program requirements. Job description and program models do not typically readjust to changes in the people being served. In fact, the primary characteristic of such a program is its continuity of service and process. In this paradigm, the ability to provide continuity of service and process is what distinguishes one program from another.

In the early 1990s, some service providers and planners argued that the content of work (what staff do) should be based on what people with disabilities expect from services and supports rather than on what the program offers. Staff members would identify people's priorities for services and supports by listening to the people whom they serve. Staff, families, and friends then could perform those work tasks that would facilitate those personal priorities. This personal futures planning paradigm refocuses the definitions of work tasks from the perspective of the person rather than from the program.

The work subsystem category can be applied to our Thanksgiving dinner. As younger children grew into adulthood, the traditions began to evolve. They brought new ideas and suggestions for the menu, new cooking activities into the kitchen, and new discussions after dinner. Because Thanksgiving focused on family, the family frequently changed the work.

Job Task Inventories   The analysis of work requires a listing of the tasks that individuals, teams, and organizational units perform. The reason for the performance of each task then is identified. The analysis determines whether the task is performed as a program process requirement or whether it promotes an individual's priority outcome. Individuals, teams, and organizational units are encouraged to list work tasks on paper, then identify on a person-by-person basis which work tasks are and are not directly related to outcomes (see Figure 10.2 for an example at a service organization).

Task	Program process	Individual outcome
Laundry	x	
Meal preparation	x	
Accompany Al, Ray, and Ellen to the grocery store	x	
Accompany Ray, Ellen, and Ruth to the recreation center		x
Arrange transportation to the mall for Alan	x	
Discuss sexuality and sexually transmitted diseases with Ruth		x
Work on budgeting with Ellen	x	

Figure 10.2.   Job task inventory (part-time supported living staff at service organization).

The job task inventory is completed by identifying the most important tasks in terms of facilitating outcomes, the tasks that take the greatest amount of time, and the tasks that consume the greatest amount of resources. Figure 10.3 identifies the same tasks as presented in Figure 10.2 by importance to outcome, by time, and by cost. The job task analysis generally reveals that the tasks of greatest importance to outcomes are not those that consume the most resources or time. Many of the tasks rest on an interpersonal relationship with the individual and a willingness and ability to determine what is most important to the individual.

Work Method Subsystem (How We Do Our Work)

The work method subsystem identifies how we work and how the individualized organizational processes facilitate outcomes for people. Work processes are not important in and of themselves; they are important only if they facilitate outcomes for people. Think back to my Thanksgiving dinner. Watching football, bowling, or going to the movie theater were examples of how we accomplished the work of keeping children and men out of the kitchen. In a similar manner, the goal of cooking could be attained by using a charcoal grill; a gas stove; or, unfortunately, a microwave.

Task	Outcome	Time	Cost
Laundry	L	M	L
Meal preparation	L	M	L
Accompany Al, Ray, and Ellen to the grocery store	L	H	M
Accompany Ray, Ellen, and Ruth to the recreation center	H[1]	H	H
Arrange transportation to the mall for Alan	L	L	L
Discuss sexuality and sexually transmitted diseases with Ruth	H[2]	L	L
Work on budgeting with Ellen	H[3]	L	L

Figure 10.3.   Job task inventory (part-time supported living staff at service organization). (Key: H, High; L, Low; M, Medium.)
[1]Martial arts are Ray's major motivation for social interaction. Staff accompany Ray to the center to assist him in registering for classes.
[2]Ruth's desire for an intimate relationship is impeded by her lack of understanding about contraception and sexually transmitted diseases.
[3]Ellen wants the opportunity to express financial independence by maintaining her own checking and credit card accounts.

The differences between work task and work process are illustrated by the distinction between form and function. Consider the task or the work of sweeping the floor of an apartment. The functional outcome is to clean the floor. The form of cleaning or how we clean the floor can vary. We could, for example, use a broom, a carpet sweeper, or a vacuum cleaner. In another example, staff develop plans of services and supports for people served by the organization. The functional outcome is an effective plan. The form of planning or how the staff conduct the planning process also can vary. The staff can adapt a form of goal planning, design a plan that incorporates the requirement of active treatment, use a form of person-centered planning, or construct an individual service plan. Finally, consider Ann, a woman who has oral-motor impairments that complicate her mealtime routines. She must accomplish the functional outcome of maintaining an adequate nutritional intake. The form of accomplishing that nutritional intake can vary. Staff may assist Ann to cut her food into small pieces, to purée the food, or to take her nutrition through a feeding tube. Table 10.1 illustrates additional distinctions between work content (i.e., task or function) and work process (i.e., form).

There is no universal best process for performing tasks. The manner in which a task is performed is based on the individual and his or her desired outcomes. The role of staff is to identify the processes that will work best for each individual. This individualized approach means that different people will require *different* processes to accomplish *common* outcomes. People with different challenges and disabilities often will require *different methods* to achieve their definition of the *same outcome category*. The difference is in the methods not the outcomes.

Work Process Clusters   Different methods for accomplishing work tasks often are clustered into familiar categories. Some of these categories are professional skills and approaches, service prototypes, innovative methodologies, adaptive equipment, assistive work processes, office equipment, and information networks.

Professional Skills and Approaches   Professional disciplines are based on the acquisition of specialized skills and expertise. For example, special educators, occupational therapists, nutritionists, and speech-language therapists provide different processes and techniques for facilitating person-centered outcomes.

Table 10.1.   Form versus function

Outcome, task, or function	Process, work process, or form
1. Eliminate self-destructive behavior.	Positive behavior intervention Chemical restraint Aversive conditioning Physical restraint
2. Communicate with teacher and classmates.	Speech Sign language Speech synthesizer Picture board
3. Teach community living skills with positive reinforcement.	Continuous schedule Fixed ratio Variable ratio Fixed interval Variable interval
4. Prepare for employment opening.	Train in workshop, then find a job Find job opening, then provide training and support

Service Prototypes   Services often are organized around different work processes. Supported employment and the workshop cite the same ends but employ rather different work processes to accomplish those ends. Restoring functional daily living skills for people with ongoing mental illness can incorporate behavioral, psychopharmacological, and counseling approaches. Thus, psychosocial rehabilitation, vocational education, education, medical rehabilitation, day treatment, and vocational rehabilitation approaches can characterize organizations. Each approach rests on a different set of work processes or technologies. The outcomes expected from services and supports may be remarkably similar; the work processes are different.

Innovative Methodologies   Promising new practices are continuously emerging from research and demonstration projects. New forms of person-centered planning, functional assessment and analysis, psychopharmacology, strategic planning, service brokerage, and organization management offer new alternatives and opportunities for facilitating outcomes for people.

Adaptive Equipment   Occupational therapists, rehabilitation engineers, therapeutic recreation specialists and other clinicians, inventors, and tinkerers have created greater access for people with disabilities. Special grips on eating utensils, plate guards, motorized wheel chairs, bowling balls with collapsing handles, jigs, and grips to increase eye–hand coordination are a few examples of adaptive equipment.

Assistive Work Processes   Assistive work processes refer to the use of sophisticated electronic devices to solve problems faced by people in day-to-day living. The use of various input devices such as a light pen, mouthstick, touch-sensitive screen, joystick, or mouse enter data into a computer. Specialized software then processes the information through output devices that greatly increase control over the environment. Eye blinks can control lighting, temperature, sound, and data entry, information storage, and retrieval. With the right equipment and devices, every person can prepare a Thanksgiving dinner!

Office Equipment   Modem office equipment is transforming not-for-profit, human services organizations into contemporary communication centers. Service coordinators and case managers work with beepers and cellular telephones. Laptop computers at work stations enable staff to add real-time information to the main record. Staff schedules, resource allocations, and monthly calendars for staff, people with disabilities, families, and friends can be updated on a daily basis and automatically directed to designated locations.

Information Networks   Families and self-advocates are linking and organizing through e-mail systems and the Internet. This information linkage and personal communication are phenomena in the virtual world of the 1990s. It is not surprising that families and self-advocates have seized the latest work processes to increase their own communication capabilities, find common bulletin boards, and organize for action.

People Subsystem (Who)

The people subsystem consists of the individuals who make up the organization. This people subsystem is simple to understand because it is about people; but it is difficult to analyze because people are unpredictable and not always as they appear. There are four aspects of this subsystem—skills and abilities of the people, leadership philosophy and style, a formal person subsystem, and an informal person subsystem.

Skills and Abilities of the People   Developing competent employees requires some combination of effective recruitment, ongoing staff development, good supervision, and opportunity for individual growth and development. In our Thanksgiving traditions, the older women gradually introduced teenage girls to the tasks of cooking and baking. Except for the instance in which Ginger microwaved the turkey, adolescent women went through a supervised, multiyear development program.

Leadership Philosophy and Style   A leader's philosophy and style are related to the manner in which decisions are made, information is communicated and coordinated, and the degree of concern for human values within the organization. The concern for human values applies to both staff and people receiving services and supports.

Formal Person System   Personnel functions such as staffing, promotion, rewards, performance appraisal, bargaining processes, and systems for due process and appeal represent the formal person system. The formal system is encoded in the organization's policies and procedures. Many aspects of the formal system are required by federal and state law. The formal system is designed to address the programmed or routine activities that take place on a recurring basis. During Thanksgiving, the formal person system included the family hosting the dinner, the women in the kitchen, and the men leading the bowling trips. This formal system evolved over time but never disappeared.

Informal Person System   The informal part of the people subsystem contains the values, norms, and assumptions that govern group behavior. They define the unwritten rules of how the organization works and explain the value and status of people with disabilities, their families, and the direct support and service staff. This informal system is seldom detailed in writing, and it may not be immediately acknowledged in discussion among staff. In some cases, the values and principles articulated by the formal system may well be out of synch with the real values, norms, and assumptions buried in the informal system.

This informal system existed within our Thanksgiving. Smokers, banished from most homes, met over the years in backyards and garages. They developed their own communication and values system. Young teenagers, particularly males, also functioned as an informal system that was incomprehensible to the rest of the family. Even the older teenagers could not understand the actions of the 12- and 13-year-olds.

The informal part of the people subsystem is the launching ground for significant change. Changing values, norms, and assumptions are preconditions for organizational change. Norms, values, and assumptions, however, cannot be changed by typical management or supervisory methods. Training alone will not change norms and assumptions. Merely sending key staff to conferences and seminars will not work. The management of change requires focused, often painful, open discussion of key issues by the very people who will be most affected by the proposed change. Successful leaders understand the power of norms and assumptions contained in the informal system. Significant organizational change cannot take place unless the proposed change is consistent with the norms and assumptions in the informal people system.

Structure Subsystem (Organization)

The structure subsystem is the most visible part of the organization. This subsystem consists of the grouping of the organization such as units, departments, or divisions. It also includes the work rules, the authority system, and the processes for sanctions and rewards for work performance. Finally, the structural subsystem contains procedures for communicating, planning, coordinating, and decision making.

The structural subsystem—which identifies the extent of formalization, centralization, and standardization within the organization—determines how the organization operates.

Formalization   Formalization refers to the written documentation required by the organization. Some types of organizations such as air traffic control systems, nuclear power plants, and hospitals require a high degree of documentation because they contain potential for high-risk situations. Other organizations such as independent home maintenance contractors, supported employment contractors, and county recreation programs require less formalization. For Thanksgiving, most women cooked and baked with a lot of written documentation. Sister Ginger, however, used detailed schedules, recipes, and other reminders to get through the day.

Centralization   Centralization refers to the focus of decision-making responsibility. Organizations with a high degree of centralization restrict decision making to the top of the organizational hierarchy. In decentralized organizations, decision making is located as close to the final consumer as possible.

Standardization   Standardization is a measure of uniformity of practice throughout the organization. Some organizations, such as McDonald's, stress the need for uniformity and standardization throughout their worldwide locations. In fact, the anticipation of uniformity at any location throughout the world is a marketing strategy for the McDonald's corporation. In contrast, universities are organized around the autonomy of individual degree-granting colleges and programs.

SYSTEMS CONNECTIONS AND LEADERSHIP OPPORTUNITIES

Understanding the interconnections between and among the subsystems is more important than analyzing individual subsystems. The interconnections reveal the ambiguity and subtlety in organizational dynamics. Systems thinking enables leaders to recognize the following five points:

1. Depending on organizational characteristics, the outside environment, and individual skills, *leaders can initiate change and quality improvement in any of the subsystems.* Some leaders begin with a change in norms, values, and assumptions in the people system. Some organizations begin with a discussion of goals and mission statement. Other organizations begin the change by altering the way they work through the introduction of new technology. Finally, some leaders promote change by simplifying structures and rules.
2. *Successful quality improvement and change efforts will cross into other systems* and eventually will reach throughout all systems. Some organizations make changes in norms, values, and assumptions by introducing new work processes that identify personal futures, prioritized personal outcomes, or other simi-

lar planning processes. Simplifying structures and rules in the structure subsystem leads to redefinition of employees' tasks in the work content subsystem and greater flexibility in the people subsystem.

3. *Efforts to define quality improvement and change within the context of a single subsystem or to contain the change to a single subsystem will fail.* Different forms of individual planning represent changes in the work process subsystem. Training staff to interview people with personal outcome measures takes change into the formal person subsystem and work process subsystem. Yet to be successful, leaders must examine the possible changes that need to occur in the structural and informal person subsystems. This explains why the simplest occurrence could cause such confusion on Thanksgiving. When Aunt Helen cooked, dinner was always late. This caused problems among the other women who then each proposed different work tasks and structures to compensate for the delays and to make up for lost time. The children arrived back from the movies with no additional work tasks to perform, and Grandfather tried to take advantage of the confusion and put chestnuts in the dressing. It seemed that the simplest occurrences threw the family into chaos. Confusion was seldom contained in one subsystem.

4. *Understanding the consistency among subsystems and relationships between and among subsystems are more important than analyzing a single subsystem.* For example, do the mission and goals support the outcomes that people with disabilities want from services and supports? Do employees have the skills and abilities to perform the work processes to do the tasks that facilitate the outcomes that people want in their lives? Does the organizational structure support the employees in their efforts to facilitate outcomes? In our family, we used existing structures to keep Grandfather out of the kitchen. We recognized that the work of cooking the turkey was influenced by the skills of the women in the kitchen and the manner by which they chose to cook the turkey.

5. *Mission, principles, and values are important; but they are just the beginning point for change.* Leaders must explore the multitude of hard issues that lie in the connections among organizational structure, the people, the work tasks that are performed, and the work processes. Systems thinking reveals that we can begin with values, assumptions, and norms; but the change and quality improvement will require solid skills, interpersonal skills, understanding of the work and work processes, commitment, and endurance.

SYSTEMS DYNAMICS

Quality in services, leadership, and organizational behavior can be analyzed through clusters of organizational subsystems. Different clusters reveal patterns of causation, influence, and connections. The alignment and combination of some clusters counters the influence of other clusters. These clusters can be grouped as follows: reasons why staff training fails, funding sources and regulators are to blame, words have not been translated into actions, all systems need to be put into gear, and rigidity of the organizational structure.

Reasons Why Staff Training Fails

Organizations often attempt to implement person-centered planning by focusing attention on the work content and on the skills of the staff. As such, the organization offers education programs that identify the tasks and procedures for person-centered planning and the set of skills and abilities that staff will need to implement the new planning approach. The focus on the work content and formal people clusters, however, ignores the impact of the presence of the structure and informal people clusters.

In non–person-centered programs, the existing organizational structure of departments, units, and programs defines the range of services and supports. The program structure of these organizations, rather than person-centered priorities, generally determines the range and scope of services. Introducing person-focused planning and outcomes as simply another assessment methodology does not challenge the existing organizational structure or hierarchy. The successful introduction of person-centered approaches rests on a thorough reexamination of organizational structure. There is a strong connection among the introduction of person-focused planning and outcomes and redesigning organizational structures. In addition, the introduction of outcome-based approaches to service delivery challenges the people subsystem at both the formal and informal levels. On the formal level, the outcome-based approach turns the decision about individual priorities from staff to the individual. People with disabilities, rather than staff, identify outcomes. Staff then use their skills, experience, and professional training to facilitate the outcomes as defined by the person. For some professionals, this represents a loss of professional status and authority. Finally, in many instances, the informal aspects of the people cluster, values, norms, and assumptions were developed to support the program model in operation. The successful change effort that allows for service selection on the basis of priority outcomes will require successful transformation of the personal belief systems in the informal people subsystem.

Funding Sources and Regulators Are to Blame

Organizations often cite regulatory requirements and rate-setting and reimbursement formulas as barriers to quality enhancement. Outmoded process requirements, excessive paperwork, and nit-picking state inspectors are frequently named as reasons for maintaining the status quo. In a similar manner, organizations cite continued loss of federal and state support or the lack of additional funding as barriers to quality enhancement. In some cases, these regulatory and financial barriers may be significant. In other instances, however, the focus on the external environment masks the more significant issues in the informal people subsystem. The significant barriers may rest not in the regulatory and financing agencies of state government but with the values, norms, and assumptions of the organization's employees. The existing set of beliefs may simply not support new work tasks and work processes associated with personal outcomes.

Words Have Not Been Translated into Actions

Organizations often incorporate the language and symbols of quality enhancement in their mission statements and goals. In some instances, however, those values are not cemented into the informal people system—the older values, norms, and assumptions remain unchanged. As a result, the symbols and language of the mission and goals are never transformed into organizational action. The language of quality enhancement is present, but the implementation actions resemble sentences with poor syntax.

Organizations face two challenges. They must base the organizational mission on sound values, and they must ensure that the employees fully integrate those values, norms, and assumptions in the belief systems. Without internalization of the right values, norms, and assumptions, organizational missions remain unrealized and the work content does not change.

All Systems Need to Be Put into Gear

The identification of person-centered outcomes and the design of individualized organizational processes to facilitate those outcomes direct attention to the work task/work process subsystems. The goals, people, and structural subsystems are designed to maximize an individualized approach to service design and delivery. The planning and implementation of a person-centered approach to service rests on well-developed goals, people, and structural subsystems. The mission and goals of the organization should clearly communicate the priority attached to person-centered outcomes. The commitment to these values is evident in the informal people subsystem in which new values, norms, and assumptions have been cemented. In addition, employees develop new professional roles as outcome facilitators and develop skills to help people identify their outcomes and then to facilitate those outcomes. Finally, the structure is decentralized to allow for as much work task/work process decision making as possible throughout the organization.

Rigidity of the Organizational Structure

The processes that employees use to perform work tasks are influenced by the tasks themselves, the people, and the structure. In successful, people-oriented organizations, staff members individualize the organizational process to facilitate outcomes for people. Quality is enhanced and outcomes are realized when organizational processes are individualized for different people. Rigid structures, however, prevent individualization and insist that organizational processes remain consistent and homogeneous. Program structures reinforce this rigidity because consistency in organizational process and the repetition of the same techniques highlight the program approach to services and supports. The development of nonprogrammed organizational processes that are driven by person-centered outcomes require flexible structures and people.

CONCLUSIONS: AFTER VALUES AND PRINCIPLES, IT IS ABOUT PEOPLE AND STRUCTURE

The focus on person-centered outcomes suggests a sequence in the design and development of organizational systems. The organization's systems might evolve in the following manner:

1. A mission and organizational goals are established that are consistent with the forces in the external environment and the priorities of people receiving services and supports.
2. The organization identifies the work tasks that will facilitate outcomes.
3. The organization then identifies the individualized work processes that will accomplish the work tasks.
4. The organization identifies and hires the employees that can accomplish the work tasks through the designated methods to facilitate the outcomes.

5. Finally, the organization identifies structures that maximize employees' capabilities to perform work and facilitate outcomes. In this model, structure is the last subsystem to evolve. The form, or structure, of the organization flows from the nature of the work performed.

This model of systems evolution suggests that changes in mission, work task, or process, or even people, might result in a shift of equilibrium among the systems and cause a change in the structural system. The other possibility is that the structural system is so rigid that it inhibits change and adaptation in the work task and work process systems. Bureaucratic organizations often operate in this manner.

Finally, there is a connection between the structural subsystem and the informal people system. The official rules that address communication, feedback, supervision, promotion, and organizational justice in the structural subsystem must be consistent with the informal values, norms, and assumptions of the people system. The importance of the people's connections to the other subsystems appears obvious, but some organizations attempt to make changes in those systems as though there were no people involved. For example, boards of directors and senior managers change structure and tasks frequently without examining the impact that these changes will have on the employees. Changes in work task and work process raise questions of staff training and support. In addition, the informal people system of values, norms, and assumptions may be compatible with one structure, set of tasks, and work process but not with proposed changes in those systems.

The basic compatibility among the people, work task, and work process subsystems must be present to facilitate outcomes for people. Staff members require the capability, motivation, and opportunity to perform work. Employees need specific skills to individualize organizational processes to facilitate outcomes for people. These nonprogrammed processes require greater independence and autonomy than the reapplication of uniform procedures and methods.

REFERENCE

French, W., & Bell, C. (1984). *Organization development: Behavioral science interventions for organization improvement* (3rd ed.). Upper Saddle River, NJ: Prentice-Hall.

11

Reframing

Robert L. Sandidge and Anne C. Ward

The meaning of any situation or of any set of circumstances is found in the frame within which we view it. One of our favorite old stories is one based on the simplest question of frames: When something happens, is it good or is it bad? The story goes like this:

A Russian farmer in the 1800s was plowing his fields one spring day, and as he unhooked the plow from his horse, his horse leaped and galloped out of his fields and into the forest. The man walked back to the village that evening and told of the event. His friends and neighbors gathered around him and remarked about his misfortune, saying what an unlucky day this was for him. The man said only, "You never know."

Not more than 2 weeks later, the man and his son were slowly plowing the spring fields by themselves when the farmer's horse trotted back into the field along with another horse, a wild horse. When the farmer and his son arrived in the village at the end of the day, riding one horse and leading the second horse, all of their friends and neighbors gathered around them and talked about how fortunate it was that their horse went into the wild, because now they had two horses on the farm. Once again, the thoughtful farmer said only, "You never know."

Several days later, the farmer's son broke his leg when he was thrown from the wild horse while trying to break it and train it for farm work. That night, the villagers cursed the unfortunate day that the wild horse came to the farm. The farmer said, "You never know."

Not long after, the entire village shook when the Cossacks came roaring across the plain, going from house to house, and conscripting every man of fighting age into service until they came to the farmer's home, where they left his son with his family because of his broken leg. That night, a mourning village came together to console themselves and each other and to tell the farmer how lucky he was that the wild horse had broken his son's leg. The farmer looked at all of his neighbors and said only, "You never know."

The villagers in the story were very quick to place meaning on every event, to interpret it, and to place it in the scheme of things past and future. The "frame" of meaning through which they gazed let them know how they were to feel, what was to be done next, and what to watch out for in the future. The farmer in the story saw life and circumstances through a very different lens. He extracted no meaning from events and went from event to event, from moment to moment, giving what was called for and taking what was given.

Reframing takes the same situation and the same circumstances and then gives those "facts" a different meaning. This different meaning allows us to take a different approach and gives us new possibilities for the actions that we might take and the responses we might make.

REFRAMING EXPLAINED

Reframing is about changing perception by understanding something in another way. Bandler and Grinder explained reframing in the following manner:

> What reframing does is to say, Look, this external thing occurs and it elicits this response in you, so you assume that you know what the meaning is. But if you thought about it this other way, then you would have a different response. Being able to think about things in a variety of ways builds a spectrum of understanding. None of these ways are 'really' true, though. They are simply statements about a person's understanding. (1982, p. 43)

BASIC TYPES OF REFRAMING

There are two basic kinds of reframes: context reframing and content reframing. Both can alter our internal representations of events or situations, which permits us to experience the events in other, hopefully, more resourceful ways.

Context Reframing

Bandler and Grinder noted that "every experience in the world and every behavior is appropriate, given some context, some frame" (1982, p. 9). *Context reframing* offers an understanding of how we make meaning through the environment—physical, intellectual, cultural, historical, and emotional—in which a situation occurs. It can also provide a pattern of thinking that helps us see the value in every situation regardless of any perceived downside.

Context reframing is taking an experience that seems to be negative, not useful, and distressing and showing how the same behavior or experience can be useful in another context. Children's stories are full of reframes that are designed to show children how what might seem a liability can be useful in another context. For example, the other reindeer made fun of Rudolph's bright, red nose; but that funny nose made Rudolph the hero on a dark night.

Context reframing can be used as a "perceptual filter," taught and practiced until it becomes an integral and habitual way of organizational thinking. It is a very useful tool in business as it is a way of thinking that gives one the ability to make lemonade from those unexpected (and unwanted) lemons. Creativity, new visions, and innovations are commonplace for those who know how to reframe and recontextualize problems and obstacles into opportunities and resources. The following stories are prime examples of this ability to reframe and recontextualize.

An executive director at a human services agency was looking for inexpensive raw materials to make dried flower arrangements for the agency gift shop. He called the local funeral parlors and asked what they did with flowers after the funerals. As expected, the funeral parlors disposed of the flowers. The parlors agreed to give the agency the flowers at no cost. The agency transforms the flowers into beautiful arrangements to sell in the agency gift shop at a good profit. Throwing away dead flowers may not seem like an opportunity to many, but when you can reframe them into another context, you have created free raw materials.

Safety-Kleen in Elgin, Illinois, was one of the fastest growing and most successful companies in the mid-1970s and 1980s. Its founder noticed that garages threw out the oil when they made oil changes. It was not only a bad ecological practice, it was wasteful. What other use could there be for used motor oil? The management of Safety-Kleen answered that question. Waste oil could be used in asphalt and other oil-based building materials. It also could be cleaned and recycled. Safety-Kleen built a multimillion dollar business by putting out a fleet to pick up used oil. They were one of the first to collect the used oil and resell it; they also charge the operator for the service.

Viewing organizations, individuals, and the world with reframing tools opens us to potential rather than locking us into our perceived limits. An entrepreneur is fundamentally an expert reframer—that is, he or she is someone who can add value to resources and convert them into wealth.

Content Reframing

The second type of reframing is content reframing. *Content reframing* is simply changing the meaning of a situation—that is, the situation or behavior stays the same, but the meaning is changed. For instance, a famous army general reframed a distressful situation for his troops by telling them that "We're not retreating, we're just advancing in another direction." Another example is the reframing of death. Death is a life event that has different meanings in different cultures, and even many individuals deal with this event in vastly different ways. Some are forever grieving the loss, whereas others are joyous at the now eternal presence of the person's spirit. In other words, different people attach very different meanings and interpretations to the concept of death.

REFRAMING AS A COMMUNICATION SKILL

Bandler and Grinder noted that "as a communicator you want to have the ability to shift the frames that people put around anything" (1982, p. 33). Learning to reframe is essential in learning to communicate effectively with others and even with ourselves. In every field of endeavor, it is the person who sets the frame who defines the playing field and, therefore, the scope of the "game" to be played. The framer defines the focus of attention and sets the frames that define the presuppositions of the activity or conversation.

In politics, professionals who specialize in setting frames and in reframing situations are called spin doctors. Although this group may need to do a little "spinning" to gain a better perception of what they are saying, what they are doing is not new; it just has been given a name. Politics, marketing, sales, and effective communication of any type is about perception not about any objective truth. For example, you may recall the age issue raised when Ronald Reagan ran for president against Walter Mondale. In a television debate, Mondale made a comment that implied Reagan's age was an issue. Reagan replied that he did not think age should be an issue and that he had no intention of making an issue of his opponent's youth and inexperience. In that one comment, he totally reframed the question in a way that ensured that it would not be a major factor in the race.

This ability to reconceptualize and reframe concepts so that others alter their own perceptions is a concept prevalent in marketing. Reis and Trout (1981) explored the concept in their now-classic marketing book called *Positioning: The Battle for Your Mind.* In a more recent book, Trout defined *positioning* as "not what you do to the product, but what you do to the *mind* . . . the ultimate marketing battleground is the mind, and the better you understand how the mind works, the better you'll understand how positioning works" (1995, p. ix, italics in original). Trout identified two basic types of organizations with problems: those that have lost their focus and those that have lost touch with the marketplace. In both cases, he prescribed "repositioning" as the answer.

Losing focus and losing touch with the marketplace are problems that confuse the consumer's perception of a company. In the first case, the market does not know what the company does. And in the second case, being out of touch with a changing world leaves the company positioned to fill needs that no longer exist. In both cases, repositioning requires redefining the company's purpose, what it is doing, and how it is being perceived. Organizations should remember that it is perception that motivates behavior, nothing else. Reframing, which is accomplished through communication, is a tool for changing perception.

Learning to Communicate

Reframing starts by recognizing how each of us processes our experiences. Reframing is not just a pattern to apply to the world "out there" but needs to be a resident program in our mental operating system. We tend to accept our perceptions at face value and use reasons like "that's just the way I am" as the rationale for continuing to proceed with the same thought patterns.

To overcome our reluctance to challenge our perceptions, the personal challenge is to learn to communicate with ourselves with all the purpose, direction, and persuasiveness that we offer in a business presentation. How we think, or the structure of our thinking, affects the content in the same way that how we drive affects the safety and security of our passengers. In practice, reframing is widely used in the therapeutic context. When a counselor asks an individual to "see it another way" or "think about it differently," he or she is attempting to reframe events to get him or her to see the problem in another light.

THEORY AND PRACTICE FOR INDIVIDUAL REFRAMING

Reframing is a key to the puzzle of self-fulfilling prophecies—the concept that your beliefs tend to unconsciously manifest themselves in your actions and decisions. Self-fulfilling prophecies have been called the Pygmalion effect from a play that later became *My Fair Lady*. In the play, Professor Henry Higgins won a wager that nurture was more powerful than nature. He trained a commoner, Eliza Doolittle, to have the manner and speech of a woman of the upper class. The story demonstrates that our self-perception, or who it is we learn to think we are, is a primary determinant in how we will fare in life. There is story after story about classroom experiments in which teachers were told that a group of randomly chosen students were gifted and that another random group were slow; sure enough, at the end of the experiment, the students tested just that way.

Perceptions define our experience. Meaning is created in our brains from our experiences. Behavior is given meaning based on what we learned the behavior meant in the past. We have a past frame into which we fit current behavior in order to identify and understand it. The understanding comes not from the behavior itself but from the particular frame through which we chose to view it. Each of us perceives the world as filtered into our awareness through our frames of perceptions. Thus, each of us experiences and finds different and unique meaning in our world.

Reframing, then, is expanding our own or others' perceptions by providing a new frame through which to view a life situation. What is a disastrous problem to one person is a challenging growth opportunity for another. Victor Frankl (1963), who survived a Nazi concentration camp, recounted that although most of his fellow inmates lost hope and subsequently died, Frankl kept hope and planned for the lectures that he would give after his release. In his own mind, he turned a potentially hopeless situation into a source of rich experiences that he could use to help others overcome hopeless situations. Fortunately, we do not have to be in such dire circumstances for reframing to be useful. Every moment of every day, there is opportunity to see things in another way. To see them through another frame of perception can give us hope and a better perspective of ourselves and others.

A major implication of this concept is that there are no correct or right frames of perceptions. There are only useful frames and not so useful frames, depending on the particular context. A useful reframe is to understand that all perceptions are useful in some context. Given that, you can always ask yourself or someone else, "where would this perception be useful, or where would it make sense?"

Reframing in Practice

Celebrated medical hypnotherapist, Milton H. Erickson, M.D., mastered reframing in a therapeutic setting (Rosen, 1982). When an individual would come to him with a problem such as procrastination, Erickson would immediately congratulate him and declare the individual an expert on procrastination. He then would enlist the person to teach him how to become a master Procrastinator. By reframing what was perceived as a lifelong liability into a skill, Erickson helped each individual see this former liability as a positive attribute and as an ability to be valued when used in the appropriate contexts. The person then could view his or her behavior not as something to avoid or get rid of but as a resource that has value when used appropriately. Two possible contexts in which procrastination could be useful are postponing dessert when dieting or delaying the expression of rage when angry. This ownership and mastery of, in this example, procrastination, gives the individual options to choose to use this skill in an appropriate context.

The ability to reframe virtually any issue into a positive attribute establishes an atmosphere of acceptance and cooperation rather than one of "expert and subject." Genuinely accepting every person's ideas, attitudes, and behaviors as positive and useful is to open one's own perceptions to the potential rather than the limitations of any situation.

Seligman (1990) noted that people who were more realistic (i.e., less optimistic) were accurate in their assessments of objective reality but were less happy and did not live as long as people who chose to be optimistic. Often people who are great optimistic reframers are discredited as being Pollyannas and criticized for being naïve. Although the accusations may be true in a sense, it would appear that the Pollyanna and naïve perceptions are actually more life-sustaining than those of the realist.

Reframing is more than a technique to resolve a difficulty. Reframing is an operating system for the organism. Once it becomes a habit, the whole world and everyone in it are seen in terms of "what is right" rather than "what is wrong." This is a fundamental shift in our cultural paradigm in that we are encouraged and rewarded to be problem solvers from an early age. American culture gives great accolades and much money to those who can solve the big problems. We learn to measure our self-worth in terms of our ability to solve problems. Seeing oneself through the filters of being a problem solver sets one's perceptual filters to "scan for problems." Life is then seen primarily as a source of problems being served up so that we can maintain our status as master problem solver. Problem solving is a dominant theme in schools, psychotherapy, management, and counseling. We continue our fascination with problems although we know that success is what creates success. Success stimulates success in people and in organizations. Yet, we spend much of our personal and organizational time looking through the frame of "problem elimination or solution." How many of us as children learned that we got more attention from adults when we brought them a problem to solve? How many of us carry this unconscious pattern into everything we do today? Management consultants, managers, and employees often see their roles as problem solvers. This orientation can hide from us the small successes that if noticed and nurtured, can lead to a creative spirit of continuous improvement and success. An individual attitude of reframing problems into potential and opportunity is more than just "sleight of mind." It is a way to change the perceptions of ourselves, those we serve, and the organizations we lead.

THE QUALITY REVOLUTION AS A REFRAME IN BUSINESS

The total quality management movement in business was a major, across-the-board reframe. It affected the ways that businesses thought about every important relationship, from relationships with customers to relationships with suppliers and employees. One of the primary changes brought about by the quality revolution was in the relationships between companies and their employees.

An example of a new covenant between employer and employee comes from Jack Stack of Springfield Remanufacturing. Stack (1992) explained that he shares all of Springfield's production and profit numbers with every person in the plant and in the office. He even offers classes to his employees to teach them what every number means and how the financial reporting process works. This is a massive reframe in a business world that still tends to operate on a need-to-know basis. Since Stack started opening his books to his employees, Springfield's sales have soared, as have profits. Employee turnover is extremely low, whereas employees hold themselves and each other to the highest of standards. Stack wrote that

> We have a company filled with people who not only are owners, but who think and act like owners rather than employees. . . . Owners, real owners, do not have to be told what to do—they can figure it out for themselves. They have all the knowledge, understanding, and information they need to make a decision, and they have the motivation and the will to act fast. (1992, pp. 15–16)

All employees want to find meaning in their work. If managers act as if this "frame" were true and if they hold it as part of their covenant with employees, then how will they think differently about what information they share with associates and team members? How will managers help employees to organize their work? What demands will managers make of their teams and of themselves to uphold the values that they have chosen to be the nonnegotiable elements in the organizations? How will managers go about choosing team members—their partners in service?

One of the most important reframes in the quality revolution is the definition of quality itself. The new definition is simple: *Quality is what the customer says it is.* Looking through this lens has been a big change for many enterprises. Moreover, the new ways of thinking continue to take on new frames as companies reckon with the challenges presented by the quality movement. Roles have shifted. Companies, in the demand for defect-free products, increasingly have started demanding the same of their suppliers. An organization committed to delivering the highest quality service or product needs to align itself with supplier companies and individuals who share this dedication to high-quality standards. This has led to more long-term relationships between companies and suppliers. Demming noted that "in long-term relationships both supplier and customer have a chance to learn from each other" (in Latzko & Saunders, 1995, p. 58). In this context, an organization's relationship with its suppliers is similar to the organization's relationship with its end-use customers. In other words, a firm that establishes a long-term, mutually beneficial relationship with suppliers is more likely to maintain consistently high quality.

And, if all of this information about quality and the changes that it has wrought in business has made us start to wonder about the cost of this reframe, Philip Crosby (1979) suggested that we think about that in another way, too. He reframes the entire nature of the cost of quality in the title of his seminal book, *Quality Is Free.*

MAJOR REFRAMES IN THE FIELD OF HUMAN SERVICES

How we think about what is most important in our work with people with disabilities are the frames that determine what values we
espouse, what we choose to do, and what we choose to learn. These
frames have been changing significantly in almost every area of
human services. For example, we heard a professional in the field
of developmental disabilities offer, by way of definition of the disability, "What we know is that these people learn more slowly."
This frames the entire nature of developmental disabilities as well
as the definition of learning, the process of learning, and, therefore,
the nature of our work with people "who learn more slowly." How
will we know if our work is successful? Using this professional's definition, we will watch for evidence of change, no matter how small,
no matter how long it takes. We will watch for evidence of learning,
and so we may pay more attention to what is to be learned and,
therefore, to what we will teach. Within this definition, our roles
are primarily as teachers and facilitators for those we support as
learners. We are the links to the world, the entire environment,
and those who are learning more slowly to more fully join in that
world. Our roles shift slightly from being primarily providers of
care to teachers. This definition affects what we will choose to learn
ourselves.

The Reframe of Person-Centered Planning

If we assume the roles of teachers and facilitators, what is it that we
are to teach, and what is it that we are to learn? This is where the
new frames of person-centered planning and the theory and practice
of the outcomes chosen by each individual become important. When
we have the concept of a "learner," it becomes important to know
what it is that the learner wants to learn so that we can provide the
necessary experiences and facilitate his or her interactions with the
environment. Only when we have this information can we teach
what the learner wants to learn, and therefore, help individuals
move toward those outcomes that they have chosen as the most important in their lives.

In this frame, we reframe the past in terms of what we did not
yet know. We reframe the future in terms of what we choose to learn
and the goals we set. The present is for providing experiences that
will give us the opportunity to learn in order to move toward important outcomes. Neither the past nor the future is who we are.
The learner is who we are. This is an empowering reframe because
no matter where we find ourselves, we will always determine what

is to be learned right here, right now. And we will go about setting goals for ourselves and designing learning experiments.

New Frames for Thinking About Environment

If we think of the immediate environment around a person as a "container" of that person, then we must immediately recognize that the container we provide for people with developmental disabilities is one that we are constantly attempting to grow and enlarge. This container—a known environment—is the place in which a person has the most safety, has the most familiarity, can move with ease, has the most defined choices, and knows the expectations of the environment and the people in it. Within this container, he or she can adjust expectations accordingly, with some real knowledge of cause and effect.

The concept of enlarging this space around a person with a disability is a major reframe. Knowing that the larger the container, the less predictable the environment, society historically has attempted to further and further restrict and constrict the containers provided for people with all types of disabilities. This is where the importance and the complexity of increased choice become apparent. The larger the container in which we live, the more choices we will be called on to make for ourselves. The larger the container, the more personal responsibility we have. The larger the container, the more information about choices is required. The container also must be large enough to allow for some real self-expression. Yet we must actually have a boundary to the container—the security of a known space—to have the comfort of ritual and the comfort of expectations that we can assume will be met.

The reframe here—that is, the change in mindset—is one of quality of life as opposed to the safety of imposed restriction. Just trying on this mindset, to the extent that it is different, will change our thinking, which will tend to change our behavior.

THEORY AND PRACTICE FOR ORGANIZATIONAL REFRAMING

Covey (1989) used the concept of a paradigm to explain how the way we see a situation and how we interpret its meaning determine our possible choices of response. Covey would give a drawing to participants in workshops that, depending on how one looked at it, could be a drawing of either a very young, smartly dressed woman or of a very old, haggard woman. He has his students write stories about the woman in the drawing and has the participants share their stories with each other. Students who saw the old woman in the drawing are in shock and disbelief when they hear stories about the young woman in the picture. Each group wonders about the sanity and sensory acuity of the other group. The perceptions of each group are so firm by the time they invent their stories that it takes a long time for each group to demonstrate to the other group that their eyes are seeing an accurate picture. Each section of the drawing must be explained in terms of the picture that they are seeing until the other group suddenly cries out, "Oh! I see her now." The lines and the shadows on the page had not changed, but only through reframing is each participant able to see two distinctly different pictures in those lines and shadows.

How an organization interprets the meaning of a situation will determine its choices and responses. Schwarz and Volgy (1985) challenged (and reframed) the meaning that the Reagan Administration put on the economic difficulties of the early 1980s. The authors used the analogy of a patient who was experiencing symptoms of the heart and respiratory system. These symptoms might indicate that the patient was having a heart attack. If that were the case, the patient would need immediate, drastic measures in order to pull through. They used this interpretation to explain the drastic, rather painful, measures of supply-side economics that the Reagan economists were proposing.

Schwarz and Volgy (1985) then took the exact same heart and respiratory symptoms and explained them as the symptoms of a person who was in the last half mile of a marathon race. The marathon runner had been taxing his physical systems in order to finish a highly unusual event that required great strength and stamina. Moreover, although the runner had used up all reserves in his physical system, the recommendation to the runner would be to rest for a period and then start building reserves again. If the symptoms of the runner were confused with those of a heart attack victim, the measures taken by doctors would either kill the runner or seriously damage his health.

The authors then went on to argue that the economy had just run a marathon, that it had demonstrated its strength and stamina in a difficult time, and that it was now time to rest and build reserves; it was not a time to take drastic measures in an experiment to find out what would "trickle down" to those who had already been called on to give their all and who had given it faithfully.

Analogies and metaphors can be useful tools in the challenge to see a business situation in a new way, through a new lens. Take the common example of interdepartmental strife. Imagine a situation in which accusations, mutual blaming, and miscommunication in a growing organization are escalating into a situation that could affect the quality of customer care. It can be useful to try on several different frames as a way of both gathering information and generating potential possibilities for intervention between noncooperating departments. One might look at such a situation through a number of lenses, such as family systems, complexity or self-organizing systems, organizational values and goals, intentions and expectations, organizational structure, and time and space.

Family Systems

If we look at a situation through a family-systems theory lens, we might gather information by asking the following questions:

- *Triangulation:* Is there a pattern of people drawing others into their interpersonal (or interdepartmental) conflicts? Is there a tendency to encourage people to take sides?
- *Distance:* Is communication among people in the departments becoming less frequent? Has communication been cut off altogether?
- *Over-focus:* How much organizational energy is focused (unproductively) on this particular conflict? What effect is this intense focus of attention having on other parts of the organization? On the conflict itself?

Complexity of Self-Organizing Systems

In 1992, Margaret Wheatley brought the new scientific theories of chaos and complexity into the world of business when she wrote *Leadership and the New Science.* Wheatley wrote about the nature of self-organizing systems in which

> Small, local disturbances are not suppressed; there is no central command control that prohibits small, constant changes. The system allows for many levels of autonomy within itself, and for small fluctuations and changes. By tolerating these, it is able to preserve its global stability and integrity in the environment. (1992, p. 95)

In light of this lens, or interpretation, we might bring the noncooperating departments together; make sure that it is clearly understood that organizational values will be upheld; ensure that the quality of care and service will be held to our highest standards; and then make resources of time, space, trust, and leadership available to both departments. We also would expect them to reorganize themselves in order to better serve both their customers and the overall organizational values.

Organizational Values and Goals

In viewing a conflict through an organization's values and goals, managers can ask the following questions:

- What is really most important in the organization—being right or meeting outcomes?
- To which organizational values could the conflict be giving voice?
- Does everyone involved know what the organizational values are? How do they know?

Intentions and Expectations

To ascertain the employees' intentions and expectations, managers can ask the following:

- What are the deeper intentions and expectations?
- What skills are required to meet those intentions and expectations?

Organizational Structure

A manager who views departmental conflict through an organizational structure lens might ask these questions:

- How does the current organizational structure foster the conflict?
- How is power being used in the conflict?
- Where is the organization's energy going? What is getting lost in the conflict? How can it be found again?

Time and Space

Changing the context of a situation often changes its meaning, which changes expectations, imagined possibilities, and choices of behavior. One way to change context is to expand, contract, or in some other way change the time and space within which a situation unfolds. A manager who views interdepartmental conflict through the lenses of changing time and space could explore conflict resolution options in the following ways:

- *Change the context.* Imagine that the conflict continues to escalate over the next year. What will it be like a year from now?
- *Imagine that the conflict has been solved* and that communication throughout the entire organization has improved as a result of steps taken and information generated. How did that happen? What was necessary?

Schwartz (1991) discussed the ability to try on different ways of making meaning by shifting time. He takes teams through a process of imagining what changing circumstances might mean. As the groups develop their stories of what they think will happen because of what is currently happening, they determine the best course of action based on that interpretation. Schwartz then has them put that one interpretation aside, take the same set of circumstances, apply a completely different meaning, and develop an appropriate course of action based on the new meaning given the same circumstances. The result of this kind of thinking and rethinking is a greatly increased ability on the part of team members to be able to see multiple potential interpretations of circumstances with which they are presented; and they develop a deeper wisdom about possible choices.

REFRAMING AND SYSTEMS THINKING

Systems thinking is described by Senge:

> Business and other human endeavors are . . . systems. They . . . are bound by invisible fabrics of interrelated actions, which often take years to fully play out their effects on each other. Since we are part of that lacework ourselves, it's doubly hard to see the whole pattern of change. . . . Systems thinking is a conceptual framework, a body of knowledge and tools that has been developed over the past fifty years, to make the full patterns clearer, and to help us see how to change them effectively. (1990, p. 7)

Senge introduced a tool for diagramming systems that shows cause and effect as a way to "see" what is actually happening graphically (i.e., how the elements of a system are related). This allows us to "step back" and see the situation portrayed outside of ourselves so that we can more objectively move things around, play with the variables, and make predictions. Any method we use that gives us more objectivity will help us to get out of our current frames of meaning and, therefore, to have more choices with which to experiment.

We invite consultants into our organizations in the hope that they will help us see our situations in new ways. Consultants can do this precisely because they are not deeply or historically involved in the organization. They tend to see in terms of patterns. Because they are detached from the organization, consultants are often able to discuss organizational patterns in objective terms. This, in turn, can teach the members of the organization to reframe their thinking into more objective language. An experienced consultant is also likely to have seen and worked with similar organizational patterns before, and we expect him or her to help the organization change frames with confidence.

Leadership and Management Issues

A frame's usefulness can be evaluated by the following seven objective variables: inclusiveness, connection to organizational values, positive focus, systemic in nature, uses strengths over weaknesses, emphasizes learning and possibility over failure or impossibility, and the new frame fits the mindset of the organization and participants.

Inclusiveness   A useful frame will tend to be more inclusive. This viewpoint will be able to incorporate many different, perhaps even disparate ideas. Helgesen (1995) offered a major reframe of the way organizations are organized. She contrasted the architecture of a web with the typical hierarchical structure of many organizations. She said that "the 'dynamic connectedness' of the web means that web organizations reflect organic rather than mechanical principles; that is, *they work in the same way that life does*" (1995, p. 16, italics in original).

Connection to Organizational Values   Organizational values can be fully supported by and connected to the most useful frames. These frames will tend to allow the most long-term thinking that will actually carry the organization's values through time.

Positive Focus   The most useful frames will be positive in focus and in language. Goals framed in terms of where we want to go are more achievable than those framed in terms of what we do not want to happen. Robbins noted that "reframing in its simplest form is changing a negative statement into a positive one by changing the frame of reference used to perceive the experience" (1986, p. 293).

Systemic in Nature   Frames fit not just one part of the organization but the organization as a whole. The frame takes into account the systemic nature of all decisions through time. Making use of systems diagramming is often helpful in determining the through-time effect of a way of thinking.

Uses Strengths over Weaknesses   As Clifton and Nelson stated, "The greatest chance for success lies in reminding people or organizations of an existing strength, and getting them back on track while instituting a management strategy for the weaknesses" (1992, p. 17).

Emphasizes Learning and Possibility over Failure or Impossibility   The concept of organizational learning is an empowering one. In fact, reframing "failure" into "learning" allows us to use the concept of continuous feedback and continuous learning while we make our way toward our goals and outcomes and strive to take our organizational values into the world. Kouzes and Posner (1993) had this to say about the importance of learning and leadership: "Developing capacity requires that leaders provide a climate conducive to learning. . . . A prime requirement for people to be capable of learning—able to change and develop new skills—is an environment in which they feel safe. They must be able to trust the system and the people involved" (p. 168). Developing good feedback systems for continuous learning is one of the prime responsibilities of leadership.

New Frame Fits the Mindset of the Organization and Participants
Senge introduced the notion of "mental models" and noted that

> One thing all managers know is that many of the best ideas never get put into practice. . . . We are coming increasingly to believe that this 'slip 'twixt cup and lip' stems, not from weak intentions, wavering will, or even nonsystemic understanding, but from mental models. More specifically, new insights fail to get put into practice because they conflict with deeply held internal images of how the world works, images that limit us to familiar ways of thinking and acting. That is why the discipline of managing mental models—surfacing, testing, and improving our internal pictures of how the world works—promises to be a major breakthrough for building learning organizations (1990, p. 174).

Reframing is a leadership and organizational skill that will go further than any other in allowing us to change mental models and to share useful mental models. In order to do this, the person or group attempting to reframe a situation must have a deep understanding of the current mental models in practice.

Reframing in Practice—Encountering Difference

Difference of opinion is difference in models. A difference in models produces a difference in framing and perceived or projected meaning on a given situation. In the field of disabilities there are many different mental models in practice. To understand what frames others are using and how they are making sense of the world through those frames, it is useful to examine and understand the prevalent models in the field (see Table 11.1). It is not surprising, then, that how one frames disabilities has everything to do with how he or she responds both personally and professionally. The frame influences the thinking in every aspect of approaching the person with a disability, and it affects all the systems and surroundings. Each frame offers a different view of the nature and source of the problem, evidence procedures, impact of the problem on the individual, solutions sought, and strategies employed.

In Daniel's (1991) model, the individual defect paradigm frames the desired outcomes in terms of improved functional capacity, return to work, and improved personal adjustment. The focus is on

Table 11.1.   Frames of reference

Paradigm/frame	Focus and emphasis of the frame
Individual defect	The patient, client, person with the disability
Community and social unit	The family, community, service system, decision makers
Technology/ecology	Systems of information, financing, implementation and development of assistive technology
Individual rights	Society, laws, regulations, relationships

Source: Daniels (1991).

fixing the individual. The community and social unit paradigm places value on stronger relationships, fuller life for all citizens, and community ownership of problems and solutions. The focus is on building community and family capacity to support people with disabilities. The technology/ecology frame uses filters to enhance individual choice and control through the use of technology. Access to information and technology is key to self-determination. The individual rights paradigm frames the rights and responsibilities of full citizenship. Disability is viewed in the frame of an ongoing civil rights struggle.

Each frame has its own language, cultural heroes, and advocates. It is easy to see that each paradigm or cluster of ideas puts a different frame on and shows a different picture of the same situation. Each view is not necessarily right or wrong, just a different point of view that is typically used by the advocates to sway public thinking and support.

MANAGEMENT PARADIGMS

Management is thought and subsequent behavior that is based on theories and ideas. How we do everything we do is based on a conscious or unconscious paradigm. We are full of assumptions, theories about how we work, how the world works, why people behave and misbehave the way they do, and how organizations work. Although many of these ideas are not conscious, they drive the frames that we put around each management situation.

Leaders draw on a variety of ideas and paradigms as they work to improve and change their organizations. Since the early 1970s, social scientists have focused on the ideas about how organizations work. The theory base is diverse, but four frames emerge (Bolman & Deal, 1991): rational systems, human resources, political, and symbolic.

Rational systems theorists focus on goals, roles, and technology. For them, the frame is about developing structures to support organizational purposes. Organizations establish purposeful goals and then select structure, policy, and procedure to accomplish those goals.

Human resources theorists focus on how to get a better alignment among people's needs, skills, values, and formal relationships. The frame emphasizes interdependence. Human resources theorists often are bored by discussions of structure and policy. In contrast, they place the priority on understanding one another.

Political theorists see the world through the filters of power, conflict, and the distribution of scarce resources. For them, organizations are like the wilds in which success comes to those who understand the uses of power, coalitions, bargaining, and conflict. Whereas rational systems theorists would design new structures to reduce conflict and human resource theorists would encourage people to talk it out, the political theorists would accept conflict and move on to building a larger coalition to exert more influence.

Symbolic theorists are concerned about problems of meaning. The frame here is that managers must rely on images, drama, magic, and luck to manage the meaning of events in the organization. Symbolic theorists are consummate reframers.

CONCLUSIONS: MAKING SENSE OF ANOTHER'S FRAMES

Understanding where others are "coming from" requires the ability to step outside one's own mental structures to perceive the situation through another person's frames. To find the sense in the situation that someone else sees, you have to look at it through his or her frame. Once you do that, you will have some ground for redirecting his or her attention to looking at it another way or through another frame.

Reframing is a tool, which when skillfully applied, can bring greater understanding of those who think and act differently than oneself. Knowing that there are different possible frames and paradigms will give us a way to engage those different models of the world in a deeper, more accepting way. We then can realize that those who disagree with us are speaking and acting from within a different frame, perhaps a different theory of disabilities, or a different theory of management.

By using reframing skills, we can explore the other person's views to find the frame of reference from which they are thinking and operating. Only then can we reframe the situation and move on to creating a frame that will allow the deeper intentions of both people to guide our plans and actions to mutually beneficial outcomes.

REFERENCES

Bandler, R., & Grinder, J. (1982). *Reframing.* Moab, UT: Real People Press.
Bolman, L.G., & Deal, T.E. (1991). *Reframing organizations: Artistry, choice, and leadership.* San Francisco: Jossey-Bass.
Clifton, D., & Nelson, P. (1992). *Soar with your strengths.* New York: Delacorte Press.
Covey, S. (1989). *The seven habits of highly effective people: Restoring the character ethic.* New York: Simon & Schuster.
Crosby, P. (1979). *Quality is free.* New York: McGraw-Hill.
Daniels, S. (1991). *Disability paradigm.* Unpublished manuscript, Washington, DC.
Daniels, S. (1993). *Disability paradigm.* Unpublished manuscript, Washington, DC.
Frankl, V.E. (1963). *Man's search for meaning: An introduction to logotherapy.* New York: Penguin USA.
Helgesen, S. (1995). *The web of inclusion.* New York: Currency/Doubleday.
Kouzes, J.M., & Posner, B.Z. (1993). *Credibility.* San Francisco: Jossey-Bass.
Latzko, W.J., & Saunders, D.M. (1995). *Four days with Dr. Deming: A strategy for modern methods of management.* Reading, MA: Addison-Wesley.
Ries, A., & Trout, J. (1981). *Positioning: The battle for your mind.* New York: McGraw-Hill.
Robbins, A. (1986). *Unlimited power.* New York: Fawcett Columbine.
Rosen, S. (1982). *My voice will go with you: The teaching tales of Milton H. Erickson.* New York: W.W. Norton.
Schwartz, P. (1991). *The art of the long view.* New York: Currency/Doubleday.
Schwarz, J.E., & Volgy, T.J. (1985). The myth of America's decline. *Harvard Business Review, 63,* 98–107.
Seligman, M. (1990). *Learned optimism.* New York: Alfred A. Knopf.
Senge, P.M. (1990). *The fifth discipline: The art and practice of the learning organization.* New York: Currency/Doubleday
Stack, J. (1992). *The great game of business.* New York: Currency/Doubleday.
Trout, J. (1995). *The new positioning.* New York: McGraw-Hill.
Wheatley, M.J. (1992). *Leadership and the new science.* San Francisco: Berrett-Koehler.

RECOMMENDED READINGS

Anderson, W.T. (1990). *Reality isn't what it used to be.* San Francisco: HarperCollins.
Carse, J.P. (1986). *Finite and infinite games.* New York: Ballantine Books.
Collins, J.C., & Porras, J.I. (1994). *Built to last.* New York: HarperCollins.
Crum, T.F. (1987). *The magic of conflict.* New York: Simon & Schuster.

DeBono, E. (1990). *I am right; you are wrong*. New York: Penguin USA.

Dobyns, L., & Crawford-Mason, C. (1991). *Quality or else*. Boston: Houghton Mifflin.

Dykstra, A., Jr. (1995). *Outcome management*. East Dundee, IL: High Tide Press.

Felts, B. (1993). Interview with Richard Bandler. *NLP Network News, 1*(4), 1–11.

Goldstein, J. (1994). *The unshackled organization*. Portland, OR: Productivity Press.

Hagen, S. (1995). *How the world can be the way it is*. Wheaton, IL: Quest Books.

Hardy, R.E., & Swartz, R. (1996). *The self-defeating organization*. Reading, MA: Addison-Wesley.

Kelley, R. (1992). *The power of followership*. New York: Currency/Doubleday.

Kohn, A. (1993). *Punished by rewards*. New York: Houghton Mifflin.

Lynch, D. (1984). *Your high performance business brain: An operator's manual*. Upper Saddle River, NJ: Prentice-Hall.

Lynch, D. (1988). *Strategy of the dolphin: Scoring a win in a chaotic world*. New York: William Morrow & Co.

Lynch, D., & Neenan, D. (1995). *Evergreen: Playing a continuous comeback business game*. Lakewood, CO: Brain Technologies Corporation.

Muldoon, B. (1996). *The heart of conflict*. New York: G.P. Putnam's Sons.

Ray, M., & Myers, R. (1986). *Creativity in business*. New York: Doubleday.

Ray, M., & Rinzler, A. (Eds.). (1993). *The new paradigm in business*. New York: Jeremy P. Tarcher.

Watzlawick, P. (1978). *The language of change*. New York: W.W. Norton.

Watzlawick, P. (1984). *The invented reality*. New York: W.W. Norton.

Watzlawick, P., Weakland, J., & Fisch, R. (1974). *Change: Principles of problem formation and problem resolution*. New York: W.W. Norton.

Wheatley, M.J. (1992). *Leadership and the new science*. San Francisco: Berrett-Koehler.

12

Quality Performance and Person-Centered Outcomes

Data as a Leadership Tool

Michael S. Chapman

Since the late 1960s, The Council on Quality and Leadership in Support for People with Disabilities (The Council) has designed and published quality-in-services standards for organizations supporting people with disabilities. In 1990, The Council decided to take a fresh look at quality and standards. The result was the publication of the *Outcome Based Performance Measures* in 1993. These measures redefined *service quality* by changing the focus of quality from compliance with organizational processes to responsiveness to individual outcomes. This new definition of service quality challenges service providers to redefine quality in terms of personal outcomes rather than program effectiveness. Defining quality in terms of personal outcomes requires a reorientation to quality enhancement. This new definition of quality poses challenges to the traditional forms of quality assurance.

QUALITY AS A DESIGN VARIABLE

The traditional quality assurance systems in human services organizations are derived from inspection and compliance models developed in industry. In these systems, quality is defined by the extent
of compliance with organizational process standards. But the measurement of noncompliance with organizational process is not necessarily connected to outcomes for people. Inspections identify but
do not contribute to the correction of deficiencies. From an outcomes
perspective, however, quality is a design variable that shapes and
supports services at the point of initiation. Outcome measures enable organizations to identify priority outcomes for each person and
then arrange supports and services to assist the individual to
achieve the outcomes. Services and supports for people with disabilities must be designed correctly from the beginning. A faulty
design results in supports or services of poor quality. Inspection will
only confirm that the design is incorrect, so improving quality requires moving beyond inspection. Quality results from the design
and redesign of services and supports around personal outcomes.

CONTEXT FOR OUTCOME MEASUREMENT

Program evaluation generally measures accomplishment of program
goals. Measures of efficiency and effectiveness are indicators of goal
attainment. Traditional program evaluation, however, is limited because program goals are set by management or funding sources and
not by the people receiving the services. As such, the program evaluation determines whether the program meets its own goals rather
than the outcomes of the people receiving the services and supports.

Person-focused outcomes are not measures of program efficiency or effectiveness. Person-focused outcomes are centered on the
individual not on programs or program categories. Person-focused
outcomes challenge program designs because they consider outcomes that fall outside of the program's boundaries. The measures
of success move from how well the professionals and the programs
are doing to how well the individual is doing in those areas (beyond
program boundaries, perhaps) that are most important to him or
her. Person-focused outcomes require that we establish direct connections among resources, processes, program goals, and person-
focused outcomes.

Measuring Quality—One Person at a Time

The Council's (1993) *Outcome Based Performance Measures* provide
an interview, observation, and document review protocol that en-

ables the service/support provider to identify each person's desired outcomes. Each person with a disability defines the specific meaning of each outcome measure for him- or herself. Although the definition of the outcome is subjective, the determination of whether the outcome is present—in the form and extent as defined by the individual—is objective.

The *Outcome Based Performance Measures* enable the service provider to measure whether the outcomes, as identified by the individual, are present. Once the individual identifies his or her personal outcome, the outcome can be defined and measured. Finally, the *Outcome Based Performance Measures* ask the service provider to identify the individualized organizational supports that facilitate each outcome for each person.

National Outcomes Database

Since the initial introduction of the *Outcome Based Performance Measures* in 1993, The Council has maintained a database of individuals who have participated in interviews during accreditation reviews. As of 1998, 1,861 individuals across the United States are included in the database. A separate database is maintained on the reliability of the instrument. These two databases continue to serve as the foundation for numerous statistical studies at various points in the instrument's evolution. Studies of the *Outcome Based Performance Measures* have found the instrument to be reliable and valid. The overall reliability of the instrument is .88 (Gardner, Nudler, & Chapman, 1997). Table 12.1 presents the validity data and factor loadings.

Through factor analysis studies, The Council has demonstrated the feasibility of measuring quality in terms of personal outcomes rather than in terms of compliance with organizational process or attainment of a score on a standardized outcome scale. The 24 variables load onto 7 constructs (see Table 12.1). These constructs include identity, autonomy, affiliation, attainment, rights, health, and safeguards. These 7 constructs represent a model for better understanding the person with disabilities, including people with mental illness. Analysis of the data provides information on each outcome and associated organizational supports and serves as the foundation for the revised *Personal Outcome Measures* (Gardner et al., 1997). Table 12.2 identifies the national statistics obtained for each outcome and associated organizational supports for the revised edition.

The data presented in Table 12.2 suggest that some outcomes are harder to obtain than others. Some outcomes are difficult to achieve, which is defined as being present in less than half of the sample; conversely, some outcomes are more than likely present for

Table 12.1. Factor loadings, commonalities (h^2), percents of variance and covariance on *Outcome Based Performance Measures* items

Outcome	1	2	3	4	5	6	7	h^2
				Factors[a]				
29	.75							.62
30	.74							.62
13	.51							.47
3	.44							.57
4	.32							.57
1	.32							.50
20		.73						.57
18		.63						.53
24		.44						.45
7		.35						.51
11			.74					.62
9			.55					.63
10			.51					.59
25			.42					.62
17			.41					.50
8			.40					.61
6				.66				.57
2				.64				.58
14					.70			.55
28						.75		.72
16						.67		.63
22						.30		.40
23							.82	.72
12							.39	.52

[a]Factors are, respectively, 1, Identity; 2, Autonomy; 3, Affiliation; 4, Attainment; 5, Rights; 6, Health; 7, Safeguards.

individuals (see Table 12.2). In a similar manner, many organizations lack supports or procedures for ensuring the attainment of outcomes for people; whereas many organizations have systems in place that facilitate the attainment of outcomes (see Table 12.2).

Analyses of the data in Table 12.2 suggest that the presence of strong individualized organizational supports result in the attainment of outcomes for individuals supported by the organization. Conversely, weak or absent individualized organizational supports result in outcomes that are not present for individuals. Further analyses suggest that higher-order items or those items associated with self-fulfillment (e.g., choice, social roles, rights) are more difficult to attain, whereas basic supports or safeguards (e.g., safety, continuity and security, freedom from abuse and neglect) are more often present.

These findings are more than likely directly attributed to the evolution of the service delivery system since the 1960s. Reports of mistreatment or even no treatment as described by Blatt and Kap-

Table 12.2.   Personal Outcome Measures: Accreditation and evaluation systems

Construct	Variable	Outcome (% present)	Process (% present)
Identity	People choose personal goals[a,c]	36.2	35.8
	People choose where and with whom to live[a]	44.1	57.3
	People choose where they work[a,c]	35.0	45.2
	People have intimate relationships	68.8	62.9
	People are satisfied with services [b]	85.7	68.5
	People are satisfied with their personal life situations [b]	82.4	78.5
Autonomy	People choose their daily routines [b,c,d]	81.1	82.0
	People have time, space, and opportunity for privacy [b,d]	87.0	90.8
	People decide when to share personal information [b]	87.9	75.7
	People use their environments [d]	76.4	83.0
Affiliation	People live in integrated environments[a,c]	26.6	34.3
	People participate in the life of the community[a,d]	85.2	87.1
	People interact with other members of the community	63.7	65.0
	People perform different social roles[a,c]	29.9	28.6
	People have friends	60.4	57.0
	People are respected	71.5	73.6
Attainment	People choose services[a,c]	43.8	45.9
	People realize personal goals[b,d]	84.9	84.5
Safeguards	People remain connected to natural support networks[d]	72.0	80.7
	People are safe[b,d]	88.5	81.7
Rights	People exercise rights[a,c]	25.9	27.5
Health	People have the best possible health	69.5	72.0
	People are free from abuse and neglect [b,d]	87.0	88.5
	People experience continuity and security [b,d]	88.4	92.7

[a] Outcomes that are more difficult to achieve (defined as occurring in less than 50% of the sample).
[b] Outcomes that are more often achieved (defined as occurring in more than 80% of the sample).
[c] Outcomes that many organizations lack processes or procedures for attaining (defined as occurring in less than 50% of the sample).
[d] Outcomes that many organizations have processes or procedures for attaining (defined as occurring in more than 80% of samples).
Note: Review of national statistics ($N = 1,861$).

lan (1966) and Trent (1994) resulted in strict state and federal regulations over the provision of care for individuals with disabilities.
These regulations often addressed the health, safety, and welfare of
individuals with disabilities and the requirements of organizations
to safeguard these areas. The data suggest that the field has made
progress in those areas. Yet, moving beyond these basic safeguards
presents many challenges to organizations as they identify strategies for assisting individuals to become self-sufficient.

The national database on outcomes also contains demographic
data on the individuals participating in the interview process and
descriptive data on organizations that support people with disabilities. Maintaining data in this manner, The Council is able to analyze data from a variety of different perspectives. For example, the
data suggest the following (Figures 12.1 through 12.4 describe additional findings from these data):

- As the age of the population increases, the number of outcomes
  in six categories—goals, choice, social inclusion, relationships,
  dignity, and environment—decreased significantly; whereas
  there were no significant changes in the health, security, satisfaction, and rights categories.
- People with profound mental retardation have significantly
  lower scores than those with all other disabilities.
- People with severe mental retardation have significantly lower
  scores than those with mild mental retardation, cerebral palsy,
  autism, or mental illness.
- When the level of disability is held constant, people with the
  most severe disabilities achieve more outcomes in Supported

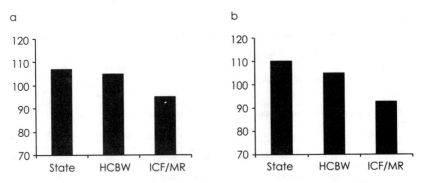

Figure 12.1.   Mean summation score: a) by source of funding; and b) by source of funding,
entire sample.

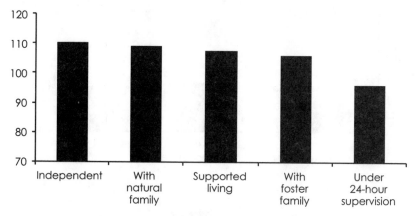

Figure 12.2.   Mean summation score—by living arrangement, entire sample.

Living settings than in Intermediate Care Facilities for the Mentally Retarded (ICFs/MR).

- Individuals for whom the staff was the source of information scored higher than those for whom the family or the person him- or herself was the source of information.
- Individuals who received the following services—case management, early intervention, family support, and/or supported employment—scored higher than those who did not.
- People who are in work activity centers and workshop settings scored lower than those who were not in those settings.

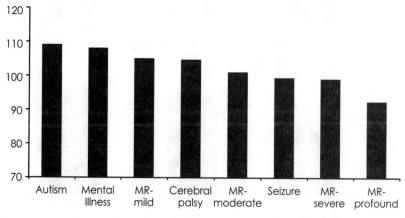

Figure 12.3.   Mean summation score—by primary disability, entire sample (MR, mental retardation).

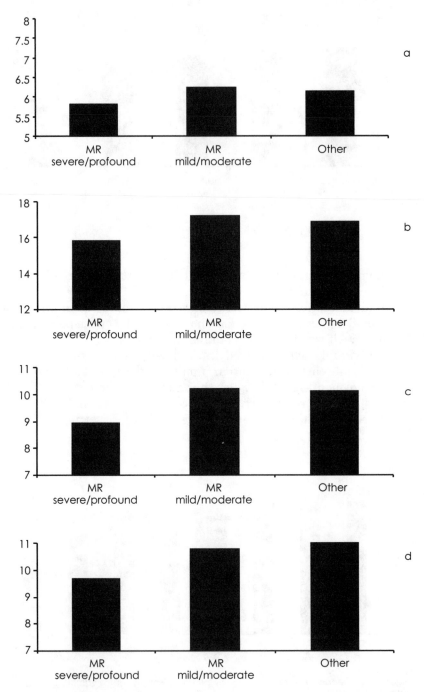

Figure 12.4.   Mean summation score—by outcome: a) goals, b) choice, c) social, and d) relationships (MR, mental retardation).

DATA AS A LEADERSHIP TOOL

As illustrated in the previous section, data and the presentation of data are powerful management tools. The leaders of organizations need data. If data are to be useful to organizations, then a data management strategy must be developed. Many organizations collect hoards of data on the premise that they might be needed someday. Data collection, storage, and retrieval is an expensive proposition for most organizations. Absent a data management strategy, organizations waste considerable time and effort. Each data element collected has a price tag associated with it. Therefore, the prudent leader develops clear strategies for data use and reporting. Figure 12.5 presents a data management strategy. Each element in Figure 12.5 builds on the previous one and is discussed in the next section.

Define the Need for Data

A data management strategy begins with clearly defining the need for data. Whether the organization is pursing personal outcomes or tracking its expenditures, clearly defined informational needs and the corresponding data will assist leadership with assessing organizational effectiveness. As stated previously, collecting data can be expensive. Therefore, this first step—defining the need for data—is a critical one. Leadership needs to plan to collect enough data to answer strategic organizational questions at a reasonable cost but not collect too much that the data burden staff and incur undo cost. Leadership needs to clearly define what questions are to be addressed through the gathering of data. For example, organizations pursuing personal outcomes may want to know which

- Outcomes are occurring with the greatest frequency
- Outcomes are occurring with the least frequency
- Organizational processes support achieving outcomes
- Organizational processes hinder attaining outcomes
- Departments within the organization are aligned with personal outcomes
- Consumer characteristics present challenges to organizations in achieving outcomes

There are multiple needs for data within an organization. A list of written questions will assist with organizing data flow for the organization.

Define the Audience for the Data

The next step is to define the audience for the data. Audiences change from situation to situation and may include the organiza-

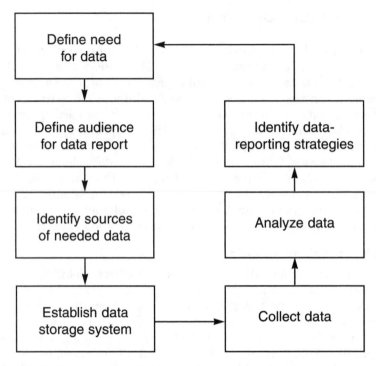

Figure 12.5. Data management strategy.

tion's board, consumers and their parents, the general public, fiscal auditors, state governmental officials, elected officials, or the federal government, to name a few. Each of these groups may have different data reporting needs. Understanding the audience and their need for data will help to ensure that the correct data are collected and reported.

Identify Sources of Data

Data exist at various locations within an organization. Some rest within a computer program, spreadsheet, or database; some within consumer records; and even other data within the heads of staff. Accessing data becomes an important and time-consuming organizational process. In a strategic data management system, sources of data are directly linked or mapped to the need for the data, whereas staff members are identified to maintain data and the data's accuracy. Developing a data source book helps to ensure that all data collected are known to the organization's leadership. Through this process, the leaders are able to evaluate the appropriateness of each data element and its utility to the organization. By developing a coherent process of collecting and evaluating data, management can ensure that staff recognize the process as essential to organizational activity. The process of data collection and evaluation, or organizational mapping, continues for each data element collected by the organization. It is also helpful to survey the staff to determine whether databases unknown to management exist within the organization. These databases, although potentially helpful, may contain duplicated data that result in redundancy and inefficiencies. Figure 12.6 provides an example of an organizational mapping system.

Establish a Data Storage System

Different data elements require different storage capacities. Some data are best stored in a computer database, whereas for other data, pencil and paper work best. The essential element of this step is to avoid duplication of effort by tracing sources of data directly to their storage systems. For example, many organizations collect demographic data on each person receiving services as a part of their admissions procedures. The same data often are repeated in the financial system and in the service coordinator's database. Duplicated data storage systems are expensive and increase the possibilities of data errors.

Collect Data

Some data are collected on an ongoing basis, whereas other data are collected only periodically. Having defined data collection protocols for each needed data element will aid in setting the staff's expecta-

Data element	Type of data	Location	Responsible staff
Date of admissions	Numerical	Mainframe computer	Lauren Reed
Individual's age	Numerical	Mainframe computer	Lauren Reed
Individual's goals/ progress	Alphabetical	ISP database— Service coordinator's personal computer	Kate Logan
Last physical exam	Alpha-numerical	Medical record— Section 2-A	Sally Kees

Figure 12.6.   Sample organizational mapping system.

tions. It also will help to ensure that data will be available when they are needed. Equally important is helping staff to understand why they are being asked to collect data. Without a clear understanding, the integrity of the data may be compromised as staff may not take the data collection process seriously.

Analyze Data

All data are open to interpretations. Whether using a calculator or a sophisticated statistical software program, data analysis is used to put an order to the data collected. Analysis helps to organize data in a way that makes interpretations possible. As in the previous step, analysis may be required on an ongoing basis or only periodically, depending on the question that is being addressed. Developing expertise in data analysis will help organizations to interpret data and to improve the organization's internal quality enhancement process. Some staff members often believe that listing data is, in itself, the same as analysis. Data analysis, however, requires an in-depth review and interpretation of listed data. The process of understanding what the data mean or how the results were obtained enable staff members to better understand the organization. It also enables the staff to more effectively develop organizational improvement plans.

Identify Data Reporting Strategies

The presentation of data helps organizations to effectively communicate with their defined audience. Tables, figures, or graphs are commonly used strategies for reporting data. Organizations using one of these to report data should adopt simplicity as a guide to reporting data. Many organizations put too much data in a single reporting format. This often confuses the audience. Rather, it is best to report data results that directly address a particular question. Multiple reporting strategies also may serve to help the defined audience to view the results from a variety of different angles. This may result in an increased understanding of what the data analysis results tell the organization about its services and supports.

Implement the Strategy

The primary goal of developing and implementing a data management strategy is to ensure an integrated data utility system within the organization. Yet, this can only be achieved when the organization's leadership addresses three issues for making information useful to others: timeliness, accuracy, and relevance. These three issues directly reflect the value that useful data have to others within or outside the organization.

Timeliness   Timeliness of data reporting is crucial. Many staff members within an organization develop a sense of what is occurring within the organization from the daily performance of their duties. Data not reported in a timely manner often are viewed as old news or outdated by the time they reach staff. The timeliness of data reporting affects staff members' abilities to effectively respond to issues and to their confidence that the right issue has been addressed. The organization's leadership must ensure timely data in order for the staff to be effective.

Accuracy   Managers and staff members also must have a level of confidence in the accuracy of the reported data. Without data accuracy, the data are useless. Determination of accuracy means that the right numbers were collected and analyzed but also that the analysis consisted of appropriate measurement strategies. Defined audiences, and especially staff members, must trust the accuracy of the data. The data reported must mesh with people's daily observations in order for the data to have any real meaning.

Relevance   Data relevance must be addressed if the data reports are to have meaning. Relevance is strengthened by timeliness and accuracy yet must relate to a need-to-know relationship within the organization. Relevance often is confounded by data reports that are too detailed or complicated to understand. Relevancy best relates to the business of the organization and focuses on measuring the right things for the right reasons. These reasons are typically articulated in the organization's mission statement. All targeted audiences (e.g., staff members in performing their day-to-day activities, consumers in achieving personal outcomes, legislatures in determining value in services and supports) must find the data reports useful and relevant.

CASE STUDIES

The following case studies present various strategies for analyzing data collected using the *Personal Outcome Measures* (The Accreditation Council, 1997) during a self-assessment workshop. These cases, which are fictional conglomerates of typical service organizations, are designed to illustrate data as a leadership tool.

L & K Services, Inc.

L & K Services, Inc., is a day and residential care provider located in a southeastern state. At the time of the self-assessment workshop, L & K was operating six group homes in scattered supervised apartment settings and providing supported employment services.

A total of 65 individuals were receiving services from the company. All individuals were between the ages of 18 and 60 years and had varying degrees of mental retardation and support needs (requiring intermittent supports, 32%; limited supports, 22%; extensive supports, 41%; and pervasive supports, 6%). In addition to mental retardation, 14% had cerebral palsy, 28% had a seizure disorder, 45% had vision impairments, and 19% experienced difficulty with mobility. The accreditation review was conducted over a 3-day period. A total of six randomly selected individuals participated in the interview process using the *Personal Outcome Measures*. Table 12.3 shows the number of personal supports and individualized process measures that were present for the six individuals in the sample.

Analysis of the data in Table 12.3 may take one of several directions. Analysis may focus on each individual within the sample, the group as a representative sample of the organization, or the individual and/or group as compared with available national statistics. Regardless of the direction that the analysis may take, it is important to remain focused on the intent of an analysis—which is organizational performance improvement. Without a clear focus or context for the analysis, it is possible that the analysis will be meaningless and, thus, will result in no changes for people supported by the organization. It is impossible to make changes in one subsystem without considering its effect on each of the other subsystems. Attention to each subsystem increases the possibility of successful organizational performance improvements. (Chapter 10 presents a discussion of organizational analysis. Figure 10.1 shows the interconnectedness of each of the subsystems.)

For the purpose of the data presented in Table 12.3, analysis of the group as a representative sample of individuals supported by the organization follows. First, it is helpful to identify those areas of organizational strength. This is defined as those areas in which the personal outcomes and associated organizational processes are present for the majority of people in the sample. It is also helpful to convert the number to percentages to better analyze the impact of the area on the total number of individuals supported by the organization.

An analysis of strengths is important to an organization. It provides an opportunity to review with staff those organizational supports that produce desired organizational outcomes. It also provides an opportunity for celebration and recognition, whereas it enables leaders to target organizational improvement efforts and to establish benchmarks for organizational behavior. Table 12.4 demonstrates areas of strength. For example, the strengths presented in Table 12.4 are present in the majority of people supported. Closer

Table 12.3. Number of personalized supports and individualized process measures: L & K Services, Inc.

Construct	Variable	Outcome (number)	Supports (number)
Identity	People choose personal goals	0	0
	People choose where and with whom to live	4	2
	People choose where they work	1	1
	People have intimate relationships	5	3
	People are satisfied with services	6	4
	People are satisfied with their personal life situations	6	5
Autonomy	People choose their daily routines	6	6
	People have time, space, and opportunity for privacy	6	6
	People decide when to share personal information	4	4
	People use their environments	6	6
Affiliation	People live in integrated environments	0	0
	People participate in the life of the community	6	6
	People interact with other members of the community	6	5
	People perform different social roles	2	0
	People have friends	4	4
	People are respected	4	4
Attainment	People choose services	0	0
	People realize personal goals	6	6
Safeguards	People remain connected to natural support networks	5	5
	People are safe	5	5
Rights	People exercise rights	1	2
Health	People have the best possible health	5	3
	People are free from abuse and neglect	4	5
	People experience continuity and security	4	4

Note: Number of outcomes and processes present (N = 6).

analysis of each variable, however, may suggest a level of dissatisfaction with the results obtained; for example, consider the outcome *People have friends.* The personal outcome and associated personal organizational supports are present for 67% of the people supported. Although an outcome may be present in the majority of the group, leaders still must determine whether the results are

Table 12.4.   Areas of strength: L & K Services, Inc.

Variable	Outcomes (number)	(%)	Supports (number)	(%)
People are satisfied with services	6	100	4	67
People are satisfied with their personal life situations	6	100	6	100
People choose their daily routines	6	100	6	100
People have time, space, and opportunity for privacy	6	100	6	100
People decide when to share personal information	4	67	4	67
People use their environments	6	100	6	100
People participate in the life of the community	6	100	6	100
People interact with other members of the community	6	100	5	83
People have friends	4	67	4	67
People are respected	4	67	4	67
People realize personal goals	6	100	6	100
People are free from abuse and neglect	4	67	5	83
People experience continuity and security	4	67	4	67
People remain connected to natural support networks	5	87	5	87
People are safe	5	87	5	87

acceptable. In doing so, for example, leaders must identify whether there are situations in which not having friends is acceptable. Having friends, clearly, is important. It would not be acceptable to exclude individuals from establishing friendships if they chose to develop friendships. If this opportunity is not available to consumers, then leaders must determine where the system is breaking down and establish a clear course of action for the staff to follow to fix the system. This is where the organizational analysis provides the leader with a system for review. Walking through each subsystem and responding to a series of questions should reveal where the problem(s) are and where organizational improvement efforts may be directed. Continuing with this example, consider the area of having friends for each subsystem—the organization's mission, work tasks, work methods, structure, and people.

The Organization's Mission

- Is the mission clear, concise, and understood by all employees?
- Are the underlying values clear, concise, and shared by all employees?

- Does the mission statement energize staff?
- Are all services and supports provided permissible within the mission?

Discussions with the staff during the self-assessment indicated that establishing and maintaining friendships are values of L & K Services, Inc. Staff members believe in encouraging friendships among the supported individuals. Further analysis, however, indicated that encouraging individuals to develop friendships is an unspoken value that was not clearly identified as part of L & K's mission statement or philosophy. Organizational improvement efforts were directed toward making explicit the value of friendships in the organization's mission and philosophy statements.

Work Tasks

- Do work tasks flow from the mission statement?
- Are staff members clear about what the work of the organization is?
- Do staff members and consumers have input into determining the work tasks of the organization?
- Does each staff member understand the contribution of his or her work to the overall work tasks of the organization?
- Is there a fit between what staff members do on a day-to-day basis and the overall work of the organization?
- Are work tasks openly discussed on a defined basis?

The implicit nature of having friends resulted in episodic connections for people. It was determined that friendships were present for those individuals whose support staff believed it to be important and who encouraged a process for developing friendships for the person. Further analysis indicated that the majority of these connections were between the person and other people supported by the organization or between the person and staff member. Staff members had not looked beyond the organization for possible friendships. Following discussions, the L & K staff concluded that the work task of each team member is to encourage the development of friendships, not only those with other individuals supported or staff but also those outside the service program.

Work Methods

- Are staff members clear about how they perform their work tasks?
- Are staff members clear about the various elements of the work they do?

- Are the communication links about how staff members do the work open?
- Is there a system of continuous feedback for staff members regarding the work they do?
- Is there an open system for reviewing how work is done?
- Are the work methods producing the desired results?

The process of assisting others to establish and to maintain friendships was unclear to the majority of L & K staff members. Suggestions to start a Friends Club were discussed and then later dropped. Final recommendations were to pursue friendships person by person. This included staff members' having discussions with each person, identifying the person's desires for friendships, identifying other people with whom the person has an interest in developing friendships, and discussing strategies for working with each person to pursue friendships. The staff further agreed that possible relationships beyond those within the organization should be included in this process.

Structure

- Is the organization structured in a way that promotes the accomplishment of the mission, work tasks, and work methods?
- Is the organizational structure clear to the staff?
- Is the organizational structure free of unnecessary bureaucratic layers?
- Are the staff members clear on how the various layers relate to one another?
- Are the right people performing the right duties at the right time and place?
- Is there an ongoing system for monitoring the efficiencies of the organization's structure?
- Is the organizational structure supportive of the work methods in producing the desired results?

A review of L & K's structure supported a system in which staff members would work with each person to establish friendships. Each individual was assigned to a team of other individuals, and each team was assigned support staff. In addition, each individual received natural supports and was provided access to situations that would foster the development of friendships.

People

- Is the right person performing the right job?
- Are staff members competent to perform assigned duties?

- Do staff members receive training to increase competency?
- Do staff members receive ongoing meaningful feedback regarding performance?
- Do staff members feel supported to complete assigned duties?
- Do staff members understand the boundaries in which to operate?

The self-assessment process suggested that staff members did not feel competent to support the outcome of having friends. Friendships are not part of any staff development efforts sponsored by the organization. It was recommended that outside consultants offer a series of workshops to assist all staff members with defining and refining strategies for maintaining friendships. It was also recommended that this become a requirement for new staff orientation.

This review process is completed for each area of strength needing an organizational improvement effort. In addition to analyzing strengths, the leaders also must conduct a more in-depth analysis of identified areas of weakness (see Table 12.5 for those variables applicable to L & K).

An analysis of organizational challenges requires energy and fortitude. It presents many challenges to the leaders and staff of an organization. Yet, the benefits of conducting an organizational analysis of challenges will have a significant impact on the organization and on the individuals receiving supports as the organization pursues improvement efforts. From a broad perspective of comparing areas of strengths and challenges, it is readily apparent that Maslow's (1970) concept of self-actualization composes the bulk of identified challenges. Control and influence over one's own life is the essence of self-actualization. It is incumbent upon leaders not only to ensure the health, safety, and welfare of each person under their care but also to ensure that each person has control and influence over his or her own life.

Leaders complete the same organizational analysis steps as defined in the previous section with one exception. In contrast to the areas of strength, in which the emphasis is probably on refining existing organizational supports, the identified challenges will require reframing major areas of the organization (see Chapter 11). This will be especially true of those personal outcomes and associated personal organizational supports that are not present for the entire group. Reframing is not easy and will require considerable work on the part of staff. The leaders must give close attention to each subsystem in the development of an organizational improvement strategy.

Table 12.5.   Number and percentages of outcomes and supports: L & K Services, Inc.

Variable	Outcomes (number)	(%)	Supports (number)	(%)
People choose personal goals	0	0	0	0
People choose where and with whom to live	4	67	2	33
People choose where they work	1	17	1	17
People have intimate relationships	5	83	3	50
People perform different social roles	2	33	0	0
People live in integrated environments	0	0	0	0
People choose services	0	0	0	0
People exercise rights	1	17	2	33
People have the best possible health	5	83	3	50

Community Support Services, Inc.

Some leaders prefer to conduct organizational analyses by converting the number of personal and organizational outcomes to percentages and comparing these data to national statistics. Community Support Services (CSS), Inc., is a day and residential provider located in a midwest state. At the time of the self-assessment, they supported 265 individuals in residential and day services programs. Residential supports included a large dormitory and scattered apartments. Day services consisted of 2-day activity centers, vocational development, prevocational development, and a senior citizens program. All individuals were between the ages of 18 and 75 years and had varying degrees of mental retardation (requiring intermittent supports, 13%; limited supports, 20%; extensive supports, 33%; and pervasive supports, 34%). In addition to mental retardation, 2% had autism, 23% had cerebral palsy, 28% had a seizure disorder, 10% had hearing impairments, 13% had vision impairments, and 23% experienced difficulty with mobility. The self-assessment was conducted over a 5-day period. A total of 15 randomly selected individuals participated in the interview process using the *Personal Outcome Measures* (Gardner et al., 1997). Tables 12.6 and 12.7 show the percentage of personal outcomes and individualized process measures present for the 15 individuals in the sample and the national statistics, respectively.

It is helpful to organize the data into organizational strengths and challenges. The data in Table 12.8 represent a summary of the outcomes present for CSS. In Table 12.8, the left column represents those personal outcomes obtained at CSS that exceed the national statistics, whereas those on the right fall below the national statistics. Areas of challenge are obviously of concern. Several of these areas are significantly below the national statistics. The data suggest that the organization is grounded in traditional services and supports—specifically those that promote health, safety, and welfare. CSS, given the significant differences between the national statistics and the organization's data, should seriously reevaluate

Table 12.6.   Percentage of personal outcomes present compared with the national statistics: Community Support Services, Inc.

Construct	Variable	National data (%)	CSS data (%)	+/−
Identity	Choose personal goals	36.2	40	3.8
	Choose where and with whom to live	44.1	47	2.9
	Choose where they work	35.0	27	−8.0
	Intimate relationships	68.8	67	−1.8
	Satisfied with services	85.7	100	14.3
	Satisfied with their personal life situations	82.4	100	17.6
Autonomy	Choose their daily routines	81.1	60	−21.1
	Time, space, and opportunity for privacy	87.0	100	13.0
	Decide when to share personal information	87.9	93	5.1
	Use their environments	76.4	60	−16.4
Affiliation	Live in integrated environments	26.6	20	−6.6
	Participate in the life of the community	85.2	67	−18.2
	Interact with other members of the community	63.7	47	−16.7
	Perform different social roles	29.9	20	−9.9
	Have friends	60.4	53	−7.4
	Are respected	71.5	27	−44.5
Attainment	Choose services	43.8	13	−30.8
	Realize personal goals	84.9	93	8.1
Safeguards	Remain connected to natural support networks	72.0	80	8.0
	Are safe	88.5	93	4.5
Rights	Exercise rights	25.9	13	−12.9
Health	Have the best possible health	69.5	80	10.5
	Free from abuse and neglect	87.0	100	13.0
	Experience continuity and security	88.4	100	11.6

Table 12.7. Percentage of processes present compared with the national statistics: Community Support Services, Inc.

Construct	Variable	National data (%)	CSS data (%)	+/−
Identity	Choose personal goals	35.8	40	4.2
	Choose where and with whom to live	57.3	60	2.7
	Choose where they work	45.2	27	−18.2
	Intimate relationships	62.9	87	24.1
	Satisfied with services	68.5	100	31.5
	Satisfied with their personal life situations	78.5	100	21.5
Autonomy	Choose their daily routines	82.0	67	−15.0
	Time, space, and opportunity for privacy	90.8	100	9.2
	Decide when to share personal information	75.7	93	17.3
	Use their environments	83.0	60	−23.0
Affiliation	Live in integrated environments	34.3	27	−7.3
	Participate in the life of the community	87.1	80	−7.1
	Interact with other members of the community	65.0	60	−5.0
	Perform different social roles	28.6	13	−15.6
	Have friends	57.0	80	23.0
	Are respected	73.6	27	−46.6
Attainment	Choose services	45.9	13	−32.9
	Realize personal goals	84.5	93	8.5
Safeguards	Remain connected to natural support networks	80.7	93	12.3
	Are safe	81.7	93	11.3
Rights	Exercise rights	27.5	13	−14.5
Health	Have the best possible health	72.0	93	21.0
	Free from abuse and neglect	88.5	100	11.5
	Experience continuity and security	92.7	100	7.3

its commitment to personal outcomes. (See Chapters 1 and 2 for a discussion of suboptimization as an organizational barrier.) One must consider whether CSS has, in fact, become proficient at performing the wrong task. Organizational improvement efforts for CSS should begin with a values audit. The data suggest that the basics of respect, choice, and rights are far below the national statistics. CSS is in clear need of leadership to guide the organizational change process. Once the values audit is completed, the organiza-

Table 12.8. Summary of outcomes (strengths and challenges): Community Support Services, Inc.

Outcome (Strengths)	+/−	Outcome (Challenges)	+/−
Satisfied with their personal life situations	17.6	Are respected	−44.5
Time, space, and opportunity for privacy	13.0	Choose services	−30.8
Satisfied with services	14.3	Choose where they work	−8.0
Free from abuse and neglect	13.0	Choose their daily routines	−21.1
Have the best possible health	10.5	Participate in the life of the community	−18.2
Experience continuity and security	11.6	Use their environments	−16.7
Realize personal goals	8.1	Exercise rights	−12.9
Remain connected to natural support networks	8.0	Interact with other members of the community	−16.7
Are safe	4.5	Perform different social roles	−9.9
Decide when to share personal information	5.1	Have friends	−7.4

tion should review each organizational subsystem as illustrated by the first case study.

LEADERSHIP AND INFORMATION MANAGEMENT

Data and information extend leadership capabilities, but they do not substitute for leadership. They cannot replace the need for compelling vision, effective human resources management, solid business practices, and a commitment to quality. Data and information, however, do maximize leadership effectiveness in all of these areas.

Vision and values define the future for the organization. Leadership energy and action move the organization toward the vision and values. Data and information define the road to be traveled and measure the progress of the journey; furthermore, they increase the leader's ability to

- *Measure and communicate organizational progress toward goals and objectives.* Nonpersonal, objective feedback enables the leader to focus feedback on data not on personality. The feedback is not directed at any individual. Rather, the leader uses the information to speak for itself.
- *Measure and count data.* In human services, what the organization measures and counts—whether it be placements, square footage of buildings, or personal outcomes achieved—is what the organization tends to accomplish.

- *Present an argument or position without carrying a personal message.* Without expending precious leadership capital to advance a position, the leader can allow the data to make the case and conserve valuable political capital and "IOUs" for later expenditures.
- *Build credibility.* There is so little solid data and information in human services systems that the use of data and information is, in itself, striking. Coupled with human interest and personal anecdotes, data builds credibility in reports, grant proposals, and fund-raising efforts.
- *Acquire funding.* In a contest over funding allocations, the organization or the part of the organization with data prevails. "In God we trust; all others must present data" is an apt description of state legislative skepticism.
- *Focus issues.* Organizational debate that is focused on issues and grounded in data and information is less likely to fall victim to clashes of personality or feuds based on personal issues.

CONCLUSIONS

Data are excellent resource tools for leaders and staff of organizations, but data collection for the sake of data collection is a waste of time and energy. For data to have significant meaning, the organization must have a data management strategy. A strategy ensures that the right data are collected by the right people about the right issues. Analysis of data can provide a road map to guide and evaluate organizational improvement efforts. Data collected and analyzed on the organization's efforts to ensure personal outcomes for the individuals whom it supports provides a balance between organizational processes and the effects of those processes on the attainment of personal outcomes.

Data guide organizational behavior. They also provide a means for group diagnosis and problem solving within an organization. Taking critical data elements and conducting an organizational analysis assists leaders with problem solving and planning for the future. The organizational analysis consists of reviewing each subsystem of the organization, including mission statements, work tasks, work methods, structure, and people. Making changes in one subsystem requires a review of each subsystem to ensure the successful implementation of a quality improvement effort.

Finally, data will not replace the collective years of staff wisdom. Data analysis must be considered within the context of organizational fit. Do the data fit with what the staff believe to be true?

This is not to say that staff members will dismiss data that are uncomfortable, but rather data validate what staff members know to be true about the organization.

REFERENCES

Blatt, B., & Kaplan, F. (1966). *Christmas in purgatory: A photographic essay on mental retardation*. Needham, MA: Allyn & Bacon.

Gardner, J.F., Nudler, S., & Chapman, M.S. (1997). Personal outcomes as measures of quality. *Mental Retardation, 35*(4), 295–305.

Maslow, A. (1970). *Motivation and personality* (2nd ed.). New York: Harper & Row.

The Accreditation Council on Services for People with Disabilities. (1993). *Outcome Based Performance Measures*. Towson, MD: Author.

Trent, J.W. (1994). *Inventing the feeble mind: A history of mental retardation in the United States*. Berkeley: University of California Press.

13

Managing Organizations and Maximizing Choice

Tina Campanella

Supporting choice is a requirement when moving organizations from the traditional service framework to supporting people to live within communities. The support model is built on the belief that the most effective services promote each person's choices and unique characteristics. Individualized supports for people in service organizations require that organizations commit to learning the best ways to support each person. Typical program activities that operate on generalizations about people's disabilities or functional challenges do not produce the responsiveness to individual preferences needed to maximize opportunities for personal choice.

Professional protocols and program procedures create conflicts between personal needs and established procedures. Given choices between adhering to protocols and searching for creative processes to support individuals, human services personnel often prefer the former. Management and quality assurance practices that looked for employee consistency in service activities have reinforced this adherence to the known and familiar. For the individuals receiving services, service customization is limited to choosing from among existing options available within the program or service organization. When options are not available, individuals do not have choices. Systems that rely on control mechanisms and group orientation in human services management have not produced individualized supports for choice making. Successful implementation of a support framework that accommodates individual choice occurs through new ways of approaching the task of organizing and managing services.

UNDERSTANDING CHOICE

Although the concept of choice in business and services is a relatively new phenomenon, for most people, choice is an expected part of everyday life experience. Individual choice is the foundation principle around which most people build their lives. The choices people make direct the course of their life events and reflect what is important to them. Whether choices are made consciously, people define their life outcomes through an ongoing series of big and small choices. Restructuring service management to support choice requires an understanding of the dynamics of choice.

Choice is a difficult concept for many people to understand and operationalize because they focus on choice as the "event" of choosing. Attention is drawn to the point in time when a choice or decision is expressed or acted upon. But personal choice considered in the context of a person's life is not an isolated event. Although we can identify specific time frames during which some major decisions in life are made (e.g., where to work, where to live), personal decision making is an ongoing process. Larger life decisions are built on the many personal choices made every day. Simple choices about food, clothing, and how we use our time are made routinely. These personal choices reflect our personal set of values and an ongoing process of personal assessment and decision making. These choices also provide information and experience for larger life decisions.

When choice is seen as an event, people divert their attention from the range of experiences, interactions, and deliberations that are involved in the personal decision-making process. Furthermore, there is a tendency to emphasize the capacity of the person to evaluate and choose from different options in a given situation. This leads to questions about the abilities of people with intellectual and emotional disabilities to assume the role of primary decision maker for themselves.

Capacity for decision making, however, is only one variable in personal choice. In the personal context, *choice* is best defined as an expression of preference, opportunity, and control (Smull, 1995). Individual *preferences* reflect things the person likes and desires. *Op-*

portunity can be defined as gaining an array of varied personal experience. With opportunity, the person gains knowledge about different options from which to choose. Opportunity also provides the potential for expressing choice and for acting on individual preferences. *Control,* the final variable, provides the person with the support and authority to act. Supporting choice means making a sustained effort to understand the person as a whole person through seeking information about his or her preferences, dreams, and desires.

Personal choice involves intuition and instinct as well as intellectual processes. Choices in life are made in response to real circumstances and experiences. People make choices from the available options, which are typically defined by the person's life situation and personal resources. When framed as an essential part of the person's life, personal choice is a means for creating individual identity and exerting personal autonomy. The successes or products of personal choices are evaluated over time based on the course of each person's life events.

CHOICE AND DECISION MAKING

Assisting people to direct the greatest range of decisions in their lives communicates a fundamental respect for each person. Individual choices, both small and significant, are reflections of the person's unique preferences, priorities, and life experiences. Although decision making is associated with complex thinking ability, everyone has the potential to participate in decisions concerning life choices. Choices can be individualized to the person through attention to the person's expression of personal preference.

Different types of decision making are used for different life situations (Sundram, 1994). Some decisions, such as those about where we live and work, can be life defining and can involve the consideration of many variables. Personal choices in these areas are interrelated with many other aspects of life. For example, where we live may promote or limit access to friends, family, and community events and services. The choice of work typically influences economic resources, personal schedules, and opportunities for learning and personal growth.

Other choices made during the course of life experience are more spontaneous and less significant in terms of consequences. On a regular basis, people make decisions about routine events such as meals, clothing, personal activities, and preferences. Often, we make these choices in a spontaneous way based on how we feel at the moment. Knowledge, experience, and critical thinking play an important but supporting role in these decisions. The process used for decision making around these events may not meet the formal criteria for informed choice given the nature of the impact and scope of these situations. These choices are driven (or informed) mostly by preference and personal experience.

OVERCOMING BARRIERS

Service organizations that facilitate opportunities for choice must address both real and perceived barriers to individual decision making. The typical challenges of competency, competition, and limited resources for supporting desired outcomes naturally inhibit choice for anyone. In addition, the poverty, isolation, and functional limitations experienced by many people with disabilities present significant and very real barriers to achieving personal goals and desires in life.

Family and professional concerns about the validity and reasonableness of individual choices are frequently identified as reasons why a person's choice cannot be supported. Examples of individuals expressing desires to be a doctor, an airline pilot, or the president are used to discount the possibility of responding to individual choice for some people. These examples trivialize the task of supporting choice by presuming that it is a process of doing whatever the person says. Supporting and facilitating personal choice is a complex process that requires the engagement of both the person and support staff in the exploration of personal desires.

Some professionals are apprehensive about supporting choice because of the uncertainty and lack of direct control that accompanies the process of working in partnership with people to determine the nature of services and supports. The idea of partnership includes a balancing of power and responsibility. This contrasts sharply with the history of professional control over service decisions. Partnership requires that professionals restructure their interactions with people to include more opportunity for exploring personal desires through dialogue and experience. Working in partnership does not mean that people always get what they want (Block, 1993). In contrast, partnership means that we make sure that there is opportunity for listening to what people want and that we respect and value what they say.

Support for personal choice is grounded in a process of discovering and respecting individual identity. People with disabilities often lose this sense of individual identity when they enter the service process. Assessment, diagnosis, and placement in programs emphasize the similarities among people. But, preserving individual identity in the service process requires attention to the uniqueness of each person. Designing services that support personal choice demands that we respond to each person's uniqueness and use this information to individualize supports.

SUPPORTING CHOICE AND RESPONSIBILITY: A BALANCING ACT

Any discussion of choice is incomplete without consideration for the person's responsibility for achieving individual life priorities. With freedom for personal choice comes a parallel responsibility for action. Just as people are expected to make choices that set a direction for their lives, they also are responsible for participating in the process of making their dreams come true. Attention that is focused on assistance, support, and protection of people in the human services organization often limits opportunities for people to assume responsibility for personal achievement. In addition to asking "What is most important in your life?", we must also ask "And what can you do to sustain or achieve these personal life priorities?"

The structure of the service process can facilitate or limit personal capacity for choice. If others respect and/or acknowledge a person's behavior, the individual learns that he or she can exert some control over what happens to him or her. If nothing that an individual does has any impact on his or her personal situation, however, he or she may experience a sense of helplessness and become lethargic and passive (Seigleman, 1990). This means that interactions in a support relationship can have a positive or negative effect on the behavior of a person being supported. People can learn through interaction that their preferences and desires are not important and do not influence what happens to them. This makes the process of supporting choice more difficult.

The process of assisting people to assume personal responsibility and control within their lives takes consistency and repetition, especially when trying to overcome past experiences of nonresponsive relationships. Service and support interactions with people must consistently convey the expectation that what each person thinks, feels, and wants is important—even if what the person is saying is not fully understood.

Responsibility and Social Roles

Personal responsibility also is connected to social position and active participation in community life. Responsibility enables people to live together in harmony. People are acting responsibly when the obligations and promises made to others are fulfilled.

The concept of responsibility often has little meaning for people with limited knowledge or access to different and valued social roles. Social roles provide a context for individual choice and decision making. Supporting people with disabilities to be responsible citizens requires ensuring access to the full range of opportunities within their community and enabling people to learn about the demands and requirements associated with those opportunities.

People learn responsibility through a combination of example, opportunity, and experience. In most cultures, parents teach responsibility to their children. The roles that individuals fill, first within families, and later within the larger community, define expectations for behavior. Learning about accepted behavior and living up to those expectations is a lifelong endeavor. The nature of what is expected changes with time as individuals form new relationships and begin new experiences.

The elements of learning responsibility—*example, opportunity,* and *experience*—can be used to shape efforts to support people with disabilities. People learn most effectively when others who are significant to them set *examples* of desired actions in natural environments. Providing concrete examples of responsible behavior enables people to learn through modeling and shared experience. *Opportunity* refers to the chance to try out responsible behaviors. Opportunity for trial allows the person to experiment with different actions and to individualize general concepts and ideas to one's own life experiences. *Experience* is repeated opportunity over time. This enables the person to practice and perfect the behaviors associated with responsibility.

Responsible behavior is a learned choice, a reflection of the social roles each person assumes and values. Most people choose to live up to the expectations of the roles that they play because they value the benefits and acknowledgment received in return. Others reject typical social roles, choosing instead to be guided by what they believe will provide them with the most benefit and reward, showing little concern for others. Encouraging responsibility means that we support people in choosing social roles and conducting activities associated with those roles.

People with disabilities may experience real difficulty in assuming responsibilities associated with different social roles because of the specific challenges with which they live or because of their limited life experiences. The service process, however, can assist people to overcome barriers to active social participation. Although teaching specific skills and behaviors are important, gaining access to opportunity, information, and assistive technology can significantly influence meaningful social participation. People cannot learn about the complexities of individual responsibility without the competency gained through active participation in community life.

Organizational Responsibility for Supporting Choice

Organizational support that focuses on choice and individualization for people with disabilities represents a shift in human services. Promoting individual respect, autonomy, and choice in service interactions challenges old assumptions about people with disabilities. In fact, some of the most common assumptions about organizing services prevent individualization.

Organizational practices that encourage treating large numbers of people in the same fashion conflict with principles for individualizing services and supports. Although policies and rules that restrict movement, access to personal possessions, or control of personal finances may provide protection for some people, they are unnecessary limitations for others. Generalized practices that require all people to complete minimum training, acquire specific skills, or get approval from teams for personal goals place more importance on process than on supporting the person.

Personal choice also can be limited by the way organizations structure services. Large numbers of people living together or limited types of work opportunities reduce options by tying resources to specific activities or services. The logistics of managing services for large numbers of people require benefits for the larger group to be balanced with individual concerns. The challenge for organizations supporting people with disabilities is to organize services and supports so as to allow for recognition of individual difference and to impose the least amount of limitation in people's lives.

Changing organizational patterns to support choice also requires re-examination of basic assumptions about people and practices. In traditional service organizations, service providers' generalized assumptions about the capabilities, needs, and supports required by people with disabilities prevents the use of truly personalized information to direct the supports and services. If the person is the primary focus of the service process, then the organization should design services around each person. Limitations do not provide an excuse for not addressing choice and preference as part of the service process. The following operating principles can guide staff to support choice and personal expression about desired personal outcomes.

- *Each person sets his or her own priorities.* Traditional services have relied on professional assessment and judgment to identify individuals' needs for services. People with disabilities were invited to participate in team meetings, but professionals set goals and determined priorities. Supporting choice requires just the opposite. The individual sets the priorities, and the professionals listen. Professional expertise facilitates the personal outcomes that people have chosen for themselves.

- *It is more important to be respectful and responsive than to always do things the "right" way.* Professional standards were intended to assist practitioners in providing the right services for people. Specific processes and procedures were followed in the belief that these would lead to positive outcomes for the person. This quest for "correctness" in process, unfortunately, often has left little room or time for real individualization. Good service is characterized by listening to the person and respecting the person's perspective and experience. Seeking to understand the person before making recommendations for services ensures that services address the person's priorities.

- *Listen with ears, eyes, head, and heart.* Our ability to communicate with and learn from each person served is very important when the "quality" of services is judged by responsiveness to people. Service staff must not only hear suggestions from the person, but they must also actively seek information from the person about personal needs and preferences. This kind of interaction and active listening is a skill. The interpersonal skills needed for establishing relationships with people are as important as professional skills.

- *Use guidelines as supports.* Although standards for practice and professional guidelines are important resources, they do not provide the "answers" for people. The person's life priorities are known only by the person and must be discovered through interaction and experience. Because change is one of the primary products of human services, the discovery process must be flexible. A constant flow of information about the person and his or her interests, preferences, and circumstances enables the service process to continue to meet the person's requirements. Service staff must be ready to change anything at any time, revising plans and actions based on new information from the person. Adherence to practices that do not serve the person— just because they are "the professional standard"—is not compatible with supporting choice or the definition of quality as responsiveness to the person.

- *Support choice not abandonment.* The mandate for respecting and supporting individual choice does not mean that staff cannot or should not intervene when the choices that people make are potentially dangerous or harmful. Staff assistance and support should remain available as a safeguard for people. The challenge is to direct staff members' attention to identifying situations that warrant intervention.

These principles provide a foundation for working in partnership with people to support the achievement of personal goals. Partnerships balance responsibility. In partnership with those who support them, people with disabilities share responsibility for the choices about outcomes in their lives. Like business partnerships, each partner is considered an agent for the other and is liable for the actions and outcomes that occur as a result of the partnership. Staff members do not "give up" accountability for acting in ways that are supportive of people. Staff make room for each person to share responsibility for what happens in his or her life. Partnership creates joint interest and responsibility for what happens.

Making Choice a Reality in Organizations

Responding to the individual needs and preferences of many people simultaneously seems an impossible task. The goal of organizational support for choice is to acknowledge and respect the personal choices people make. Orientation to individuals means that the preferences, needs, and desires of each person are identified and recognized as important, even if existing resources do not allow for immediate support. Even in situations in which resources are limited and few choices are available, identifying preferences and priorities remains the foundation of supports and services.

Supporting choice in service organizations begins with identifying the preferences and priorities of the people using the services offered. Decisions about the type and intensity of services that are to be provided are guided by the knowledge of the people using the organization's supports and services. A means for learning and collecting information about people and personal choices enables managers to direct resources in response to identified needs.

Learning about each person begins at the point of service initiation through direct interaction with the individual and people who know him or her best. Gathering information about personal priorities through questioning and listening provides a baseline for beginning the service relationship. It enables staff to assess the match between individuals and the supports available through the organization.

Making this assessment at service initiation can prevent many difficulties. Serving people who require supports that are not consistent with the organization's current resources can create friction.

The person who wants a job in the community but who is supported by an organization that does not provide that type of support is likely to be dissatisfied. Similarly, people who want to live independently and who require direct support to do so may be misplaced in an organization that is not designed to provide intensive in-home living support. A poor match between the person and the service organization—and not between the person's desires and disabilities—is often responsible for the ensuing difficulties.

The process of learning about people must continue throughout the service relationship. Both formal (e.g., assessments, interviews) and informal (e.g., observations, shared experiences) means of gathering information provide a continuous flow of information about the person's changing needs. This information is used to change supports in accordance with individuals' changing needs.

Assessing individual life priorities takes direct contact and interaction. This learning interaction provides different information from that which is acquired during typical assessment and training activities. This learning requires asking questions and listening to the person without having a predetermined expectation for outcome. The Council's *Personal Outcome Measures* (1997) provide a tool for accomplishing this goal. The outcomes identify areas around which questions are asked, and interactions with the person are sought. The questions assist in the process of defining individual priorities but do not limit what people identify as personal priorities. This helps to maintain a primary focus on what people want instead of what the service organization can do to assist the person to achieve personal outcomes.

DIRECT SUPPORT ROLE

The role of direct support personnel influences choice and decision making. Opportunities for making choices will be limited if support staff do not believe that personal choice is possible. Organizational leadership can reinforce the importance of individual responsiveness by designing systems that promote staff actions consistent with support for individual choice. Systems for program planning, employee supervision, and resource management unfortunately, frequently shift attention from individual to organizational concerns.

In organizations that opt for environments that encourage individual choice, the role of the support worker becomes more vague and complex. Direction for staff responsibilities that was typically provided by clear and general policies and guidelines must now be gleaned from knowledge of individual preference, capability, and desire. There can be fewer and different absolutes regarding "right and wrong" actions when individual situations are a priority.

Person-Centered Planning

Person-centered planning is one process to engage the people who work most closely with the person being supported in a collaborative effort to identify opportunities for promoting the achievement of personal goals and choices. These planning processes direct staff attention to the person's priorities as the foundation for service activities. Person-centered planning alone cannot drive all of the changes needed to support individual choice. Creating supports that enable people with disabilities to direct the service process requires staff and organizations who are willing to learn through results. Managers must define expectations for performance and set limits around what is and is not the direct responsibility of the support staff. Focusing on desired accomplishments and describing results in the most explicit and observable terms provide a benchmark against which staff can measure the effectiveness of their behavior.

Managerial Support for Choice

Direct support staff can only support choice with the involvement and support of middle and executive management. The organization of services determines what happens to and for people. When people do not achieve outcomes, supervisors must help to identify the barriers.

Policy and procedures that support choice assist staff to identify the purpose and priorities for service interactions. They guide staff behavior by defining the expectations and boundaries for acceptable performance. Effective procedures also clearly identify situations that require extra staff care and caution. For example, policy can direct attention to situations that pose potential for personal harm, or another policy may require that restrictions of individual rights are referred to supervisors and support teams for review.

Through interactive management and supervision, the rule of "person first, process follows" can be realized without total chaos. Interactive supervision is also a process that supports staff in problem solving when typical options fail to meet people's needs. Staff members learn the range of support options to which they and the people who they serve can readily gain access.

LEADERSHIP AND RESOURCE MANAGEMENT

Organizational systems create the conditions to support choice in the lives of people receiving services. The organization's leadership is responsible for providing the raw materials that enable and sustain commitment to choice. The behavior and practices of leaders (e.g., showing respect, listening) must exemplify the important principles, because employees learn what is important through their observation of senior management behavior. Commitment to the principles of choice are conveyed by the interactions and relationships between leaders and support staff in the creation of the service delivery system.

Organizational leaders make vision and values come to life for everyone in the organization by leading a process of inquiry and dialogue about key issues related to individual responsiveness. Rather than providing the answers, the leaders must help staff to define the following issues:

- Who is the primary customer?
- What role do people with disabilities play in setting the boundaries of organizational responsibility?
- How are resource limitations addressed?
- How important is it to seek solutions for unmet needs?

The management of human and fiscal resources reflects the organization's commitment to people with disabilities as the primary beneficiary of services and its support for personal choice. Senior management ensures that resources are matched to individual support requirements. Effective use of resources is difficult in any organization. This task becomes even more difficult as the size of the organization increases. Attention to personal preferences and priorities contribute to efficient use of resources by ensuring that services provided meet but do not exceed individual requirements for support. There are three major elements to the resource management task: 1) managing existing resources; 2) making use of available, yet untapped resources; and 3) acquiring new resources.

Managing existing resources requires changes in the type, intensity, and configuration of physical and human resources that are allocated for services to people according to individuals' needs for support. This may include actions such as changing service activities, reassigning staff, or moving the location of service. The goal is to ensure that the use of existing resources (e.g., money, time, expertise, activity, buildings) is directed toward processes and actions that support the outcomes desired by people using the service system.

Making use of resources that are available but yet untapped is a process of continuous reassessment of how all resources contribute to people's outcomes. This requires thinking outside of the usual patterns of resource allocation and crossing traditional boundaries of programs, divisions, and tasks. For example, teaching skills to people is typically associated with the direct support role; others in the organization, however, may have more skill and be better resources for learning. Accounting and financial staff may be better suited to teaching money management and budgeting. Even better teachers may be found in community locations such as the library, adult education courses, senior volunteer programs, mosques, churches, or synagogues.

Acquiring new resources is usually the most difficult strategy to implement. Resource development is best undertaken with top management support and leadership. Resource development, however, is not the sole responsibility of managers. Managers often are "trapped" by the limitations of the service system. Service coordinators and direct support staff often have the experiences and relationships within the community to leverage potential resources for support.

Everyone within the organization contributes to resource management. The direct support staff are responsible for allocating their time and assistance among the people they support. Service coordinators link people with available resources throughout the system. When people's needs for time and resources exceed what is available to them, middle and executive managers can facilitate the search for new sources of support.

Maximizing resource utilization requires information about the priorities of people within the service system. Resource management goals also are advanced by detailed information about the effectiveness of organizational process in supporting people to achieve desired priorities. This information, combined with creativity, forms the foundation for ensuring effective use of existing and potential resource opportunities.

Senge proposed that the manager's role in this new framework might be called "manager as researcher and designer" (1990, p. 299). In this model, the manager's primary responsibilities are gathering information that produces an understanding of how the system works and designing a process that empowers and directs staff to learn new ways to use resources to produce desired results. This is a dramatic departure from the role of "manager as director." A director, as in producing a movie, controls all major decisions and instructs people on how to deliver what is needed. The room for individual creativity and action in this approach is limited.

LEARNING AS A WAY OF ORGANIZATIONAL LIFE

Organizational cultures that value everyone's learning are the most successful in supporting choice. Respect for individuality and choice thrives in an environment that invites questioning and tolerates not knowing all the answers. Staff cannot be told or taught everything that they need to know about making choices, decision making, or supporting people with disabilities. They must be guided to recognize the connection between their actions and the results achieved. This process of learning connects how we act with the results we achieve. Real learning occurs through reflecting on our successful and unsuccessful actions.

Evaluation of individual outcomes is the best way to measure success in ensuring that service practices accommodate individual differences. There is no substitute for measurement that produces rich information about personal or organizational challenges and successes. But what we measure and how we use data can affect the success of our measurement efforts. Measurement can be used to support ongoing improvement or to control (Block, 1993).

Learning organizations support opportunities for people to openly examine, without fear of punishment, what is not working. Argyris (1993) observed that learning occurs when we detect and correct an error. He describes a process of learning through action that is designed to help people compare ideas about what should be happening with the reality of what is happening. This data-based approach to management often produces more questions than answers—a maddening experience for many people. The process of testing and questioning current assumptions with data about the outcomes of practice, however, makes learning possible.

Measurement used as a discipline to define and describe reality is a powerful motivator. When data are used to serve the purpose of learning, they identify issues that need further exploration. All data are subject to interpretation. Measurement that supports choice affirms success or difficulty in implementation of vision and values and stimulates additional learning.

Systems that support learning include opportunity for dialogue and reflection throughout the organization. Organizations practice these disciplines through gatherings, storytelling, and celebration. The traditional opportunities for coming together (i.e., meetings) can be used as a forum for sharing stories and clarifying priorities for future action.

CONCLUSIONS

Supporting choice reflects a value placed on respect for each person as a unique individual. It requires commitment to learning about the best ways to provide support for people who use services. Although this value is easy to envision in one-to-one, personal relationships, it is the antithesis of our typical and personal experience within organizations.

The realities of how choice and personal decision making operate in life must be incorporated into the practice of human services organizations. Systems for supporting choice will not consistently produce results for everyone all the time. Even good choices and well-defined supports can fail to satisfy personal desires. There is no prescription for organizational behavior that will produce answers for every situation—only principles and ideas to guide our learning about what does and does not work in different situations. Service professionals and organizations must learn to live with the uncertainty of not knowing the specific result of service efforts before action is taken.

Creating systems that allow the sharing of control and power about decisions that will affect the lives of people makes support for choice possible. Block (1993) observed that our tendency has been to associate giving up control with abdication. Supporting choice for people with disabilities requires working in partnership. Success is found through working together to discover ways to accommodate individual difference while satisfying organizational responsibilities.

REFERENCES

Argyris, C. (1993). *Knowledge for action: A guide to overcoming barriers to organizational change.* San Francisco: Jossey-Bass.

Block, P. (1993). *Stewardship: Choosing service over self-interest.* San Francisco: Berrett-Koehler.

Seigleman, M.E.P. (1990). *Learned optimism.* New York: Pocket Books.

Senge, P. (1990). *The fifth discipline: The art and practice of the learning organization.* New York: Doubleday.

Smull, M. (1995). Revisiting choice: Part 1. *AAMR News and Notes, 8,* 3–5.

Sundram, C.J. (1994) *Choice and responsibility: Legal and ethical issues in services for persons with mental disabilities.* Albany: New York State Commission on Quality of Care.

The Council on Quality and Leadership in Supports for People with Disabilities (The Council). (1997). *Personal Outcomes Measures.* Towson, MD: Author.

IV

Quality and
Leadership at Work

The four chapters in Section IV bring into focus the issues and
themes presented in previous sections. The perspectives of local service providers and state government and regional collaborative
demonstration projects offer the reader an understanding of the
problems, challenges, and solutions of leading a quality improvement effort. The chapters in this section contain the common theme
that values, vision, and leadership contribute to quality in services
and supports. In addition, these chapters demonstrate that organizations can draw from different competencies and orientations in
implementing a personal outcome structure.

In Chapter 14, Popp, Aman, and Braun describe how a coordinated information system links technology, communication, and decision making at the Black Hills Workshop in Black Hills, South
Dakota. The management information system links staff in more
than 25 locations and provides staff with real-time access to the information that they need to provide services to people. The authors
demonstrate that information technology as a quality enhancement
implementation methodology rests upon well-articulated values
and assumptions about people served and visions for the organization and on high expectations for the human resources system.

In Chapter 15, Lakin, Bast, Hewitt, O'Nell, and Sajevic present
a review of the Minnesota Alternative Quality Assurance Demon-

stration. The demonstration project was managed from the ground up and organized around consensus building among the key constituencies. The performance-based contracting project demonstrates the feasibility of using outcomes for the consumer as the basis for service improvement, redesign, and development. The authors focus attention on the challenges of moving from a centralized and highly controlled system to a more local and flexible system of quality management.

In Chapter 16, Rich approaches personal outcomes from the perspective of trying to change the criteria of quality for a workshop within a regional service system. The region's change process was linked to total quality management methods and techniques. Rich describes their successes and shortcomings and analyzes the role of personal outcomes in making large-scale change at the regional and state level. She concludes that values and vision are the foundation for both quality and leadership.

In Chapter 17, Donaldson discusses innovative service strategies that enable people receiving services and supports to achieve their own expectations. Donaldson describes a virtual organization that exists through connections with other businesses and civic organizations in the community. The Rock Creek Foundation developed value-adding marketing positioning and promotion strategies that both gained employment for people and facilitated their priority outcomes.

These four chapters note the importance of involving in the planning and direction of the change the people on whom the change process has an impact. Lakin, Bast, Hewitt, O'Nell, and Sajevic point to the work group that devoted almost a year to develop consensus on issues such as the feasibility of the demonstration, the alternative designs that the demonstration might take, and which agencies might participate. Rich discusses her successes and failures in communicating with and involving staff in the regional service system's change process. For example, line staff were included on all subcommittees. This both increased the "buy in" from other line staff and communication outside of the subcommittee meetings. Along these same lines, Donaldson begins his discussion of change at the Rock Creek Foundation with an overview of the Mission and Values Clarification process that involved teams of employees. These annual reviews evolved into a 2-day meeting in a National Guard armory in which 250 people with disabilities, employees, and community representatives sorted out personal and organizational priorities.

The chapters in this section illustrate that values, vision, and an orientation toward people are important in delivering quality services to people with disabilities. But, by themselves, values, vision, and an orientation toward people are not enough. The leaders who directed these change activities possessed unique skills and abilities—information communication, community organization, continuous quality improvement, and value-added marketing—that were used to promote high-quality services and personal outcomes. With the need for an anchor in vision, values, and an orientation toward people, the paths to quality and personal outcomes may be as varied and as many as the signature competencies that can be embedded in organizations.

14

Quality Performance and Information Communication

Dennis E. Popp, Michelle D. Aman, and Vince Braun

Peter Drucker noted that "the first question[s] in increasing productivity in knowledge and service work [have] to be 'What is the task? What do we try and accomplish?'" (1992, p. 98). The Black Hills Workshop and Training Center (BHW) has defined their task as enabling people with disabilities to live and work as part of our community. BHW measures its success by the outcomes of the people served and supported—in terms of home, job, money, and independence. The staff are proud of their results as hundreds of people with disabilities enjoy their homes, their work, and their lifestyles.

Our organizational experience indicates that many variables can interact to support people with disabilities, but a good job is the cornerstone of independence. A good job is also a mark of quality service delivery. A colleague noted, "$9.25 an hour buys a lot of inclusion." Quality performance in community support services is a synergistic combination of knowledge; skills; information; systems; facilities and equipment; behavior; and most important, the outcomes that people with disabilities experience. An organization that strives for quality should remain focused on the supports and services that move the lifestyles of people with disabilities forward. People with disabilities provide the rationale for the organization—they are the organization's reason to exist; the organization depends on them. The people within an organization need to have a strong desire to strengthen the organization to facilitate personal outcomes. Relationships with the people whom the organization serves are rooted in human and personal values. The business should be managed to ensure that the organization produces a valued outcome for all stakeholders (e.g., people with disabilities and their families; staff; community, licensing, and funding agencies).

BHW has changed the community's view of disability, which has enabled people with disabilities to use their abilities, compete for jobs, and succeed. Covey noted that the universal mission of human services organizations is "to improve the economic well being and quality of life of all stakeholders" (1991, p. 296). Both the staff of the organization and the people with disabilities can work in partnership to accomplish this mission. BHW documents its successes in performance data and in the personal stories of the people receiving services and supports.

IDENTIFYING INFORMATION PRIORITIES

BHW identifies two types of information critical to its success—outside information and inside information. With regard to outside information, the organization needs to be knowledgeable about the world and its place in it. BHW also uses outside information to interpret, evaluate, and connect its business and operations within the context of what other business, economic development, and commercial activity is occurring. This comparison with external norms is often referred to as *benchmarking*. The second type of information that the leaders need to operate effectively and efficiently is inside information—information processed from internal data (sometimes combined with outside information) and distributed to various users so that they can learn, plan, evaluate, make decisions, and act.

Many companies struggle with the increasing proliferation of both kinds of information. Effective leaders constantly monitor the information-gathering by asking, "What has happened or may happen as a result of this information?" The answer places a value on the information as the organization decides whether to continue to collect, use, store, or discard various data and information.

POSITIVE USE OF INFORMATION

Information can either be reactive or proactive depending on its content and the context in which it is received. Information that contains disappointing news and is received late can become reactive information. Reactive information looks back (i.e., is historical). The response can be harsh because the information is often questioning, critical, and judgmental; and nothing can be done to change what has happened. Reactive information is impossible to eliminate, but every organization should work to reduce it as much as possible and replace it with proactive information.

Proactive information is information received early enough to guide organizational decision making. Thoughtful goals, plans, or budgets that look forward, preview a future expectation, or define future expectations are examples of proactive information. Proactive information used in an environment that encourages critical thinking builds confidence. Proactive information provides encouragement rather than the discouragement that often accompanies reactive information.

By reframing reactive information into a question (e.g., "I see what's happening, now what do we need to do?"), one can convert it into proactive information. Reframing information promotes a safe learning environment in which growth and development are encouraged. The following story told by one of our service managers illustrates this reframing.

I dealt with a situation once in which a support person (Matt) had taken an individual (Tom) to a concert and dropped him off. Tom had a significant visual impairment and had a difficult time finding his seat and getting around at the arena. Another support person came to me and said, "What a cruel thing to do." How could anyone leave Tom at a rock concert to fend for himself? Tom must have bumped into everything and been scared that he would get hurt. I agreed with the support person and set out to talk to Matt. I was thinking that I would need to give Matt a written reminder for being neglectful and for not providing adequate support. Before I went to talk to Matt, my supervisor suggested that I first gather information. I talked to Tom to get his perspective on what had happened. Through our conversation, it turned out that Tom had not been frightened or even upset about the concert. He saw it as somewhat of a risk but then he asked me, "Have you ever been to a rock concert?" We then talked about the atmosphere of a rock concert. There was excitement in the air, lights, sounds, people bumping into each other—both accidentally and intentionally. Tom had eventually connected with his friends, and they had supported him through the concert. I did have that conversation with Matt, but the focus changed from using incomplete information and information that was defensive to a proactive conversation. The conversation proved to be effective in moving toward asking questions such as, What learning took place with the individual? How can we incorporate those experiences into our everyday work? We used the situation to plan and make decisions about how can we provide the best service and supports to each other and, in particular, for Tom.

TIME DIMENSIONS OF CHANGE

People are often quick to react to major changes but respond slowly to small, subtle changes that are spread over time. This phenomenon has implications for information management. In addition, for people to be able to respond to data and information in a timely and adequate manner, they need to learn to see patterns as early as possible. The parable of the boiled frog illustrates this concept.

A group of villagers caught a frog. One day, the villagers decided that they wanted to boil the frog, so they built a big fire and placed a big pot of water on the fire. Once the water boiled, they threw the frog into the pot. The frog jumped out of the boiling water. The villagers, being persistent, threw the frog back into the boiling water again and again, but each time the frog jumped out faster than he had been thrown into the pot. The villagers became weary and stopped to rethink their predicament. After a few minutes, they came up with another approach. They built a new fire that was much smaller than the first one. They then filled the pot with lukewarm water, threw some rocks on to the bottom, and set it on the low fire. They lowered the frog into the lukewarm water where he sat comfortably on the rock enjoying the attention and soothing water until that poor frog boiled.

The moral of the story is that small changes can erode quality without anyone noticing until it is too late. Conversely, quality improvement can quietly but steadily enhance organizations. This strategy of taking small steps toward a greater good is called *plussing*.

USE OF TECHNOLOGY

The leadership of BHW recognized the soundness of Drucker's call for asking, "What is the task?" (1992, p. 98). The leadership has defined *the task* as facilitating people's outcomes in community settings. The leadership also recognized the importance of proactive information in promoting this task. As a result, the leadership and staff of BHW have used technology as a means to manage data and information to accomplish the task.

Information about people receiving services and supports changes on a daily basis. Staff members are continually looking for new community opportunities and alternatives, building and strengthening relationships, and finding new resources. This growth and change in information requires a fully integrated set of applications and equipment. A comprehensive, managed information system for an agency is characterized as an Intranet. The Intranet makes possible integrated information processing and distribution that supports and promotes organizational growth and development. Figure 14.1 provides a conceptualization of how webs of communication and information/knowledge combine to form community relationships.

Communication Infrastructure

Communication infrastructure is one important priority in the allocation of organizational resources. Most private for-profit organizations rely on quick, accurate data and multiple layers of communications as they do business throughout the community, state, and world. The communication linkage, information flow, and constant increase of knowledge requires a flexible and comprehensive communication system. As a human services organization, BHW requires diverse information, which enables individuals to reach their desired outcomes.

Comprehensive Approach to Managed Information Systems

A comprehensive approach to managed information systems (MIS) requires systems analysis, regular daily programming changes, procurement of new hardware as well as software updates, increased expansion of the documentation for easy input and retrieval, and continuous training of staff so that they can access the system. The corporation must demonstrate flexibility as it responds daily to

| Webs of communication | + | Information and knowledge | = | Community relationships |

Figure 14.1. Basic formula for enhancing community relationships through webs of communication and information/knowledge.

webs of ever-changing needs, resources, and environments; and the information system is meant to permit this flexibility.

Most staff members view an MIS as a menu of options on individual terminals that directs them to the point of information for input or retrieval. In an Intranet, information databases often are fully integrated with e-mail, local and remote terminal installations, electronic customer support, on-line documentation, integrated word processing, and multilevel security configurations. BHW has invested resources to ensure that its information system has sufficient processing speed and storage capacity to meet the MIS challenge. The host system provides all of the on-line support services for more than 350 staff members, who provide support and services to more than 520 individuals with disabilities living and working in community settings. The information management system works in real time as people change jobs and living alternatives and as they receive a variety of ever-changing services and supports. The information system contains many applications for the storage, analysis, retrieval, and dissemination of data and information. Components and capabilities include the following: e-mail, electronic customer support, on-line documentation, integrated word processing, multilevel security configurations, on-line optical storage, electronic signatures, downloading/uploading portable computers for field personnel, full-page scanners, and integrated calendars.

BHW has tied together 25 different physical locations for computer access through modems. Over the years, the staff have developed more than 3,000 application programs, which include individual habilitation plan (IHP) reports, scheduling supports, medication profiles, social histories, health maintenance reports, building and vehicle maintenance reports, bulletin boards, personnel data, admission data, accounting programs, and federal/state reports. Staff continue to upgrade and change these programs each year at the request of various customers. The first customer is the staff, who must communicate with each other in a comprehensive manner by distributing relevant information. The second customer is the person who receives services and supports so that he or she can better control his or her own life and make choices from a variety of options. The third set of customers is the funding and regulatory agencies with whom BHW works. Finally, the fourth group of customers includes the community at large and the various agencies and individuals who relate to and interact with both the staff and the people receiving services and supports.

BHW's priorities for the comprehensive management information service are to gain access to and to share information in a timely manner. These objectives are accomplished by implementing computer programs that are easy to use and functionally efficient. The MIS department's training services ensure that each staff member has a thorough working knowledge of the programs that he or she uses. Computer staff average more than 800 requests each month for technical assistance to improve and upgrade the MIS system. One of the organization's priorities is to accommodate all the demands for information; the goal of the MIS staff is to maximize the efficiency with which it is done.

TECHNOLOGY AS SUPPORT FOR PEOPLE

Technology has enabled many individuals with disabilities to function in jobs (e.g., operating cash registers, calculators, and electronic pads for relaying orders) that they would never have been able to perform if traditional teaching methods were used. One such technological advance allows individuals to use a cash register: A person can look at the register, see the picture of the order, punch the picture, have the order sent automatically to the kitchen, and have the dollar amount recorded so that the customer and cashier can see it. Once the payment is made, the change is calculated automatically. This reduces errors and increases the various roles and responsibilities that people with cognitive limitations can achieve.

The emerging technology can complement traditional sources of service and support for people with disabilities. For example, Sue, a woman with disabilities, uses electronic transfer at her bank. BHW helped Sue to develop the appropriate skills, and the bank has been willing to assist with her personal finances. She can direct her salary to the bank and make her monthly payments electronically. This new-found independence gave her the confidence and the community presence to learn even more skills that are directly tied to achievement at her job. These new skills include gaining access to transportation, dressing for success at the job, maintaining a friendly public face and attitude, and responding to varied customers requests and demands.

Technology and Human Services Work

Despite the predictions of social forecasters that employees would become slaves to industrial machinery, information technology, instead, has liberated workers from the drudgery of repetitive tasks and has enabled them to think more critically about how to perform their work in more efficient and effective ways. Zuboff noted that

A powerful new technology, such as that represented by the computer, fundamentally reorganizes the infrastructure of our material world. It eliminates former alternatives. It creates new possibilities. It necessitates fresh choices. . . . Work becomes more abstract as it depends upon understanding and manipulating information. (1988, pp. 5–6)

The leadership at BHW is discovering the beginnings of changes in work resulting from the new technology. Although new technologies, such as point-of-sale cash registers with pictures, have enabled individuals to be more productive, computers have also helped employees to be more creative and to do critical thinking as they increase their productivity. Computers have enhanced team work and relationship building because information flows more easily and is more accurate and timely.

Davis (1987) used the term *mass customization* to describe the use of new technology to customize on a mass scale. Danaher and Rust noted "in service settings, . . . quality is defined as being different every time, to meet customer quality" (1996, p. 85). This means that we can individually customize the information bases through enhanced communications, which leads to relationship building, resource attainment, and the actualization of these resources focused on the individual's desired outcomes. In managing customer perceptions, employees can design strategies that go beyond predetermined or current procedures and standards. With better information and with increased knowledge, employees can exercise judgment and continually discover new and better ways to assist the customers.

The communication infrastructure of any agency must allow for the employees to develop methods or techniques for self-managed work teams that are centered around the individual. The BHW leadership promotes organizational learning through self-managed work teams. The teams use technology to measure inputs, processes, and outputs around each customer's needs and desired outcomes. The use of technology to further the vision for the organization, the values and assumptions about people with disabilities, and the customized and individualized nature of quality in services and supports indicate potential future advances in human services. The National Council on Disability (1996) noted that a national information infrastructure is being designed to be more pervasive, faster, and more convenient than the Internet of the late 1990s. This parallels a major trend toward the convergence of various communication instruments, telecommunications, and computers, which will have very minimal distinction among them by the early part of the 21st century. Another major organizational trend is toward the client/server or net-centric model, which, in essence, has a large data storage area on a central system. In this model, the form of access to the national information infrastructure will change as it will include information appliances, personal digital assistance, set-top boxes for facilitating access to the television, public service terminal or kiosks, and public service vending/transaction terminals and smart cards. There is also a concept of a universal identity, or telephone number, that would follow people throughout their lives. All of these developments have major implications for individuals with disabilities and will greatly increase their access to the community and the world. As the 20th century ends and the 21st century begins, many barriers will remain. To the extent feasible, accessibility to all products that connect to the community will have built-in capabilities so that assistive technology could continue to be minimized. This advanced and built-in technology would account for hearing, vision, speech, motor control, and average cognitive skills.

Technology and Knowledge Creation

Nonaka and Takeuchi described two different types of knowledge—tacit and explicit. They defined *tacit knowledge* as

> Highly personal and hard to formalize. . . . Subjective insights, intuitions, and hunches fall into this category of knowledge. . . . Tacit information is deeply rooted in an individual's action and experiences, as well as the ideals, values, or emotions he or she embraces. (1991, p. 8)

People use tacit knowledge when they learn about another person in the process of forming a relationship. Tacit knowledge in the human services system exists in the consciousness of the service providers who interact with people receiving services and supports, community resources, families, and co-workers.

Explicit knowledge, in contrast, "can be expressed in words and numbers" (Nonaka & Takeuchi, 1991, p. 8). Explicit knowledge is information that has been analyzed, formalized, and officially deposited into the database of our own brains, the organization's files, or in some form of communication. Explicit knowledge in the human services system exists, for example, in the organization's files, in the case records, or in the IHPs.

Nonaka and Takeuchi (1991) defined part of the knowledge-creation process as moving tacit knowledge to the explicit knowledge category. From the perspective of human services, a form of knowledge creation occurs when organizations capture in the organization's database the intuitive and impressionistic understanding of the direct services staff. The widespread use of portable computer inputs enable the staff to record anecdotal information that would otherwise be buried in the pages of the daily log. With an integrated information system, the anecdotal information is entered in real time at a terminal, then stored and distributed within the organization. With this technology, the organization can maintain and analyze the equivalent of multiple daily logs from geographically disperse settings of supports and services.

Computer technology and knowledge creation contribute to the promotion of outcomes in people's lives. As employees better understand the people for whom they are providing services and supports, the staff members can develop greater understanding of their distinct roles of learners and facilitators. An employee who is learning is more likely to listen, observe, question, and discover before making decisions. With this bountiful amount of information about people's priorities and choices, employees are more able to communicate a broader variety of alternatives and methods that they might employ to facilitate people's priorities and choices.

As employees better understand the volumes of ever-changing information, they are more able to understand their professional identities. Employees—connected by technology to the people who they serve and support, to community businesses and resources, and to other employees—identify their own values and assumptions and then keep them in focus as they facilitate the acquisition of alternatives or options for the people who they serve and support.

Technology and Webs

The knowledge-based, postindustrial society in the United States is also characterized by a decline in hierarchy and bureaucracy. Rigid organizational structures with defined chains of authority and communication are becoming obsolete. The emerging symbol or metaphor for the new organizational form is the web. Helgesen (1995) described the web of inclusion; and Capra (1996) explored the web of life, pointing to knowledge as a network, and Helgesen wrote:

> The emphasis upon top-down power thus continues to be eroded; networked technology reflects and hastens the trend. As organizations adapt to new understandings, leadership will begin to flourish in places and ways we can hardly imagine. (1996, p. 24)

BHW is noticing the emergence of a web that has communication strands going in all directions, some of which are thick and strong and some are lean and narrow. These strands represent communication linkages or information flow, both disseminated and retrieved. These strands also represent relationships that break off or are added. They definitely represent a community and its potentially thousands of available resources. These webs emerge around people in the form of community support relationships and communication, and the webs emerge around staff as they communicate with other staff in the community. Finally, different webs begin to overlap and to integrate.

Webs around people, staff, and businesses enable the leadership to understand the organization as a system that is part of an even larger system. All organizations are connected through a variety of relationships and marketing, sales, and information exchanges. Successful leaders see and understand this interconnected system. For example, relationships with other business members on a Chamber of Commerce Committee can assist staff members with learning which new businesses are opening or are expanding their labor forces. Through committee participation, personal relationships are established in which participants gain trust in one another, which ultimately adds value to a service organization's employment, marketing, procurement, and vocational operations. For example, community committee participation can lead to marketing efforts to promote employment for people supported being more readily accepted by potential employers. Numerous networks enable employees of community businesses to share information on service costs and quality. Civic club meetings, neighborhood meetings, and social gatherings operate at various levels of formality; but all enhance open communication. The ability to find resources and to be innovative affect the organization's perception and standing among other political, financial, and service systems.

CHANGING AND SUSTAINING STAFF BEHAVIOR

Technology is no substitute for competent staff. Technology cannot replace values and vision. In the authors' experience, a majority of the people whom we hire have little or no knowledge or experience in human services businesses. They are often young, and human services is their first "real" job. They have unlimited potential but very little experience and no frame with which to interpret events in confronting day-to-day challenges. BHW depends on promoting shared values, building relationships, and providing guidance to develop staff capabilities.

BHW's values are clearly and concisely written. They are consistently displayed in our policies and procedures, systems, tools, training, conversations, and goals. They are also observable in our daily actions and decisions, which ensures that our culture and operations are congruent with our values. Mixed messages, or big differences between what is said and done, create ambiguous environments that make it difficult to direct, support, and reinforce behavior.

Efforts to change and maintain staff behavior begin with choosing people who share similar values. Each program area completes the hiring process. The employment interview procedure begins with a screening of applicants. The first interview follows, during which the interviewer asks a series of situational and open-ended questions that encourage the applicants to discuss values and past behavior. BHW has found that past behavior is the best predictor of future behavior. During the second interview, the applicant is given a tour and spends time visiting with potential co-workers and with people receiving services and supports. The final steps are job and personal reference checks.

Once an applicant is hired, the organization uses what was learned during the hiring process to plan and schedule the person's orientation and training. The organization individualizes the person's learning experience, which includes review of written policies, agency guidelines, job procedures and support information, and personal and group instruction. The new employee is matched with a mentor who is connected to a learning network. The mentor and learning network provide ongoing feedback. Orientation training is delivered in "bite-size" pieces of learning in which instruction, study, and practice follow interactions with people receiving services and supports. The employee is also given performance reviews that directly relate to job procedures and work behaviors.

The organization, however, must remember that requirements change; knowledge becomes outdated; competition strengthens; processes improve; new tools are developed; information increases; and, as Dykstra observed, "people leak and people stray" (1995, p. 12). People forget what they once knew, and individuals and organizations stray from guiding visions and goals. Individually or in combinations, these factors create constant change and make retraining and new learning a daily concern.

Technology and Systems Thinking

BHW uses a systems-thinking approach to help people develop, sustain, and change their performance. A *systems approach* is simply an understanding that outcomes result from the outputs of numerous systems. An example is a training session that has the desired outcome of a person being able to send an e-mail message. This outcome requires the outputs of the biological systems of the people involved, computer hardware systems, computer software systems, the electrical system, the structural systems of the facility housing the training, telephone systems, and the teaching systems. Using systems thinking helps to identify, develop, and understand the whole while teaching and sustaining it in bite-size pieces. Covey (1989) observed that everything is created twice; first there is the mental creation, and then there is the physical creation. BHW follows this concept by using process models and procedures to display organizational thinking and detailed process reviews to evaluate performance. The senior management then uses outcome standards to evaluate and communicate results.

It is the authors' experience that people like the concept of change but do not like to change personally; so people will often sabotage or delay progress by holding to or reverting back to familiar ways of behaving. When new opportunities present themselves or threats develop, project teams often employ systems thinking.

The following vignette illustrates the ramifications of change on a service organization. The state of South Dakota decided to close one of its two state institutions. Closure was scheduled to occur in 6 months. The institution being closed served people with profound cognitive and physical disabilities. BHW was contacted and asked to decide within a couple of days as to whether it would participate in the closure as a community services provider. This was an opportunity for the people residing in the institution to move into a community and for BHW to broaden its service options. The opportunity also contained considerable financial and political risks. BHW's leadership evaluated the needs of the people, the capacity of its facilities, equipment, resources, skills, and community resources. The leaders talked with people in the community, state government, and personal and professional networks, then decided to participate.

To develop an implementation plan, BHW convened a project team that consisted of clinical, management, computer, financial and maintenance staff. The team began its work by gathering outside and inside information to identify and select the necessary service components. These components are displayed in the formula in Figure 14.2. The project team next focused on the success side of the

$$\text{Service Plan } \mathbf{X} \ \frac{\text{Environments + Equipment + Supplies + Protocols}}{\text{(Staff + Training + Skills + Knowledge + Information) Motivation}} \ \div \ \frac{\text{Management}}{\$} \ = \ \text{Success}$$

Figure 14.2. Formula for providing successful service.

formula to develop a clear understanding of the desired outcomes (see Figure 14.3).

The components on the left side of the formula then were developed by assigned project team members until the following overall service model emerged (see Figure 14.4). From this model, structural and environmental changes were made, procedures were written, staff training was designed and completed, and detailed process reviews were implemented. The work of the project team resulted in 14 people moving from the institution to the community with the support and training they needed. This was accomplished ahead of the original time line and below projected cost.

LEADERSHIP AND MANAGEMENT ISSUES

The employees of BHW enable people with disabilities to have productive, meaningful lives in the community. BHW has connected people within the community through strong values and computer technology. The organization has capitalized on technology and information to build networks of connections to accomplish the organizational mission. The leadership keys to quality are as follows:

- Employees who share common values and are knowledgeable, skilled, and committed
- Infrastructure that addresses the needs of all people
- Technology that provides the communication aids necessary to compete and thrive (especially computer technology that connects people and information)
- Community relationships that result from connections to business and social webs within the community
- Employee training that operationalizes service and support to ensure improvements
- Strong personal relationships

Figure 14.3.   Formula for the definition of success.

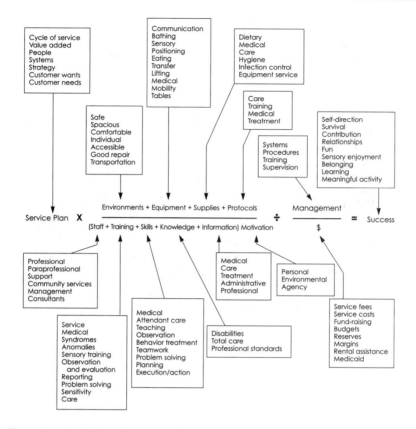

Figure 14.4.   Definition of the success formula's components.

CONCLUSIONS

Keeping pace with change requires constant communication. This requires systems and personal skills to support teams. Operationally, BHW uses teams to accomplish results. Computers, communication and network software, and training are essential to providing quality services. They connect people to internal and external information, create knowledge, and form webs of information and relationships. Technology, however, is only an instrument; quality flows from people and the values that they hold.

REFERENCES

Booth, N. (1997). *Thriving on change: The art of using change to your advantage.* San Diego: Harrison Acorn Press.

Capra, F. (1996). *The web of life: A new scientific understanding of living systems.* New York: Doubleday.

Covey, S.R. (1991). Principle-centered leadership. Arlington, TX: Summit Books.

Davis, S.M. (1987). *Future perfect.* Reading, MA: Addison-Wesley.

Drucker, P. (1993). *Managing for the future: The 1990s and beyond.* New York: Talley Books/Plume.

Danaher, P.J., & Rust, R.T. (1996). Rejoinder. *Quality Management Journal, 3,* 85–88.

Dykstra, A. (1995). *Outcome management: Achieving outcomes for people with disabilities.* East Dundee, IL: High Tide Press.

Helgesen, S. (1995). *The web of inclusion.* New York: Currency/Doubleday.

Helgesen, S. (1996). Leading from the grass roots. In F. Hesselbein, M. Goldsmith, & R. Beckhard (Eds.), *The leader of the future* (pp. 19–24). San Francisco: Jossey-Bass.

National Council on Disability. (1996). *Access to the information superhighway and emerging information technologies by people with disabilities.* Washington, DC: National Council on Disability.

Nonaka, I. (1991, Nov–Dec). The knowledge creating company. *Harvard Business Review,* 96–104.

Zuboff, S. (1988). *In the age of the smart machine: The future of work and power.* New York: Basic Books.

15

A Demonstration to Test Performance-Based Outcome Measures as the Foundation of a Quality Assurance/ Quality Enhancement System

K. Charlie Lakin, Janet Bast,
Amy Sue Hewitt, Susan N. O'Nell, and Peter Sajevic

The evolution of American society's response to people with developmental disabilities since the late 1960s has been driven primarily by the images of dismal conditions in large institutional settings. Those images were created through the vivid written, spoken, and visual essays on institutions by scholars such as Burton Blatt (1970, 1973), politicians such as Robert Kennedy ("Where the Toys Are Locked Away," 1965), and media figures such as Geraldo Rivera

(1972). Learning of the conditions of institutional life in the early 1970s caused considerable moral outrage and kindled a national commitment to get and/or keep people with developmental disabilities out of institutions and permit them opportunities to live in the same communities from which they once were removed. As a result, the number of people with developmental disabilities housed in large public institutions decreased from a national total of 228,500 people in 1967 to 59,000 people in 1996 (Prouty & Lakin, 1997). The "community side" of this rapid social change is captured in the fact that in 1989, for the first time, the balance in residential services had shifted so that more people were living in settings with 15 or fewer residents than were living in larger residential institutions (16 or more residents). Then, in 1995, just 6 years later, more than half of all people with developmental disabilities receiving residential services were living in places with six or fewer residents. On the national level, the residential care system has become primarily a community system. In Minnesota—the focus of this chapter—these changes started a little earlier and progressed a little faster but have generally mirrored these national trends (e.g., state institution depopulation began in 1965, and a majority living in homes with 15 or fewer residents was achieved in 1986) (Prouty & Lakin, 1997).

Although such milestones have been symbols of accomplishment, they have also been reminders to pause and attend with care to the actual products of the institution-to-community movement. Such reflection includes first and foremost asking what being "in the community" has meant to people with developmental disabilities. Considerable experience, validated by a number of research studies (Abery & Fahnestock, 1994; Bercovici, 1983; Burchard, Hasazi, Gordon, & Yae, 1991; Hill et al., 1989), has shown that presence in the community alone is not sufficient to foster meaningful participation and satisfying lifestyles. As a result, there has been growing interest in approaches to community living that assist people to control more of their own lives, improve the quality of their lives, and enhance their membership in the communities in which they live.

The commitment to move people and services from institutions to homes in the community was based on an assumption that people's lives would be qualitatively different than if they remained or were placed in institutions. Articulating the precise qualitative differences that should be evident in community services, however, often has been difficult. Establishing these differences has been particularly difficult for agencies whose roles are to define, measure, and monitor quality in services. These difficulties derive both from the traditional assessments and processes used by monitoring agencies and from the ambiguity in the definitions of quality. As a result, in the late 1990s, community Intermediate Care Facilities for the Mentally Retarded (ICFs/MR) operate with standards remarkably similar to the 1969 institutional standards of the Accreditation Council on Developmental Disabilities. The bulk of those standards were adopted in 1974 by the Health Care Financing Administration (HCFA) for its new ICF/MR program in an attempt to improve the scandalously poor conditions that then were common in state institutions. The legacy of this initial attempt to define and regulate quality of services is present in the late 1990s. Although less than one in five people with developmental disabilities who reside in community residential settings actually live in an ICF/MR (Prouty & Lakin, 1997), the reality is that in many states, including Minnesota, the ICF/MR standards and approaches to defining and monitoring quality in services have shaped most community quality assurance programs.

ISSUES OF IMPORTANCE TO MINNESOTA

A 1992 independent assessment of Minnesota's Medicaid Home and Community Based Services (HCBS) program for people with developmental disabilities observed that

> With respect to regulation there appears to be a nearly universal perception that services are over-regulated, that the current regulations have too little to do with quality of life and that the current approach is poorly suited to respond to the dramatic increase and dispersal of small service sites. (Lakin, Burwell, Hayden, & Jackson, 1992, p. 104)

This was not an atypical observation nor was it relevant only to Minnesota.

In 1992, Minnesota experienced widespread concern about the contributions of its quality assurance system to the quality of life of its residents. Not only were 2,600 of Minnesota's 7,300 community residential service recipients still living under the institutional standards of the ICF/MR program, but 2,300 of Minnesota's 2,900 Medicaid HCBS waiver recipients were living in residential settings governed by standards that were largely modeled on the inspection-of-standards approach of the ICF/MR program. The realization was dawning on state officials that compliance-based, process-oriented regulation was not playing a significant role in improving the quality of life for people receiving services. In addition, compliance-based, process-oriented regulation of this form of the existing quality assurance system was labor intensive, expensive, and unable to keep up with the continuing growth of community services. As a result, discussions were initiated by staff of the Minnesota Department of Human Services (DHS) and an advisory group about the need for and requirements of reinventing quality assurance to suit the purposes and goals of community services. In those discussions it soon became evident that the comprehensive nature and the substantial refocus of the desired approaches would require a federal Medicaid waiver to the many ICF/MR standards if it were to include individuals from among Minnesota's 2,500 residents of community ICFs/MR. A successful application for such a waiver of existing Medicaid rules (under the Section 1115 demonstration authority of the Social Security Act Amendments of 1965 [PL 89-97], which allows waiver of any provision of Medicaid for demonstrations "likely to assist in promoting the objectives" of Medicaid) required making a case that the existing ICF/MR standards and, by association, other similar compliance-based approaches to quality assurance for community services, created substantial impediments to the realization of Minnesota's goals for its citizens with developmental disabilities.

In authorizing the DHS to proceed with the waiver request, the Minnesota Legislature defined five goals: 1) protecting personal health, safety, and comfort (e.g., appropriate medical and dental care, preventative health practices, reasonable provisions for physical safety, access to prostheses and equipment as needed); 2) supporting the individual's personal growth, independence, and productivity (i.e., opportunities to learn new things and develop new skills that add to one's personal competence in skills of personal value, that fulfill one's interests, and that develop one's ability to communicate and act out one's individuality); 3) promoting and integrating individual choice and control over daily life decisions (i.e., opportunities to affirm one's personhood through acting out one's desires and preferences and developing one's independence); 4) improving consumer, family, and service coordinator satisfaction with services (i.e., using people's direct evaluations to assess and modify services, empowering people to have and act on their personal perceptions of the quality of services in meeting their needs and preferences); and 5) supporting community inclusion, such as social relationships and participation in valued community roles (i.e., facilitating daily interactions with people the individual enjoys and with others in the community; ongoing relationships with friends; maintaining relationships with the significant individuals in one's life; participating in valued societal roles and transactions that provide respect, economic benefits, and communicate individual abilities). The application to HCFA noted that the current rules impeded the realization of such goals for Minnesota's citizens with developmental disabilities, and it also emphasized the importance of national issues in quality assurance that needed attention through trying out new concepts and methodologies in defining, assessing, and improving quality.

NATIONAL ISSUES RELEVANT TO
REDESIGNING QUALITY ASSURANCE

A number of factors were identified in Minnesota's application to HCFA as being a part of a broader crisis in the adequacy and acceptability of existing methods of "quality assurance." They included the following: the challenge of the rapid growth and dispersion of community services, quality assurance was technically invalid and unrelated to prevailing perceptions of quality, the sense that quality assurance should contribute to improved services, the need for unified and renegotiated roles in quality assurance, the maintenance of the commitment to protecting vulnerable people, and the acceptance that quality is measured in "outcomes."

Challenge of the Rapid Growth
and Dispersion of Community Services

Since the early 1980s, human services systems, most notably reflected in residential services, have become extremely dispersed. This has greatly increased the challenges facing government quality assurance monitoring efforts. In 1982, there were about 15,600 separate households in the United States in which people with developmental disabilities received out-of-family residential services. By June 1996, that number had exploded to 86,200 separate settings (Prouty & Lakin, 1997). This rapid growth of service settings continues, and in light of budgetary limits facing most states, service settings will continue to grow more rapidly than the number of people responsible for monitoring such programs. On the national level, the effects of such pressures were evident in the "deficiencies" noted by the staff of the U.S. House Subcommittee on Regulation in a background analysis of quality assurance for community services for people with developmental disabilities:

> Deficiency #1: Many states perform inspections infrequently and usually give prior notice.
>
> Not surprisingly homes pass inspection by making special preparations before scheduled on-site visits. But performance and a home's appearance during an inspection may indicate little about staff conduct during the rest of the year . . .
>
> Deficiency #2: Staffing levels on inspection and auditing teams are too low to perform comprehensive and frequent examinations.

Unscrupulous providers recognize that only the most blatant abusers will be targeted by state agencies. Merely by keeping a low profile, home operators can avoid careful scrutiny. Furthermore, in many states case managers—the first line of protection, are over burdened with too many cases and unable to effectively oversee the services provided to persons with developmental disabilities. (Wyden, 1993)

As Minnesota looked to its future in 1992, it was increasingly apparent that to be viable, quality assessment and enhancement systems would need to become more efficient in the use of their resources and more open to being monitored by people other than the traditional quality assurance personnel (i.e., DHS, licensing and inspection personnel). Efficiency meant that systems had to reduce expectations to the essential and important while eliminating redundancy in administrative reviews. In essence, they had to get everyone on the same page, and it had to be the right page. In addition, efficient use of resources beyond those available within traditional monitoring agencies had to occur. In Minnesota, as elsewhere, efficiency and effectiveness were vital as the number of service recipients per case manager continued to grow from 50 to 75 and sometimes more (Prouty & Lakin, 1991). It seemed apparent in Minnesota that even if the traditional quality assurance approach had once worked well, the existing system was no longer tenable given the pressures of community services' growth and dispersal. The promise of quality assurance obviously could not rely on case managers who saw individuals only once per year.

Quality Assurance Was Technically Invalid and Unrelated to Prevailing Perceptions of Quality

Most of the concern about Minnesota's existing "quality assurance" approach was that for all its attention to detailed standards, it was not attending to what mattered most to people. For instance, programs were monitored for things like the number of times that a person left the facility or the exact weight of a slice of bologna on his or her sandwich rather than measuring aspects of services that were related to those desired by individuals and their families (e.g., choosing where one lived and worked, living with friends or having freedom and privacy). The Minnesota legislature realized, as did the vast majority of class members in federal court rulings and settlements since the mid-1970s, that facilities could be in compliance with hundreds of detailed ICF/MR standards but still could be unconstitutional. It seemed apparent that quality assurance needed to get closer to the real-life needs and wants of individuals. Minnesota, like other states, was publicly articulating specific goals related to inclusion, independence, and self-determination, but its quality assurance system lacked validity as a measure of the attainment of such goals.

The standard of quality of life is increasingly viewed as being the necessary standard for evaluating community services in Minnesota and elsewhere. As discussions of quality of life have become more sophisticated, there has been a recognition that there is no single standard, but that each individual's needs, interests, and preferences make up his or her definition of quality of life. But whether defined simplistically as the score of one's participation in a range of activities, relationships, and circumstances or more complexly as the congruence of those activities, relationships, and circumstances with one's preferences, Minnesota consumers, family members, advocates, service providers, and government officials were ready to try to design a quality assurance system based on meaningful definitions of quality. They were also ready to define quality not as a commodity to be scored and certified but more realistically as a continuing quest—a quest in which a person with disabilities, his or her family and friends, service providers, and other people important to the person would articulate daily preferences and longer-term goals, establish a plan for reaching those goals, and work productively toward those ends. Quality would be viewed not only in the achievement of desired outcomes but also be present in the steps that led to desired outcomes.

The Sense that Quality Assurance Should Contribute to Improved Services

A 1990 report of the U.S. General Accounting Office, focusing on quality assurance in health care, contained an observation that was highly relevant to quality assurance for services to Minnesota residents with developmental disabilities:

> Quality assurance systems typically concentrate on quality assessment and the identification of the relatively small number of providers whose care is obviously unacceptable. They do comparatively little in attempting to directly improve the overall levels of quality provided by the majority of health professionals . . . If we think of performance of health care providers in terms of the bell-shaped curve of a normal distribution, the challenge is to devise a quality assurance strategy that not only deals appropriately with the outliers but also assists in moving the entire distribution to a higher level of quality. (p. 8)

There was a sense in Minnesota that the effectiveness of a quality assurance approach should be judged not only by its ability to maintain minimum standards but also by the support and assistance it provided to improve the quality of the services. Therefore, a responsive quality assurance system was viewed as needing mechanisms and resources that could contribute to quality improvement. When considering service enhancement or improvement, it was clear that Minnesota's quality assurance system had very limited capacity in 1992. Most Department of Health (DOH) inspectors and DHS licensing staff typically did not have the training or background to move from highly prescriptive inspections to highly personal and individual reviews of quality, much less have the ability to assist agencies in developing services that satisfied or even "delighted" their customers.

The Need for Unified and Renegotiated Roles in Quality Assurance

In Minnesota, as in other states, there was remarkable disparity among quality assurance systems' requirements for community services depending on which agency or program financed them. Nationwide, this has produced a situation in which an individual state's decisions about funding services had become a major determinant of the definitions, monitoring, and enhancement of the quality of services. In Minnesota, both the people providing and receiving services found this focus on funding incongruent with pervading ideas about people having real homes and receiving supports reflecting their individual wants and needs. Therefore, it seemed important in the redesigning of quality assurance systems that the quality of people's lives should not be differentiated by the program that financed their services. But it was not just that different monitoring agencies focused on different things or even that they all seemed to focus on the wrong things, there was also substantial frustration in Minnesota because several different agencies monitored the same things. Streamlining quality assurance would require renegotiation of existing roles, and increasing the cost effectiveness and relevance would require that knowledgeable, nontraditional members be included in the quality assurance teams.

Maintaining the Commitment to Protecting Vulnerable People

While there was a willingness to accept the challenge of personalizing definitions, assessments, and improvements of quality, there was also recognition that replacing the responsibilities of quality assurance should not be done carelessly. The documented record of abuse, neglect, and exploitation was clear; and it happened within the scope of the quality assurance efforts that were in place in the early 1990s. Furthermore, maltreatment could continue or even worsen under alternative approaches (Hurst, 1989; Mitchell, 1988; Wyden, 1993). Therefore, in improving approaches to quality assessment and enhancement to address the more personalized aspects of quality of life, adherence to basic health and safety standards had to continue. These standards were meant to ensure that appropriate and sufficient steps were taken to protect individuals and/or to guarantee the actual delivery of contracted supports, services, training, and/or other opportunities. In Minnesota, there was substantial agreement with Congressman Ron Wyden, who observed at hearings on quality assurance in community services in March 1993, that "it is possible to have enhanced standards of care for the vulnerable while still keeping the regulatory gate open for the development of innovative programs" (p. 3).

Among many people in Minnesota, there was an expectation that effective attention to an individual's safety and well-being was no less a person-centered planning activity than was attending to quality in one's social life. In the commitment that no one's health and safety would be compromised in the name of desired "outcomes," assurances were made that existing quality assurance standards related to health and safety would not be broadly amended. Variances to existing protections, however, could be sought and granted if there was sufficient specification as to how the protections of a specific rule would be maintained through an alternative approach. Such a compromise attended to more protective instincts while also recognizing that universal standards for ideal levels of health and safety did not exist. Health and safety protection should be tailored to a person's abilities, general physical condition, unique health problems, the safety of the neighborhood, a person's social and intimate relationships, and the person's tolerance for risk and protection. Beyond protecting individuals with developmental disabilities, however, it was recognized that documenting health and safety practices also protected service providers and administrative authorities, as well. Because changes to health and safety standards would carry the highest risk for all parties, they were the most closely negotiated.

Accepting that Quality Is Measured in Outcomes

Writing about quality in medical care in the 1960s, Donabedian (1966) developed a three-dimensional framework for the assessment of quality that included the following: 1) structures, 2) processes, and 3) outcomes. In his model, *structures* (also referred to as inputs) included administrative and related resources that support and direct the provision of care. These included things such as the availability and quality of physical facilities and equipment, the number and qualifications of staff, the administration of the agency and its fiscal arrangements, and so forth. *Processes* were defined as largely administrative creations that document whether established practices and procedures are followed, such as records of assessment of skills and needs, records of services provided and their implementation, records on individual crises and staff responses, medical needs, services received, staff training, and so forth. Structural and process assessments of quality share the characteristic of viewing quality as being within the organization. *Outcomes* were viewed as being produced by the interaction of the organization with the individual. In Donabedian's model, which primarily focused on medical care, outcomes included current health status, changes in health, functional skills, personal comfort, and satisfaction with intervention.

Outcome orientations created some challenging paradoxes. More was not necessarily better. For example, structural improvements (e.g., greater numbers and qualifications of staff) were not necessarily related to desired outcomes (e.g., greater independence, better health). In Minnesota in the late 1990s, increasing numbers of people are advocating, as Donabedian did 30 years before, that if you must choose a way to look at quality, the quality of services is ultimately the services' outcomes, and not the condition of the buildings that house them, the training of the staff that deliver them, and so forth. Buildings, staff, and other resources, ultimately, may contribute to quality but to confuse them with quality makes them the "end" when they should be the "means."

For Minnesota residents with developmental disabilities under the demonstration of an alternative approach to quality assurance authorized by Minnesota's legislature, quality would be defined by outcomes in social skills developed and practiced, social relationships established and maintained, types and frequency of community participation, hours of employment and earnings, choices made and honored, consumer and family satisfaction, and so forth.

In Minnesota's experiences of trying to respond to the ideas and challenges presented in the previous paragraphs, it has become very clear that, although there is an elegant simplicity in outcomes as a basis of quality, creating outcome-based quality assurance systems is much more difficult than creating structure- or input-based systems. It is much easier to ensure that a person has a bedroom of a specified square footage (structure) or that service recipients are assessed and, that based on that assessment, individual programs were developed and implemented (process), than it is to determine that people increased their social network of relationships that they value or are more satisfied with their lives (outcome). The complexity of creating outcome-based quality assurance systems is compounded by the desire to have those systems also serve a quality enhancement function.

THE MINNESOTA ALTERNATIVE QUALITY ASSURANCE DEMONSTRATION

The following paragraphs discuss Minnesota's approach to an integrated program of outcome-based quality assurance and quality enhancement through a project called the Minnesota Performance Based Contracting Quality Assurance Demonstration.

Conception and Development

Developing an approach to quality assurance/quality enhancement that improved on the circumstances discussed in the previous paragraphs was viewed by government officials, service providers, advocates, and consumers as extremely important to the future definition, design, and implementation of quality assurance in Minnesota. The commitment to design, implement, and evaluate a new approach to quality assurance in human services was supported by specific commitments of the DHS and the Minnesota Legislature to facilitate solutions to the perceived problems with quality assurance in Minnesota.

In Minnesota, representatives of key constituencies were brought together by the DHS to establish parameters for appropriate, reliable, valid, and useful procedures for redefining quality in human services. These representatives were also responsible for developing approaches for assessing the quality of the procedures and for using this assessment information to improve the quality of lives of individuals and the contributions of quality assurance to these ends. This working group proposed a demonstration project that would promote alternative quality assurance systems in community ICFs/MR as well as other types of licensed homes. As mentioned previously, it was clear that a federal waiver of existing Medicaid ICF/MR standards would be required.

Medicaid's provision for demonstration of alternative, cost-effective approaches to achieving Medicaid goals fit well with Minnesota's desire to conduct a carefully monitored and evaluated demonstration of contracts for performance as the foundation of an alternative quality assurance/quality enhancement system. An important design aspect of this proposed demonstration was that by operating without ICF/MR standards, participating service agencies would be able to avoid substantial required expenses for specialized personnel, paper compliance, and accounting procedures that were of no benefit to the outcomes of importance to people. As a result, at least a 5% savings could be expected to result from a new approach. Through a federal demonstration grant, the equivalent of about 80% of the projected federal savings from the rate reduction would be provided for use in training, technical assistance, and organizational development to make the system not only one of quality assurance but also one of quality enhancement. Cost effectiveness and quality enhancement became key components of the demonstration goals.

A critical initial aspect of this demonstration was the nearly 1 full year devoted by a work group comprising representatives of the key constituencies to analyze and develop a consensus about 1) the feasibility of a demonstration in this area (i.e., Were alternative quality assurance approaches feasible?), 2) the nature of the demonstration (e.g., What were the alternatives, and in which areas were these alternatives possible, what kinds of agencies/entities should be permitted to develop alternative approaches, what kinds of services should be included?), 3) the size of the demonstration (e.g., How many individual agencies and how many service recipients should be allowed to participate?), 4) the most feasible way to recruit the most capable agencies and associated local governments, and 5) the conditions for participation. With guidance from the working group, the DHS proposed a legislative package (which was approved with modification to exclude day/vocational services) to authorize waiving state rules, obtaining endorsement of a DHS staff position for the demonstration, and seeking the necessary federal waivers for implementation.

Goals of the Demonstration

The Performance Based Contracting demonstration project was specifically designed to afford selected agencies located in cooperating counties the opportunity to offer residential and other support services under an alternative outcome-based, performance-sensitive quality assurance system for a period of up to 4 years. During that period, with federal approval, existing federal standards (e.g., ICF/MR) as well as non–health- and safety-related state rules would be waived in lieu of an alternative approach approved under the following projected goals:

- To redesign quality assurance to increase the influence of consumers and families in defining, monitoring, and improving the quality of services

- To establish and test measures of service quality in terms of desired outcomes for the consumer and to allow those preferred outcomes to be the basis for service improvement, redesign, and development
- To enable providers to assume more direct responsibility for the quality of their services and for quality enhancement activities, including implementing agency total quality management practices
- To increase the role of the state in technical assistance and support to enhance quality, while decreasing the focus on strict regulatory compliance and sanction processes
- To renegotiate the roles of existing state licensing and health monitoring personnel and to provide needed training to assist them in fulfilling their new roles of outcome monitoring
- To design and describe the effects of different approaches to outcome-based quality assurance that represent models for individual agency and state designs for reinventing quality assurance
- To recommend to the Minnesota Legislature and other state and national audiences new designs and approaches to quality assurance that improve the person-centeredness, outcome-orientation, quality-of-life relevance and individual empowerment of service recipients through reliable and valid procedures

Selecting Participating Agencies

In response to the work group recommendation to develop a demonstration of an alternative quality assurance system, the DHS and the University of Minnesota's Institute on Community Integration (ICI) sponsored a Quality Fair and invited service providers from across the state to attend. Information was provided at this fair regarding the demonstration project and various quality assurance practices and resources. Following the fair, interested agencies responded to a Request for Proposal put forth by the DHS Division for Persons with Developmental Disabilities. Only providers in "good standing" with existing review processes and who delivered community ICF/MR services were eligible to participate in the demonstration. Eleven agencies submitted responses to the Request for Proposal, which included a plan for implementing alternative quality assurance programs within their agencies. Five agencies were chosen. They ranged in size from serving 12 people in two ICFs/MR to serving more than 300 people in a variety of service models including ICFs/MR, HCBS Waiver, Semi-Independent Living Services (SILS), and in-home family support. One selected agency is located in north central rural Minnesota, and the four other agencies deliver services in the metropolitan Minneapolis/St. Paul area.

THE CHALLENGE OF THE DEMONSTRATION

Any reform that moves from centralized control of a highly regulated system to a more local and flexible system is not easy and does not occur without major hurdles, confusion, and differences of opinion. The following sections describe the development, challenges, and lessons learned regarding seven key components of the demonstration: 1) procuring state and federal regulatory variances; 2) cost cutting at the agency level; 3) developing local collaborative work groups; 4) designing and implementing an external, outcome-based quality assurance methodology; 5) designing and using performance-based contracts; 6) implementing technical assistance and training; and 7) completing a comprehensive evaluation. Although the project is just nearing a midpoint as of this writing, a number of lessons have been learned, and significant changes have occurred at the individual, agency, and systems levels.

Procuring State and Federal Regulatory Variances

The first step in the process was to procure waivers and variances at the state and federal levels and to secure support for the project from various agencies.

Obtaining a Federal Waiver and Demonstration Support   In March 1994, Minnesota submitted its request for a federal waiver that would allow it to use a person-centered, outcome-based quality assurance approach in ICFs/MR in place of federal ICF/MR standards. That application to the HCFA was, however, substantially delayed by Minnesota's request to HCFA for funding to support quality assurance and quality improvement activities. The funding requested was, in essence, a request for the return of a substantial portion of the federal savings from the 5% reduction in ICF/MR reimbursement rates. This request reflected the state's position that money saved from dispensing with an unsatisfactory system should be reinvested in efforts to create a more satisfactory system. Although the HCFA could not directly earmark such savings to this purpose, the argument contributed to HCFA's awarding Minnesota a separate demonstration grant to allow indirect allocations of reduced expenditures to go toward alternative quality assurance and quality enhancement activities. Subsequent to the grant approval, demonstration participants had to endure several more months of delay as the HCFA considered the request of Minnesota's DHS for waiver of specific Medicaid rules that HCFA was authorized to grant under its demonstration authority in Section 1115(a) of the Social Security Act. But once free from the federal bureaucracy—indeed with all requested support from it—it became readily apparent that the problems in defining quality and designing a quality assurance system based on the outcomes of importance to people were not primarily problems associated with federal bureaucratic control.

Obtaining State Rule Variances   One of the most challenging and divisive activities of the project has been the issue of which state rules should be waived or which rule provisions should have variances. One of the primary motives provider agencies had for project participation was that they would be freed from many of the state and federal regulations that they perceived as impeding their ability to provide the supports wanted by their consumers. Although a blanket federal waiver for all ICF/MR regulations was approved as a part of the demonstration, participants were surprised to learn that no agreements had been reached to grant blanket variances for the many state rules and regulations that govern ICF/MR, Home and Community Based Waiver, and SILS in Minnesota. As a result, agencies and work groups involved in the demonstration submitted line-by-line requests for variances for each component of every regulation and rule that governed the services that they provided. They spent months preparing written variance requests and reported that it seemed that once approval was made on one rule variance, another rule that needed variance was uncovered. The participating agency staff, county representatives, and local work group members variously referred to the experiences as "going around in circles," "dealing with a quagmire," and "taking apart the web of interrelated regulations."

A particular problem was the expectation by providers that the state Supervised Living Facility (SLF) rule, which applies to ICFs/MR and contains many of the same provisions as the federal ICF/MR regulations, would be waived. The unsuccessful outcome to the laborious process of making a specific request for variance and the response of the DOH, which many providers perceived to be inflexible and disrespectful, did much to damage relationships between the state and other participants. It was not until months later that state officials pointed out a little known, and last minute, addition to the legislation and federal waiver request, which specified that this rule would remain in effect.

There were other discrepancies between regulations and the waivers that caused confusion and difficulties. For example, parts of the SLF rule consisted of regulations and provided for inspections that apply to ICFs/MR but for which there were no corresponding regulations or inspections that applied to services funded under the HCBS waiver. Participants were frustrated that, despite these inconsistencies and the perceived promises made for the demonstration goals, they still could not get waivers. Nevertheless, important regulatory relief was finally obtained by the participating service providers.

Spreading Quality Assurance Statewide   Despite the limitations of regulatory accommodation within the project, the efforts of the participants to examine and revise regulatory rules have made a significant difference. A successful statewide rule consolidation effort that has derived guidance from the demonstration appears likely to provide for substantially more efficient and flexible systemwide quality assurance. Minnesota's managed care pilot projects for people with disabilities (in which counties are accepting a managed care role) are building off of the concepts of the demonstration. In the southeast region of Minnesota, a 10-county consortium has proposed legislation to give it control of quality assurance following the basic principles of the demonstration. They have been able to look at the arguments provided and the issues raised in this project to inform their efforts. And, it is hoped, if the providers are able to demonstrate successful outcomes with this level of regulatory relief, the system will bend to provide a greater level of relief in the future.

Cost Cutting at the Agency Level

A goal of this project is to demonstrate that a measure of cost effectiveness can be attained through reducing regulatory requirements and by implementing outcome-based quality assurance and quality improvement approaches. As noted, each provider in the demonstration project agreed that, as a condition of their participation, they would take a 5% reduction in their existing ICF/MR service rates. These reductions were implemented by the state even before obtaining the federal waiver and considerably before the project officially began. This administrative accomplishment was such that one provider noted to be remarkably faster than any of the others. Following their one-time, initial 5% reduction, providers have received typical annual cost-of-living increases.

Although the federal waiver had not been granted at the time of the initial 5% rate cut, providers were released from an elaborate state cost-reporting rule for ICFs/MR. This waiver has allowed the providers to save a substantial amount of money in accounting costs. As the project has progressed, service providers have reported a variety of other ways in which they have compensated for the 5% rate reduction. These include the following:

- More creative and efficient use of funds has occurred, which previously had been discouraged because providers were paid for what they spent rather than given the money to allocate where it was most needed. Cost-cutting techniques have ranged from refinancing vehicles and mortgages on existing homes to clipping coupons and attending more carefully to energy expenditures.
- Reduction in paper-processing requirements have enabled many Qualified Mental Retardation Professionals (QMRPs) to take on additional consumer support and staff support responsibilities.
- Flattening of administrative structures or shifting staff responsibilities have been made possible by less need for QMRPs' review of programs and management oversight of rule compliance.
- Reductions in expenditures for nursing, pharmacy, and similar services have occurred because of elimination of unnecessary medical service requirements of the federal ICF/MR regulations (e.g., quarterly nursing reviews).
- A shift in the focus of quality assurance has eliminated the benefits of "mock surveys" and documentation "clean up," which occupied many QMRP, nursing, and administrator hours.

Developing Local Collaborative Work Groups

A significant component of the demonstration project is the development of local (i.e., county) work groups. These work groups vary depending on the agencies and counties involved. For example, some work groups are county based and consist of all of the agencies that are involved in the project and provide services in that particular county. One work group is agency based and includes representatives from the two counties in which the agency provides services. In addition to agency and county representatives, efforts have been made to involve advocates, family members, consumers, and vocational/day training providers. These work groups provide advice and oversight for the agencies' involvement in the project, and they have spawned ideas for the development of training products, collaborative purchases of training and technical assistance, and the development of consumer satisfaction evaluation methods. To these ends, the groups were allocated resources from the federal grant based on size and number of demonstration participants. Work groups often use meetings as a forum to share ideas, tell stories, and collaborate on strategies that promote improved consumer outcomes. The activity level of the local work groups has ranged from one county and provider that have preferred to meet only on an "as needed" basis to two work groups in which participants have raved about the collaboration and mutual understanding that has emerged from their monthly meetings.

Designing and Implementing an External Outcome-Based Quality Assurance Methodology

In the initial planning of the demonstration, it was envisioned that multiple models of quality assurance would be developed and that the locus of the new quality assurance approach would be "local monitoring teams." These teams would consist of people who were part of the focus person's support network or "quality circle" as well as members of the "local work group" (e.g., service providers, family members, advocates). The original "local monitoring team" concept allowed for each locality to define the quality assurance methodology to be used; determine which training was needed; and decide how, where, and when quality reviews were to be conducted. As the project evolved, the concept of multiple local monitoring models became viewed as infeasible because of concerns about consistency and an insufficient understanding of how the local groups would be organized, trained, paid for, and coordinated with the monitoring of remaining regulations.

Shift from a Local Monitoring Concept to Centralized Quality Review   To coordinate the various local agencies, a single projectwide concept of quality review was implemented. It came to be managed by the DHS. Localities retained the freedom to adopt their own preferred quality assessment approach in addition to the statewide system, as desired.

An intention remains, however, that as the methodology becomes better established and as the participants become increasingly confident, skilled, and organized in their outcome assessment and quality improvement roles that the program will be able to integrate a more localized community involvement and increased participation by providers, families, and consumers. Indeed, one of the important realizations in the project thus far has been the difficulty of adopting a stakeholder-monitored, performance-based outcome system, because it requires a great deal of training and sophistication. Furthermore, it can be difficult to find reviewers, either professional or community volunteers, who have the time to acquire the needed training and perform the reviews.

Quality Enhancement Team   The *Outcome Based Performance Measures* and associated methodology developed by The Council on Quality and Leadership in Support for People with Disabilities (The Council) is the base of Minnesota's alternative quality assurance program (Council on Quality and Leadership, 1993). A review team, called the Quality Enhancement Team (QET), was established to participate in in-depth and comprehensive training on the use of the Council's outcome methodology. Although the QET trainees initially had some concerns about the methodology, there was also a great deal of enthusiasm. They liked the focus on outcomes and issues that were important to service recipients; the shift from a focus on paperwork to interviews with people receiving services, family members, and staff who know them; and the possibility of linking quality assessment and quality improvement. It was decided that the concerns of the QET trainees did not warrant spending the time and effort necessary to "reinvent the wheel," and The Council's methodology was used without change.

The QET consists of volunteers that include representatives from the DOH, the DHS Division for Persons with Developmental Disabilities, the ICI, county case management, The Arc, day program providers, and agencies participating in the project. Family representatives were sought, but it was not possible to find people who were able to accommodate the time demands of the activity. Self-advocates were not included in the initial review team training. It remains a goal of the demonstration to successfully recruit, train, accommodate, and include family members and self-advocates as the demonstration continues.

A decision was made, because of the limited number of reviewers, that the volunteer nature of QET membership and the fact that this was an ICF/MR demonstration project under a Section 1115(a) waiver to complete the reviews only in ICF/MR programs. Pairs of QET members conducted the reviews and presented summation reports that cited commendations and recommendations organized around the 10 general outcome categories. Many agency representatives commented on how good it was "to hear the good along with the bad."

The agencies' performance on the QET reviews has improved dramatically since the first practice reviews and the first year's official reviews. QET reviewers attribute the higher level of performance to the agencies' adopting person-centered planning and changing other organizational processes as they focus more on facilitating outcomes for individuals.

Concerns and Issues   The experience with the QET alternative quality assurance design and implementation has been difficult yet valuable. Moving from an "inspection mentality" with clearly articulated criteria and interpretive guidelines to a more fluid, less-defined enhancement system is not easy. Some emergent concerns and issues to address as the demonstration project continues include the following:

1. Despite consistencies that have come from increased experience and training, there are still concerns about subjectivity and the lack of specified criteria for decisions about whether a specific outcome is considered to be present.

2. Some participants are concerned about the lack of direct use of information for service improvement. They are concerned about the lack of follow-up on information received in interviews and believe that it is unfair to spend 2–3 hours with a person, asking him or her about his or her life and uncovering concerns, and then to only use the information for an agency rating. Not only is it viewed as critical to provide individual follow up on important issues in a person's life, but it is also crucial to be able to follow up on matters of concern in agency performance.

3. There is concern about the extent to which residential providers should be accountable for those outcomes over which they do not have full control; and conversely, there is concern about holding the system (state, county) accountable for the outcomes that these entities prevent or impede (e.g., state and county agencies often affect people's opportunities to find new homes; day programs and vocational services agencies often control where people may work).

4. There is concern about the possibility of assessing appropriate and potentially beneficial efforts toward an outcome, in those instances in which the outcome is not present (e.g., for outcomes such as "people have friends" or "people have intimate relationships," residential providers have a responsibility to help people achieve the outcome, but in the absence of the actual outcomes on it can be difficult to determine whether the "process" in place to achieve the outcome is sufficient).

5. Some participants question whether certain outcomes should be more heavily weighted based on their importance to the individual or their socially perceived importance (e.g., Is having health care services equally important as having a variety of social roles?).

6. There is concern about whether the intrusiveness of interviews (e.g., length, number of people at the interview, the fact that strangers complete the interviews) is reasonable and fair to the individual. Instead, should the process be made shorter or less intrusive by allowing people who know and care about the indi-

vidual to complete portions of the interview, or should the individual decide on the nature of and participants in the interview?

7. There is concern about the variation in QET member's interviewing skills (in some cases it was reported to be "like an interrogation") and a question as to whether compliance-oriented inspectors and others of arguably incompatible backgrounds can be trained to perform personal outcome reviews.

8. Some participants question whether there is a need and a method to determine if the focus person's responses are always reliable and valid (e.g., responses may not be consistent with what the focus person says at other times or with what people who know him or her say the responses mean) and whether providers or people who know the individual well should have input before the determinations are made about an outcome.

9. A related question is whether outcomes should be judged on information that is obtained at one point in time or whether it would be more valid to obtain information over a period of time.

Designing and Using Performance-Based Contracts

Performance-based contracts are a central component of the demonstration project. In Minnesota, a performance-based contract is a three-party agreement among the state, the county in which the service is being delivered, and the participating provider agency. It includes the current provider's performance on the achievement of outcomes based on the QET reviews and a quality improvement plan.

The first step in the development of these contracts was to review results of the initial QET review and establish a baseline level of performance. Once this was completed, performance targets were negotiated for the second year of the project. The contracts also included information on necessary state rule variances, identified training and technical assistance needs for the agency, and any other necessary amendments as determined and agreed upon by the three parties. This process will be repeated the second and third years of the project. It is important to recognize that the performance-based contracts used in this demonstration are designed to serve as a quality enhancement tool and are not being used in any punitive manner.

Quality Improvement Plan   Quality improvement is a central component that is designed into the alternative quality assurance approach. When the QET results indicate problem areas, the intention is to focus on identifying the barriers and providing the necessary technical assistance to overcome them. This commitment to quality improvement is reflected in the development of a Quality

Improvement Plan (QIP) that is incorporated into the performance-based contract. The QIP includes outcome areas that need improvement as identified by the provider, local work group, and consumers and their families. QIPs also may include requests for related variances and technical assistance. Within the demonstration, however, no negative sanctions exist for not meeting the performance targets set forth in the QIP. Incentives for meeting QIP performance targets have been discussed and possibilities being considered include the following: 1) Space QET reviews farther apart from DOH and DHS inspections and licensing reviews, 2) provide small financial grants to be used for specific agreed-upon purposes, and 3) provide positive public acknowledgments.

Implementing Technical Assistance and Training

One important benefit of participation in the demonstration that providers have noted has been the access to a wide range of training and technical assistance made available to them through the federal grant funds. This technical assistance has helped agency staff to see their services and supports through the eyes of the consumer and has helped them to visualize creative possibilities for the future. The project has developed tools and strategies to plan and provide more person-centered services, and organizations have been able to take advantage of organizational change strategies that assist with the effective implementation of new person-centered, outcome-focused strategies for quality improvement.

The project has facilitated extensive agency staff training and has provided a wide range of technical assistance. Specific training has included agency participation in Frameworks for Accomplishment seminars, Essential Lifestyle Planning, Personal Futures Planning, workshops on facilitating friendships, and development and delivery of curricula on self-determination and exercising of rights. The project has provided technical assistance on many topics, ranging from the facilitation of an 18-month organizational redesign and planning effort in the largest agency to more short-term efforts such as developing new agency mission and vision statements. Agencies have received assistance in developing new competency-based training programs for their staff and in designing QIPs. They have received assistance facilitating consumer focus groups within agencies and linking consumers to People First groups outside of the agencies. Seven hundred project participants in many roles from agency director to direct support staff to consumers and family members attended and contributed to a 2-day "Putting People First" conference. The conference was designed to share information on the activities, interests, and challenges of administration, staff, and consumers and to present local and national speaker's ideas on how to increase the person-centered, outcome-orientation of services.

The Council also has taught computer skills such as how to use e-mail and the World Wide Web to more efficiently acquire and disseminate information. Projectwide technical assistance has been available to establish a World Wide Web home page, to begin the development of a Consumer Information System, and to develop software to guide the development of individualized planning. In addition, the training and technical assistance available from The Council on the performance-based outcomes has proved to be very useful to agencies, community work groups, and QETs.

Although the bulk of training and technical assistance has been focused at the agency and county level, training and technical assistance has also been available at the state and consumer/family levels. Consumer and family technical assistance activities have included informational meetings about personal outcomes planning and the demonstration project, in establishing local self-advocacy groups, and in the facilitation of dozens of person-centered planning processes.

Completing a Comprehensive Evaluation

An independent evaluation of the Performance Based Contracting Project is being conducted by staff of the ICI. The evaluation consists of a quantitative outcome component and a qualitative process component.

Quantitative Component   The purpose of the outcome component of the evaluation is to obtain quantitative information on consumer outcomes in the five areas specified by the Minnesota Legislature as areas to which an alternative quality assurance program should attend. These areas are 1) health, safety and comfort; 2) community inclusion, including social relationships and participation in valued social roles; 3) personal growth, independence, and productivity; 4) individual choice and control over daily life decisions; and 5) consumer satisfaction. It was determined that the Council's 30 outcomes could also be linked with these five categories, thereby allowing additional comparison with QET review results.

Survey instruments that address the five outcome areas were developed for consumers and for a close acquaintance (e.g., family member, friend) of the consumer. As of this writing, information on consumers' characteristics is being derived from the Inventory for Client and Agency Planning. These data will be used to compare outcomes for consumers in the project with matched samples of consumers participating in other studies of community services in Minnesota, as well as to compare outcomes for consumers at Year 1 of the project with those reported near the end of the project.

Qualitative Component   There are three levels of analysis in the qualitative process component of the evaluation. In addition to describing the development of the project as a whole, evaluators are compiling case studies of each on the participating agencies and on several of the individuals receiving services from these agencies. At the conclusion of the project, a cross-case analysis of the different processes and outcomes of the agencies and individuals will be made.

WHAT HAS CHANGED AND WHAT HAS BEEN LEARNED THROUGH THE MINNESOTA EXPERIENCE?

The Minnesota demonstration has completed several years of planning, start up, and 1½ years of official implementation. Perhaps at this point in the project there are more questions than answers; however, there have been changes made and lessons learned at all levels (e.g., systems, agency, individual) of this project. Real changes in the system have been few, but the lessons learned from attempts at creating systems change have been significant. Agency changes are rapidly emerging, and the lessons learned within these agencies are beginning to show increasing specificity. It is, however, at the individual and family level that changes have been the most dramatic.

Systems-Level Change

At the systems level, some changes have occurred in the way programs are reviewed and in the way in which quality is measured. In addition, lessons have been learned about the difficulty of achieving substantial systems change within a demonstration project, the importance of collaboration, and the need for technical assistance and training.

The Performance Based Contracting demonstration project has proven to be extremely complex, and the changes that were made possible by the project have not always been clear. In an interview about the project, one provider reported frustration with the complexity of the project and the belief that reform was slower than expected. In the absence of total and immediate reform at the onset of this project, providers and state-level agencies have struggled with the reality of running dual systems (e.g., continuing to function as an ICF/MR while awaiting a federal waiver, obtaining variances, receiving commitments from counties, and developing person-centered plans for consumers). In addition, most project participants had expectations of extensive deregulation, and few realized that many of the potential options in this area had been squelched by last-minute changes in the authorizing legislation. As a result, few regulations were actually waived, and multiple forms of regulatory and quality oversight by state agencies have continued.

Other needs identified in the project have been those of providing resources and support for change-related activities as well as the need for participation of day providers, family members, and consumers at all levels of planning and implementing systems change. The resources targeted for training and technical assistance within this project have been managed by the DHS, Division for Persons with Developmental Disabilities. This component of the project has illustrated the invaluable nature of providing information and support to agencies that are trying to move from prescriptive, regulatory-focused services to those that are person centered and outcome oriented. In addition, the demonstration project process has made it clear that without the involvement of families, consumers, and day providers, difficulties arise in being able to support individuals in realizing outcomes, and the opportunity to gain needed industry support to sustain the project past the demonstration period are jeopardized.

This project has also challenged the roles and perceptions of state agencies. Historically, little trust has existed between state systems personnel and the provider community; thus, developing trust between these groups proves challenging. Providers came in to the project expecting decisions to be made collaboratively and were discouraged when some decisions were made in isolation by state agencies. In addition, changing the roles and perceptions of various state personnel in monitoring and regulating services has been difficult. As time has passed and as state personnel have begun participating in and observing the work of local work groups, the QET, and other project-related activities, however, this tension and mistrust has begun to subside.

Perhaps the biggest change at the systems level within this project has been the creation and implementation of the alternative quality assurance design—that is, the QET. This process has resulted in a better, although not perfect, system of monitoring quality.

Agency-Level Change

Agencies participating in this project have benefited tremendously from the challenge. The project has provided them with the opportunity to examine their processes and their ways of doing business, and it has offered them the opportunity to make valuable changes designed to create outcome-oriented and efficient services.

The agencies within the Performance Based Contracting demonstration project have all moved toward some form of person-centered planning and supports. They have realized that moving toward person-centered services means changing more than just agency assessment and program planning processes. This change process affects everything within the organization including the mission, training, personnel practices, internal quality assurance mechanisms, and so forth. It requires an agency to focus more on the individual people served than on the system and its rules and regulations. Staff within the participating agencies report that moving toward a person-centered approach to providing services has made their jobs more meaningful and provides them with more personal satisfaction. Families and service coordinators have reported satisfaction with the planning and reporting processes associated with new person-centered approaches (i.e., receiving narrative reports on what the person likes and is doing versus deficiency-centered, goal-based traditional annual and quarterly reports).

The Performance Based Contracting project has also challenged agencies to address difficult issues around protecting individuals with disabilities versus honoring their choices, rights, and opportunities to take risks. The system of licensing and regulating in Minnesota has historically put protection ahead of individual rights. This project has enabled providers to move beyond a focus on protection by questioning their practices and looking at restrictions in a different manner (i.e., as a violation of rights). For example, because a person overspent his or her money, should staff keep the money locked in a cabinet (provide protection), or should they let him or her keep it, choose how to spend it, and learn from mistakes (learn how to take risks)?

This project has also challenged providers to see the importance of strong relationships with day programs. Person-centered teams have been greatly enhanced when both residential and day provider members began focusing on what was important to the individual. This has made these relationships stronger through better communication, mutual goals, and a sense of more purposeful and meaningful participation. It has proved difficult at times to strengthen relationships, however, because, as a fundamental flaw of this project, day and residential providers are working under different systems with different requirements and regulations.

Individual- and Family-Level Change

The Performance Based Contracting demonstration has already affected the lives of the individuals participating in the demonstration. Perhaps the most significant effects have come as a result of person-centered planning approaches and the provision of services that focus on what people want. Many individuals initially expressed suspicion toward these new processes. They were not quite certain how to respond to being asked about what they wanted and if they were satisfied with services. But as the project progressed, they and their family members began to feel that they were being listened to and that what they say does make a difference and actually has an impact on the services that they receive.

It is also evident that individuals participating in the Performance Based Contracting demonstration are being allowed the dignity to make choices and to direct their own services. Many of these choices might seem commonplace to others, but the individuals participating in this project have often been denied these opportunities in the past. For example, people are choosing to go out to lunch at work with a friend, to live with a new housemate, to have a private bedroom, to participate in religious services and service clubs, and to volunteer and develop special interests—all choices that in the past had been denied or made by others.

REFERENCES

Abery, B.H., & Fahnestock, M. (1994). Enhancing the social inclusion of persons with developmental disabilities. In M.F. Hayden & B.H. Abery (Eds.), *Challenges for a service system in transition: Ensuring quality community experiences for persons with developmental disabilities* (pp. 83–119). Baltimore: Paul H. Brookes Publishing Co.

Bercovici, S. (1983). *Barriers to normalization: The restrictive management of retarded persons.* Baltimore: University Park Press.

Blatt, B. (1970). *Exodus from pandemonium: Human abuse and reformation of public policy.* Needham Heights, MA: Allyn & Bacon.

Blatt, B. (1973). *Souls in extremis.* Needham Heights, MA: Allyn & Bacon.

Burchard, S.N., Hasazi, J.E., Gordon, L.R., & Yae, J. (1991). An examination of lifestyle and adjustment in three community residential alternatives. *Research in Developmental Disabilities, 12,* 127–142.

Donabedian, A. (1966). Evaluating the quality of medical care. *Milbank Memorial Fund Quarterly, 44,* 166–206.

Hill, B.K., Lakin, K.C., Bruininks, R.H., Amado, A.N., Anderson, D.J., & Copher, J.I. (1989). *Living in the community: A comparative study of foster homes and small group homes for people with mental retardation.* Minneapolis: University of Minnesota, Research and Training on Community Living.

Hurst, J. (1989, January 8). Private care for the retarded—a gamble. *Los Angeles Times,* 22–26.

Lakin, K.C., Burwell, B.O., Hayden, M.F., & Jackson, M.E. (1992). *An independent assessment of Minnesota's Medicaid Home and Community Based*

Services waiver program (Project Report #37). Minneapolis: University of Minnesota, Research and Training Center on Community Living.

Mitchell, G. (Chair). (1988). *Hearing before the U.S. Senate Subcommittee on Health on the Medicaid Home and Community Quality Services Act of 1987* (S. Hearing 100-817, March 22, 1988). Washington, DC: U.S. Government Printing Office.

Prouty, R.W., & Lakin, K.C. (1991). *A summary of states' efforts to positively affect the quality of Medicaid Home and Community Based Services for persons with mental retardation and related conditions.* Minneapolis: University of Minnesota, Research and Training Center for Community Living.

Prouty, R.W., & Lakin, K.C. (Eds.). (1997). *Residential services for persons with developmental disabilities: Status and trends through 1996.* Minneapolis: University of Minnesota, Research and Training Center on Community Living.

Rivera, G. (1972). *Willowbrook.* New York: Vintage Books.

Social Security Act Amendments of 1965, PL 89-97, 42 U.S.C. §§ 1115 *et seq.*

The Council on Quality and Leadership in Supports for People with Disabilities. (1993). *Outcome Based Performance Measures.* Baltimore: Author.

U.S. General Accounting Office. (1990). *Quality assurance: A comprehensive national strategy for health care is needed.* (GAO/PEMD-90-14BR). Gaithersburg, MD: Author.

Where the toys are locked away: Senator Kennedy's indictment of New York State's institutions for mentally retarded children. (1965, September 29). *Christian Century,* 1179–1180.

Wyden, R. (Chair). (1993). Staff memorandum: Residential programs for the mentally retarded. In *Growth of small residential living programs for the mentally retarded and developmentally disabled; Hearing of the Committee on Small Business, House of Representatives, March 29, 1993* (House Serial Report No. 103-8). Washington, DC: U.S. Government Printing Office.

16

Changing Regional Service Systems

Combining Personal Outcomes and
Total Quality Management Techniques

Christine Rich

In the early 1990s, the Connecticut State Department of Mental Retardation (DMR) began to explore the concept of assisting people with developmental disabilities to identify and pursue personal outcomes. State and regional office personnel recognized the need to do business with greater efficiency and with a greater focus on the needs of people receiving services and supports. As a result, the DMR also began to explore the philosophies and techniques of total quality management (TQM).

At the time, Connecticut was divided into six service delivery regions. Residential and day services throughout the state were provided by a mixture of both publicly administered programs and private, not-for-profit agencies. The Eastern Region comprised the eastern section of the state and provided services to approximately 2,000 people with developmental disabilities. This chapter describes the management of organizational and systemic changes in the regional service delivery system.

In February 1993, the Region made the decision to concentrate on the people employed in the large, publicly run sheltered workshop. Although Connecticut had embraced the concept of supported employment in the early 1980s and had committed almost all new development money since then to fund this type of support, more than 100 people worked in the segregated site. Lack of community jobs, individual and family resistance to change, unclear administrative direction, and an overall organizational inertia and reluctance to change contributed to the workshop's continuation.

GETTING STARTED

The Region began the process of change by linking the workshop's closure with thoughtful planning that took into account the needs of all workshop employees, family concerns, and input from line staff. A project team was selected that included representatives from all levels of the organization, including line staff, line supervisors, and administration, as well as representatives from the business office and staff development department. The project team, unfortunately, did not initially include a consumer or family member, although all subsequent subcommittees did. A project team leader and a quality advisor were appointed, and the team began to use TQM tools and techniques in its planning efforts. Team members were able to participate in training on TQM and facilitation skills.

The project team's first task was to develop a vision statement as a guide for the months ahead. The project team believed that the vision statement should (Albin, 1992)

- Be a clear and compelling picture of its ideal future
- Be a rallying point for future decision making
- Provide direction for prioritizing goals and identifying strategies and action steps

After much debate, the following initial vision statement was adopted: "To develop optimal day programs for all individuals reflective of their interests, abilities, and needs." At the time, members of the project team thought that this was a vision statement beyond reproach because it took into account individual preferences. The project team's self-confidence, however, did not last very long. Shortly after the project team was formed, several members of the team attended a 2-day conference on "Applying Total Quality Concepts in Human Service Settings and Using Outcome Measures to

Improve Quality." They returned and convinced the team that it was headed in the wrong direction with its focus on developing *programs* instead of *personal outcomes* for individuals. The project team quickly shifted the focus away from program development to personal outcomes. The project team realized the following flaws in the first vision statement:

- Focusing on programs would mean that the project team would be making assumptions about what people needed and wanted.
- Programs and program "slots" develop lives of their own that last long past any true need on the part of consumers.
- Programs often are driven by "politics" not by consumers.
- Programs create "turf" that staff and/or agencies then defend.
- Programs do not often change their services or levels of support in response to changes in their customers' needs and interests (Gaebler & Osborne, 1993).
- Quality must start with the person, not with the service or program.

A NEW BEGINNING

The new revised vision statement reflected one small but crucial change. It was changed to read, "To develop optimal day *outcomes* for all individuals reflective of that person's interests, abilities, and needs." This small change in wording turned out to be much more than a case of semantics or jargon. The commitment to personal outcomes for the people employed in the sheltered workshop influenced every subsequent decision in the months to come. The use of personal outcomes moved the project team from a focus on process to a focus on personal career choices for people.

The project team also emphasized the guiding principle of TQM: Know and listen to your customers. When the project team began to view workshop employees as customers, it realized that listening to people's definitions of what they wanted out of their careers was a nonnegotiable necessity. In addition to a customer focus, the project team also attempted to adhere to the following TQM principles:

- Leadership commitment
- Data-based decision making
- Participative involvement and staff empowerment
- Continuous improvement
- Systems perspective

SETTING UP THE SYSTEM:
USING TOTAL QUALITY MANAGEMENT TECHNIQUES

The project team used a variety of techniques to further their vision within the organization. This section explores these techniques and provides step-by-step directions on how the team implemented each technique.

Affinity Diagram

Having settled on the vision statement, the project team began planning by using a brainstorming methodology known as an Affinity Diagram (Brassard, 1989) to explore the following question: *"What are the issues involved with developing optimal day outcomes for each individual based on that person's choices, abilities, and needs?"* The Affinity Diagram (see Table 16.1) is a creative tool that gathers large numbers of ideas (or opinions, issues, etc.) and organizes them into groupings based on the natural relationships among them. An Affinity Diagram is best used when the following conditions are present:

- Chaos exists.
- The team is drowning in a large volume of ideas.
- The issue seems too large or complex to grasp.
- The team needs to find new patterns of information or solve solutions.
- Broad issues/themes must be identified.

The sequence of steps in using the Affinity Diagram includes the following:

1. Assemble the right team (four to six people with varied perspectives, creative thinkers).
2. Phrase the issue to be considered (broad, neutral statement, clearly stated).
3. Generate and record ideas. (Follow brainstorming guidelines and record each idea on cards. There should be no one-word cards.)
4. Randomly lay out completed cards (e.g., place on flipchart using self-adhesive notes or on table).
5. As a team, sort the cards into related groupings. (Groupings should be done in silence using only gut reactions. This should be a quick process; if members disagree, move cards but do not discuss.)
6. Create the Header Cards. (Header Cards should be concise but complete with no one-word headers. They should make sense

standing alone and capture the essential link among subordinate cards. Establish subthemes.)

7. Draw the finished Affinity Diagram. (Draw lines connecting headers and subheaders [the subthemes in Step 6] with all the cards beneath them, and bring together related groupings. Review diagram as a team, then have other people outside of the team review diagram.)

This particular technique allowed the group to generate a number of ideas that were then sorted into categories as illustrated in Table 16.1. The project team also used two other TQM tools known as the Nominal Group Technique and the Pareto Analysis, which enabled the team to identify those issues that should be addressed first and would produce the largest impact.

Table 16.1.   Affinity Diagram

What are all of the issues involved with developing optimal day outcomes for each individual based on that person's choices, abilities, and needs?

Program development/expansion
    Sufficient resources in terms of staffing to support individualized outcomes
    Development of nonvocational alternatives (e.g., retirement)
    Community job development
    Transportation options
    Economy in Northeast Connecticut
    Relationships with other human services agencies

Workshop: present/future
    Shift in resources from in-house programs to community supports
    Maintain quality services in workshop while downsizing
    Decreased cash flow due to decrease in subcontracts
    What to do with present vendors

External and internal concerns
    Fear and resistance to change from individuals and families
    Resistance from agency staff
    Union issues with job descriptions
    Need for buy-in from line staff to concept of outcomes
    Need for buy-in from interdisciplinary teams to the concept of outcomes

Quality-of-life issues
    Need for workshop employees to have greater awareness of realistic options
    Need to develop a tool to help people determine career choices
    Concern about impact of increased wages on entitlements
    Need for safety net for when people are between jobs and cannot stay home

Nominal Group Technique

The Nominal Group Technique (Albin, 1992; Brassard, 1988; Scholtes, 1988) is a method for obtaining input in a structured format from a group. The technique helps a group to narrow down a list of options and establish priorities. Organizations can best use the Nominal Group Technique to prevent any one person from dominating the decision-making process and to prioritize a list of recommendations. The Nominal Group Technique includes the following steps:

1. Introduce and clarify the topics (use an open-ended question format such as the Affinity Diagram).
2. Generate ideas individually and silently.
3. Collect ideas on a flipchart (do not discuss at this point, clarify only).
4. Reduce number of items to 50 or fewer (e.g., combine ideas, remove least important ideas through consensus).
5. Give each participant from four to eight file cards. The number of cards is a rough fraction of the number of items still on the list. Hand out 4 cards per person for up to 20 items; 6 cards for 20–35 items; 8 cards for 35–50 items.
6. Members individually identify their preferences from the list and write one preference on each card.
7. Have members assign a point value (highest is most important) to each item, based on their preferences. The value depends on the number of items selected (four, six, or eight). In an eight-card system, the most preferred item is numbered 8, and the least preferred item is numbered 1.
8. After each participant has given point values to the items selected, the cards are collected and the votes tallied. The item that ends up with the highest point total is the group's selection.
9. The group reviews the results, discusses reactions, and decides next steps.

Pareto Analysis

Another TQM technique is a Pareto Analysis (Albin, 1992; Brassard, 1988; Scholtes, 1988) (see Figure 16.1), which is a special form of bar graph that helps to determine which problems to solve in what order. The name is derived from the Pareto Principle, a principle that recognizes that a small number of variables often account for the majority of outcomes (e.g., 80% of the trouble comes from 20% of the problems, or 20% of the employees accomplish 60% of the work). A Pareto Analysis contributes to an organizational process

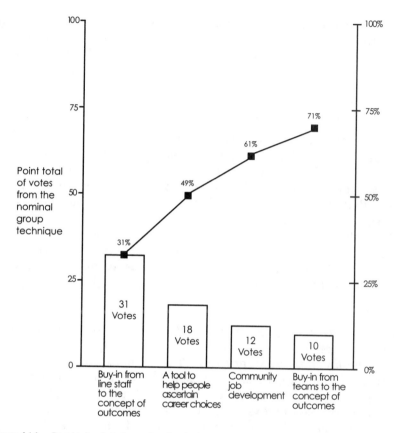

Figure 16.1.   Pareto Analysis: Issues involved with developing optimal day outcomes.

when it is used early in a project to determine which problems should be studied first. It can be used later in the project to narrow down which causes of a problem should be given first priority. Facilitators use a Pareto Analysis to identify those factors that will have the greatest impact (known as the "vital few"). Finally, it builds consensus in a group by drawing attention to those "vital few." A Pareto Analysis is performed as follows: Once the data are collected, order the data on a bar graph in descending frequency of occurrence so that the categories with the highest frequency of occurrence are to the left and the categories with the lowest frequency are farthest to the right (see Figure 16.1). For maximum effectiveness, limit categories to 10 or fewer. Also, it is often helpful to include cumulative percentages within the bar graph. For example, the Pareto Analysis in Figure 16.1 indicates that four issues re-

ceived 71% of the votes and that by concentrating on these four topics, the team would make the greatest contribution to achieving the
vision statement. The next section presents a detailed discussion of
these four issues and action steps taken to address those issues.

PRIORITY ISSUES IDENTIFIED BY THE PROJECT TEAM

Using a Pareto Analysis, the project team had prioritized the four
issues that would help them to implement the organization's vision
statement. The following section isolates each priority and discusses the tools and methods used to develop each issue. The priorities that the group identified were 1) develop internal support from
line staff for the vision statement and concept of personal outcomes,
2) develop a method for assisting people in the identification of desired career outcomes, 3) develop a community job network, and
4) develop support from the interdisciplinary teams for the project
and the vision statement.

Priority Issue #1

*Develop internal support from line staff for the vision statement and
concept of personal outcomes.*

Quality Improvement Tools   To accomplish the goal of developing internal support for the vision statement and the concept of
personal outcomes, the project team used a Tree Diagram (Brassard, 1989) (see Figure 16.2) to systematically map out the full
range of tasks. A Tree Diagram is employed when broad objectives
must be broken down into more specific detail. It allows for options
to be explored and for the creation of assignable tasks. The Tree Diagram contains the following steps:

1. *Choose the Tree Diagram goal statement.* The goal statement
   can be chosen from different sources: from the Header Cards
   from the Affinity Diagram or from "scratch" (i.e., from open discussion with no use of other tools).
2. *Assemble the right team.* Choose action planners with detailed
   implementation knowledge.
3. *Generate the major tree headings.* Headings should indicate the
   broadest implementation paths that the team wants to pursue.
   Headings can be generated using one of two options: 1) Create
   an Affinity Diagram from the goal statement, or 2) use brainstorming. If using an Affinity Diagram, use the Header Cards
   as the major headings; if brainstorming, lay out cards until
   broadest level of detail emerges.

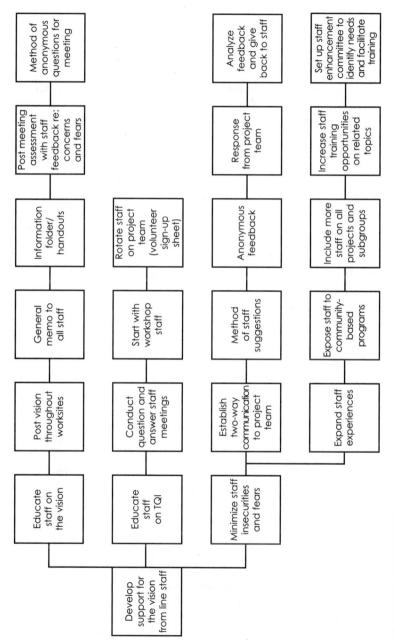

Figure 16.2. Tree Diagram.

4. *Complete the Tree Diagram under each major path.* Place the goal statement and the major headings to the extreme left, right, or top of paper or other work surface. Ask of each level of detail, "What needs to happen/be addressed to resolve/achieve this problem/goal statement?" Use existing cards or create new ones to fill in details at all levels.

5. *Review the completed Tree Diagram for logical flow.* Check logic at each level of detail. Going from specific to general ask, "Will these actions actually lead to these results?" Then, moving from general to specific ask, "If I want to accomplish these results, do I really need to do these tasks?"

Drawing from the Tree Diagram, the team scheduled and implemented the following action steps to build support for personal outcomes:

- Posting and publicizing the vision statement
- Conducting meetings with all involved staff
- Developing a "4C Form" (the 4 Cs are Comments, Concerns, Criticisms, and Cures) for all involved to use
- Including line staff on all subcommittees
- Training line staff on outcomes and TQM
- Conducting yearly staff surveys to assess progress

The response to the vision statement from line staff was varied. Because the project team was adamant about not rushing into change and because it took time to train in TQM philosophy and methodology, line staff initially only knew that a "team" was planning a change. The line staff considered the project team a "secret society." Therefore, the initial response on the part of line staff was anxiety and unrest. As a result, the new initiative to develop internal support had inadvertently generated opposition. The lesson learned is that any organization planning changes should communicate broadly, rapidly, and frequently. The reality, however, is that no team can communicate simultaneously to all members of a large organization. Someone will inevitably always be the last to know.

Reaction of line staff to specific action goals also varied. For example, only a few line staff used the 4C Form. Although the team had strived for rapid, positive responses, the 4C Form did not provide a major communication medium, and after a few months it was rarely used. Inclusion of line staff on all subcommittees was a major and more successful initiative in getting buy-in. *Buy-in* is a term that is generally used to mean "I understand the vision and am willing to work on it." As line staff met face to face with project team members, they were able to better understand the newly proposed initiatives and felt included in shaping the project goals. As inclusion on subcommittees grew, so too did the communication outside of meetings. Informal employee discussions became as important as the formal planning and implementation meetings.

Meetings with all line staff were held periodically. The presenters at these staff meetings always included the managers on the project team. This communicated the importance and organizational support of the project. This strategy successfully counteracted staff members' suspicions that the project was "packaged" as a personal outcomes project but was really management's plan to close the workshop, privatize the new initiative, and lay off the public sector employees. This fear was not totally unfounded because part of the project was unfolding as state government debated privatizing DMR day services. Privatization, however, did not occur.

Priority Issue #2

Develop a method for assisting people in the identification of desired career outcomes.

Quality Improvement Tools   A subcommittee prepared a flowchart and analyzed the effectiveness of the existing system within the workshop for determining people's choices about desired career outcomes. The subcommittee also collected and analyzed information about personal planning methods that were in use elsewhere (e.g., vocational interest inventories, career planning, person-centered planning formats).

Flowcharts are step-by-step schematic pictures used to describe an existing situation or to plan a new desired sequence (Scholtes, 1988). The four major types of flowcharts are as follows:

1. A *top-down flowchart* is a fast and efficient way to provide a picture of the major steps in a process. It forces people to narrow their thinking to only those steps absolutely essential to the process. To construct a top-down flowchart, first list the six or seven basic steps in the process. Below each step, list the major substeps.
2. A *detail flowchart* includes a lot of information about what happens at every step. These are helpful when trying to identify inefficiencies and redundancies. These are used sparingly because the amount of detail is often unnecessary.
3. A *work flow diagram* is a picture of the movement of people, materials, and information in a process. It is created by tracing

these movements on a floor plan. It is useful in analyzing inefficiencies and unnecessary movements in a process.

4. A deployment chart shows both the flow of a process or project and which people or groups are involved or responsible at each step. These charts are used to keep track of what each person or group is supposed to do, where the people involved fit into the sequence, and how they relate to the other players at that stage. To construct a deployment chart, list the major steps of a project or process vertically on a page. List each of the players—individuals or groups—across the top, and draw lines to create columns under each heading. Then mark the key action at each step in the appropriate column, denoting which person or group is responsible for that step (symbols can be helpful to indicate varying roles).

After completing a top-down flowchart, the project team developed and implemented a two-part planning system that included conducting one-to-one interviews with the organization's consumers as well as a person-centered brainstorming meeting for each individual. This process enabled consumers to tell staff of their individual career preferences and expectations.

The one-to-one interview provided the individual with a relaxed, nonthreatening atmosphere in which to talk about future dreams. The project team discovered that the typical interdisciplinary team meeting often put people on the spot and forced them to make important personal decisions in the presence of too many people. Interviewing the person a week or two before the meeting allowed staff to gather unbiased information.

Choosing the correct person to facilitate the brainstorming meeting was also paramount to the success of individual outcomes planning. People often came to the brainstorming meetings with preconceived ideas about the person and his or her prioritized outcomes. The facilitator must enable the planning group to discover information that reflects the person's priorities as well as the perspectives of the staff and family. The facilitator must also secure a commitment to the personal outcome planning process. All participants must understand that personal outcomes planning is not just a high-energy brainstorming session that ends with the plan on a flipchart. The planners are stakeholders who have an ongoing role in the process. They need to stay energized long after the initial meeting ends. Indeed, the plan identifies participants as *partners* to show their relationship to the person who they met with and will support.

Often the facilitator works with the meeting participants to overcome the belief that "if it's not broken, don't try to fix it." The sheltered workshop was, in many respects, highly successful. Workers liked going there, and parents supported it. Staff were kind and supportive. As a result, the facilitator needed to nudge the staff to continue the quality journey to personal outcomes, which is far different than fulfilling their job descriptions. The challenge for the project team was to elicit a response from the person receiving services, such as "they asked me and I told them what I would like to do, but no one had ever asked before. Now I'm doing something that I've always wanted to do."

Priority Issue #3

Initiate improved methods for community job development.

Implementing the Career Action Plan In terms of organizational response, the project team initially decided that the staff member who supported the individual in the workshop should implement the career action plan for securing a community job. The project team, however, recognized that not all direct support staff possessed skills and experience in job development. Supervisory staff, experienced job developers, and a staff training committee provided just-in-time training to staff who lacked the skill or motivation to support people in their community job search.

Action Steps The project team established a marketing committee that exercised the following responsibilities to assist staff with developing better methods for assisting individuals with identifying desired career outcomes:

- Update all marketing brochures and development of presentation kits.
- Involve local business representatives in a focus group to determine local employment needs.
- Develop individual résumés for all workshop employees.
- Invite local Labor Department and Bureau of Rehabilitation Services to make presentations.
- Train staff on the Americans with Disabilities Act (ADA) of 1990 (PL 101-336).
- Expand networking with local organizations (e.g., Chamber of Commerce).
- Set up databank systems to collect information about individuals' job interests and employment opportunities.

Even with these supports, many staff balked at leaving the worksite to enter into the unknown arena of community job development. The project team recognized that "cold calls" were not an effective job development tool and that there was a common perception (based somewhat on reality) that few jobs were available in the depressed economy in northeast Connecticut.

Experience indicates that the best approach to job development is to identify staff who are self-initiators and who are already connected to the local community and give them the tools and supports to become job developers. The project team, then, refocused the staff so that their goal was to build career bridges from the workshop to community jobs and allow the natural networks to grow by word of mouth from business to business, from family member to family member, and from community organization to community organization.

Priority Issue #4

Develop support from the interdisciplinary teams for the project and the vision statement.

    Quality Improvement Tools   To help them to develop support for the project and the vision statement, the interdisciplinary team conducted a force field analysis (Albin, 1992; Brassard, 1988; Scholtes, 1988) (see Table 16.2) to identify those driving and restraining forces that had an impact on buy-in from teams, families, and other departments within the region. The team prioritized those forces into the "vital few" issues that could be addressed and that would have the greatest impact on implementation.

Force field analysis is a brainstorming technique for identifying the driving (positive) forces and the restraining (negative) forces of any specified change. The force field analysis is suited to situations in which there are many different forces that prevent the desired change and in which the problem is related to people or organizational (not technological) problems. Construction of a force field analysis includes the following steps: 1) Define the question (What are the forces related to. . . ?), 2) assemble the right team, 3) facilitate brainstorming, 4) list positive and negative forces in opposite columns (similar to a balance sheet), then 5) prioritize factors and determine a starting point for action.

    Action Steps   Following the force field analysis, the project team initiated the following action steps:

- Placed articles in the regional newsletter
- Included family members and interdisciplinary team members in all subcommittees

Table 16.2.   Force field analysis

What are the forces related to buy in from interdisciplinary teams for the concept of optimal day outcomes?

Driving forces	Restraining forces
• Vision statement	• Fear about possible loss of entitlements
• Mission statement	
• Administrative/steering committee support	• Transportation issues
	• Resistance to change
• "Pioneer spirit"—some people may embrace vision	• Impact on social activities (e.g., dances/Special Olympics)
• Emphasis on person-centered planning	• Lack of consensus on what is "optimal" day outcome
• Individual's own enthusiasm—individual choice	• Economy—in case of lay off and person not at work during day creates residential/parental challenges
• National movement out of segregated workshops	
• Leadership of project team	• Security of workshop versus risk of normal employment
	• Medical/medication administration issues
	• Lack of knowledge regarding vision
	• Nonacceptance of nontraditional day programs and other than first shift hours
	• More resource intensive

- Established constant and public support from the Regional Director, Regional Steering Committee, and State Commissioner of Mental Retardation
- Made presentations at the Region's Family Advisory Committee, to private agency forums, and to all departments
- Conducted regionwide training on the impact of increased wages on entitlements and arranged regionwide training by The Accreditation Council on "Moving from Organizational Process to Outcomes for People." The organizational response indicated that the same problems that existed with buy-in from direct-line staff also existed with personnel in other departments. Some staff members were aware of person-centered planning and TQM and eagerly embraced the implementation process. Others were skeptical and waited for this personal outcome fad to wane.

The project team chose to work initially with the teams or service coordinators who expressed early interest in the project. Because of the need to demonstrate early success, the team selected workers who most easily could move to a community job. Of course, some staff criticized the easy success and challenged the team to achieve success with people who were less ready for the community. Some teams complained that the process was too slow, and other teams viewed the process as an addition to their already over-burdened work load.

To combat negativism, the project team devised ways to speed up the process. It put a skeptical influential service coordinator on one subcommittee and continued to publicize the team's successes. More important, the project team responded to customer feedback, which resulted in continued gains in outside support.

The next sections discuss how staff implemented the new para-digm and vision statement to enhance personal outcomes for the individuals who they served. The organization developed a career profile process and used a variety of tools to ensure that once per-sonal outcomes were identified, staff could turn these desires into actual jobs.

THE CAREER PROFILE PROCESS:
HOW WE HELP PEOPLE PLAN FOR THEIR FUTURES

To assist individuals with developing a career profile, the organiza-tion developed an interview team. To ensure that the job attained met the actual desires and expectations of each individual, the or-ganization also developed person-centered outcomes facilitators who would be present at each career profile meeting.

The organization developed a pool of volunteers (both workshop staff and other interested parties) trained in interview skills. An in-terviewer was assigned to a person who worked in the sheltered workshop. The interviewer would follow the protocol set forth in Table 16.3 in order to make the interview as comfortable and mean-ingful as possible and to respect any confidentiality issues. The con-tent of the interview is summarized in Table 16.4.

The organization also maintained a pool of people who were trained in facilitating person-centered planning meetings. These fa-cilitators would help the individual to identify the people who he or she would like to attend the career profile meeting. The project team found that the person who the individual being served really wanted at the meeting was not necessarily the typical interdiscipli-nary team member. The individual often identifies family members and friends as well as past supervisors or co-workers. The project team found that these people are often the most committed to help-

Table 16.3.   Interview protocol

1. Interviewer is assigned to an individual.
    • Interviewer must check for biases and conflicts of interest before begin-
      ning the interview.
2. Contact the service coordinator.
    • Obtain information about the individual's interactive style and any perti-
      nent information that would facilitate the interview process. Inquire
      about guardian status.
    • Determine who are the significant people in the person's life who will
      also need to be interviewed.
    • Contact guardian (if appropriate) to obtain consent and to explain the
      process.
3. Schedule the initial interview with the individual.
    • Call ahead. Give ample time, and consider privacy and where the per-
      son is most comfortable.
4. Conduct the interview.
    • Explain confidentiality issues and obtain consent to share interview re-
      sults with team.
    • If the person is unable to communicate, observe him or her in a familiar
      environment and interview significant others.
    • If the person does not want to participate, terminate the interview and
      find out if it is okay to return another time. (Is it okay to meet and inter-
      view significant others? Would the person prefer to meet in a different
      setting? Would the person prefer a different interviewer?)
5. Schedule and conduct interviews with significant others.
    • Ideally, someone from the individual's home and current day program
      should be interviewed as well as anyone else that the individual
      suggested.
6. Interviewer's task is finished and the interview booklet is forwarded to the
    Career Profile Coordinator.

ing the individual achieve his or her personal outcomes. The meeting is held wherever the person feels the most comfortable, usually
avoiding use of agency facilities.

The following items were prepared and reviewed prior to the
career profile meeting:

• Personal history/background
• Social characteristics: Who is this person?
• Relationships and community networks
• Physical/health considerations
• Educational history
• Work history
• Personal attributes: work skills, strengths

Table 16.4.   Interview content

Section	Content
1	Introduction, explanation, and consents; determine who the person wants to attend the planning meeting
2	Personal profile (e.g., general questions about where the person lives, works, hobbies)
3	Schedule/hours (e.g., preferences regarding schedules, hours per day, endurance, need for breaks)
4	Work environment (e.g., indoor/outdoor work, climate, noise level, equipment skills, physical demands, fine and gross motor skills, sedentary or active work)
5	Social environment (e.g., proximity to others, preference not to work with other individuals with disabilities, type of co-workers, type of supervisor, supports needed to adjust to new job)
6	Job skills, interests and work habits (e.g., interests, need for change or repetition throughout day, work pace, need for task completion, desire to help others)
7	Outcomes from work (e.g., questions about desired wages and benefits, preference for challenging work or the opportunity to be creative, job security, community inclusion, opportunity to make friends, opportunities for advancement)
8	Preferred time frames for a change

- Personal interests and hobbies
- Situations that work and that do not work for that person

Brainstorming during the meeting resulted in a description of the person's ideal day. Information was posted on wall charts and typically included the following:

- Description of what the person wants to get out of the job
- Ideal schedule
- Impact of wages on entitlements
- Transportation options
- Type of preferred co-workers
- Type of preferred supervisor/job coach
- Supports needed for community inclusion
- Other supports needed and accepted by the person
- Ideal work environment
- Preferred occupations/types of work

The preparation of materials and the brainstorming sessions were part of the development of Outcome Partnership Plans. The teams stressed the concept of partnership to underscore the belief that everyone who attends a meeting is committed to working on the plan. Most people with disabilities, their families, and professionals have spent many hours at planning meetings that resulted in very few positive changes in people's lives. To avoid this, the project team established the following accountability system:

- Periodic review meetings with the people who attended the career profile meeting
- Periodic reviews of the staff's progress toward desired outcomes
- Periodic reports of successes and/or barriers to implementation to the project team
- Annual customer satisfaction survey with each person

Service Delivery System Changes
Resulting from the Focus on Career Outcomes

Following the initiation of the Career Profile Process with the sheltered workshop employees, it became apparent that many of them had never worked outside of the workshop and had very minimal exposure to any other jobs. As a consequence, many employees were reluctant to leave the safety and comfort of the familiar workshop setting. A number of workshop employees actually turned down jobs that staff had worked very hard to procure. In an effort to overcome this reluctance, three initiatives were undertaken: career exploration, videotaped job postings, and community service opportunities.

Career Exploration   The career exploration option was similar to the work-study programs offered by high schools. The organization developed a short-term employment opportunity with a local business (5–10 days) based on an individual's stated career interests. The organization paid the individual's wages and provided a support person/job coach on site. This allowed workshop employees to try out a community job without any pressure to make a decision to leave the workshop. This has been an invaluable strategy to overcome resistance to change and to offer people expanded work experiences so that they are better able to make informed career choices. One unexpected outcome was that employers often were so pleased with the experience that permanent job opportunities developed.

Videotaped Job Postings   Whenever possible, staff videotaped job opportunities for viewing by all workshop employees. Staff discovered that many people declined job opportunities without any knowledge of the job. People who refused to visit potential jobsites were offered a chance to watch the videotapes instead.

Community Service Opportunities   Staff set up paid volunteer opportunities with local service organizations such as hospitals, nursing homes, civic associations, and town groups. The goal was to offer people a chance to participate in community environments in an effort to gain knowledge about employment opportunities and to decrease resistance to change.

CONCLUSIONS

In 1998, the workshop employed less than 50 people with disabilities. More than 50 people have moved on to community-based employment opportunities or retirement options. Although the goal of closing the workshop could have been accomplished sooner, a focus on closure might have negated the emphasis on learning and choosing. Listening to people takes time.

The region has gone through some major reorganizations, and yet the project team and its vision statement to develop optimal day outcomes for all people have remained in place. A single unit within a larger organizational structure can achieve personal outcomes on a daily basis for people with whom they are "partners." Any single unit can change its focus, can make a paradigm shift, can begin a quality journey, and can sustain the quality standards for as long as the leadership and staff decide to stay committed to and practice their mission or vision statement. TQM methods and tools were effective instruments for moving toward these values and the vision of personal outcomes; however, methods and tools alone will not suffice. It takes commitment to a clearly stated vision to accomplish organizational change.

REFERENCES AND RECOMMENDED READINGS

Albin, J.M. (1992). *Quality improvement in employment and other human services: Managing for quality through change.* Baltimore: Paul H. Brookes Publishing Co.

Americans with Disabilities Act (ADA) of 1990, PL 101-336, 42 U.S.C. §§ 12101 *et seq.*

Brassard, M. (1988). *Memory jogger.* Methuen, MA: GOAL/QPC.

Brassard, M. (1989). *Memory jogger plus.* Methuen, MA: GOAL/QPC.

Byham, W., & Cox, J. (1992). *Zapp! The lightning of empowerment.* Pittsburgh, PA: Development Dimensions International.

Crosby, P. (1979). *Quality is free.* New York: Penguin Books.

Dykstra, A. (1995). *Outcome management.* East Dundee, IL: High Tide Press.

Gaebler, D., & Osborne, T. (1993). *Reinventing government.* Reading, MA: Addison-Wesley.

Plsek, P.E., & Onnias, A. (1989). *Quality improvement tools.* Wilton, CT: Juran Institute.

Scholtes, P. (1988). *The team handbook.* Madison, WI: Joiner Associates.

The Council on Quality and Leadership in Supports for People with Disabilities. (1993). *Outcome Based Performance Measures.* Towson, MD: Author.

17

Creating and Adding Value

Redefining the Organization

Gary Donaldson

The Rock Creek Foundation is a community psychiatric rehabilitation agency in Montgomery County, Maryland. It serves people with developmental disabilities who are experiencing ongoing mental health, behavior, and neuropsychiatric challenges, as well as people with severe and persistent mental illnesses. In 1992, the management of the Foundation decided that it was time to examine how the agency was creating value for its consumers. Although there was no external pressure to change, management believed that it was time to review the agency's strategic position and make whatever changes were necessary to update the service delivery system.

EXAMINING STRATEGIC POSITION

At the time of the review, the Foundation offered the typical range of facility-based services, including psychosocial day activity programming, psychiatric day treatment, and vocational and residential services. Vocational services consisted primarily of mobile work crews and enclaves in the community. Residential services consisted of rented homes and apartments in which three consumers resided with live-in supervisors. The agency was community based with most of the service offerings partially segregated and sheltered.

Management and direct line staff participated in the strategic planning activities, which included environmental scans, strength and weakness assessments, threats and opportunities analyses, and market trend forecasting. Cross-functional information-gathering teams were formed to learn what successful organizations in various industries were doing and to learn what the experts were promoting. Staff shared the information through a series of agencywide meetings in which peers reported to peers. This approach was chosen to promote ownership of the project and to avoid placing management in the position of pushing an agenda on the direct services staff (Albin, 1992; Goldstein, 1994; Judson, 1990; Lynch & Werner, 1994; Lytle, 1991; Manzini, 1988; Melan, 1995; Meyers, 1992; Miller, 1994; Nagel, 1991; Quinn, 1990).

The basic questions that the staff explored were related to how excellent service providers were creating value for their consumers. The teams were also charged with finding out what industry leaders believed would be the next generation of service delivery strategies, including assumptions on who will be providing services, where services will be provided, and how services will be provided (Camp, 1989).

TEAM FINDINGS

The information-gathering teams learned that there were two basic types of successful organizations, both groups serving consumers with similar functional levels. The first group tended to be consumer focused. Their primary mission was achieving consumer-defined outcomes linked to community inclusion in socially valued roles. Their consumers tended to spend most of the time in the community holding down real jobs or participating in an array of learning, social, leisure, and recreational activities. The lifestyles of the consumers revolved around active participation and presence in generic community resource settings and were enriched with natural supports. Staff appeared passionate regarding their roles as facilitators and brokers on behalf of the consumers. Staff focused on helping the consumers define personal aspirations and preferences and matching these with opportunities in the community. Staff tended to be rewarded for inventing creative solutions and achieving consumer-defined results. The management styles focused on consumer, staff, and community empowerment (Lawton, 1993; Quinn, 1990).

The second set of providers defined success not by consumer outcomes but by financial performance of the organization, orderliness, and stability of operations. The organizations were making money, policies and procedures were well articulated, and the documentation was up to date. The focus was on compliance to company rules and state regulations. Many had third-party accreditation that stressed process compliance standards. Consumer outcomes were linked to long-term stability in a sheltered environment. Few consumers graduated from in-house services. Expectations were low for consumers' success in the community without ongoing, facility-based services. Consumer choice was limited to a fixed menu of services that was predetermined by the agency. Management style was more traditional, with a focus on a chain of command. Staff did not appear passionate about their roles. They tended to be most comfortable with predictable job routines and functioned more as technicians. There was little understanding or appreciation for a mission beyond getting through day-to-day work. Creativity that involved bold and innovative solutions was not encouraged.

Both organizational types were considered by the Foundation staff to be successful at what they did. The teams realized that it would be important for the Foundation to be clear on how it was to define success. The teams recommended that the definition of success needed to be based on values related to consumer, staff, and community empowerment but also reflect good management, administrative, and fiscal practices. They defined *success* for the Foundation as follows:

- Integrating services and supports into the community
- Having consumers participate in socially valued roles
- Using generic resources and natural supports
- Promoting consumers' self-determination
- Designing personalized services
- Basing services and supports on consumers' choices and preferences
- Empowering consumers, staff, and community
- Practicing fiscally sound administrative policies

It was the impression of the teams that the organizations that were facility based did not have a sense of vitality or relevance to the consumer. Consumer and staff potential were largely untapped.

MISSION AND VALUES CLARIFICATION

After soul searching and clarifying values, the management and direct line staff drafted a new mission statement for the Foundation along with a plan of action to improve services. The old mission directed the efforts of the Foundation to provide a comprehensive continuum of community mental health and psychiatric rehabilitation services. The emphasis was on movement of consumers across a continuum of least restrictive treatment environments. The focus was on symptom relief and establishing treatment environments that contained the disability.

In contrast, the new mission charged Foundation staff to assist consumers in choosing, obtaining, and maintaining fully integrated community lifestyles in socially valued roles. The emphasis was on facilitating consumer self-determination. Community inclusion and successful performance in meaningful roles in living, learning, working, and social environments were targeted outcomes. The new direction focused on conversion of facility-based operations to individualized off-site community-integrated placements. Use of generic resources and natural supports were identified as the vehicle for services.

CONSUMER LEADERSHIP

In a subsequent year, the annual planning meeting expanded to include consumers, board members, funding sources, and people from the local community. Management believed that it was time to invite consumers to give direction to the Foundation once many of the agency's stakeholders had been exposed to community-integrated options. More than 250 stakeholders attended a 2-day session in a large hall in a local town meeting center. Teams were formed that mixed and matched consumers with the other stakeholders. Participants received instructions to identify individual consumer priorities, person by person, through one-to-one interviews. The results of the interviews were shared, discussed, and recorded at the team level (Band, 1991; Bell, 1994; Lawton, 1993).

Each team presented their findings to the whole planning body. Major themes emerged from the information presented. Consumers reached consensus on major themes, and then they voted to prioritize those themes that they wanted the agency to focus on for the next fiscal year. Participants then selected members for a quality enhancement team (QET). The purpose of the QET was to establish a mechanism for consumers and frontline staff to lead continuous quality improvement initiatives (Albin, 1992; Lawton, 1993; Melan, 1995; Meyers, 1992). The first assignment of the team was to collaborate with executive management to translate the priorities into annual outcome objectives for the Foundation.

Consumers and frontline staff presented the priorities and outcome objectives to the Board of Trustees at the Foundation's annual meeting. The Board approved the recommendations and directed management to incorporate the consumers' wishes into the annual and strategic plans. Through this process, the Foundation reaffirmed its commitment to create and add value for the people served by the agency. Consumers defined value in their own terms.

Consumer priorities for the agency were as follows: 1) develop real jobs with real pay in the community, 2) help consumers to find places to live on their own with whom they wanted, 3) help consumers with using community resources, 4) help consumers with facilitating good family relationships, and 5) provide consumers with opportunities to develop friendships with people in the community. Not surprising, staff and management expressed the same goals for their personal lives.

Service Delivery Strategy

To meet consumer expectations, the Foundation had to adopt a new service strategy. It was clear that supporting 200–300 consumers in individual arrangements was not achievable by relying on paid staff as the primary source of support. The strategy moved from a focus on direct services by paid professional staff to an approach that relied on delivery of services through generic community resources with the aid of natural supports (Judson, 1990; Morton, 1991; Nagel, 1991; Porter, 1980). The new service strategy incorporated service brokering, community network facilitation and consultation, value engineering[1], and virtual staffing[2] and organizational structure through use of generic resources and natural supports.

Consumers formed a peer mentoring service so that they could begin to help each other learn skills, expand social networks, and achieve personal goals. They established a resource center in which consumers and staff could meet, establish a community resource database, explore interests, and use the Internet. The resource cen-

---

[1]*Value engineering* means helping businesses and other community resources to discover how to gain something of worth (e.g., increased revenue, decreased costs, access to new opportunities).

[2]*Virtual staffing* means using people not paid by the organization to serve as natural supports, thereby leveraging available community resources.

ter served as a home base for consumers to get a start and help each other.

Staff learned to function more as consultants to the community and as brokers for the consumers. The strategy focused on bypassing and fading from direct services roles whenever feasible. The mantra of the Foundation became "Our job is to get everyone else to do our job." This multiplied the number of available resources and virtual staff (Ashkenas, Ulrich, Jick, & Kerr, 1995; Fabian, Luecking, & Tilson, 1994; Goldstein, 1994; Huxman, 1996; Lewis, 1990; Morton, 1991; Nagel, 1991).

Moving consumers, staff, and resources out of a facility-based environment and into community-integrated settings meant that the Foundation had to redefine the concept of customer. The Foundation broadened the definition of *consumer* to include internal agency co-workers and external parties such as employers, neighbors, and other generic resources. Individuals who were being served, co-workers, employers, neighbors, and other generic resources were all considered consumers.

Systems Thinking

With this redefinition of the concept of consumer and the subsequent shift in awareness came the realization that the relationship of the consumer, generic resource setting (e.g., employer, YMCA), and the natural supports had to become the focus, not just the "client," and that these had to be harmonized. Outcome measures had to expand to incorporate the relationship. The Foundation realized that it needed to understand, articulate, and deliver value from the mutual gains of each party through the relationship. Advocacy remained centered around the individual consumer with disability. Balancing the needs of the new multiple partners, however, entered into the equation and required attention. This new perspective introduced system thinking and value-adding approaches to service delivery implementation (Goldstein, 1994; Kilmann, 1989; Meyers, 1992; Miller, 1994; Nilson, 1992).

One staff member used the example of writing a memo to explain to his colleagues how systems thinking worked for him. He pointed out that when writing a memo, he used a pen, a pad, and his hand. When these three elements worked together, they formed the process of writing. Trying to understand the process of writing by concentrating on just one of the elements, for example, the hand, did not yield a full picture. By focusing attention outside of the interdependent relationship with each of the other elements, in this case the pen and pad, he lost critical information about the real nature of the writing process.

Gathering information on the elements separate from their relationship to the whole and to each other gave a picture that was out of context. When information is out of context, it loses meaning. The relationship of the pen, pad, and hand gave meaning to these elements, and the elements gave meaning to the relationship. If he tried to improve his ability to write by focusing only on one element, then he would not have the information he needed to design the most effective strategy. He could focus on using a different type of paper, an alternative pen, or a different way of using his hand. Without understanding the relationship of the pen, paper, and hand, he might choose a grade of paper that was incompatible with the type of ink delivered by the pen; or, he might choose a pen that was not proper for the weight of the paper. The lesson he conveyed was that meaning evolved through the exchange of value among the elements. The elements could not be addressed one at a time to achieve desired outcomes. They needed to be dealt with simultaneously. The generation of reciprocal value created and maintained the relationship. The pen, paper, and hand formed a union that gave, captured, and shared value among the elements. Concurrent focus on all three elements and their value-sharing relationship optimized performance outcomes (Goldstein, 1994; Kilmann, 1989; Meyers, 1992; Miller, 1994).

Figure 17.1 suggests a schematic representation of the interdependent relationships that form a system identity. In systems in which value is exchanged, the following occur:

- Value exchange is simultaneous and reciprocal.
- Exchange is through an interdependent connection of relationships.
- Exchanges bind together to create and maintain a common whole.
- The parts simultaneously contribute to each other and the whole.
- The whole simultaneously contributes to the parts.

In order to capture value for consumers, the Foundation learned that it had to create and add value for *all* of the parties in the consumer's community support network. Advocacy on behalf of the consumer required advocacy on behalf of everyone connected to the life of the consumer. Successful outcomes came slowly when the agency focused exclusively on advancing the needs of the consumer at the expense of supporting the whole. Outcomes grew when the Foundation took time to invest in the success of organizations and people surrounding the consumer.

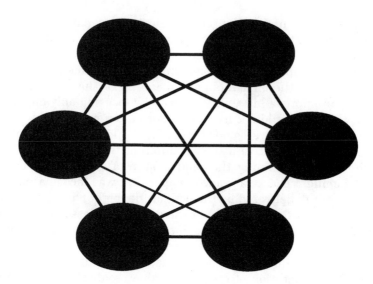

Figure 17.1.   Network of interdependent relationships that form a system identity. (*Key:* ●, value generator and receiver [part]; ———, reciprocal exchange [value].)

CONSUMER-DESIGNED COMMUNITIES

The Foundation knew that to build a sense of community member-ship, consumers needed to belong to a group. The members of the group had to participate in common practices, depend on one an-other, make decisions together, have a shared identity, and commit to each other and the group's long-term well being. The group could be self-contained as in a worksite or in a network of personal con-nections. Each connection shared a common interest in the individ-ual. Once the individual was connected to different parts of the com-munity (e.g., jobsites, YMCA, grocery store), the connections formed the consumer's personally designed community. The individually tailored networks are based on consumers' preferences; encourage community presence, participation, and social inclusion within an array of settings; and allow individuals with similar interests to share in activities (Shaffner & Anundsen, 1993).

To build consumer-designed communities, the Foundation de-cided to focus on three dimensions of community: breadth, depth, and length. With *breadth,* the Foundation expands opportunities for sharing as many facets of the consumer's life with members of the community as desired. There is a continuous initiative to expand connections with a wide range of people and experiences. The focus on *depth* fosters interpersonal closeness and reciprocal sharing of inner feelings and thoughts that build socially appropriate intimacy. *Length* refers to the developing bonds and community connections that last over time (Shaffer & Anundsen, 1993).

Helping consumers build a community and participate in typical community routines was not as simple as going out, getting what is wanted, setting up supports, and fading. Building community required finding strategies to overcome the very challenges that each consumer's disability presented.

Offsetting Limitations by Adding Value

The population served by the Foundation presents the full range of challenges one would expect with people with severe behavior and psychiatric disorders. Many consumers require individually designed protocols to make it through basic tasks of daily community functioning. Biopsychosocial functional impairments, in particular, pose significant challenges. Providing services is not a matter of giving the person what they want and placing the person in the "right" normalized environment. The psychiatric component of the disability profile cannot be trained or placed away.

The critical issue for staff is to move beyond the limitations imposed by the disability profile. The competing demands of the disability frequently inhibit opportunities for social inclusion or reliance on natural supports. The nature of the relationship among the consumer, generic resources, natural supports, and service provider has to offer mutual value that far outweighs the cost for all parties.

Adding value occurs directly by the performance of a consumer and indirectly because of the presence of the consumer (Gilbert, 1978; Lewis, 1990; Nilson, 1992; Trischler, 1996). The consumer may directly add economic value (e.g., cash value) to a service organization by producing a product. Clearing a table, filing a document, and assembling a computer board are examples. Targeted tax credits, helping generic resources to obtain access to new customers, or helping an employer rewrite job descriptions to be in compliance with the Americans with Disabilities Act (ADA) of 1990 (PL 101-336) are examples of indirect sources of value.

Value is tangible and intangible. *Tangible value* is easily observable and measurable. For example, a consumer may assemble 10 computer boards per hour. The company for which he works is able to earn $2,000 more per month because the human resources needs are fulfilled, so they can then concentrate on serving *their* customers more effectively. *Intangible value* is more difficult to isolate and measure. It tends to have a synergistic and cumulative effect. The contribution of intangible value is as significant as tangible value. Examples of intangible value are morale, team spirit, cooperation, collaboration, dependability, proactive thinking, commitment, and creativity. An employer may have the most efficiently designed work process possible yet not succeed due to intangible factors. Intangible factors can multiply the probability of successful outcomes, or they can inhibit a process. Intangible factors contribute to high performance, sustainability, and continuous improvement (Quinn, 1990).

Many win-win opportunities exist when each party in a relationship perceives a net gain in value that more than offsets the challenges presented by a disability (Gilbert, 1978). The value created by the presence and contribution of a consumer is illustrated in the following example.

The Foundation served a woman in her early thirties who had a history of multiple admissions to the state developmental disabilities institution and frequent hospitalizations in psychiatric units of local general hospitals. Before coming to the Foundation, she had been discharged from several community service providers due to their inability to meet her needs.

The consumer was considered too difficult to serve. There was not a community-based provider willing to admit her for services in the state, and she had developed a reputation that isolated her from receiving support. Providers were frightened by her sudden aggressive and uncontrollable behaviors that resulted in attacks on staff and destruction of property. The episodes lasted for several days and required hospitalization.

Through a combination of clinical and behavioral support provided by the Foundation, the individual was able to sustain her functioning in the community for periods that far exceeded her previous experiences. She continued to have periodic episodes that required hospitalization for periods up to 30 days. The flash points for her outbursts continued to be unpredictable.

Medications were helpful but not always able to contain the effects of sudden shifts in her biochemical status. The focus of the Foundation was on initial one-to-one proactive behavioral supports combined with an individually structured routine in the community. There was no guarantee that she would not suddenly become hostile and injurious to herself and others.

A representative of the Foundation contacted the regional manager of a restaurant chain to explore employment opportunities. The restaurant's regional manager agreed that the Foundation could conduct a study to determine if there were areas of performance improvement that the company could make that would increase revenues and decrease costs in their field operations. Results of the study revealed that carving out and creating the position of silverware roller would save the company thousands of dollars. The point of the study was to offer management and consulting services in order to get in the door and then carve out (or invent) a job for the individual. The Foundation also provided the employer with strategies for increasing economic value.

Traditionally, the waiters and waitresses rolled the silverware. They did this duty either before the restaurant opened or during customer hours. The waiters and waitresses were paid less than minimum wage for this part of their jobs, so they resented coming in early to prepare the silverware (they are paid below minimum wage because they would also get paid in tips, but only when waiting on customers). During customer hours, stopping to roll silverware detracted from their ability to serve customers, which, in turn, reduced their sales and tips. Ultimately, this resentment resulted in high employee turnover.

Each turnover cost the restaurant $600–$700 in recruitment, interviewing, hiring, and training costs. Furthermore, sales were lower during the initial orientation period of new employees. The lowered productivity cost the company another $200–$300 in lost revenue. The net result cost the company between $800 and $1,000 each time there was a change in employees.

The turnover in the restaurant chain was costing the regional manager $50,000–$70,000 per year throughout the greater metropolitan area. Creating the silverware rolling position saved the company a substantial amount of money. The regional manager saw tremendous savings by implementing the new position at all of the restaurant's locations. He instructed his managers at each location to hire appropriate candidates through the Foundation.

The support counselor for the woman discussed in the beginning of this case contacted one of the restaurants in the chain. She negotiated a job placement with the branch manager. She was honest regarding the consumer's needs and the consumer's behavior challenges. The subject was approached in a straightforward manner without using clinical or overly dramatic terms. The manager was told what the Foundation had learned to help the consumer perform well and told what the Foundation did to prevent, reduce, or eliminate the behavior challenges presented by the consumer's disability.

Once the risk issues were addressed to the satisfaction of the manager, he hired the consumer. He recommended that she work during periods of the day before the restaurant opened. This would cause the least disruption to operations should there be a problem. There were other employees working during this time. She was considered part of the prep crew. The counselor agreed to serve initially as the consumer's job coach every day that she worked. Due to the unpredictability and severity of the consumer's behavioral episodes, it was believed that the risk was too high to shift to natural supports immediately. The counselor also made back-up arrangements to have another consumer or staff member cover duties when the consumer was absent from her job.

The consumer handled her responsibilities well, but the manager had taken a calculated risk in hiring the consumer. On occasion, she was unable to work because of her behaviors. Only several months before employment, the consumer was considered too difficult to serve in sheltered workshops and day activity centers. The employer hired the consumer because the Foundation was able to demonstrate to the regional and branch manager that having the consumer as an employee offset any unique challenges presented by her disability.

The return on the investment far outweighed the challenges. With minor accommodations, the manager of the restaurant gained a loyal and motivated worker in addition to decreased overall operating costs and increasing employee morale. The Foundation agreed to work with the regional manager to staff the other restaurants with silverware rollers. This became part of the deal in hiring the consumer. This created more job opportunities for many other Foundation consumers as well as consumers from other service providers in the area.

The Foundation learned that the perception of adding value creates more opportunities and options than the perception of adding cost or burden. The restaurant received value by saving money. The consumers received value by expanding job opportunities. The Foundation received value by meeting its mission and achieving tangible outcomes.

The Foundation discovered that adding value created demand. Following a year of successful job placements, the Foundation did not need to use as many organizational resources to market and promote community collaborations. As the Foundation developed a positive reputation, consumers were invited into the world of others so that they could gain from the relationships. The continuous exchange of value created demand and sustained meaningful relationships (Band, 1991; DeRose, 1989; Huxman, 1996; Lewis, 1990, Nilson, 1992; Porter, 1980). Members of the Foundation learned that

- Pursuing the self-interest of the consumer without focus on another party's needs was perceived by the community as potentially adding burden, cost, and risk.
- The perception of burden, cost, and risk are conditions that interfere with creating collaborative relationships.
- Offering something of worth that meets and exceeds expectations is perceived as adding value, minimizing risk, and maximizing gain.
- Gain is attractive and to be pursued.
- Being perceived as adding value creates its own demand.

VALUE AS CURRENCY

As members of the Foundation ventured into the community, they learned that the market for services agencies was getting crowded. Multiple social services agencies were promoting the use of generic community resources. There were more than 50 workforce development agencies providing employment services in the county, not including the school system. Management felt that the Foundation needed to stand out in the crowd so that staff could secure employment and other community-integrated placements (see Porter, 1980).

An important aspect of determining value is evaluating how value is perceived by others. Value—which can be measured in terms of cost, quality, quantity, reliability, and consistency—will be perceived differently by each stakeholder. A person's perception of value is typically determined by comparisons with similar substitutes. An employer typically compares factors such as cost to acquire, cost to use, and cost to keep. Therefore, an organization needs to have a distinct favorable image in the community that stresses that there is no substitute that can replace what it has to offer. Every aspect of the organization needs to reinforce a distinct and favorable image.

The Foundation determined that in order to be distinguished from other agencies it would engage in a value-adding market positioning and promotion strategy. The Foundation would find ways to create, add, and exchange value with generic resources and natural supports. The value-adding strategy would be used as a vehicle to open doors and develop community membership for its consumers. Field operations would be aligned to support the approach and image.

Value and Worth

Exchange of value requires a recognizable form of currency. Understanding the concepts of value and perceived worth expanded the range of currency available for use by the Foundation (see Cohen & Bradford, 1990; Gilbert, 1978; Lewis, 1990; Nilson, 1992). *Advocacy* was perceived by the Foundation as an exchange of value using currency that was relevant to each party in a relationship with a consumer.

The Foundation began with the premise that value was in the "eye of the beholder"; it was not intrinsic (Lawton, 1993). This understanding opened the door to finding the resources needed to facilitate community inclusion of consumers. The Foundation did not seek infusion of additional government money to sponsor conversion to non–facility-based services. Instead, staff became fluent in their ability to identify value-adding opportunities and to convert this understanding into currency for exchange. This permitted the discovery of existing resources that were previously invisible. The forms of currency used by the Foundation are classified as task, position, personal, inspirational, and relationship.

Task Currencies   *Task currencies* are tangible resources, assets, supports, or assistance brought to a relationship that help the other party implement projects, meet deadlines, complete work assignments, or increase skills. Money, personnel, space, information, training, and consultation are examples. Task currencies may also include providing an opportunity to the other party to do tasks that increase skill and abilities as with student interns and volunteers. Rapid response, just-in-time, and just-enough support are task currencies, as well. Providing task help quickly and when needed is a currency in high demand (Cohen & Bradford, 1990).

The Career Designs Division of the Foundation supplies qualified labor and job trainers to local businesses. This task currency exchange results in businesses' 1) increasing revenue, 2) decreasing operating costs, 3) offsetting costs, 4) preventing costs, and 5) increasing cash flow (Fabian et al., 1994; Lewis, 1990; Porter, 1980; Rickards, 1974). In a unique approach, two psychosocial day service divisions—Supported Community Options (serving people with long-term mental illness) and Achievement Center (serving people with developmental disabilities and mental illness)—combined forces and went to a local town government in an adjacent jurisdiction, several miles from the Foundation. They arranged to "adopt" the town. Usually nonprofit organizations are in constant search for sponsors. This time the opposite occurred. The Foundation became a benefactor to the town.

Consumers and staff report daily to the town center instead of to the facility, and they work on projects scattered throughout the community. The projects include public landscape maintenance, sorting and filing books in the library, clerical support at the town hall, and related tasks. Consumers work either individually or as a crew based on interest, skills, and the size of the task.

By exchanging task-related currencies, the Foundation is able to get access to a variety of meaningful roles within community settings that are highly visible and socially integrated. This creative strategy increases the probability that jobs, inclusion, social networks, relationships, and functional community life skills evolve. The time, effort, and expense of job and resource development diminish because of the frequent contact with members of the community. Informal networking supplements formal channels. The return on informal networking consistently performs well. Adopting the town allowed the consumers to move from devalued, marginal statuses to the roles of altruists and good citizens —a social standing usually held by distinguished and accomplished civic leaders.

Because jobs moved to generic resource settings throughout the local community, there was a decreased need for the Foundation to rent space to provide services. By expanding this approach to other locations in the county, the Foundation estimated that it could save $48,000 per year.

In exchange for the consumers' contributions, the town receives valued services. The various volunteer assignments covered by the consumers and staff improve the quality of life in the town and allow the government to concentrate on other important priorities. The landscaping work was so valued that it eventually turned into paid employment.

Position Currencies   *Position currencies* are concerned with facilitating recognition, increasing visibility, gaining access to insider status and importance, developing important contacts, and enhancing reputation (Cohen & Bradford, 1990).

Through networking in the community, the Foundation is able to accumulate a wealth of contacts that serve as currency. It used position-related currencies to create an employment opportunity. While engaging in a labor market survey, a counselor interviewed the owner of a small store that sells balloons for special occasions. The owner had no previous experience in business or marketing services. The business was slowly developing and not in a position to hire additional employees. From the conversation, it became evident that the owner could benefit from help in expanding her customer base. A position-related currency was used when the counselor linked the owner to a general manager who was opening a new mall and needed balloons to decorate the building complex.

Reciprocal value was exchanged when the owner offered a job to a Foundation consumer because the business volume increased and new employees were needed. Because the Foundation reached out to a business as a community partner, sharing skills and connections, both parties benefited.

Personal Currencies   *Personal currency* is an expression of gratitude, indebtedness, and use of influence on behalf of another. It is also an affirmation of one's values and identity (Cohen & Bradford, 1990).

The owner of the aforementioned balloon store felt a true kinship with the Foundation because it had helped her at a critical stage of her business development. As the owner expanded her business and became more active in the local community, she remembered the help that she had received. Although she had hired a consumer, she wanted to do more. On her own initiative, she used her position to promote the hiring of Foundation consumers to other potential employers. At chamber meetings, business gatherings, and through her business contacts, she spoke of the benefits of hiring Foundation consumers and providing other forms of support. A personal currency was used by the storeowner as a form of gratitude for helping her expand her business.

Inspirational Currencies   *Inspirational currencies* are concerned with having the opportunity to do what is right by a higher standard, serving for the greater good of the community, fulfilling a calling, or having a chance to make an important contribution (Cohen & Bradford, 1990).

The Student-Volunteer Department of the Foundation has a highly established presence in the community. The director has recruited corporate, university, and community volunteers. For example, she established a linkage with the University of Maryland Best Buddies program through which college students commit to form a 1-year, one-to-one peer relationship with consumers.

The experience is a true peer relationship. It is based on the mutual participation of each person in each other's life. The student does not have a set of habilitation goals and does not work from an individual habilitation plan. Instead, the student and the consumer develop a friendship, which provides a normalized relationship experience. The contacts offer opportunities for the students to serve as natural mentors, facilitators, and community builders on behalf of the consumers. The exchange is two way; consumers actually help the students to grow. The relationship helps the students learn to transcend the typical caste system that frequently separates people with severe disabilities from others. The experience teaches an important lesson regarding genuineness and sharing common ground despite initial differences. The students also have the opportunity to contribute to the greater good of the community.

Relationship Currencies *Relationship currencies* focus on expressing understanding; listening to another's concerns; demonstrating acceptance; validating personal worthiness; and offering opportunities for inclusion, emotional closeness, friendship, and personal support (Cohen & Bradford, 1990).

During the course of daily events, the Foundation has a variety of contacts with community members through formal meeting and informal social networking. These encounters offer an opportunity to connect with other people. On occasion, these encounters grow into emotional bonds by one or both parties. The bond usually contains relationship-related currency exchange.

At a business meeting at which a Foundation member was present, an employer unveiled a new initiative for mentoring youth. After the formal presentation, the Foundation member talked to the presenter. There was enough of a personal connection that both agreed to have lunch the following week. As each party became familiar with one another on a more personal level, the employer talked about the challenges that he faced in his corporate environment. The Foundation member listened, communicated empathic understanding, provided emotional support, and helped the employer develop a problem-solving strategy around one of the issues.

Several days later, the Foundation staff person received a telephone call from the employer regarding a social opportunity for consumers. A collection of individuals were forming a group to pursue common interests in outdoors activities such as camping, canoeing, fishing, and hiking. The person offered to connect consumers to members of the group. A relationship currency was exchanged. The connection between the two parties continued with both sharing ideas and leads between each other for mutual benefit.

Increasing Returns

Exchanging currency sets in motion a system of increasing returns. The Foundation learned that adding value has a ripple effect. The immediate effects of the value-adding transaction spreads to stakeholders of the targeted generic resource, employer, or natural support. Each community partner has a web of relationships that involves value exchanges. Figure 17.2 provides a schematic representation of the interrelationship among these value exchanges. Table 17.1 describes the steps to increasing returns. Keeping an inventory of the ripple effect provides a very strong database of real

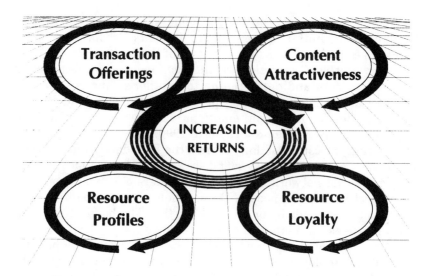

Figure 17.2.   Schematic representation of the interrelationship among value exchanges. These exchanges—transaction offerings, content attractiveness, resource profiles, and resource loyalty—lead to increasing returns.

outcomes that are useful to share when developing other potential resources. Being able to demonstrate concrete outcomes increases the probability of successfully obtaining more community partners and offers leads to unexpected opportunities (DeRose, 1989; Lewis, 1990; Nilson, 1992; Porter, 1980). The following vignette is an example of the increasing returns process in action.

A local recreation service offers adult education classes. The Foundation approached the recreation service to formalize arrangements for referring consumers to classes. This meant that the recreation service could receive at least $10,000 of business through payment of fees for classes. The recreation service was receptive but was unclear how the consumers could fit into their classes. Many of the subjects offered appeared to be too difficult for consumers to participate. For example, one series of classes was in bicycle repair. The subject matter required class participants to calculate gear ratios. Clearly, many of the consumers were not capable of doing the math required.

The instructors at the center are part-time faculty. The classes they teach are based on their personal interests and skills. The Foundation arranged to pay the instructor of the bicycle repair course for his time to redesign the curriculum so that it would be accessible to Foundation consumers. This showed respect for his time,

Table 17.1.   The increasing returns process in action

1. A provider offers a value-adding transaction to a generic community resource or natural support.
2. The transaction outcome meets or exceeds expectations and is viewed as attractive.
3. Attractive outcomes breed loyalty to the provider.
4. Loyalty opens the door to a closer relationship.
5. The closer relationship reveals further profile information on the evolving needs of the same and similar generic resources.
6. The increased insider information leads to expanded opportunities to design and offer other relevant value-adding transactions.
7. The increased opportunities broaden the range of community options available to consumers while strengthening the bond between the provider and the community.
8. The increased bonds facilitate easier and expanded access to further community resources.
9. Increased linkages with community resources facilitate the opportunities for consumer inclusion in socially valued roles.
10. Expanded bonds, linkages, and socially valued roles lead to geometric progression in development of self-organizing and self-managing support networks for the consumer and the provider.

did not place a burden on the instructor, added a benefit by broadening the range of people who could take the course, and expanded his revenue.

A consumer became interested in taking the repair course. The Foundation assigned a staff member to work with the instructor. Once the curriculum was modified, the consumer was able to participate, at his own level, side by side other participants. In this case, during the evening that involved gear-ratio theory, the instructor had the participants bring in their gears so that the consumer could clean them while they were doing the math calculations.

Instructors' pay and the recreation service revenue are linked to enrollment: Instructors receive 60% of the fees collected, and the service receives 40%. The instructor received an hourly rate for redesigning the curriculum and had new members join his course. This value-adding intervention also created an opportunity for the recreation service to expand their client base not only to the Foundation but also to many of the other programs serving people with severe disabilities.

The impact of the Foundation partnership has the potential of even going further. Notices for classes are sent to the general public 6 weeks before they are held. Classes are limited in size and require prior registration. Many of the Foundation consumers cannot read or understand the class descriptions, but the consumers make the most effective personal choices when they are able to see first-hand what the classes look like. The announcements for the classes inadvertently block accessibility.

The Foundation has made arrangements for the core classes to be videotaped and distributed to libraries throughout the county. This way, consumers (from the Foundation as well as general community) will be able to view the content in advance. This will help in their choice making. It will also facilitate use of a generic community resource, the public library system.

Using a value-adding strategy contributes to personal gain for the consumer. It also creates opportunities for others. As this lesson has become increasingly clear, the Foundation is looking to redefine its role in the community. The focus is no longer on disability. It is broadening to include wider civic issues. The Foundation and its staff are beginning to emerge as community-building entrepreneurs.

SEEKING OPPORTUNITIES

Experience has taught management and staff of the Foundation two important lessons: 1) When we argue for our limitations, they become our reality; and 2) that which receives attention tends to grow. The challenge is to discover where to look and how to mobilize the necessary resources to achieve consumer-defined community outcomes (Lynch & Kordis, 1990; Lynch & Neenan, 1995). Integrating creative and innovative thinking into day-to-day problem-solving activities broadens our options. The community holds many treasures that can be used to advance the well-being of our consumers. Using a strategy based on creating and adding value facilitates approaches that generate increasing returns for all parties.

REFERENCES

Albin, J.M. (1992). *Quality improvement in employment and other human services: Managing for quality through change.* Baltimore: Paul H. Brookes Publishing Co.

Americans with Disabilities Act (ADA) of 1990, PL 101-336, 42 U.S.C. §§ 12101 *et seq.*

Ashkenas, R., Ulrich, D., Jick, T., & Kerr, S. (1995). *The boundaryless organization.* San Francisco: Jossey-Bass.

Band, W.A. (1991). *Creating value for customers: Designing and implementing a total corporate strategy.* New York: John Wiley & Sons.

Bell, C.R. (1994). *Customers as partners.* San Francisco: Berrett-Koehler.

Camp, R.C. (1989). *Benchmarking: The search for industry best practices that lead to superior performance.* Milwaukee, WI: Quality Press.

Cohen, A.R., & Bradford, D.L. (1990). *Influence without authority.* New York: John Wiley & Sons.

DeRose, L. (1989). *Value selling: The strategy for reaching the industrial customer, satisfying customer requirements, and competing in cost-conscious markets.* New York: AMACOM.

Fabian, E.S., Luecking, R.G., & Tilson, G.P., Jr. (1994). *A working relationship: The job development specialist's guide to successful partnerships with business.* Baltimore: Paul H. Brookes Publishing Co.

Gilbert, T.F. (1978). *Human competence.* New York: McGraw-Hill.

Goldstein, J. (1994). *The unshackled organization.* Portland, OR: Productivity Press.

Huxman, C. (1996). *Creating collaborative advantage.* Thousand Oaks, CA: Sage Publications.

Judson, A. (1990). *Making strategy happen.* Cambridge, MA: Basil Blackwell.

Kilmann, R.H. (1989). *Managing beyond the quick fix: A completely integrated program for creating and maintaining organizational success.* San Francisco: Jossey-Bass.

Lawton, R.L. (1993). *Creating a customer-centered culture.* Milwaukee, WI: ASQC Quality Press.

Lewis, J.D. (1990). *Partnerships for profit: Structuring and managing strategic alliances.* New York: The Free Press.

Lynch, D., & Kordis, P.L. (1990). *Code of the monarch: An insider's guide to the real global business revolution.* Lakewood, CO: Brain Technologies Corporation.

Lynch, D., & Neenan, D. (1995). *Evergreen: Playing a continuous comeback business game.* Lakewood, CO: Brain Technologies Corporation.

Lynch, R.F., & Werner, T.J. (1994). *Reengineering business processes and people systems.* Atlanta: QualTeam.

Lytle, W.O. (1991). *Socio-technical systems analysis and design guide.* Plainfield, NJ: Block Petrella Weisbord.

Manzini, A.O. (1988). *Organizational diagnosis: A practical approach to company problem solving and growth.* New York: AMACOM.

Melan, E.H. (1995). *Process management: A system approach to total quality.* Portland, OR: Productivity Press.

Meyers, C.H. (1992). *Improving whole systems.* Plainfield, NJ: Block Petrella Weisbord.

Miller, L.M. (1994). *Whole system architecture.* Atlanta, GA: Miller Howard Consulting Group.

Morton, M.S.S. (1991). *The corporation of the 1990s: Information technology and organizational transformation.* Oxford, England: Oxford University Press.

Nagel, K. (1991). *The six keys to company success.* Exeter, England: Fitzwilliam Publishing

Nilson, T.H. (1992). *Valued-added marketing.* London: McGraw-Hill.

Porter, M.E. (1980). *Competitive strategy.* New York: The Free Press.

Quinn, R.E. (1990). *Beyond rational management.* San Francisco: Jossey-Bass.

Rickards, T. (1974). *Problem-solving through creative analysis.* Wales, United Kingdom: Gower Press.

Shaffer, C.R., & Anundsen, K. (1993). *Creating community anywhere: Finding support and connection in a fragmented world.* New York: Putnam.

Trischler, W.E. (1996). *Understanding and applying value-added assessment.* Milwaukee, WI: ASQC Quality Press.

Index

Page references followed by *t*, *f*, or *n* indicate tables, figures, or footnotes, respectively.